enVision® Mathematics

Common Core

Volume 1 Topics 1–7

Authors

Randall I. Charles
Professor Emeritus
Department of Mathematics
San Jose State University
San Jose, California

Jennifer Bay-Williams
Professor of Mathematics Education
College of Education and Human Development
University of Louisville
Louisville, Kentucky

Robert Q. Berry, III
Professor of Mathematics Education
Department of Curriculum, Instruction and Special Education
University of Virginia
Charlottesville, Virginia

Janet H. Caldwell
Professor Emerita
Department of Mathematics
Rowan University
Glassboro, New Jersey

Zachary Champagne
Assistant in Research
Florida Center for Research in Science, Technology, Engineering, and Mathematics (FCR-STEM)
Jacksonville, Florida

Juanita Copley
Professor Emerita
College of Education
University of Houston
Houston, Texas

Warren Crown
Professor Emeritus of Mathematics Education
Graduate School of Education
Rutgers University
New Brunswick, New Jersey

Francis (Skip) Fennell
Professor Emeritus of Education and Graduate and Professional Studies
McDaniel College
Westminster, Maryland

Karen Karp
Professor of Mathematics Education
School of Education
Johns Hopkins University
Baltimore, Maryland

Stuart J. Murphy
Visual Learning Specialist
Boston, Massachusetts

Jane F. Schielack
Professor Emerita
Department of Mathematics
Texas A&M University
College Station, Texas

Jennifer M. Suh
Associate Professor for Mathematics Education
George Mason University
Fairfax, Virginia

Jonathan A. Wray
Mathematics Supervisor
Howard County Public Schools
Ellicott City, Maryland

Mathematicians

Roger Howe
Professor of Mathematics
Yale University
New Haven, Connecticut

Gary Lippman
Professor of Mathematics and Computer Science
California State University, East Bay
Hayward, California

ELL Consultants

Janice R. Corona
Independent Education Consultant
Dallas, Texas

Jim Cummins
Professor
The University of Toronto
Toronto, Canada

Reviewers

Katina Arnold
Teacher
Liberty Public School District
Kansas City, Missouri

Christy Bennett
Elementary Math and Science Specialist
DeSoto County Schools
Hernando, Mississippi

Shauna Bostick
Elementary Math Specialist
Lee County School District
Tupelo, Mississippi

Samantha Brant
Teacher
Platte County School District
Platte City, Missouri

Jamie Clark
Elementary Math Coach
Allegany County Public Schools
Cumberland, Maryland

Shauna Gardner
Math and Science Instructional Coach
DeSoto County Schools
Hernando, Mississippi

Kathy Graham
Educational Consultant
Twin Falls, Idaho

Andrea Hamilton
K-5 Math Specialist
Lake Forest School District
Felton, Delaware

Susan Hankins
Instructional Coach
Tupelo Public School District
Tupelo, Mississippi

Barb Jamison
Teacher
Excelsior Springs School District
Excelsior Springs, Missouri

Pam Jones
Elementary Math Coach
Lake Region School District
Bridgton, Maine

Sherri Kane
Secondary Mathematics Curriculum Specialist
Lee's Summit R7 School District
Lee's Summit, Missouri

Jessica Leonard
ESOL Teacher
Volusia County Schools
DeLand, Florida

Jill K. Milton
Elementary Math Coordinator
Norwood Public Schools
Norwood, Massachusetts

Jamie Pickett
Teacher
Platte County School District
Kansas City, Missouri

Mandy Schall
Math Coach
Allegany County Public Schools
Cumberland, Maryland

Marjorie Stevens
Math Consultant
Utica Community Schools
Shelby Township, Michigan

Shyree Stevenson
ELL Teacher
Penns Grove-Carneys Point Regional School District
Penns Grove, New Jersey

Kayla Stone
Teacher
Excelsior Springs School District
Excelsior Springs, Missouri

Sara Sultan
PD Academic Trainer, Math
Tucson Unified School District
Tucson, Arizona

Angela Waltrup
Elementary Math Content Specialist
Washington County Public Schools
Hagerstown, Maryland

Savvas Learning Company LLC, 15 East Midland Avenue, Paramus, NJ 07652

ISBN-13: 978-0-13-495472-1
ISBN-10: 0-13-495472-6
8 21

Digital Resources

You'll be using these digital resources throughout the year!

Go to SavvasRealize.com

Interactive Student Edition

Access online or offline.

Visual Learning

Interact with visual learning animations.

Interactive Additional Practice Workbook

Access online or offline.

Activity

Solve a problem and share your thinking.

Videos

Watch Math Practices Animations, Another Look Videos, and clips to support 3-Act Math.

Practice Buddy

Do interactice practice online.

Math Tools

Explore math with digital tools.

Games

Play math games to help you learn.

Glossary

Read and listen in English and Spanish.

Assessment

Show what you've learned.

SAVVAS realize™ Everything you need for math anytime, anywhere

Hi, we're here to help you.
Let's have a great year!

Digital Resources at SavvasRealize.com

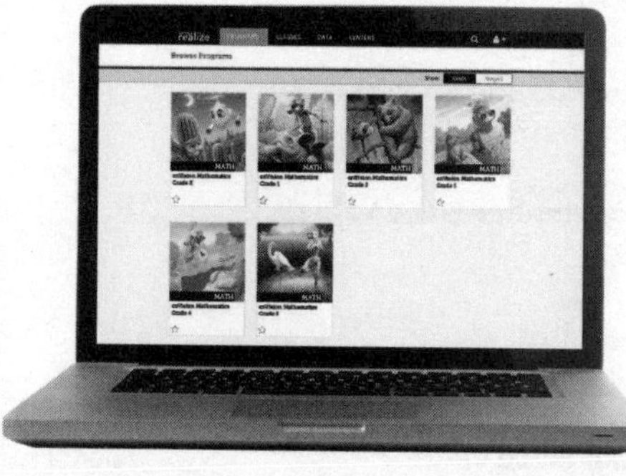

TOPICS

And remember your Interactive Student Edition is available at SavvasRealize.com!

SavvasRealize.com

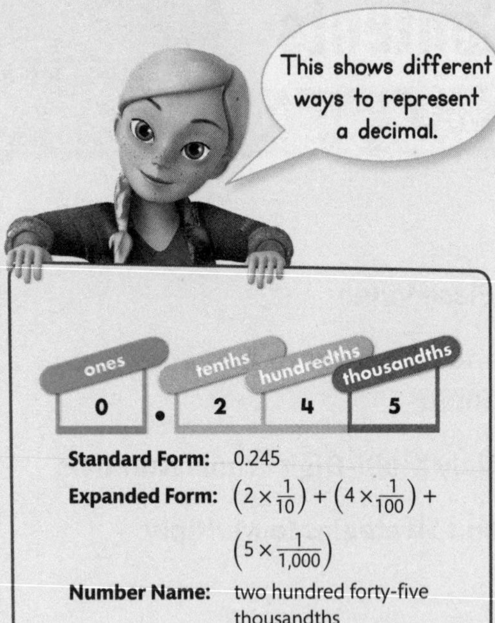

Standard Form: 0.245

Expanded Form: $\left(2 \times \frac{1}{10}\right) + \left(4 \times \frac{1}{100}\right) + \left(5 \times \frac{1}{1{,}000}\right)$

Number Name: two hundred forty-five thousandths

TOPIC 1 Understand Place Value

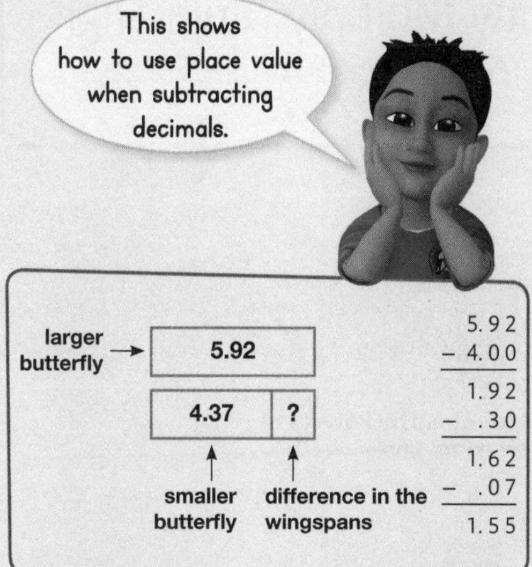

TOPIC 2 Use Models and Strategies to Add and Subtract Decimals

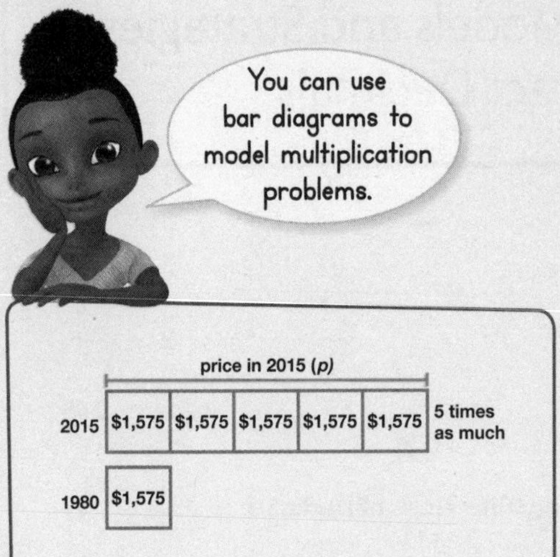

TOPIC 3 Fluently Multiply Multi-Digit Whole Numbers

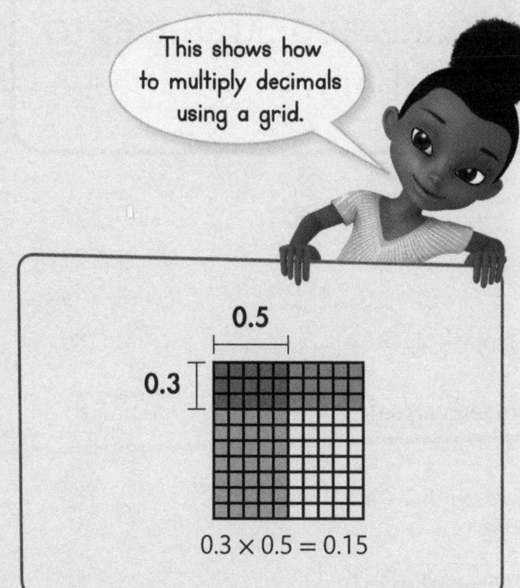
This shows how to multiply decimals using a grid.
0.5
0.3
0.3 × 0.5 = 0.15

TOPIC 4 Use Models and Strategies to Multiply Decimals

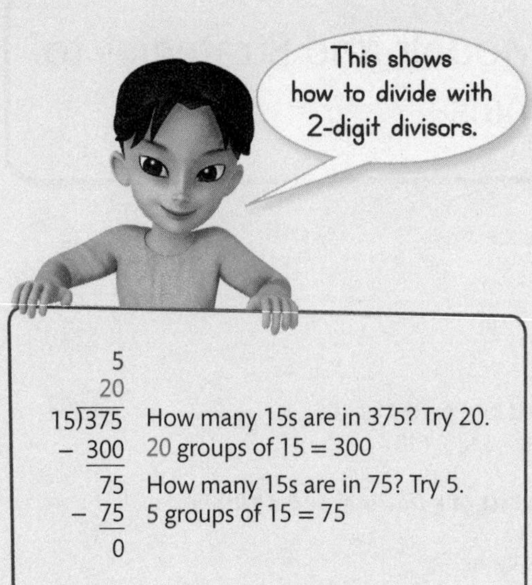
This shows how to divide with 2-digit divisors.
5
20
15)375 How many 15s are in 375? Try 20.
− 300 20 groups of 15 = 300
75 How many 15s are in 75? Try 5.
− 75 5 groups of 15 = 75
0

TOPIC 5 Use Models and Strategies to Divide Whole Numbers

TOPIC 6 Use Models and Strategies to Divide Decimals

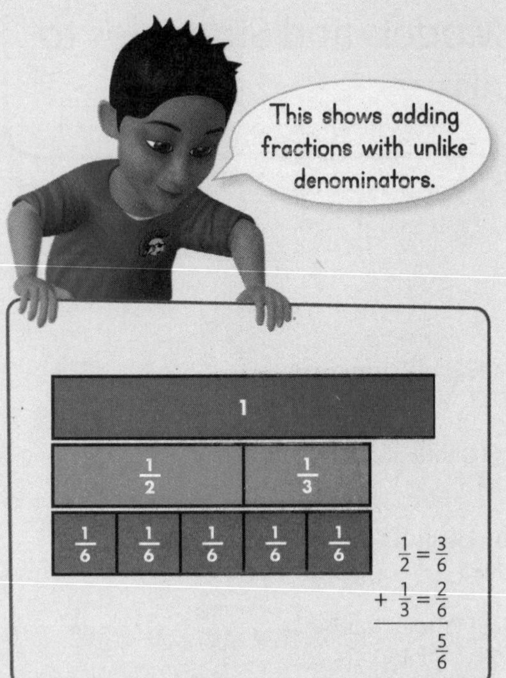

TOPIC 7 Use Equivalent Fractions to Add and Subtract Fractions

Grade 5 Common Core Standards

Dear Families,

The standards on the following pages describe the math that students will learn this year.

DOMAIN **5.OA**
OPERATIONS AND ALGEBRAIC THINKING

ADDITONAL CLUSTER **5.OA.A**
Write and interpret numerical expressions.

5.OA.A.1 Use parentheses, brackets, or braces in numerical expressions, and evaluate expressions with these symbols.

5.OA.A.2 Write simple expressions that record calculations with numbers, and interpret numerical expressions without evaluating them. *For example, express the calculation "add 8 and 7, then multiply by 2" as 2 × (8 + 7). Recognize that 3 × (18932 + 921) is three times as large as 18932 + 921, without having to calculate the indicated sum or product.*

ADDITIONAL CLUSTER **5.OA.B**
Analyze patterns and relationships.

5.OA.B.3 Generate two numerical patterns using two given rules. Identify apparent relationships between corresponding terms. Form ordered pairs consisting of corresponding terms from the two patterns, and graph the ordered pairs on a coordinate plane. *For example, given the rule "Add 3" and the starting number 0, and given the rule "Add 6" and the starting number 0, generate terms in the resulting sequences, and observe that the terms in one sequence are twice the corresponding terms in the other sequence. Explain informally why this is so.*

DOMAIN **5.NBT**
NUMBER AND OPERATIONS IN BASE TEN

MAJOR CLUSTER **5.NBT.A**
Understand the place value system.

5.NBT.A.1 Recognize that in a multi-digit number, a digit in one place represents 10 times as much as it represents in the place to its right and $\frac{1}{10}$ of what it represents in the place to its left.

5.NBT.A.2 Explain patterns in the number of zeros of the product when multiplying a number by powers of 10, and explain patterns in the placement of the decimal point when a decimal is multiplied or divided by a power of 10. Use whole-number exponents to denote powers of 10.

5.NBT.A.3 Read, write, and compare decimals to thousandths.

5.NBT.A.3a Read and write decimals to thousandths using base-ten numerals, number names, and expanded form, e.g., 347.392 = $3 \times 100 + 4 \times 10 + 7 \times 1 + 3 \times \left(\frac{1}{10}\right) + 9 \times \left(\frac{1}{100}\right) + 2 \times \left(\frac{1}{1000}\right)$.

Common Core Standards

5.NBT.A.3b Compare two decimals to thousandths based on meanings of the digits in each place, using >, =, and < symbols to record the results of comparisons.

5.NBT.A.4 Use place value understanding to round decimals to any place.

MAJOR CLUSTER **5.NBT.B**
Perform operations with multi-digit whole numbers and with decimals to hundredths.

5.NBT.B.5 Fluently multiply multi-digit whole numbers using the standard algorithm.

5.NBT.B.6 Find whole-number quotients of whole numbers with up to four-digit dividends and two-digit divisors, using strategies based on place value, the properties of operations, and/or the relationship between multiplication and division. Illustrate and explain the calculation by using equations, rectangular arrays, and/or area models.

5.NBT.B.7 Add, subtract, multiply, and divide decimals to hundredths, using concrete models or drawings and strategies based on place value, properties of operations, and/or the relationship between addition and subtraction; relate the strategy to a written method and explain the reasoning used.

DOMAIN **5.NF**
NUMBER AND OPERATIONS–FRACTIONS

MAJOR CLUSTER **5.NF.A**
Use equivalent fractions as a strategy to add and subtract fractions.

5.NF.A.1 Add and subtract fractions with unlike denominators (including mixed numbers) by replacing given fractions with equivalent fractions in such a way as to produce an equivalent sum or difference of fractions with like denominators. *For example,* $\frac{2}{3} + \frac{5}{4} = \frac{8}{12} + \frac{15}{12} = \frac{23}{12}$. *(In general,* $\frac{a}{b} + \frac{c}{d} = \frac{(ad + bc)}{bd}$.*)*

5.NF.A.2 Solve word problems involving addition and subtraction of fractions referring to the same whole, including cases of unlike denominators, e.g., by using visual fraction models or equations to represent the problem. Use benchmark fractions and number sense of fractions to estimate mentally and assess the reasonableness of answers. *For example, recognize an incorrect result* $\frac{2}{5} + \frac{1}{2} = \frac{3}{7}$*, by observing that* $\frac{3}{7} < \frac{1}{2}$.

MAJOR CLUSTER **5.NF.B**
Apply and extend previous understandings of multiplication and division to multiply and divide fractions.

5.NF.B.3 Interpret a fraction as division of the numerator by the denominator $\left(\frac{a}{b} = a \div b\right)$. Solve word problems involving division of whole numbers leading to answers in the form of fractions or mixed numbers, e.g., by using visual fraction models or equations to represent the problem. *For example, interpret* $\frac{3}{4}$ *as the result of dividing 3 by 4, noting that* $\frac{3}{4}$ *multiplied by 4 equals 3, and that when 3 wholes are shared equally among 4 people each person has a share of size* $\frac{3}{4}$*. If 9 people want to share a 50-pound sack of rice equally by weight, how many pounds of rice should each person get? Between what two whole numbers does your answer lie?*

5.NF.B.4 Apply and extend previous understandings of multiplication to multiply a fraction or whole number by a fraction.

5.NF.B.4a Interpret the product $\left(\frac{a}{b}\right) \times q$ as a parts of a partition of q into b equal parts; equivalently, as the result of a sequence of operations $a \times q \div b$. *For example, use a visual fraction model to show* $\left(\frac{2}{3}\right) \times 4 = \frac{8}{3}$*, and create a story context for this equation. Do the same with* $\left(\frac{2}{3}\right) \times \left(\frac{4}{5}\right) = \frac{8}{15}$*. (In general,* $\left(\frac{a}{b}\right) \times \left(\frac{c}{d}\right) = \frac{ac}{bd}$*).*

5.NF.B.4b Find the area of a rectangle with fractional side lengths by tiling it with unit squares of the appropriate unit fraction side lengths, and show that the area is the same as would be found by multiplying the side lengths. Multiply fractional side lengths to find areas of rectangles, and represent fraction products as rectangular areas.

5.NF.B.5 Interpret multiplication as scaling (resizing), by:

5.NF.B.5a Comparing the size of a product to the size of one factor on the basis of the size of the other factor, without performing the indicated multiplication.

5.NF.B.5b Explaining why multiplying a given number by a fraction greater than 1 results in a product greater than the given number (recognizing multiplication by whole numbers greater than 1 as a familiar case); explaining why multiplying a given number by a fraction less than 1 results in a product smaller than the given number; and relating the principle of fraction equivalence $\frac{a}{b} = \frac{(n \times a)}{(n \times b)}$ to the effect of multiplying $\frac{a}{b}$ by 1.

Common Core Standards

5.NF.B.6 Solve real world problems involving multiplication of fractions and mixed numbers, e.g., by using visual fraction models or equations to represent the problem.

5.NF.B.7 Apply and extend previous understandings of division to divide unit fractions by whole numbers and whole numbers by unit fractions.

5.NF.B.7a Interpret division of a unit fraction by a non-zero whole number, and compute such quotients. *For example, create a story context for* $\left(\frac{1}{3}\right) \div 4$, *and use a visual fraction model to show the quotient. Use the relationship between multiplication and division to explain that* $\left(\frac{1}{3}\right) \div 4 = \frac{1}{12}$ *because* $\left(\frac{1}{12}\right) \times 4 = \frac{1}{3}$.

5.NF.B.7b Interpret division of a whole number by a unit fraction, and compute such quotients. *For example, create a story context for* $4 \div \frac{1}{5}$, *and use a visual fraction model to show the quotient. Use the relationship between multiplication and division to explain that* $4 \div \frac{1}{5} = 20$ *because* $20 \times \frac{1}{5} = 4$.

5.NF.B.7c Solve real world problems involving division of unit fractions by non-zero whole numbers and division of whole numbers by unit fractions, e.g., by using visual fraction models and equations to represent the problem. *For example, how much chocolate will each person get if 3 people share* $\frac{1}{2}$ *lb of chocolate equally? How many* $\frac{1}{3}$*-cup servings are in 2 cups of raisins?*

DOMAIN **5.MD**
MEASUREMENT AND DATA

SUPPORTING CLUSTER **5.MD.A**
Convert like measurement units within a given measurement system.

5.MD.A.1 Convert among different-sized standard measurement units within a given measurement system (e.g., convert 5 cm to 0.05 m), and use these conversions in solving multi-step, real world problems.

SUPPORTING CLUSTER **5.MD.B**
Represent and interpret data.

5.MD.B.2 Make a line plot to display a data set of measurements in fractions of a unit $\left(\frac{1}{2}, \frac{1}{4}, \frac{1}{8}\right)$. Use operations on fractions for this grade to solve problems involving information presented in line plots. *For example, given different measurements of liquid in identical beakers, find the amount of liquid each beaker would contain if the total amount in all the beakers were redistributed equally.*

MAJOR CLUSTER **5.MD.C**
Geometric measurement: understand concepts of volume and relate volume to multiplication and to addition.

5.MD.C.3 Recognize volume as an attribute of solid figures and understand concepts of volume measurement.

5.MD.C.3a A cube with side length 1 unit, called a "unit cube," is said to have "one cubic unit" of volume, and can be used to measure volume.

5.MD.C.3b A solid figure which can be packed without gaps or overlaps using n unit cubes is said to have a volume of n cubic units.

5.MD.C.4 Measure volumes by counting unit cubes, using cubic cm, cubic in, cubic ft, and improvised units.

5.MD.C.5 Relate volume to the operations of multiplication and addition and solve real world and mathematical problems involving volume.

5.MD.C.5a Find the volume of a right rectangular prism with whole-number side lengths by packing it with unit cubes, and show that the volume is the same as would be found by multiplying the edge lengths, equivalently by multiplying the height by the area of the base. Represent threefold whole-number products as volumes, e.g., to represent the associative property of multiplication.

5.MD.C.5b Apply the formulas $V = \ell \times w \times h$ and $V = b \times h$ for rectangular prisms to find volumes of right rectangular prisms with whole-number edge lengths in the context of solving real world and mathematical problems.

5.MD.C.5c Recognize volume as additive. Find volumes of solid figures composed of two non-overlapping right rectangular prisms by adding the volumes of the non-overlapping parts, applying this technique to solve real world problems.

Common Core Standards

DOMAIN **5.G**
GEOMETRY

ADDITIONAL CLUSTER **5.G.A**
Graph points on the coordinate plane to solve real-world and mathematical problems.

5.G.A.1 Use a pair of perpendicular number lines, called axes, to define a coordinate system, with the intersection of the lines (the origin) arranged to coincide with the 0 on each line and a given point in the plane located by using an ordered pair of numbers, called its coordinates. Understand that the first number indicates how far to travel from the origin in the direction of one axis, and the second number indicates how far to travel in the direction of the second axis, with the convention that the names of the two axes and the coordinates correspond (e.g., *x*-axis and *x*-coordinate, *y*-axis and *y*-coordinate).

5.G.A.2 Represent real world and mathematical problems by graphing points in the first quadrant of the coordinate plane, and interpret coordinate values of points in the context of the situation.

ADDITIONAL CLUSTER **5.G.B**
Classify two-dimensional figures into categories based on their properties.

5.G.B.3 Understand that attributes belonging to a category of two-dimensional figures also belong to all subcategories of that category. *For example, all rectangles have four right angles and squares are rectangles, so all squares have four right angles.*

5.G.B.4 Classify two-dimensional figures in a hierarchy based on properties.

MATHEMATICAL PRACTICES

MP.1 Make sense of problems and persevere in solving them.

MP.2 Reason abstractly and quantitatively.

MP.3 Construct viable arguments and critique the reasoning of others.

MP.4 Model with mathematics.

MP.5 Use appropriate tools strategically.

MP.6 Attend to precision.

MP.7 Look for and make use of structure.

MP.8 Look for and express regularity in repeated reasoning.

Math Practices and Problem Solving Handbook

A **Math Practices and Problem Solving Handbook** is available at SavvasRealize.com.

Math Practices

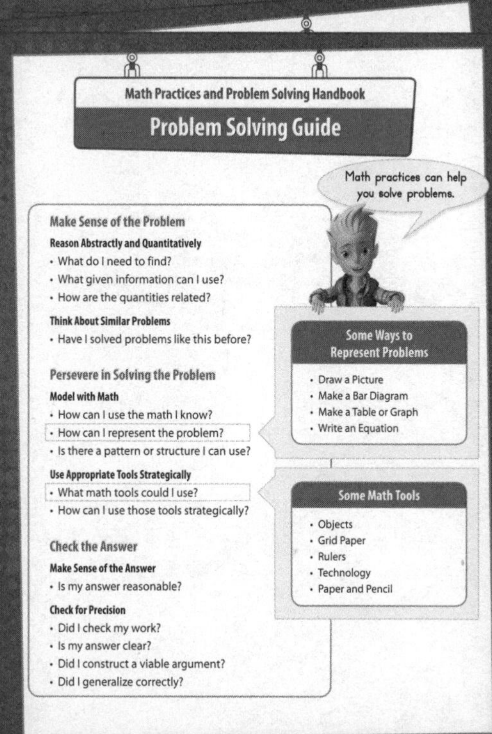

Problem Solving Guide
Problem Solving Recording Sheet
Bar Diagrams

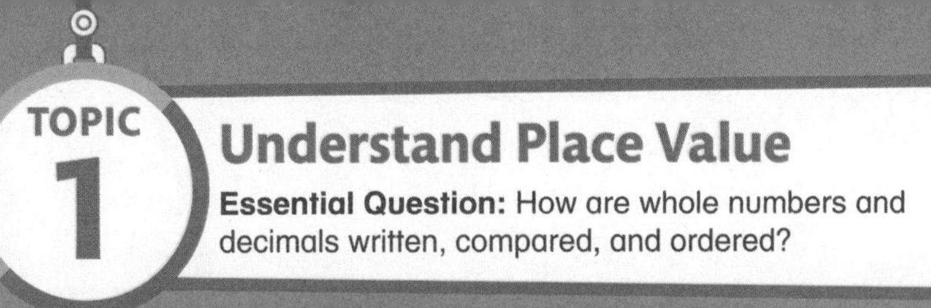

TOPIC 1 Understand Place Value

Essential Question: How are whole numbers and decimals written, compared, and ordered?

Digital Resources
Interactive Student Edition
Activity
Visual Learning
Video
Practice
Assessment
Games
Tools
Glossary

For every human on the planet there are more than 200 million insects!
Did you know pollinating insects produce $\frac{1}{3}$ of all the food and beverages we consume?
Then we better get busy as bees! Here's a project on the value of pollinating insects and their place in our world. Oops, I meant place value.

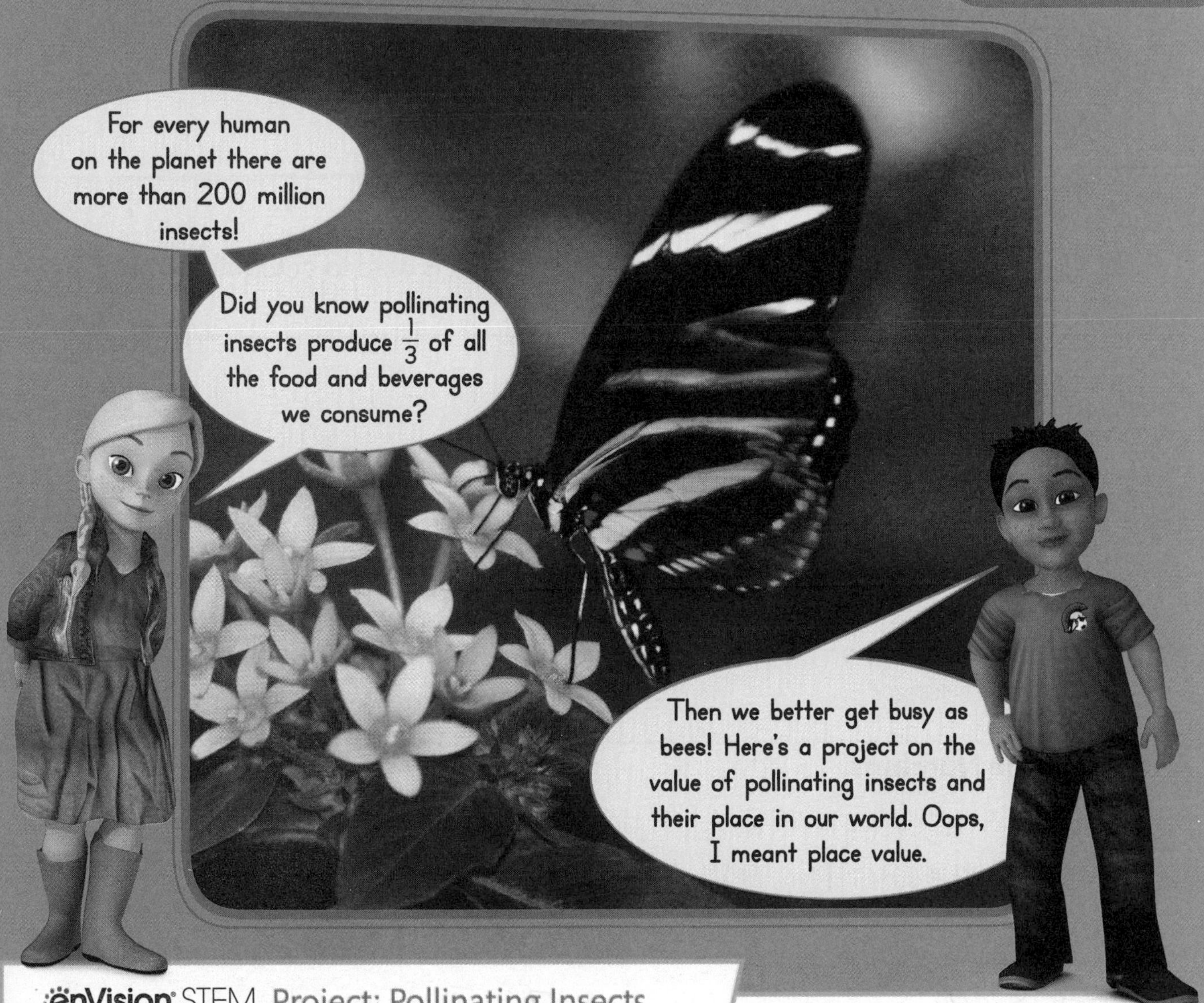

enVision STEM Project: Pollinating Insects

Do Research Use the Internet or other sources to find out more about pollinating insects in the United States. What types of insects are they? How many are there of each type? How many crops and flowering plants depend on pollinating insects in order to produce the foods we eat?

Journal: Write a Report Include what you found. Also in your report:

- Choose two of the pollinating insects. Estimate how many crop plants each type of insect pollinates.
- Estimate how many of your favorite foods and beverages come from pollinated plants.
- Make up and solve ways to compare and order your data.

Name ______________________________

Review What You Know

Vocabulary

Choose the best term from the box. Write it on the blank.

- digits
- ~~place value~~
- period
- whole numbers

1. period are the symbols used to show numbers.
2. A group of 3 digits in a number is a whole numbers.
3. place value is the position of a digit in a number that is used to determine the value of the digit.

Comparing

Compare. Use <, >, or = for each ◯.

4. 869 < 912
5. 9,033 < 9,133
6. 1,338 < 1,388
7. 417,986 = 417,986
8. 0.25 < 0.3
9. 0.5 = 0.50
10. Kamal has 7,325 songs on his computer. Benito has 7,321 songs on his computer. Who has more songs?

Adding Whole Numbers

Find each sum.

11. 10,000 + 2,000 + 60 + 1 = 12,061
12. 20,000 + 5,000 + 400 + 3 = 25,403
13. 900,000 + 8,000 + 200 + 70 + 6 = 908,276
14. 7,000,000 + 50,000 + 900 + 4 = 7,050,904

Place Value

15. The largest playing card structure was made of 218,792 cards. What is the value of the digit 8 in 218,792?

Ⓐ 80 Ⓑ 800 Ⓒ 8,000 Ⓓ 80,000

16. **Construct Arguments** In the number 767, does the first 7 have the same value as the final 7? Why or why not?

No, the first 7 is 700, the last 7 is just 7.

Name ____________________

PROJECT 1A

Manatees or sea cows?

Project: Create a Manatee Poster

PROJECT 1B

What makes a game fun?

Project: Design a Game with Place-Value Blocks

PROJECT 1C

How far are we from the sun?

Project: Research Measurements in Our Solar System

Math Modeling

Buzz In

Video

Before watching the video, think:

A minute can seem like a few seconds or a few hours, depending on what you're doing. It takes the same amount of time for me to water my plants as it does to eat lunch, but it doesn't feel that way. That's why we have stopwatches, timers, and clocks to help us keep track of time.

I can ...

model with math to solve a problem that involves comparing decimals to thousandths.

Mathematical Practices MP.4 Also MP.3, MP.6
Content Standards 5.NBT.A.3b
Also 5.NBT.A.1, 5.NBT.A.3a, 5.NBT.A.4

Name ______________________________ Activity

Lesson 1-1

Patterns with Exponents and Powers of 10

I can ...
write numbers using exponents.

Content Standard 5.NBT.A.2
Mathematical Practices MP.4, MP.5, MP.7

Solve & Share

A store sells AA batteries in packages of 10 batteries. They also sell boxes of 10 packages, cases of 10 boxes, and cartons of 10 cases. How many AA batteries are in one case? One carton? 10 cartons? ***Solve these problems any way you choose.***

You can use appropriate tools, such as place-value blocks, to help solve the problems. However you choose to solve it, show your work!

1 pack = 10
1 boxes = 100
Cases = 1,000
Carton, 10,000

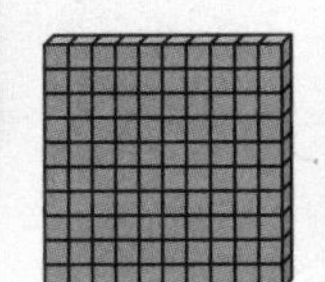

1 package = 10
1 box = 100
1 case = 1,000
1 carton = 10,000

Look Back! How many 10s are in 100? How many 10s are in 1,000? Write equations to show your work.

$100 \div 10 = 10$

$1,000 \div 10 = 100$

Essential Question

How Can You Explain Patterns in the Number of Zeros in a Product?

Visual Learning Bridge

A

Tamara's new horse weighs about 1,000 pounds. How can you show 1,000 as a power of 10 using an exponent?

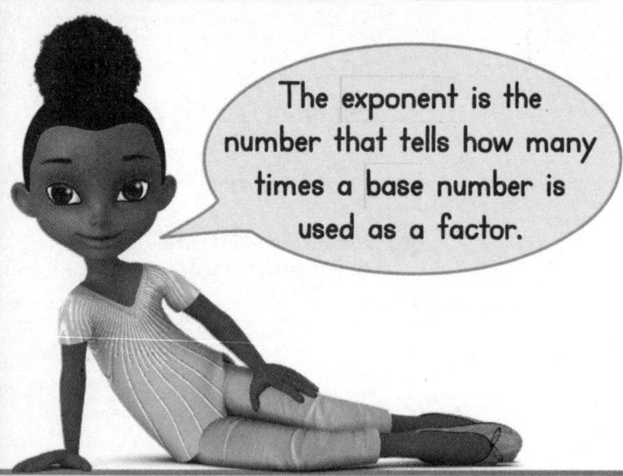

The exponent is the number that tells how many times a base number is used as a factor.

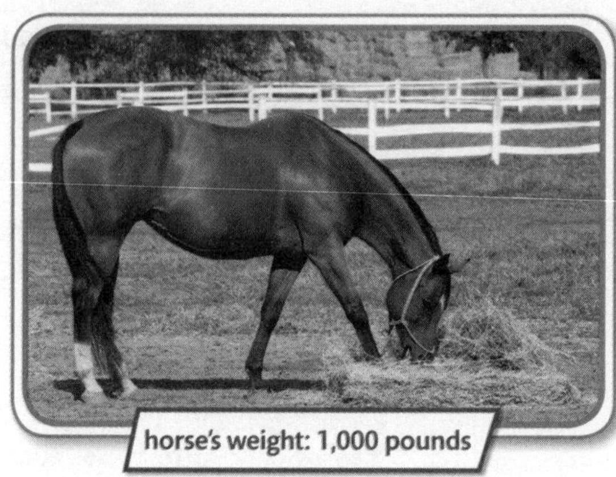

horse's weight: 1,000 pounds

B Write 1,000 as a product using 10 as a factor.

factors — exponent

$$1{,}000 = 10 \times 10 \times 10 = 10^3$$

base

The exponent, 3, shows that the base number, 10, is multiplied 3 times.

So, 1,000 is written as 10^3 using exponents.

C Tamara estimates that her horse will eat about 5,000 pounds of hay each year. How can you write 5,000 using exponents?

$5 \times 10^1 = 5 \times 10 = 50$

$5 \times 10^2 = 5 \times 10 \times 10 = 500$

$5 \times 10^3 = 5 \times 10 \times 10 \times 10 = 5{,}000$

The number of zeros in the product is the same as the exponent.

So, 5,000 is written as 5×10^3 using exponents.

Convince Me! Look for Relationships What pattern do you notice in the number of zeros in the products in Box C above?

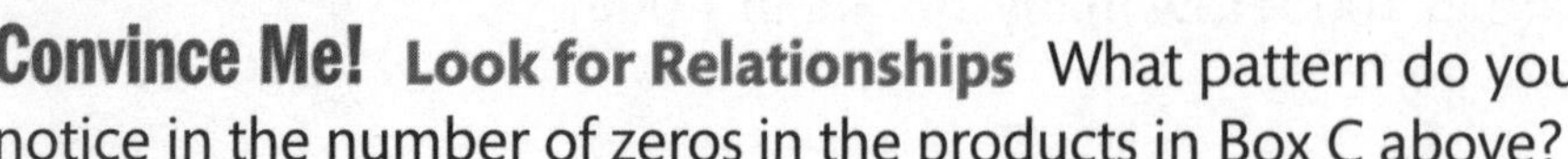

If the exponent is 10^1, then there is 1 zero. If it is 10^2, then, there are 2 zeros. 10^3 has 3 zeros.

Name

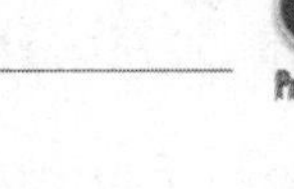

Guided Practice

Do You Understand?

1. Why are there three zeros in the product of 6×10^3?

Because 10^3 means 3 zeros.

2. Susan said that 10^5 is 50. What mistake did Susan make? What is the correct answer? Sue's mistake was she multiplied 10×5=50. The correct answer is 100,000

Do You Know How?

In **3** and **4**, complete the pattern.

3. $10^1 =$ 10
$10^2 =$ 100
$10^3 =$ 1,000
$10^4 =$ 10,000

4. 70 $= 7 \times 10^1$
700 $= 7 \times 10^2$
7,000 $= 7 \times 10^3$
70,000 $= 7 \times 10^4$

Independent Practice

In **5–15**, find each product. Use patterns to help.

5. $3 \times 10^1 =$ 30
$3 \times 10^2 =$ 300
$3 \times 10^3 =$ 3,000
$3 \times 10^4 =$ 30,000

6. $2 \times 10 =$ 20
$2 \times 100 =$ 200
$2 \times 1{,}000 =$ 2,000
$2 \times 10{,}000 =$ 20,000

7. 90 $= 9 \times 10^1$
900 $= 9 \times 10^2$
9,000 $= 9 \times 10^3$
90,000 $= 9 \times 10^4$

8. 8×10^4 = 80,000 **9.** $4 \times 1{,}000$ = 4,000 **10.** 5×10^2 = 500 **11.** $6 \times 10{,}000$ = 60,000

12. 4×10^1 = 40 **13.** 100×9 = 900 **14.** $10^3 \times 6$ = 6,000 **15.** 8×10^5 800,000

16. Write $10 \times 10 \times 10 \times 10 \times 10 \times 10$ with an exponent. Explain how you decided what exponent to write.

10^6, since we were multiplying 10, 6 times.

Problem Solving

17. One box of printer paper has 3×10^2 sheets of paper. Another box has 10^3 sheets of paper. What is the total number of sheets in both boxes?

18. A post is put every 6 feet along a fence around a rectangular field that is 42 ft long and 36 ft wide. How many posts are needed?

19. Number Sense A company had 9×10^6 dollars in sales last year. Explain how to find the product 9×10^6.

20. An aquarium has the same shape as the solid figure shown below. What is the name of this solid figure?

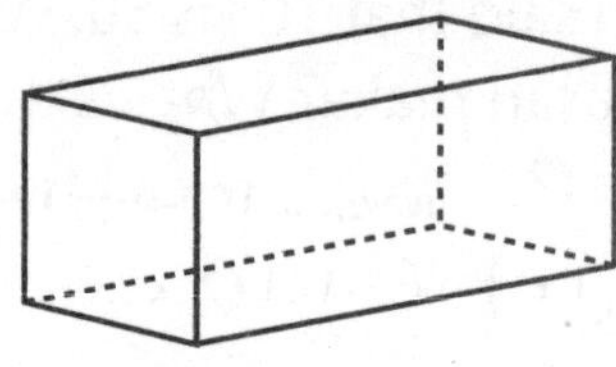

21. Model with Math Isaac takes 5 minutes to ride his bike down the hill to school and 10 minutes to ride up the hill from school. He attends school Monday through Friday. How many minutes does he spend biking to and from school in two weeks? Write an equation to model your work.

22. Higher Order Thinking Santiago hopes to buy a 4-horse trailer for about $12,000. Describe all the numbers that when rounded to the nearest hundred are 12,000.

Assessment Practice

23. Choose all the equations that are true.

- ☐ $10 \times 10 \times 10 \times 10 = 40$
- ☐ $10 \times 10 \times 10 \times 10 = 10^4$
- ☐ $10 \times 10 \times 10 \times 10 = 1{,}000$
- ☐ $10 \times 10 \times 10 \times 10 = 10{,}000$
- ☐ $10 \times 10 \times 10 \times 10 = 4 \times 10^4$

24. Choose all the equations that are true.

- ☐ $6 \times 10^5 = 6 \times 100{,}000$
- ☐ $6 \times 10^5 = 6 \times 10{,}000$
- ☐ $6 \times 10^5 = 600{,}000$
- ☐ $6 \times 10^5 = 60{,}000$
- ☐ $6 \times 10^5 = 650{,}000$

Name ____________________

Activity

Lesson 1-2
Understand Whole-Number Place Value

I can ...
understand place-value relationships.

Content Standard 5.NBT.A.1
Mathematical Practices MP.3, MP.7

Solve & Share

The population of a city is 1,880,000. What is the value of each of the two 8s in this number? How are the two values related? ***Use tools like this place-value chart to help solve the problem.***

80,000 × 10 = 800,000

Use Structure
You can use place value to analyze the relationship between the digits of a number. Show your work!

millions period			thousands period			ones period		
hundred millions	ten millions	one millions	hundred thousands	ten thousands	one thousands	hundreds	tens	ones

$\frac{14}{1} - 3\frac{5}{8}$

$\frac{112}{8} - \frac{29}{8} = \frac{83}{8} = 10\frac{3}{8}$

$\frac{14}{1} - \frac{29}{8}$

14 × 8 = 112

112 − 29 = 83

Look Back! Is the relationship between the value of the two 8s in 1,088,000 the same as the relationship between the value of the two 8s in the problem above? Explain.

Yes, because if you multihly by ten.

How Are Place-Value Positions Related?

Visual Learning Bridge

A

According to the 2010 U.S. Census, the population of Phoenix, Arizona is about 1,440,000. What is the relationship between the value of the two 4s in this number?

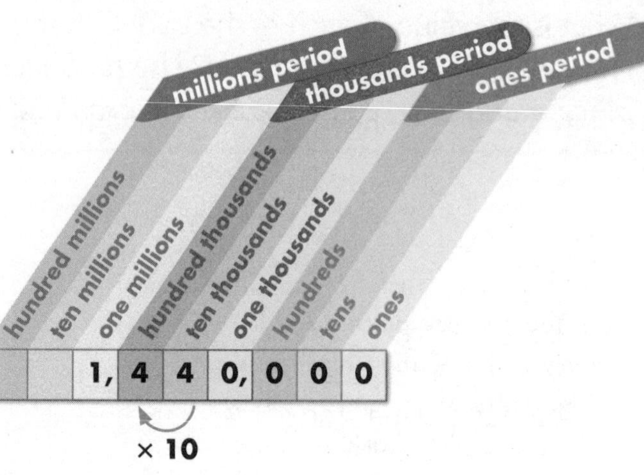

B

Look at the expanded form of 1,440,000. The value of the 4 in the hundred thousands place is 400,000. The value of the 4 in the ten thousands place is 40,000.

400,000 is 10 times as great as 40,000.
40,000 is $\frac{1}{10}$ of 400,000.

Sometimes *word form* is used instead of *number name.*

Standard form:
1,440,000

Expanded form:
$1 \times 1{,}000{,}000 + 4 \times 100{,}000 + 4 \times 10{,}000$

Using exponents, this can be written as:
$(1 \times 10^6) + (4 \times 10^5) + (4 \times 10^4)$

Number name:
one million, four hundred forty thousand

Convince Me! **Construct Arguments** Is the value of the 1 in 1,440,000 10 times as great as the value of the 4 in the hundred thousands place? Explain.

No, 1,000,000 x 10 is not the same as 400,000

Name ______________________________

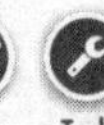

Practice Tools Assessment

Another Example

When two digits next to each other in a number are the same, the digit on the left has 10 times the value of the digit to its right.

When two digits next to each other are the same, the digit on the right has $\frac{1}{10}$ the value of the digit to its left.

5 5 5, 0 0 0

$\times 10$ $\times \frac{1}{10}$

Guided Practice

Do You Understand?

1. In 9,290, is the value of the first 9 ten times as great as the value of the second 9? Explain.

Do You Know How?

2. Write 4,050 in expanded form.

In **3** and **4**, write the values of the given digits.

3. the 7s in 7,700

4. the 2s in 522

Independent Practice

In **5–7**, write each number in standard form.

5. 8,000,000 + 300 + 9

6. $(4 \times 10^4) + (6 \times 10^2)$

7. 10,000 + 20 + 3

In **8–10**, write each number in expanded form.

8. 5,360

9. 102,200

10. 85,000,011

In **11–13**, write the values of the given digits.

11. the 7s in 6,778

12. the 9s in 990,250

13. the 1s in 2,011,168

Problem Solving

14. Write the number name and expanded form for the number of driver ants that could be in two colonies.

Up to 22,000,000 driver ants can live in a single colony.

15. **enVision® STEM** A queen ant can produce about nine million ants in her lifetime. Write this number in standard form.

16. **Critique Reasoning** Paul says that in the number 6,367, one 6 is 10 times as great as the other 6. Is he correct? Explain why or why not.

17. Jorge drew a square that had a side length of 8 inches. What is the perimeter of Jorge's square?

Remember, the *perimeter* of a shape is the distance around it.

18. **Higher Order Thinking** Dan wrote $(2 \times 10^6) + (3 \times 10^4) + (5 \times 10^3) + 4$ for the expanded form of two million, three hundred fifty thousand, four. What error did he make in the expanded form? What is the standard form of the number?

Assessment Practice

19. Colleen says she is thinking of a 4-digit number in which all the digits are the same. The value of the digit in the hundreds place is 200.

Part A

What is the number? Explain.

Part B

Describe the relationship between the values of the digits in the number.

Name ______________________________ Activity

Lesson 1-3
Decimals to Thousandths

I can ...
read and write decimals to the thousandths.

Content Standards 5.NBT.A.1
Also 5.NBT.A.3a
Mathematical Practices MP.2, MP.3, MP.7

Solve & Share

At Suzie's Sticker City, customers can buy a book of stickers, a page, a strip, or a single sticker. Provide the missing fractions in the boxes below.

How can you use what you know about powers of 10 to help you fill in the boxes?

1 book of 10 pages	1 page of 10 strips	1 strip of 10 stickers	1 sticker
	Fraction of book: ☐	Fraction of book: ☐	Fraction of book: ☐

Look Back! Use Structure Describe any patterns you notice in the fractions.

How Can You Read and Write Decimals to the Thousandths?

Visual Learning Bridge

A

A box is filled with 1,000 cubes. Amy picks out 4 cubes. How can you represent 4 out of 1,000 cubes as a decimal?

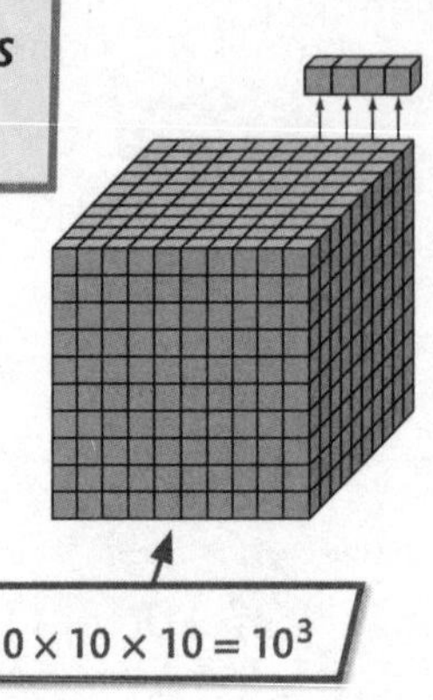

You can write 4 out of 1,000 as the fraction $\frac{4}{1,000}$.

B

The number name for $\frac{4}{1,000}$ is four thousandths. A decimal place-value chart can help you determine the decimal. Notice that the thousandths place is three places to the right of the decimal point.

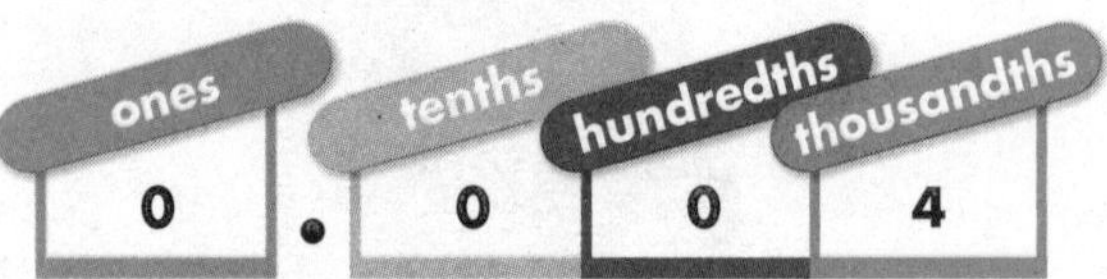

So, $\frac{4}{1,000}$ can be represented by the decimal 0.004.

C

How can $\frac{444}{1,000}$ be represented by a decimal? $\frac{444}{1,000}$ is read as *four hundred forty-four thousandths* and represented by the decimal 0.444.

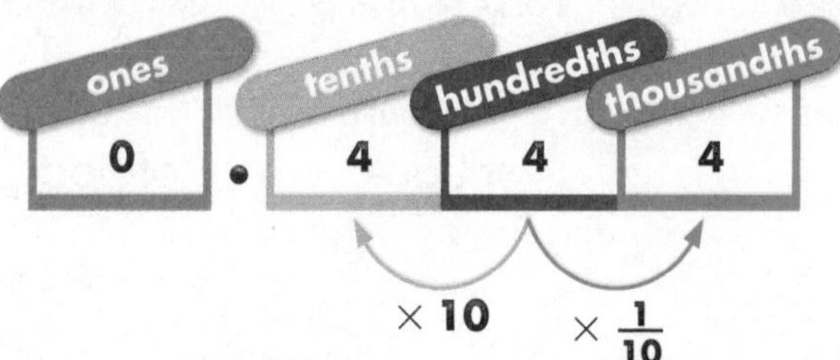

The value of the digit 4 in the hundredths place has 10 times the value of the digit 4 in the thousandths place and $\frac{1}{10}$ the value of the digit 4 in the tenths place.

Convince Me! **Reasoning** How is 0.004 the same as and different from 0.444?

Name

Practice Tools Assessment

Guided Practice

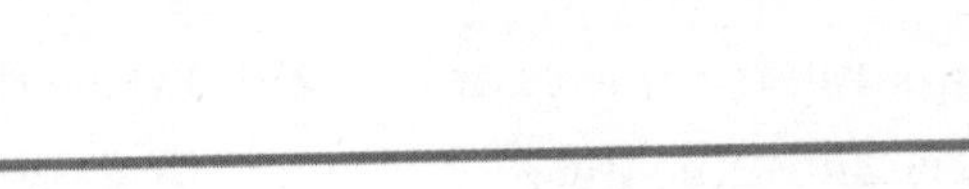

Do You Understand?

1. If four cubes are pulled from the box on the previous page, how would you write the fraction representing the cubes that are left? the decimal representing the cubes that are left?

2. 0.3 is 10 times as great as what decimal? 0.003 is $\frac{1}{10}$ of what decimal?

Do You Know How?

In **3-6**, write each decimal as a fraction.

3. 0.001 =

4. 0.05 =

5. 0.512 =

6. 0.309 =

In **7-10**, write each fraction as a decimal.

7. $\frac{2}{1,000} =$

8. $\frac{34}{100} =$

9. $\frac{508}{1,000} =$

10. $\frac{99}{1,000} =$

Independent Practice

In **11-18**, write each decimal as a fraction.

11. 0.007

12. 0.08

13. 0.065

14. 0.9

15. 0.832

16. 0.203

17. 0.78

18. 0.999

In **19-26**, write each fraction as a decimal.

19. $\frac{434}{1,000}$

20. $\frac{3}{10}$

21. $\frac{873}{1,000}$

22. $\frac{17}{1,000}$

23. $\frac{309}{1,000}$

24. $\frac{5}{1,000}$

25. $\frac{6}{100}$

26. $\frac{999}{1,000}$

27. Look at the middle 9 in Exercise 18. How is its value related to the value of the 9 to its left? to the value of the 9 to its right?

Problem Solving

28. The Palmers' property tax bill for the year is $3,513. In their first installment, they paid $1,757. How much do they still owe on their bill? Write an equation to model your work.

29. Write the fractions $\frac{22}{100}$ and $\frac{22}{1,000}$ as decimals.
How are the values of the digit 2 related in each of the decimals?

30. Simon scored 4×10^2 points in a game. Joe scored 2×10^3 points in the same game. Whose score is higher? How much higher?

31. **Higher Order Thinking** Kelly said that $\frac{97}{1,000}$ can be written as 0.97. Is she correct? Explain.

32. **Critique Reasoning** Frank reasoned that in the number 0.555, the value of the 5 in the thousandths place is ten times as great as the 5 in the hundredths place. Is he correct? Explain.

33. How many cubes are in the box? What fraction of the entire box do the 7 cubes represent? Explain your answer.

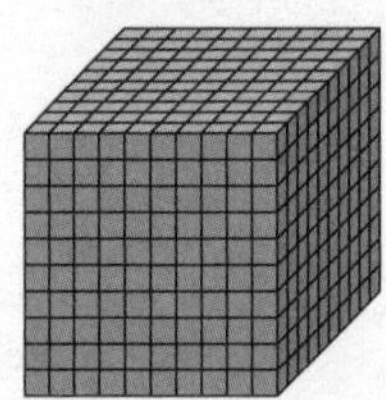

Assessment Practice

34. 0.04 is 10 times as great as which decimal?

Ⓐ 0.4
Ⓑ 0.1
Ⓒ 0.004
Ⓓ 0.001

35. 0.009 is $\frac{1}{10}$ of which decimal?

Ⓐ 0.01
Ⓑ 0.09
Ⓒ 0.1
Ⓓ 0.9

Name

Activity

Lesson 1-4
Understand Decimal Place Value

I can ...
read and write decimals in different ways.

Content Standard 5.NBT.A.3a
Mathematical Practices MP.6, MP.7, MP.8

Solve & Share

A runner won a 100-meter race with a time of 9.85 seconds. How can you use place value to explain this time? Complete a place-value chart to show this time.

Generalize
You can use what you know about whole-number place value to help you think about place value of decimal numbers.

Look Back! In the decimal 9.85, what is the value of the 8? What is the value of the 5?

Visual Learning

Glossary

Visual Learning Bridge

Essential Question How Can You Represent Decimals?

A

Jo picked a seed from her flower. The seed has a mass of 0.245 gram. What are some different ways you can represent 0.245?

You can write the standard form, expanded form, and number name for a decimal just like you can for a whole number.

B

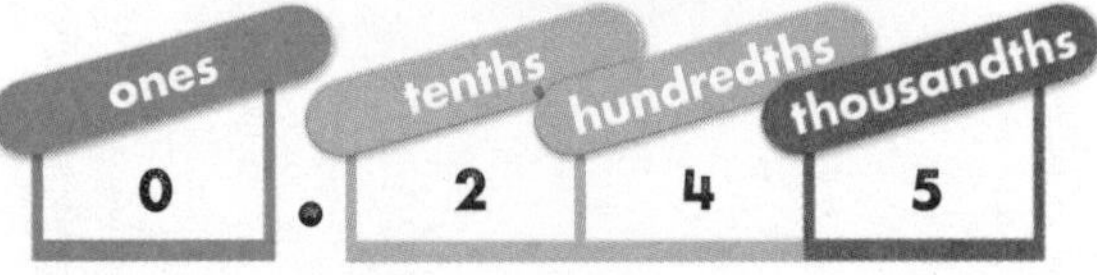

Standard Form: 0.245

The 5 is in the thousandths place. Its value is 0.005.

Expanded Form:

$\left(2 \times \frac{1}{10}\right) + \left(4 \times \frac{1}{100}\right) + \left(5 \times \frac{1}{1{,}000}\right)$

Number Name: two hundred forty-five thousandths

A place-value chart can help you identify the tenths, hundredths, and thousandths places in a decimal.

Convince Me! **Use Structure** How many hundredths are in one tenth? How many thousandths are in one hundredth? Tell how you know.

Name ____________________

Another Example

Equivalent decimals name the same amount.

What are two other decimals equivalent to 1.4?

1 hundredth is equal to 10 thousandths.

One and four tenths is the same as one and forty hundredths.

$$1.4 = 1.40$$

One and four tenths is the same as one and four hundred thousandths.

$$1.4 = 1.400$$

So, 1.4 = 1.40 = 1.400.

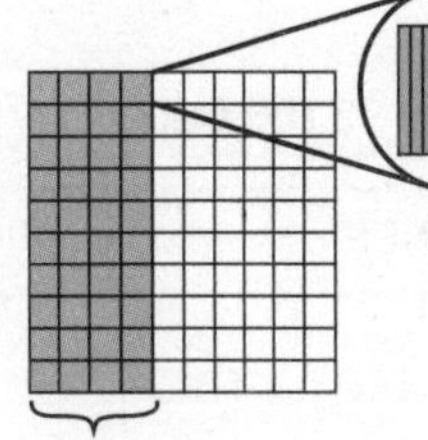

Guided Practice

Do You Understand?

1. The number 3.453 has two 3s. Why does each 3 have a different value?

Do You Know How?

In **2** and **3**, write each number in standard form.

2. $4 \times 100 + 7 \times 10 + 6 \times 1 + 6 \times \left(\frac{1}{10}\right) + 3 \times \left(\frac{1}{100}\right) + 7 \times \left(\frac{1}{1,000}\right)$

3. four and sixty-eight thousandths

Independent Practice

In **4–6**, write each number in standard form.

4. $(2 \times 1) + \left(6 \times \frac{1}{1,000}\right)$

5. $(3 \times 1) + \left(3 \times \frac{1}{10}\right) + \left(9 \times \frac{1}{1,000}\right)$

6. nine and twenty hundredths

In **7–10**, write two decimals that are equivalent to the given decimal.

7. 2.200

8. 8.1

9. 9.50

10. 4.200

Problem Solving

11. The annual fundraising goal of a charity is \$100,000. So far \$63,482 has been raised. How much more money is needed to reach the goal?

\$100,000	
\$63,482	?

12. Santiago has a rope that measures 205.95 centimeters. Write this number in expanded form.

13. How can you tell that 7.630 and 7.63 are equivalent decimals?

14. In Justin's school, 0.825 of the students participate in a sport. If there are one thousand students in Justin's school, how many participate in a sport?

15. **Be Precise** Maria incorrectly placed the decimal point when she wrote 0.65 inch for the width of her tablet computer. What is the correct decimal number for the width?

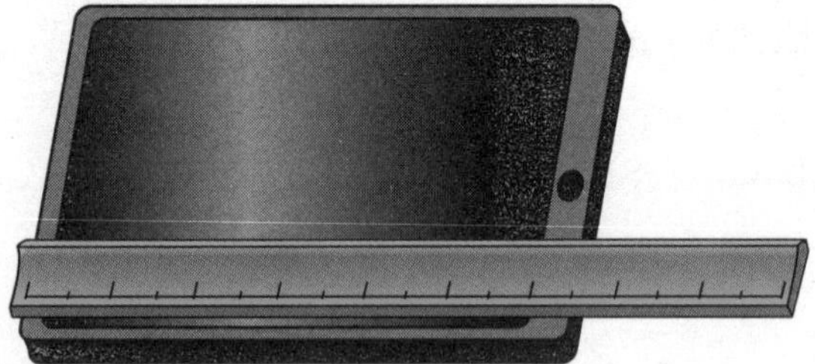

16. **Higher Order Thinking** Three boys cut out hundredths decimal models. Derrick does not shade any of his models. Ari shades half of one model. Wesley shades two models and one tenth of another model. What decimal represents the amount each boy shades?

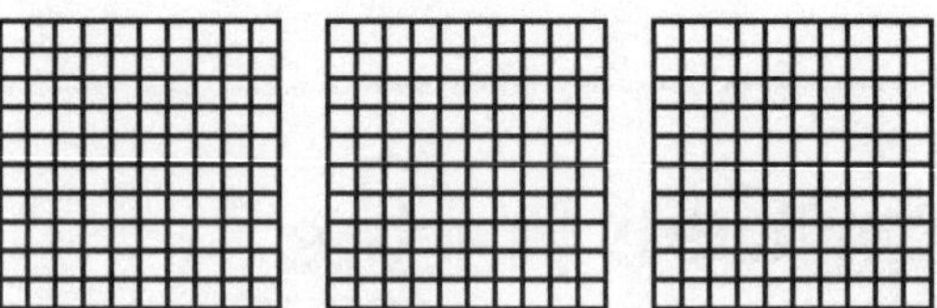

Assessment Practice

17. Find two decimals that are equivalent to $(4 \times 10) + \left(7 \times \frac{1}{100}\right)$. Write the decimals in the box.

40.7 40.07 4.7 40.070 4.70 40.70

Name ____________________

Activity

Lesson 1-5
Compare Decimals

I can ...
compare decimals to the thousandths.

Content Standard 5.NBT.A.3b
Mathematical Practices MP.3, MP.6

Solve & Share

The lengths of three ants were measured in a laboratory. The lengths were 0.521 centimeter, 0.498 centimeter, and 0.550 centimeter. Which ant was the longest? Which ant was the shortest?

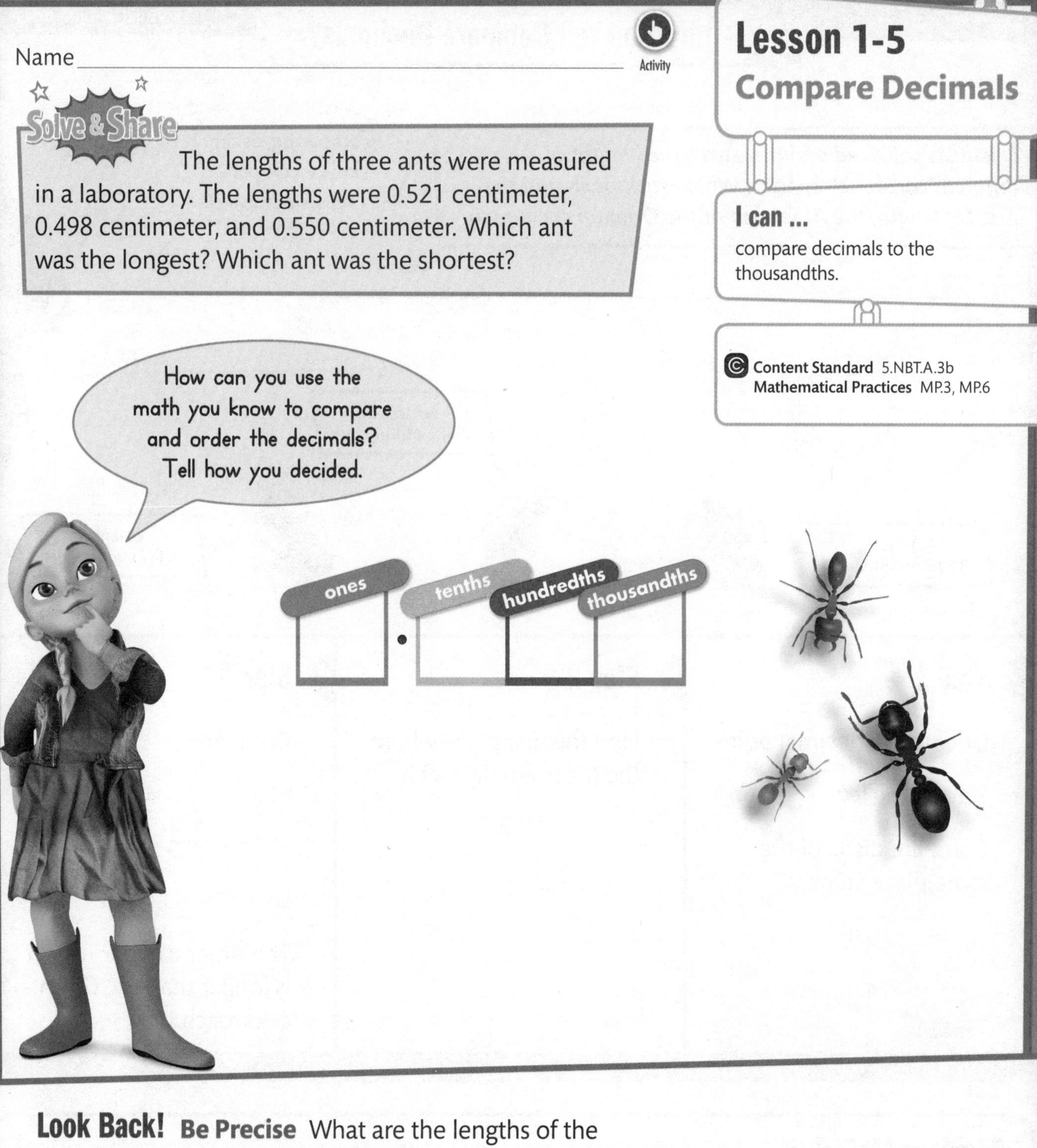

How can you use the math you know to compare and order the decimals? Tell how you decided.
ones
tenths
hundredths
thousandths

Look Back! Be Precise What are the lengths of the ants in order from least to greatest?

Visual Learning

Glossary

Visual Learning Bridge

Essential Question: How Can You Compare Decimals?

A

Scientists collected and measured the lengths of different cockroach species. Which cockroach had the greater length, the American or the Oriental cockroach?

Comparing decimals is like comparing whole numbers!

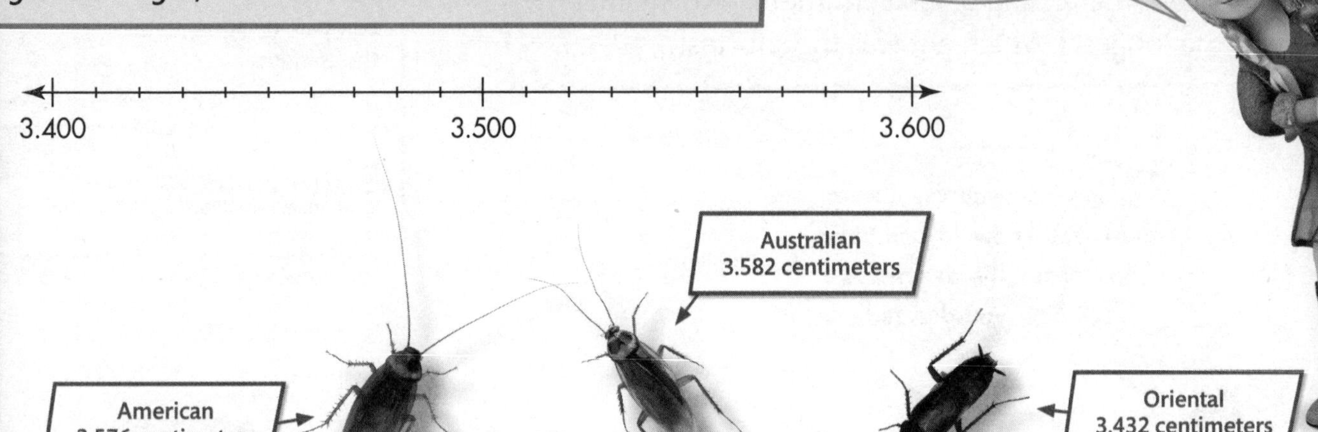

B

Step 1

Line up the decimal points.

Start at the left.

Compare digits of the same place value.

3.576

3.432

C

Step 2

Find the first place where the digits are different.

3.576

3.432

D

Step 3

Compare.

$5 > 4$

$0.5 > 0.4$

So, $3.576 > 3.432$.

The American cockroach is longer than the Oriental cockroach.

Convince Me! Critique Reasoning Valerie said, "12.68 is greater than 12.8 because 68 is greater than 8." Is she correct? Explain.

Name ____________________

Another Example

Order the cockroaches from least to greatest length.

Step 1

Write the numbers, lining up the decimal points. Start at the left. Compare digits of the same place value.

3.576
3.432
3.582

3.432 is the least.

Step 2

Write the remaining numbers, lining up the decimal points. Start at the left. Compare.

3.576
3.582

3.582 is greater than 3.576.

Step 3

Write the numbers from least to greatest.

3.432 3.576 3.582

From least to greatest lengths are the Oriental, the American, and the Australian.

Guided Practice

Do You Understand?

1. Scientists measured a Madeira cockroach and found it to be 3.44 centimeters long. Toby says that the Madeira is shorter than the Oriental because 3.44 has fewer digits than 3.432. Is he correct? Explain.

Do You Know How?

In **2** and **3**, write >, <, or = for each ◯.

2. 3.692 ◯ 3.697 **3.** 7.216 ◯ 7.203

In **4** and **5**, order the decimals from least to greatest.

4. 5.540, 5.631, 5.625

5. 0.675, 1.529, 1.35, 0.693

Independent Practice

In **6–8**, compare the two numbers. Write >, <, or = for each ◯.

6. 0.890 ◯ 0.890 **7.** 5.733 ◯ 5.693 **8.** 9.707 ◯ 9.717

In **9** and **10**, order the decimals from greatest to least.

9. 878.403, 887.304, 887.043 **10.** 435.566, 436.565, 435.665

Problem Solving

11. **Critique Reasoning** Explain why it is not reasonable to say that 4.23 is less than 4.135 because 4.23 has fewer digits after the decimal point than 4.135.

12. **Number Sense** Carlos wrote three numbers between 0.33 and 0.34. What numbers could Carlos have written?

13. **Vocabulary** Draw lines to match each decimal on the left to its **equivalent decimal** on the right.

0.75	0.750
1.50	0.075
1.05	1.500
0.075	1.050

14. Is 0.5 greater than or less than $\frac{6}{10}$? Draw a number line to show your answer.

15. **Higher Order Thinking** Ana's gymnastics scores were posted on the scoreboard in order from highest to lowest score. One digit in her floor score is not visible. List all the possible digits for the missing number.

16. Marcia's vault score is 15.050. How does it compare to Ana's vault score?

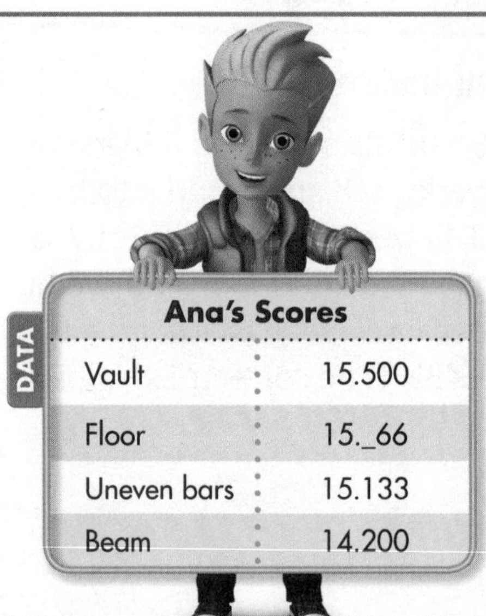

Ana's Scores	
Vault	15.500
Floor	15._66
Uneven bars	15.133
Beam	14.200

Assessment Practice

17. Which statements correctly compare two numbers?

- ☐ $0.1 < 0.125$
- ☐ $0.2 < 0.125$
- ☐ $0.125 > 0.13$
- ☐ $0.125 > 0.12$
- ☐ $0.126 < 0.125$

18. Cara weighed 4.16 pounds of apples at the grocery store. Which numbers make the statement true?

$\square > 4.16$

- ☐ 4.15
- ☐ 4.19
- ☐ 4.2
- ☐ 4.09
- ☐ 4.1

Name ______________________

Activity

Lesson 1-6
Round Decimals

I can ...
round decimals to different places.

Content Standard 5.NBT.A.4
Mathematical Practices MP.1, MP.3, MP.7

Solve & Share In science class, Marci recorded numbers from an experiment as 12.87, 12.13, 12.5, and 12.08. Which numbers are closer to 12? Which are closer to 13? How can you tell?

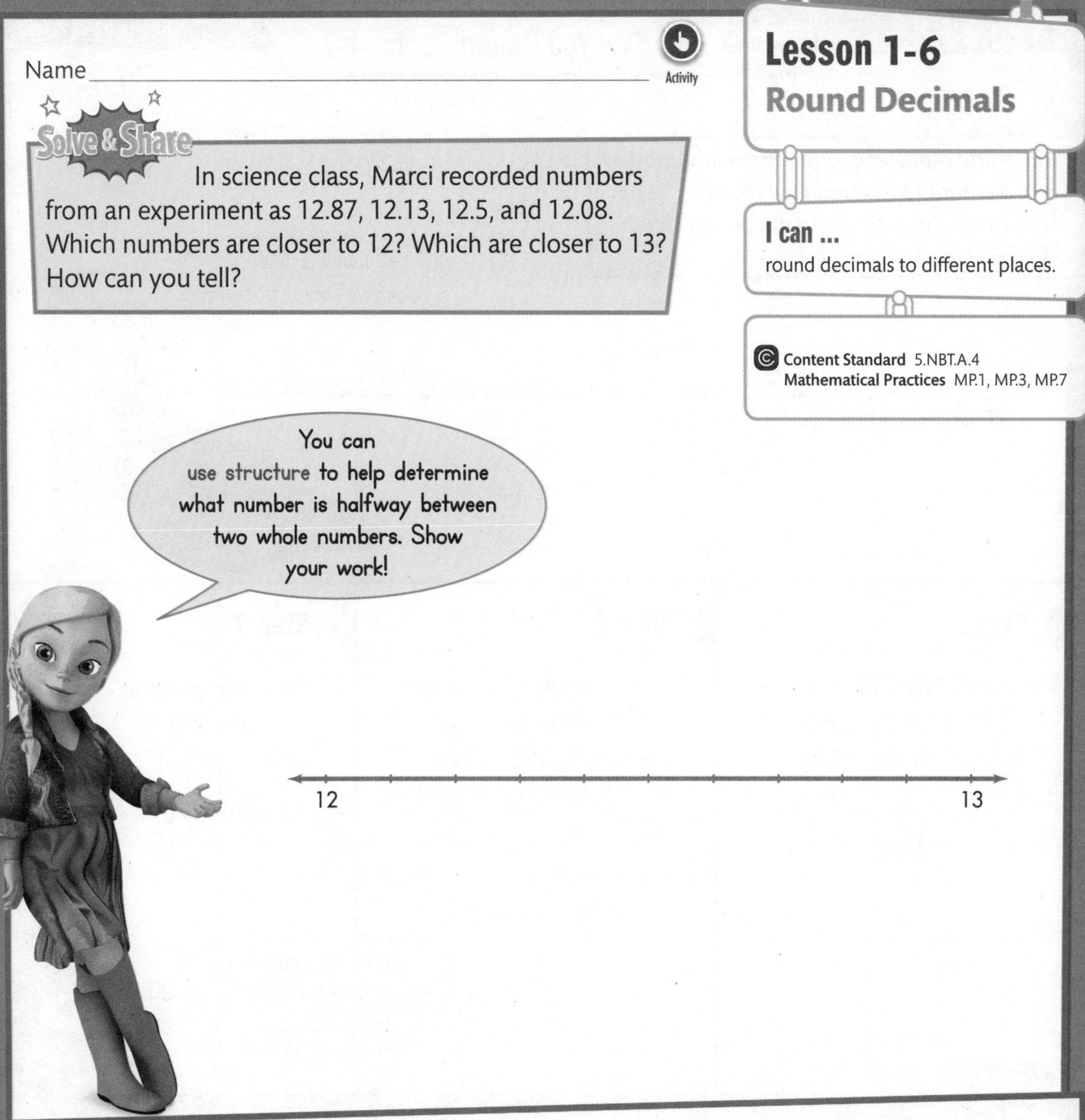

You can use structure to help determine what number is halfway between two whole numbers. Show your work!
12
13

Look Back! What is the halfway point between 12 and 13? Is that point closer to 12 or 13?

Visual Learning   A-Z Glossary

How Can You Round Decimals?

Visual Learning Bridge

A

Rounding replaces one number with another number that tells about how many or about how much. Round 2.36 to the nearest tenth. Is 2.36 closer to 2.3 or 2.4?

A number line can help you round a decimal.

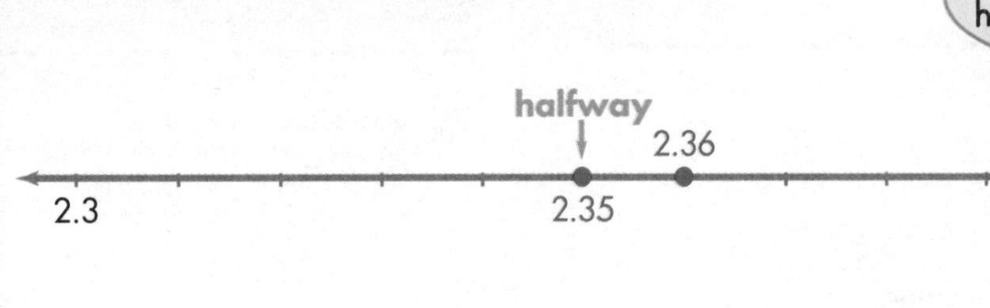

B

Step 1

Find the rounding place. Look at the digit to the right of the rounding place.

2.<u>3</u>6

C

Step 2

If the digit is 5 or greater, add 1 to the rounding digit. If the digit is less than 5, leave the rounding digit alone.

Since 6 > 5, add 1 to the 3.

D

Step 3

Drop the digits to the right of the rounding digit.

2.36 rounds to 2.4

Rounding can help you find which tenth or hundredth a decimal is closest to.

Convince Me! **Critique Reasoning** Carrie said, "448 rounds to 500 because 448 rounds to 450 and 450 rounds to 500." Is she correct? Explain. Use the number line in your explanation.

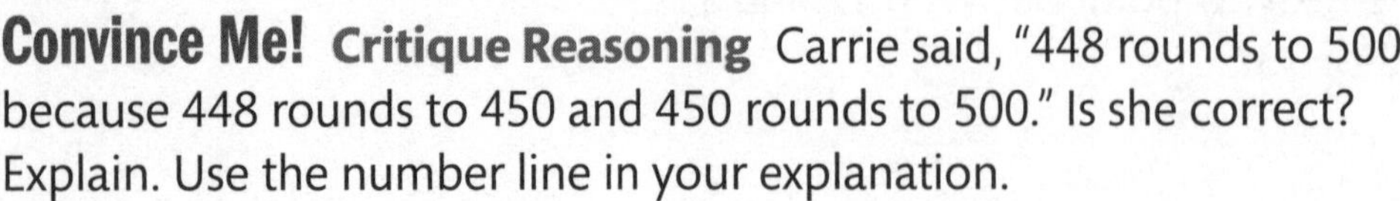

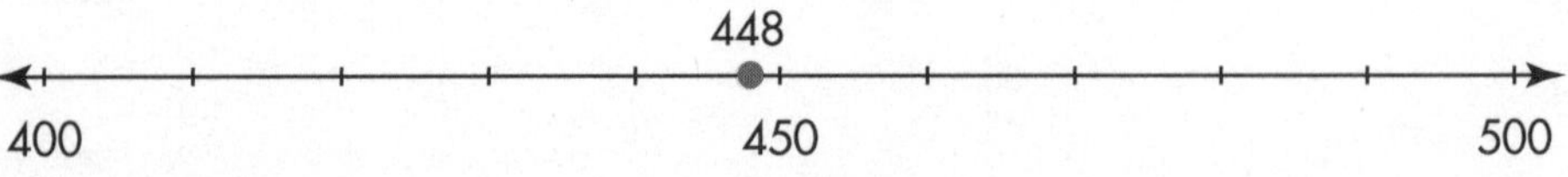

Name ____________________

Another Example

Round 3.2 to the nearest whole number.

Is 3.2 closer to 3 or 4?

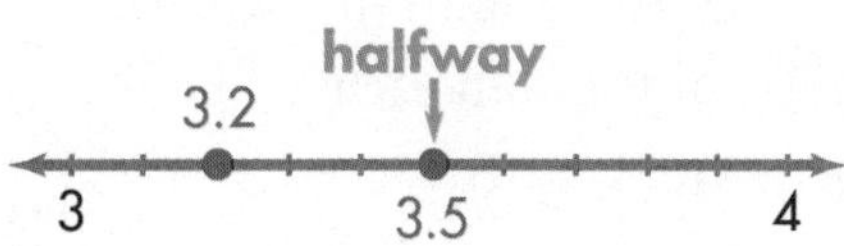

Step 1	**Step 2**	**Step 3**
Find the rounding place. Look at the digit to the right of the rounding place. $\underline{3}$.2	If the digit is 5 or greater, add 1 to the rounding digit. If the digit is less than 5, leave the rounding digit alone. Since $2 < 5$, leave 3 the same.	Drop the digits to the right of the decimal point. Drop the decimal point. 3.2 rounds to 3.

Guided Practice

Do You Understand?

1. To round 74.58 to the nearest tenth, which digit do you look at? What is 74.58 rounded to the nearest tenth?

2. A car-rental service charges customers for the number of miles they travel, rounded to the nearest whole mile. George travels 40.8 miles. For how many miles will he be charged? Explain.

Do You Know How?

In **3–10**, round each number to the place of the underlined digit.

3. 1$\underline{6}$.5 **4.** 5$\underline{6}$.1

5. 1.$\underline{3}$2 **6.** 42.$\underline{7}$8

7. 1.6$\underline{5}$2 **8.** 582.$\underline{0}$4

9. 80,547.6$\underline{4}$5 **10.** 135,701.$\underline{9}$49

Independent Practice

In **11–14**, round each decimal to the nearest whole number.

11. 4.5 **12.** 57.3 **13.** 34.731 **14.** 215.39

In **15–18**, round each number to the place of the underlined digit.

15. 7.$\underline{1}$58 **16.** 0.7$\underline{5}$8 **17.** 6.4$\underline{3}$82 **18.** 84.$\underline{7}$32

Problem Solving

19. The picture at the right shows the length of an average American alligator. What is the length of the alligator rounded to the nearest tenth?

4.39 meters

20. Name two different numbers that round to 8.21 when rounded to the nearest hundredth.

21. **Number Sense** To the nearest hundred, what is the greatest whole number that rounds to 2,500? the least whole number?

22. Draw all of the lines of symmetry in the figure shown below.

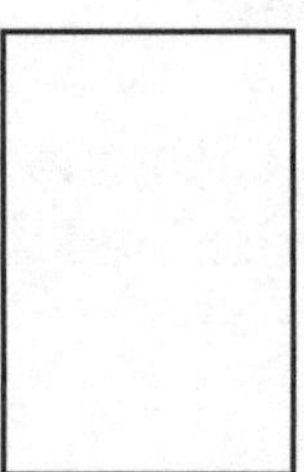

23. **Higher Order Thinking** Emma needs 2 pounds of ground meat to make a meatloaf. She has one package with 2.36 pounds of ground meat and another package with 2.09 pounds of ground meat. She uses rounding and finds that both packages are close to 2 pounds. Explain how Emma can choose the package closer to 2 pounds.

24. **Make Sense and Persevere** Robert slices a large loaf of bread to make 12 sandwiches. He makes 3 turkey sandwiches and 5 veggie sandwiches. The rest are ham sandwiches. What fraction of the sandwiches Robert makes are ham?

25. **Algebra** After buying school supplies, Ruby had \$32 left over. She spent \$4 on notebooks, \$18 on a backpack, and \$30 on a new calculator. How much money, *m*, did Ruby start with? Write an equation to show your work.

Assessment Practice

26. Find two numbers that round to 35.4 when rounded to the nearest tenth. Write the numbers in the box.

35.45 34.42 35.391 35.345 35.44 35.041

Name ____________________

Activity

Solve & Share

Angie volunteers in the school library after school. The librarian gave her a stack of books and told her to use the number on each book to shelve it where it belongs.

How can Angie arrange the books in order from least to greatest to make shelving them easier?

Problem Solving

Lesson 1-7

Look For and Use Structure

I can ...

look for and use the structure of our decimal place-value system to solve problems.

Mathematical Practices MP.7 Also MP.6, MP.8
Content Standards 5.NBT.A.3a Also 5.NBT.A.3b

Thinking Habits

Be a good thinker!
These questions can help you.

- What patterns can I see and describe?
- How can I use the patterns to solve the problem?
- Can I see expressions and objects in different ways?
- What equivalent expressions can I use?

Look Back! **Use Structure** Explain why 323.202 is less than 323.21 even though 202 is greater than 21.

How Can You Use Structure to Solve Problems?

Visual Learning Bridge

A

Analyze the chart. What do you notice that can help you complete the chart?

0.01	0.02	0.03					0.08		0.1
0.11				0.15	0.16			0.19	
0.21								0.29	
	0.32		0.34			0.37			

What do I need to do to solve this problem?

I can use the structure of the decimal place-value system to complete the chart.

You can look for patterns to find the missing numbers.

B **How can I make use of structure to solve this problem?**

I can

- find and describe patterns.
- use the patterns to see how the numbers are organized.
- analyze patterns to see the structure in the table.
- break the problem into simpler parts.

C **Solve**

Here's my thinking...

As you move down the columns, tenths increase by 1 while the hundredths stay the same.

Moving from left to right in the rows, tenths stay the same, except for the last number, while the hundredths increase by 1.

Column 1

0.01
0.11
0.21
0.31

Row 1

0.01	0.02	0.03	0.04	0.05	0.06	0.07	0.08	0.09	0.1

Convince Me! **Use Structure** Write the missing numbers. Explain how you can use structure to find the last number in the bottom row.

0.01	0.02	0.03	0.04	0.05	0.06	0.07	0.08	0.09	0.1
0.11				0.15	0.16			0.19	
0.21								0.29	
0.31	0.32		0.34			0.37			

Name ___________________________________

Guided Practice

Use Structure

Each of these grids is a part of a decimal number chart similar to the one on page 30.

1. Describe the pattern for moving from a pink square to a green square. Then write the missing numbers.

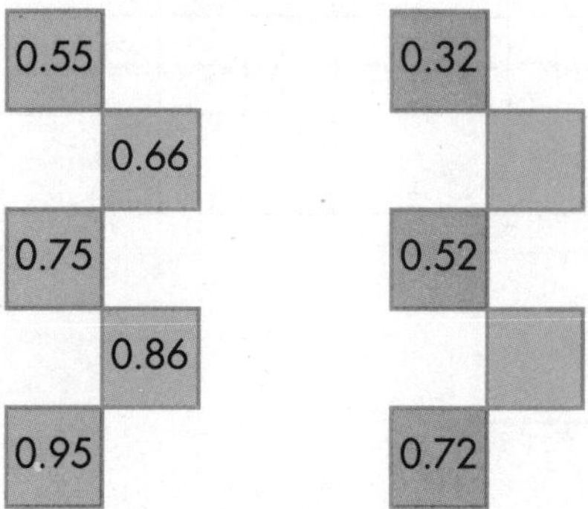

2. How can you use patterns to find the number that would be in the box below 0.52?

You can use what you know about place value when you look for patterns with decimals.

Independent Practice

Use Structure

Pamela is hiking. When she returns to camp, she passes the mile markers shown at the right.

3. Explain how you can use structure to find the decimal numbers that will be shown on the next four mile markers.

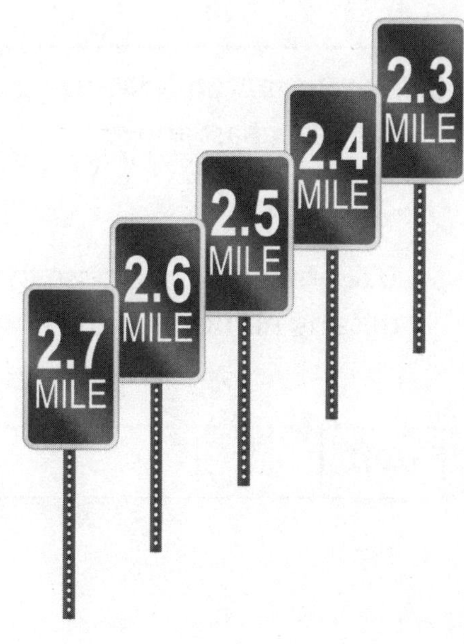

4. Pamela stops at the 1.8 mile marker. Where will she be if she walks one tenth of a mile towards camp? one mile towards camp? Explain.

Problem Solving

Performance Task

Thousandths Chart

The students in Ms. Lowell's class wrote a thousandths decimal chart on the board. Some of the numbers got erased.

0.001	0.002		0.004	0.005	0.006				0.01
0.011		0.013			0.016	0.017		0.019	0.02
	0.022					0.027		0.029	
0.031	0.032		0.034	0.035		0.037			

5. **Use Structure** Describe the pattern for moving across a row from left to right.

6. **Be Precise** How does the pattern change in the last square of each row?

7. **Use Structure** Describe the pattern for moving down a column.

8. **Use Repeated Reasoning** Write the missing numbers in the decimal chart above.

9. **Use Structure** Suppose the students add to the chart. Write the missing numbers in the row and the column below.

You can use structure to decide if decimal numbers are following a pattern.

0.071						0.077			

0.056
0.086

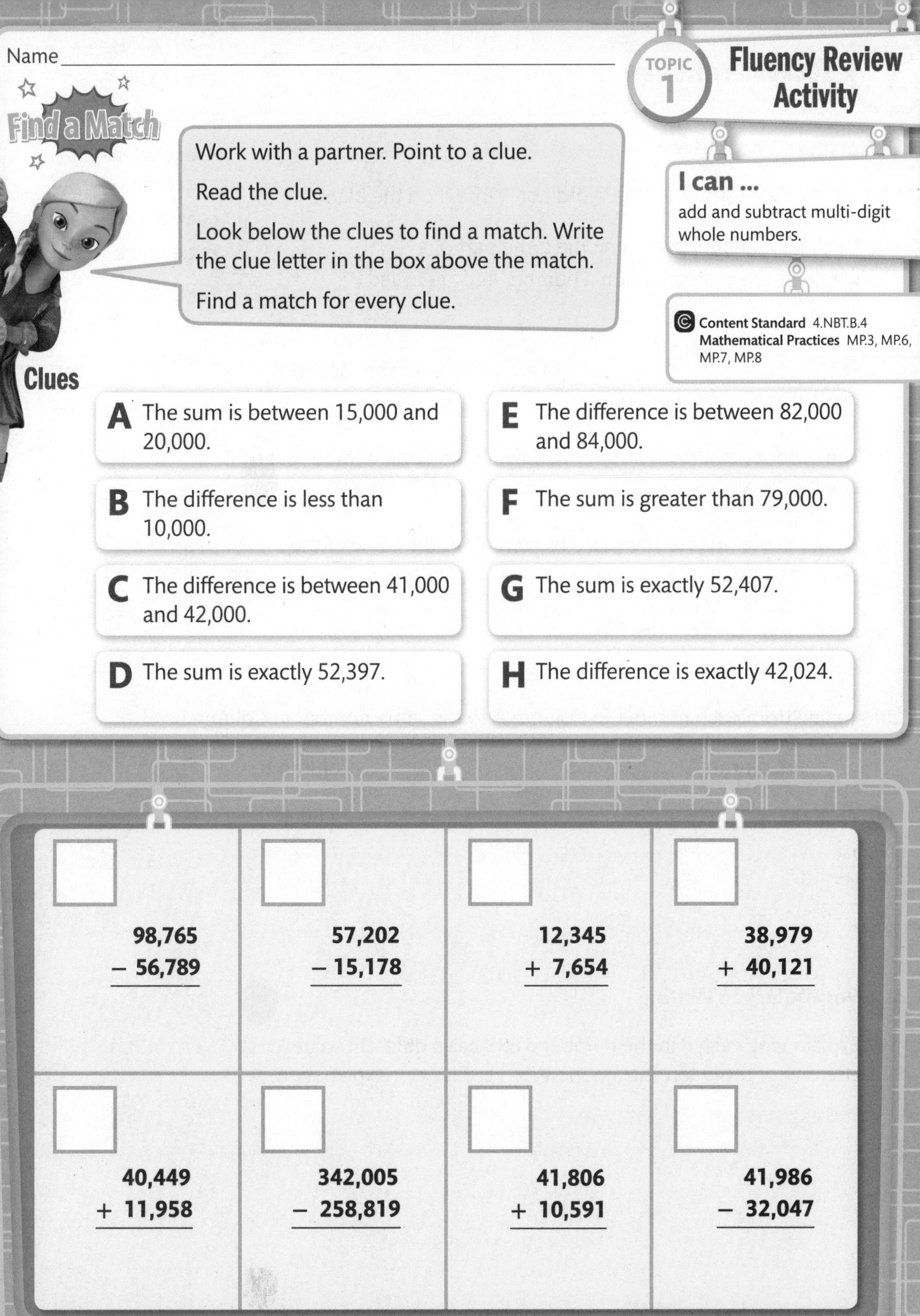

Name ____________________

TOPIC 1 Fluency Review Activity

Find a Match

Work with a partner. Point to a clue.

Read the clue.

Look below the clues to find a match. Write the clue letter in the box above the match.

Find a match for every clue.

I can ...
add and subtract multi-digit whole numbers.

Content Standard 4.NBT.B.4
Mathematical Practices MP.3, MP.6, MP.7, MP.8

Clues

A The sum is between 15,000 and 20,000.

B The difference is less than 10,000.

C The difference is between 41,000 and 42,000.

D The sum is exactly 52,397.

E The difference is between 82,000 and 84,000.

F The sum is greater than 79,000.

G The sum is exactly 52,407.

H The difference is exactly 42,024.

☐	☐	☐	☐
98,765 − 56,789	57,202 − 15,178	12,345 + 7,654	38,979 + 40,121
☐	☐	☐	☐
40,449 + 11,958	342,005 − 258,819	41,806 + 10,591	41,986 − 32,047

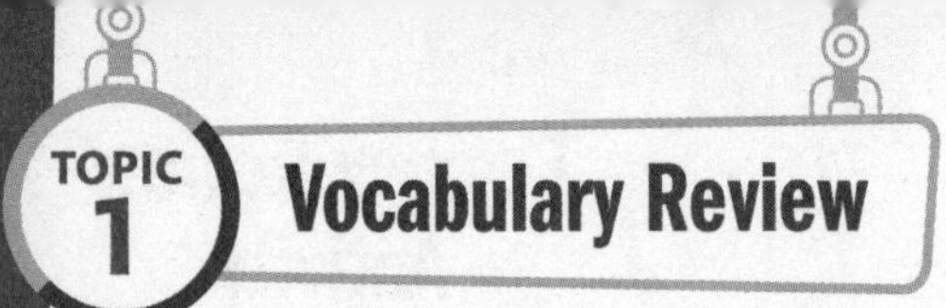

TOPIC 1 Vocabulary Review

Glossary

Word List

- base
- equivalent decimals
- expanded form
- exponent
- power
- thousandths
- value

Understand Vocabulary

Choose the best term from the Word List. Write it on the blank.

1. Decimal numbers that name the same part of a whole or the same point on a number line are called ______________.

2. The ______________ of a digit in a number depends on its place in the number.

3. The product that results from multiplying the same number over and over is a(n) ______________ of that number.

4. A digit in the hundredths place has ten times the value of the same digit in the ______________ place.

5. In 10^5, the number 10 is the ______________.

Draw a line from each number in Column A to the same number in Column B.

Column A	Column B
6. $7 \times 1{,}000 + 9 \times 10 + 2 \times 1$	4,000
7. 10^4	7,092
8. 4×10^3	10,000
9. 3.08	3.080

Use Vocabulary in Writing

10. Explain why each 8 in the number 8.888 has a different value. Use one or more terms from the Word List in your explanation.

Name ________________________________

TOPIC 1

Reteaching

Set A pages 5–8

How can you write 7,000 using exponents?

$7{,}000 = 7 \times 10 \times 10 \times 10 = 7 \times 10^3$

So, using exponents, you can write 7,000 as 7×10^3.

Remember the number of zeros in the product is the same as the exponent.

Find each product.

1. 9×10^1
2. $8 \times 1{,}000$
3. 5×10^2
4. 2×10^5

Set B pages 9–12

Write the number name and tell the value of the underlined digit for 93$\underline{0}$,365.

Nine hundred thirty thousand, three hundred sixty-five

Since the 0 is in the thousands place, its value is 0 thousands, or 0.

Use digital tools to solve these and other problems.

Remember you can find the value of a digit by its place in a number.

Write the number name and tell the value of the underlined digit.

1. $\underline{9}$,000,009
2. 4$\underline{8}$5,002,000
3. 2$\underline{5}$,678
4. $\underline{1}$7,874,000

Set C pages 13–16, 17–20

A place-value chart can help you write the standard form, expanded form, and number name for a decimal.

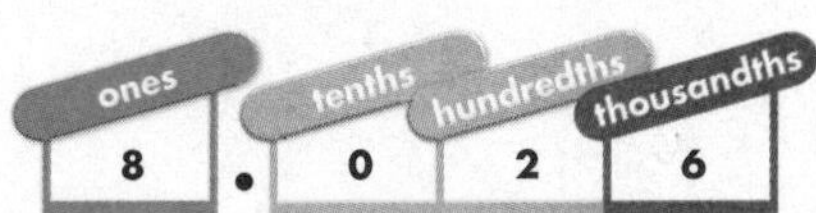

Standard form: 8.026

Expanded form: $8 + 2 \times \frac{1}{100} + 6 \times \frac{1}{1{,}000}$

Number name: Eight and twenty-six thousandths

Remember the word *and* is written for the decimal point.

1. How can you write 0.044 as a fraction? How are the values of the two 4s related in 0.044?

Write each number in standard form.

2. eight and fifty-nine hundredths
3. seven and three thousandths
4. $3 + 2 \times \frac{1}{10} + 4 \times \frac{1}{1{,}000}$

Set D pages 21–24

Compare. Write >, <, or =.

8.45 ◯ 8.47

Line up the decimal points. Start at the left to compare. Find the first place where the digits are different.

$8.4\underline{5}$
$8.4\underline{7}$ 0.05 < 0.07

So, 8.45 < 8.47.

Remember that equivalent decimals, such as 0.45 and 0.450, can help you compare numbers.

Compare. Write >, <, or =.

1. 0.584 ◯ 0.58
2. 9.327 ◯ 9.236
3. 5.2 ◯ 5.20
4. 5.643 ◯ 5.675
5. 0.07 ◯ 0.08

Set E pages 25–28

Round 12.087 to the place of the underlined digit.

$12.0\underline{8}7$ Look at the digit following the underlined digit. Look at 7.

Round to the next greater number of hundredths because 7 > 5.

12.087 rounded to the nearest hundredth is 12.09.

Remember that rounding a number means replacing it with a number that tells about how many or how much.

Round each number to the place of the underlined digit.

1. $10.\underline{2}45$
2. $\underline{7}3.4$
3. $0.1\underline{4}5$
4. $3.\underline{9}99$
5. $13.0\underline{2}3$
6. $45.\underline{3}98$

Set F pages 29–32

Think about these questions to help you **look for and use structure** to understand and explain patterns with decimal numbers.

Thinking Habits

- What patterns can I see and describe?
- How can I use the patterns to solve the problem?
- Can I see expressions and objects in different ways?
- What equivalent expressions can I use?

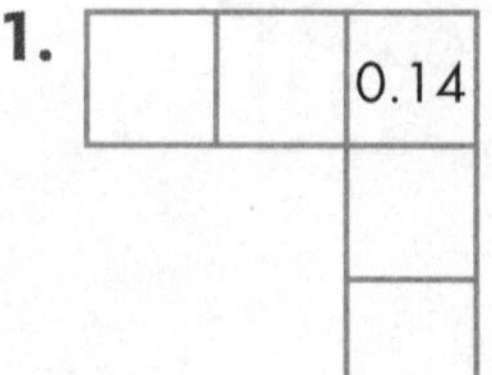

Remember to check that all of your answers follow a pattern.

Each grid is part of a decimal number chart. Write the missing numbers to complete the grids.

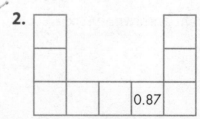

1.

		0.14

2.

			0.87	

Name ______________________________

TOPIC 1

Assessment Practice

1. Complete the sentences to make true statements.

6 is 100 times ________.

0.06 is 10 times ________.

60 is $\frac{1}{100}$ of ________.

2. A national park has eighty thousand, nine-hundred twenty-three and eighty-six hundredths acres of land. Which shows this in standard form?

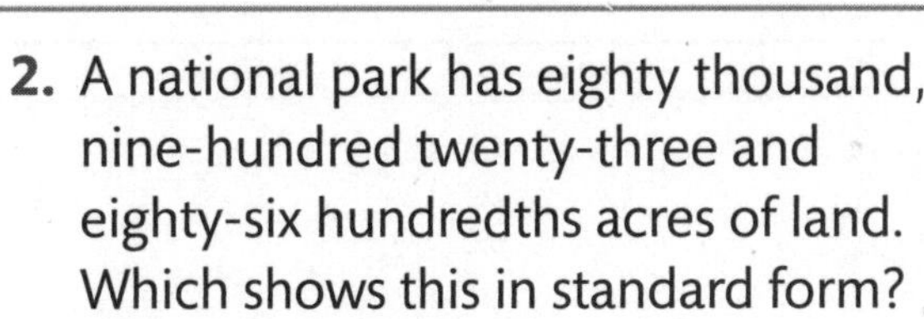

Ⓐ 80,923.086

Ⓑ 80,923.68

Ⓒ 80,923.806

Ⓓ 80,923.86

3. Which numbers have a digit in the ones place that is $\frac{1}{10}$ the value of the digit in the tens place? Select all that apply.

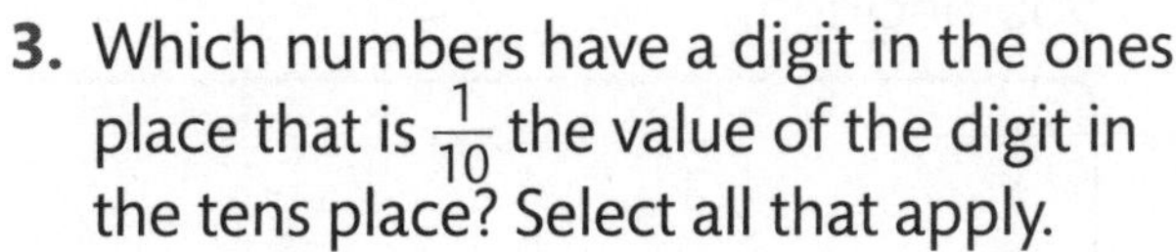

☐ 9,077

☐ 9,884

☐ 1,303

☐ 1,055

☐ 3,222

4. Mrs. Martin has $7,000 in her savings account. Alonzo has $\frac{1}{10}$ as much money in his account as Mrs. Martin. How much money does Alonzo have in his account?

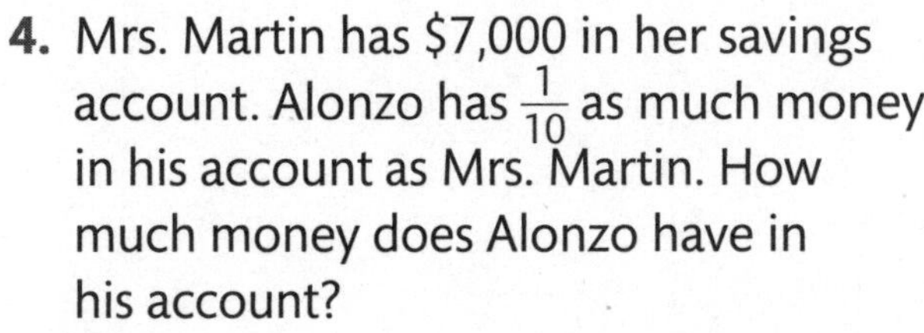

5. Select all the comparisons that are true.

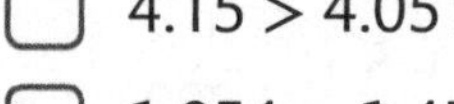

☐ 4.15 > 4.051

☐ 1.054 > 1.45

☐ 5.14 < 5.041

☐ 5.104 < 5.41

☐ 5.014 < 5.41

6. Luke shaded 20 squares on his hundredths grid. Bekka shaded 30 squares on her hundredths grid.

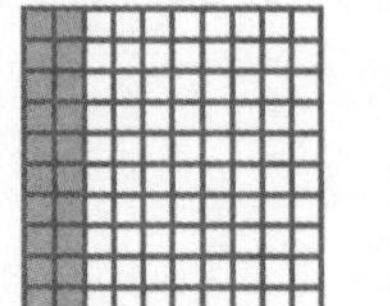

A. Whose grid represents the larger decimal?

B. Write two decimals equivalent to Luke's decimal.

7. Which statements about the values of 2.044 and 20.44 are true? Select all that apply.

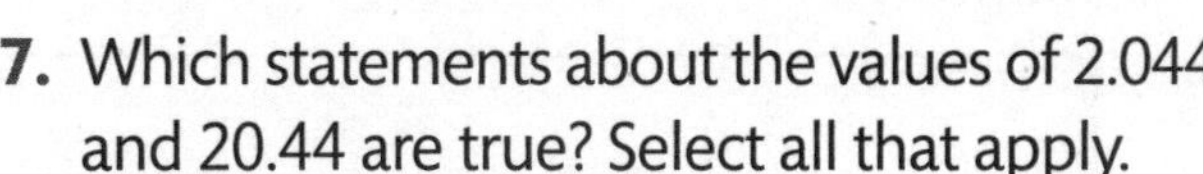

☐ 2.044 is $\frac{1}{10}$ of 20.44.

☐ 2.044 is $\frac{1}{100}$ of 20.44.

☐ 20.44 is 10 times 2.044.

☐ 20.44 is 100 times 2.044.

☐ 2.044 is 10 times 20.44.

8. The weight of Darrin's phone is 3.405 ounces. What is 3.405 written in expanded form?

Ⓐ $3 \times 1 + 4 \times \frac{1}{10} + 5 \times \frac{1}{1,000}$

Ⓑ $3 \times 10 + 4 \times \frac{1}{10} + 5 \times \frac{1}{1,000}$

Ⓒ $3 \times 10 + 4 \times \frac{1}{10} + 5 \times \frac{1}{100}$

Ⓓ $3 \times 1 + 4 \times \frac{1}{100} + 5 \times \frac{1}{1,000}$

9. Elaine has a piece of wire that is 2.16 meters long. Dikembe has a piece of wire that is 2.061 meters long. Whose piece of wire is longer? How can you tell?

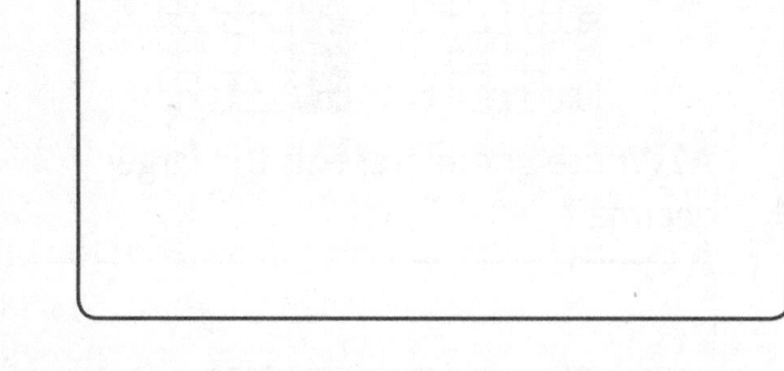

10. In a basketball tournament, Dimitri averaged 12.375 rebounds per game. What is 12.375 written in expanded form? How is it written with number names?

11. The numbers below follow a pattern.

0.006 0.06 0.6 6 ____ ____

A. What are the next two numbers in the pattern?

B. What is the relationship between the terms in the pattern?

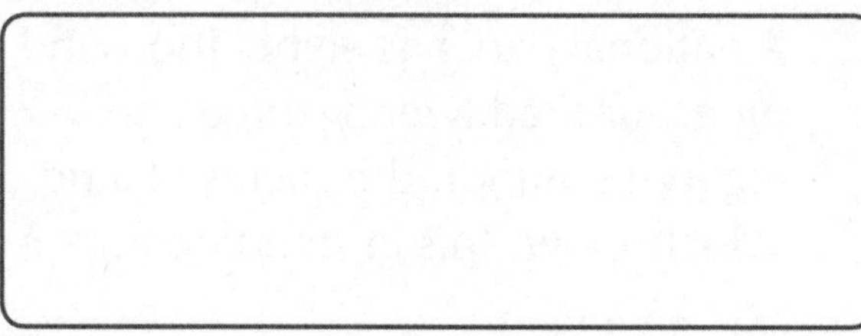

12. Kendra and her horse completed the barrel racing course in 15.839 seconds. What is this number rounded to the nearest tenth? Explain how you decided.

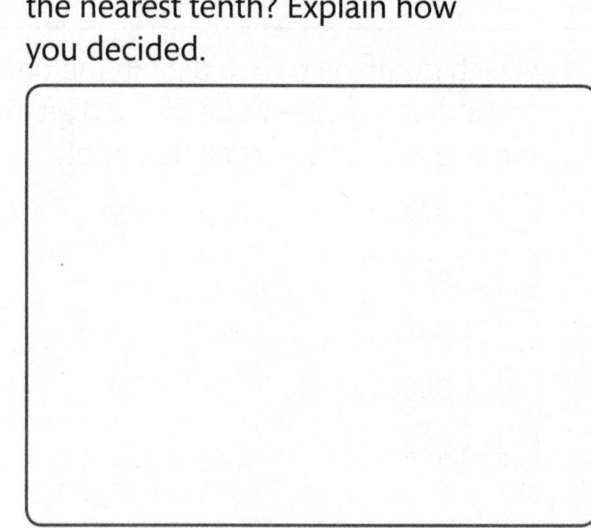

Name ______________________________

TOPIC 1

Performance Task

Fruits and Vegetables

Henry recorded how many pounds of fruits and vegetables his family bought during the past two months.

DATA

Fruit	Weight (lb)
apples	2.068
blueberries	1.07
lemons	1.031
oranges	3.502
peaches	2.608
pears	3.592

DATA

Vegetable	Weight (lb)
asparagus	2.317
beets	1.862
celery	1.402
corn	2.556
potatoes	3.441
red onions	1.861

1. Pick four fruits and list them in the table below.

Part A

Round each fruit's weight to the nearest 0.1 pound. Write the rounded weight in the next column.

Fruit	Rounded Weight (lb)	Fruit	Rounded Weight (lb)

Part B

Explain how you rounded the weights of the fruits.

2. Pick four vegetables and list them in the table below.

Part A

Round each vegetable's weight to the nearest 0.01 pound. Write the rounded weight in the next column.

Vegetable	Rounded Weight (lb)	Vegetable	Rounded Weight (lb)

Part B

Explain how you rounded the weights of the vegetables.

3. Use <, >, or = to compare the weights of blueberries and lemons.

4. When rounded to the nearest hundredth, two items will round to the same decimal. What two items are they?

5. How does writing the weight for potatoes in expanded form show why the same digit can have different values?

6. What is the relationship between the values of the two 4s in the weight of the potatoes?

7. Write the number of pounds of celery Henry's family bought using number names and in expanded form.

8. The store where Henry's family shops sold 10^3 times as many pounds of corn as Henry's family bought.

Part A

How many pounds of corn did the store sell? Write your answer in standard form and with number names.

Part B

Explain how you found your answer.

Use Models and Strategies to Add and Subtract Decimals

Essential Questions: How can sums and differences of decimals be estimated? What are some common procedures for adding and subtracting decimals? How can sums and differences be found mentally?

All living things are classified as producers, consumers, or decomposers.

Producers make food. Consumers use the food producers make or eat other organisms.

We are consumers! Here's a project on how much food consumers need.

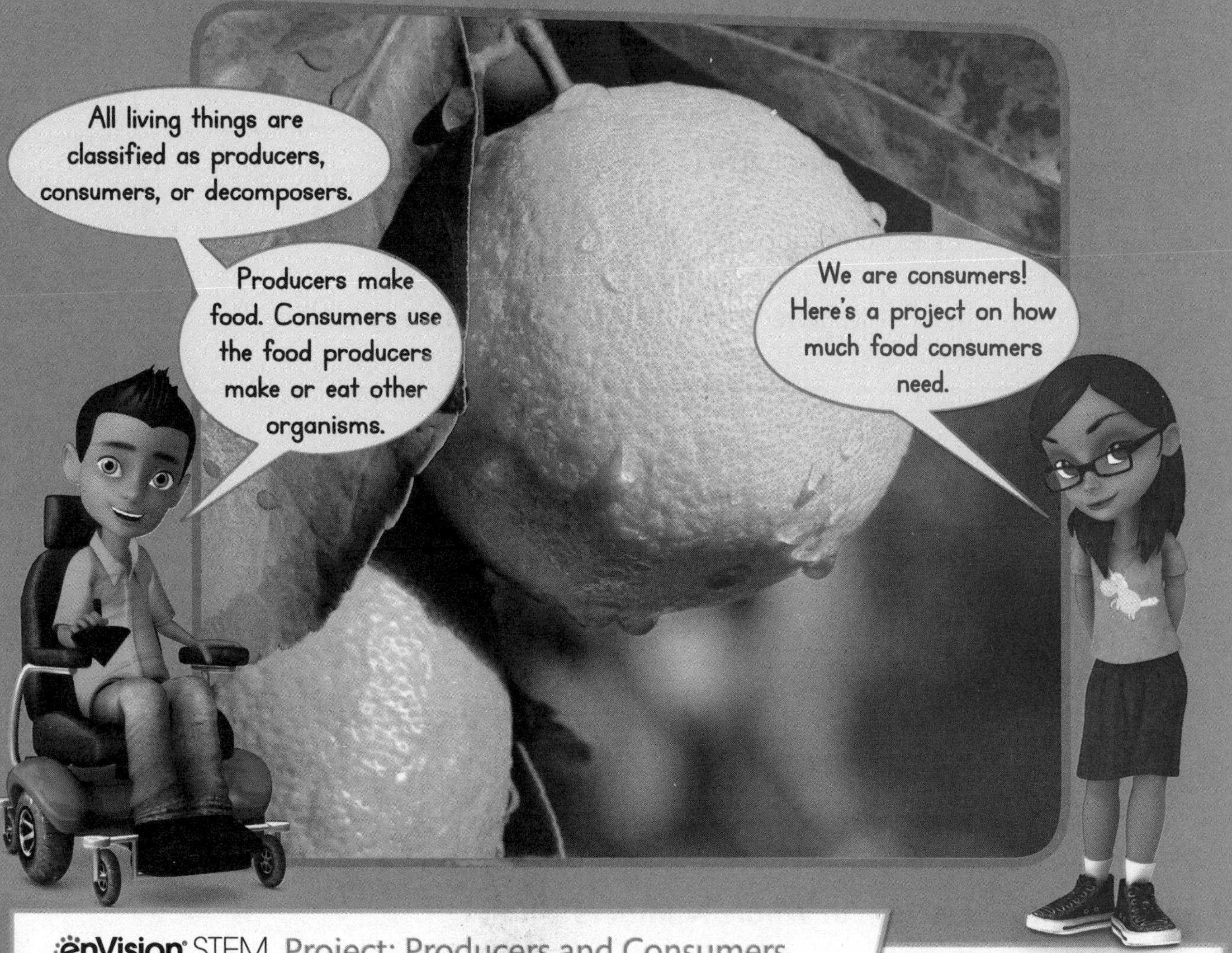

enVision STEM Project: Producers and Consumers

Do Research Use the Internet or other sources to find information about producers and consumers.

Journal: Write a Report Include what you found. Also in your report:

- What do producers need to survive? What do consumers need to survive?
- Give at least three examples of both producers and consumers.
- Write and solve decimal addition and subtraction problems for the amounts of food the consumers need.

Name ______________________________

Review What You Know

Vocabulary

Choose the best term from the box. Write it on the blank.

- addend
- difference
- equivalent
- inverse operations
- round
- sum

1. The __________ is the result of subtracting one number from another.

2. Two numbers or expressions that have the same value are __________.

3. The answer to an addition problem is the __________.

4. One way to estimate an answer is to __________ the numbers and then do the calculation.

Round Decimals

Round each number to the nearest tenth.

5. 74.362 6. 28.45 7. 13.09

Round each number to the nearest hundredth.

8. 43.017 9. 186.555 10. 222.222

Round each number to the underlined digit.

11. $8\underline{4}.59$ 12. $2.9\underline{4}8$ 13. $30.1\underline{2}5$

Addition and Subtraction of Whole Numbers

Find each sum or difference.

14. 9,536 + 495 15. 612 − 357 16. 5,052 − 761

17. Vivica sees that a printer costs $679 and a computer costs $1,358. What is the total cost of the printer and the computer?

18. The Pecos River is 926 miles long, and the Brazos River is 1,280 miles long. How many miles longer is the Brazos River than the Pecos River?

Ⓐ 2,206 miles Ⓑ 1,206 miles Ⓒ 364 miles Ⓓ 354 miles

Name ______________________

PROJECT
2A

How big are alligators and crocodiles?

Project: Compare the Sizes of Reptiles

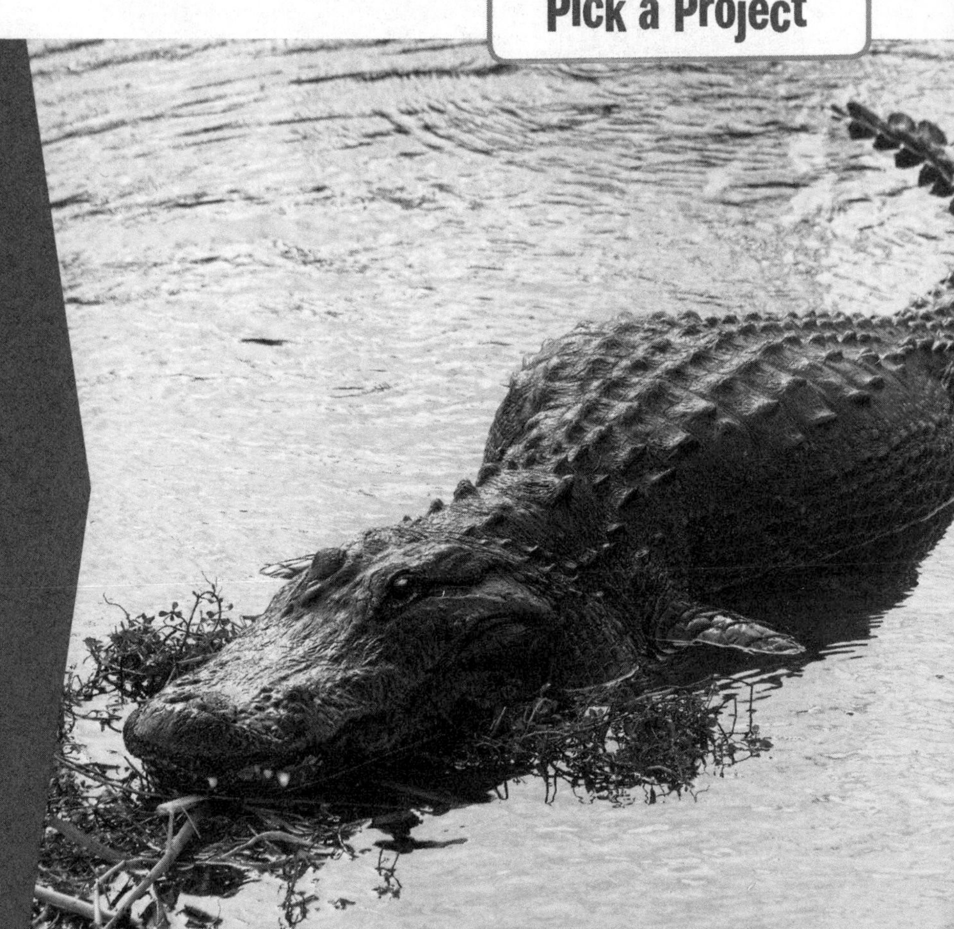

How much should a theme park ticket cost?

Project: Make a Brochure for a Theme Park

PROJECT 2C

How much and how healthy is your meal in a restaurant?

Project: Plan Your Meal

PROJECT 2D

How far was your trip?

Project: Make a Travel Journal

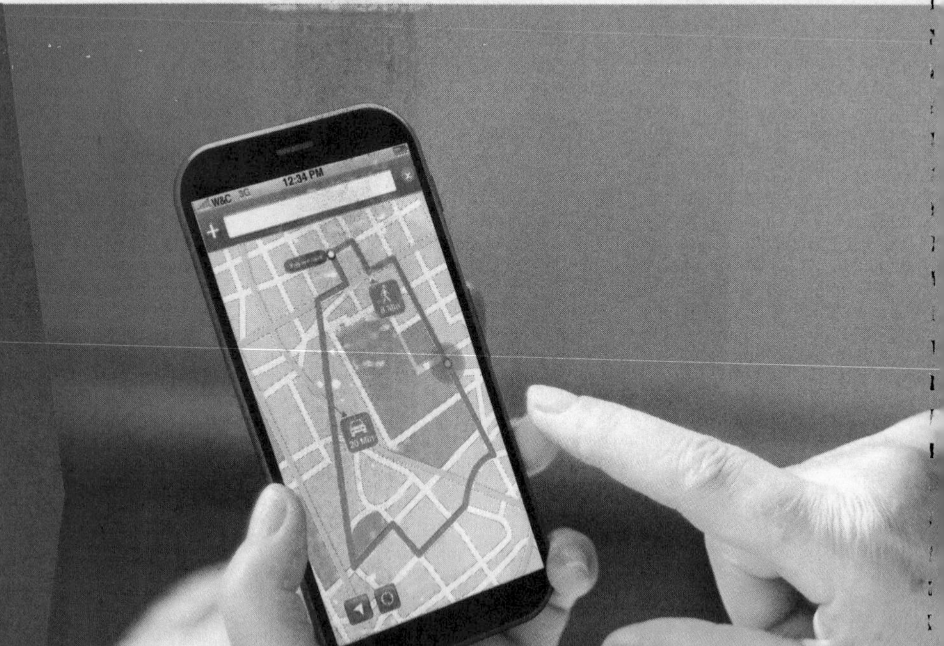

Name ______________________________

Lesson 2-1
Mental Math

I can ...
use mental math to solve addition and subtraction problems.

Content Standards 5.NBT.B.7 Also 5.NBT.A.4
Mathematical Practices MP.2, MP.3

Solve & Share

Three pieces of software cost $20.75, $10.59, and $18.25. What is the total cost of the software? ***Use mental math to solve.***

You can use reasoning to help you. What do you know about adding three numbers that will make it easier to solve this problem?

Look Back! Which two numbers above were easy to add in your head? Why?

Visual Learning

Glossary

Visual Learning Bridge

Essential Question How Can You Use Mental Math to Add?

A

Properties of addition can help you find the total cost of these three items.

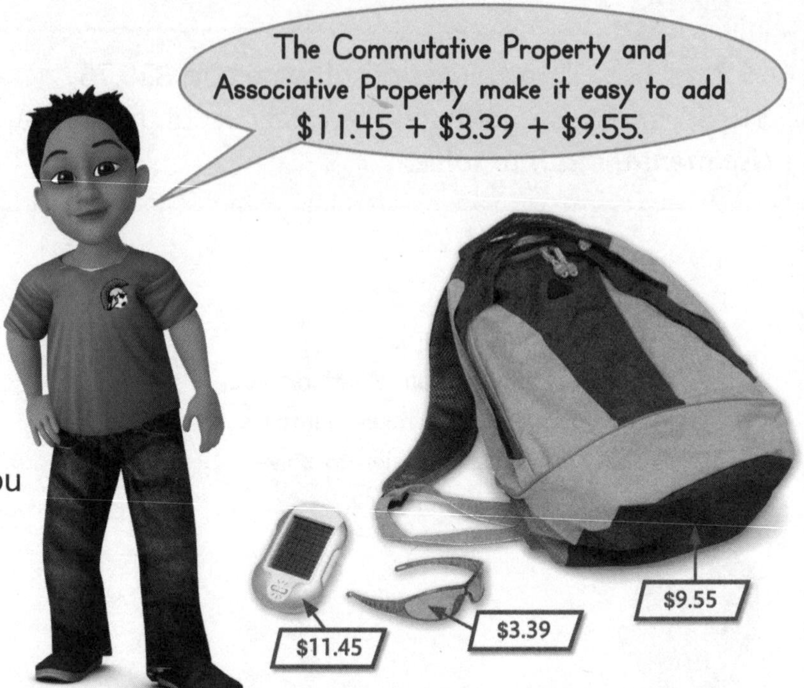

The Commutative Property and Associative Property make it easy to add $11.45 + $3.39 + $9.55.
$11.45
$3.39
$9.55

The Associative Property lets you change the grouping of addends.
($11.45 + $3.39) + $9.55 =
$11.45 + ($3.39 + $9.55)

The Commutative Property lets you add two decimals in any order.
$11.45 + $3.39 = $3.39 + $11.45

B Use the Commutative Property to change the order.

$11.45 + ($3.39 + $9.55) =
$11.45 + ($9.55 + $3.39)

Use the Associative Property to change the grouping.

$11.45 + ($9.55 + $3.39) =
($11.45 + $9.55) + $3.39

C Add $11.45 and $9.55 first because they are easy to compute mentally.

$11.45 + $9.55 = $21

$21 + $3.39 = $24.39

The three items cost a total of $24.39.

Compatible numbers are numbers that are easy to compute mentally.

Convince Me! **Reasoning** Use mental math to find the sum. Explain your thinking.

Jim earns $22.50, $14.75, and $8.50 on three different days. How much did he earn in all?

Name ______________________

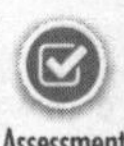

Another Example

With compensation, adjust one or both numbers to make the calculation easier. Then adjust the difference or sum to get the final answer.

Use compensation to subtract.

Find 4.25 − 0.08 mentally.

4.25 − 0.10 = 4.15

0.02 too much was subtracted. (↑ 0.10)

Compensate; add back 0.02. (↑ 4.15)

4.25 − 0.08 = 4.17

Use compensation to add.

Find \$3.47 + \$4.35 mentally.

\$3.50 + \$4.35 = \$7.85

Add 0.03 (↑ \$3.50)

Compensate; take away 0.03. (↑ \$7.85)

\$3.47 + \$4.35 = \$7.82

Guided Practice

Do You Understand?

1. Show how to use compensation to add \$3.18 and \$6.50.

2. Use properties to rewrite the expression to be easier to solve. Explain.
(13 + 4.63) + 7.4

Do You Know How?

In **3–6**, use mental math to add or subtract.

3. 12 + 3.04 + 8.28

4. 6.97 + 4.15

5. 9.04 − 6.98

6. 4.02 + 0.19 + 16.48

Independent Practice

Leveled Practice In **7–12**, use mental math to add or subtract.

7. 7.1 + 5.4 + 2.9 =
_______ + 5.4 =
____

8. 373.4 − 152.9 =
373.4 − _______ = 220.4
_______ + 0.1 = _______

9. \$18.25 + \$7.99 + \$4.75

10. 1.05 + 3 + 4.28 + 0.95

11. 2,504 + 140 + 160

12. 35.7 − 14.8

Problem Solving

13. Joanne bought three books that cost \$3.95, \$4.99, and \$6.05. How much did she spend in all? Use compensation and mental math to find the sum.

? spent → ?

\$3.95	\$4.99	\$6.05

14. Construct Arguments Use compensation to find each difference mentally. Explain how you found each difference.

A 67.9 – 29.9

B 456 – 198

15. Number Sense The table shows how many points Eduardo scored during each game. Use mental math to find how many points he scored in the first three games.

Game	Points
1	54
2	19
3	26
4	10

16. On three different days at her job, Sue earned \$27, \$33, and \$49. She needs to earn \$100 to buy a desk for her computer. If she buys the desk, how much money will she have left over?

17. A shelf can hold 50 DVDs. Jill has 27 DVDs. She plans to buy 5 new ones. Each DVD costs \$9. After she buys the new ones, how many more DVDs can the shelf hold?

18. When finding the difference of two numbers mentally, can you use the Commutative Property? Explain.

19. Higher Order Thinking Daria bought a skein of alpaca yarn for \$47.50, a skein of angora yarn for \$32.14, a skein of wool yarn for \$16.50, and a pair of knitting needles for \$3.86. How much did she spend in all? Describe how you calculated your answer.

Assessment Practice

20. Mrs. Healer's class took a field trip to a park 12.3 miles away. Mr. Dean's class drove 4.9 miles to the public library. How much farther did Mrs. Healer's class travel than Mr. Dean's class? Explain how you used mental math to determine the difference.

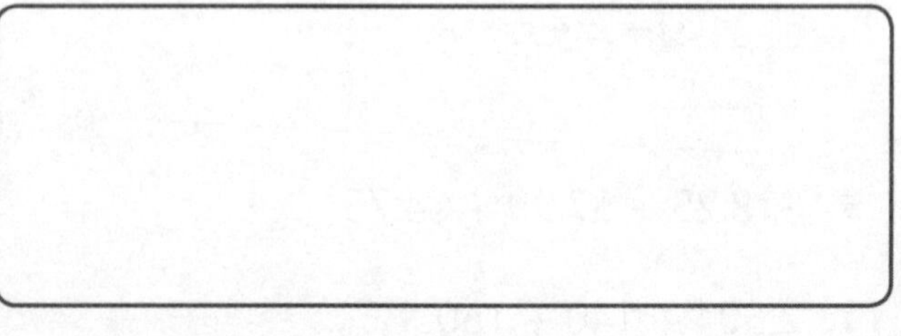

Name ______________________________

Lesson 2-2

Estimate Sums and Differences of Decimals

I can ...

estimate sums and differences of decimals.

Content Standards 5.NBT.B.7 Also 5.NBT.A.4
Mathematical Practices MP.2, MP.3

Solve & Share An amusement park has two roller coasters. One is 628 feet long, and the other is 485 feet long. If you ride both roller coasters, about how many feet will you travel in all? ***Use estimation to solve.***

You can use reasoning to decide what you are asked to find. Is the problem looking for an exact answer? How can you tell?

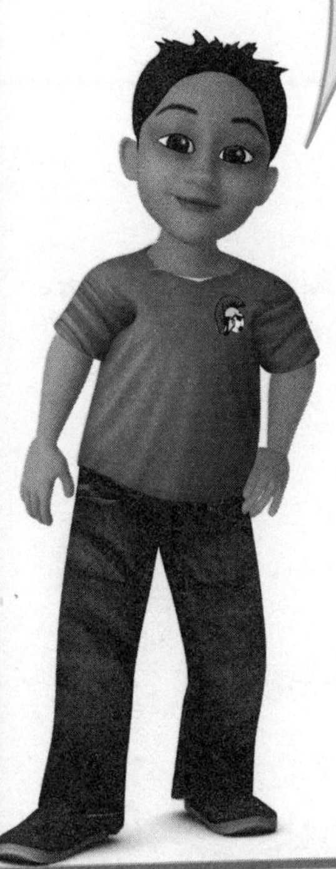

Look Back! About how much longer is the one coaster than the other? Show your work.

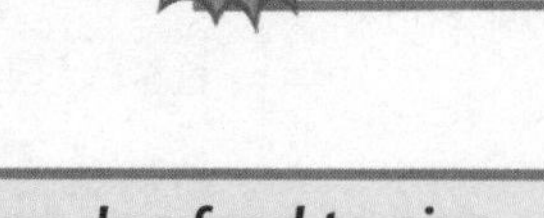

How Can You Estimate Sums?

A

Students are collecting dog food to give to an animal shelter. Estimate how many pounds were collected in Weeks 3 and 4.

There is more than one way to find an estimate.

DATA

Week	Pounds of dog food
1	172.3
2	298
3	237.5
4	345.1
5	338

B

One Way

Round each addend to the nearest hundred.

$$\begin{array}{r} 237.5 \\ +\ 345.1 \\ \hline \end{array} \longrightarrow \begin{array}{r} 200 \\ +\ 300 \\ \hline 500 \end{array}$$

237.5 + 345.1 is about 500.

The students collected about 500 pounds of dog food in Weeks 3 and 4.

C

Another Way

Substitute compatible numbers.

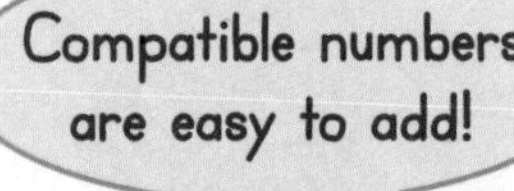

Compatible numbers are easy to add!

$$\begin{array}{r} 237.5 \\ +\ 345.1 \\ \hline \end{array} \longrightarrow \begin{array}{r} 250 \\ +\ 350 \\ \hline 600 \end{array}$$

237.5 + 345.1 is about 600.

The students collected about 600 pounds of dog food in Weeks 3 and 4.

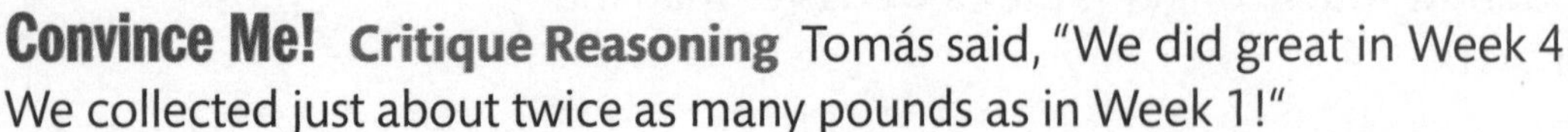

Convince Me! **Critique Reasoning** Tomás said, “We did great in Week 4! We collected just about twice as many pounds as in Week 1!”

Use estimation to decide if he is right. Explain your thinking.

Name ____________________

Practice Tools Assessment

Another Example

You can estimate differences.

Estimate 22.84 – 13.97.

One Way

Round each number to the nearest whole number.

$$\begin{array}{r} 22.84 \\ -\ 13.97 \\ \hline \end{array} \rightarrow \begin{array}{r} 23 \\ -\ 14 \\ \hline 9 \end{array}$$

22.84 – 13.97 is about 9.

Another Way

Substitute compatible numbers.

$$\begin{array}{r} 22.84 \\ -\ 13.97 \\ \hline \end{array} \rightarrow \begin{array}{r} 25 \\ -\ 15 \\ \hline 10 \end{array}$$

22.84 – 13.97 is about 10.

Guided Practice

Do You Understand?

1. In the example above, which estimate is closer to the actual difference? How can you tell without subtracting?

2. In the example on the previous page, students collected more pounds of dog food in Week 4 than in Week 3. Estimate about how many more.

Do You Know How?

In **3–10**, estimate each sum or difference.

3. 49 + 22.88

4. 86.9 – 18

5. 179 + 277.1

6. 23.2 – 9.71

7. 23.8 – 4.7

8. 87.2 + 3.9

9. 38.9 – 21.4

10. 576 + 94.6

Independent Practice

In **11–18**, estimate each sum or difference.

11. 79.1 + 32.4

12. 788.9 – 572

13. 837 + 488.12

14. 418.5 – 23.7

15. 2.9 + 3.9

16. \$12.99 – \$3.95

17. 8.1 + 3.7 + 7.9

18. 3.8 + 4.1 + 3.3

Problem Solving

19. Construct Arguments The cost of one DVD is $16.98, and the cost of another DVD is $9.29. Ed estimated the cost of the two DVDs to be about $27. Is his estimate higher or lower than the actual cost? Explain.

20. Higher Order Thinking A teacher is organizing a field trip. Each bus can seat up to 46 people. Is it better to estimate a greater or lesser number than the actual number of people going on the field trip? Why?

21. The size and shape of Golden Gate Park are often compared to the size and shape of Central Park. About how many more acres does Golden Gate Park cover than Central Park?

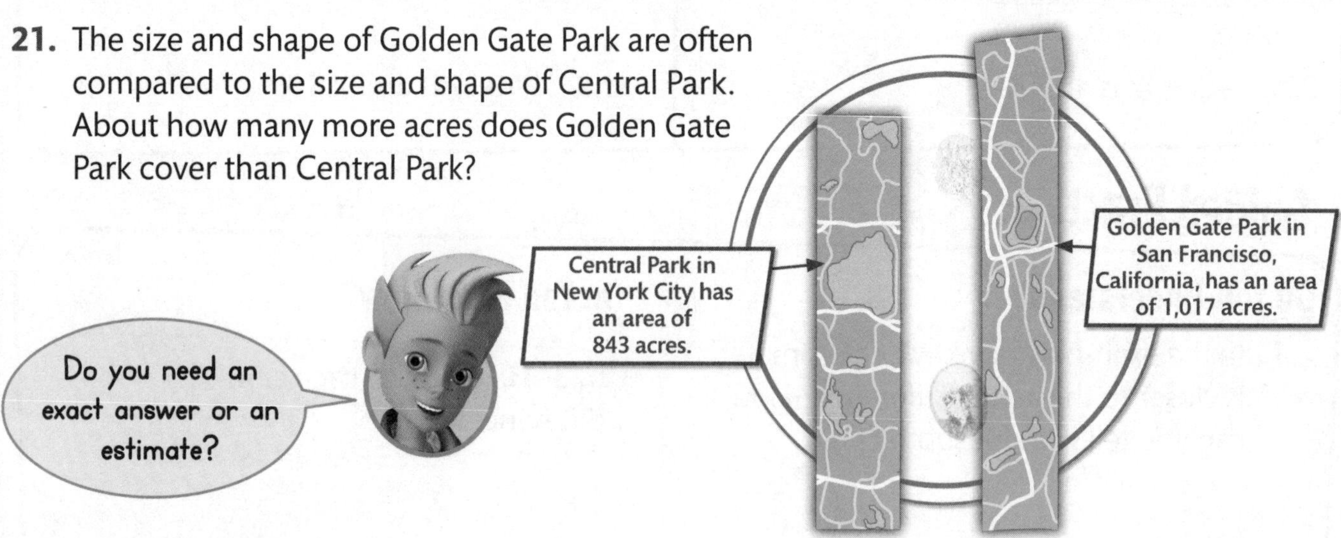

Do you need an exact answer or an estimate?
Central Park in New York City has an area of 843 acres.
Golden Gate Park in San Francisco, California, has an area of 1,017 acres.

Assessment Practice

22. Three rock samples have masses of 74.05 grams, 9.72 grams, and 45.49 grams. A scientist estimates the total mass of the samples by rounding each mass to the nearest whole number. Which lists the numbers he will add?

Ⓐ 75, 10, and 46

Ⓑ 74.1, 9.7, and 45.5

Ⓒ 74, 10, and 45

Ⓓ 75, 10, and 50

23. Umberto buys a game for $7.89 and some batteries for $5.49. He pays with a $20 bill. Which is the best estimate of how much change he should get?

Ⓐ $5.00

Ⓑ $7.00

Ⓒ $13.00

Ⓓ $17.00

Name ______________________________

Activity

Lesson 2-3
Use Models to Add and Subtract Decimals

I can ...
model sums and differences of decimals.

Content Standard 5.NBT.B.7
Mathematical Practices MP.1, MP.3

Solve & Share Gloria rode her bicycle 0.75 mile in the morning and 1.40 miles in the afternoon. How many miles did Gloria ride in all? ***Solve this problem any way you choose.***

You can use tools, such as place-value blocks, to help determine how many miles Gloria rode.

Look Back! Make Sense and Persevere How can you check that your answer is reasonable?

How Can You Use Models to Add Decimals?

Visual Learning Bridge

A

Use the table at the right to find the total monthly cost of using the dishwasher and the DVD player.

Place-value blocks can be used to add decimals.

DATA

Device	Monthly Cost
DVD player	$0.40
Microwave oven	$3.57
Ceiling light	$0.89
Dishwasher	$0.85

Use compatible numbers to estimate. $0.85 + $0.40 is about $0.80 + $0.40, so the sum is about $1.20.

B Use place-value blocks to model $0.85 + $0.40.

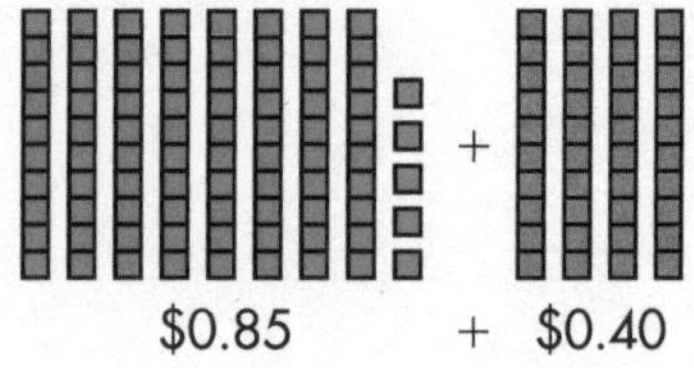

C Combine the blocks. Regroup when you can.

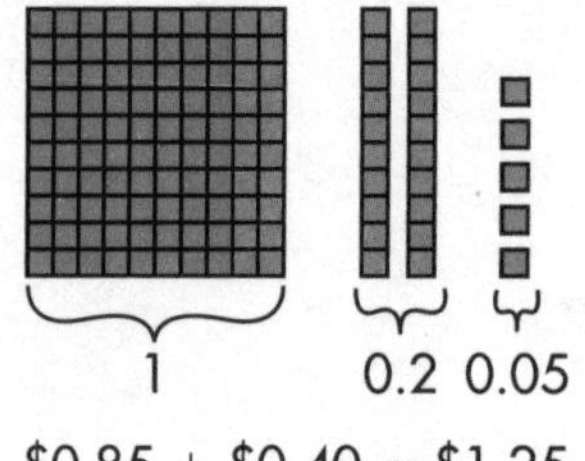

$0.85 + $0.40 = $1.25

The monthly cost of using the dishwasher and DVD player is $1.25.

Convince Me! **Critique Reasoning** For the example above, Jesse said, "The total monthly cost of using the ceiling light and the dishwasher was $0.74." Is Jesse correct? Explain.

Name ____________________

Another Example

You can subtract decimals with place-value blocks.

Find 1.57 − 0.89.

Step 1

Show 1.57 with place-value blocks.

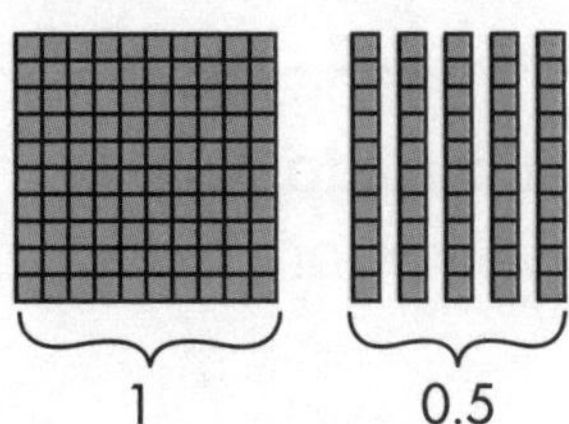

Step 2

To subtract 0.89, regroup the blocks and remove 8 tenths and 9 hundredths. The blocks remaining are the difference.

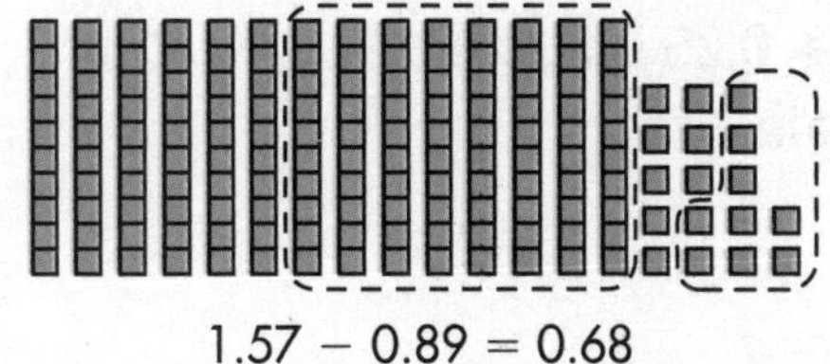

Guided Practice

Do You Understand?

1. Explain how to use place-value blocks to find the difference between the monthly cost of using the DVD player and the dishwasher. Then find the difference.

Do You Know How?

In **2–7**, use place-value blocks to add or subtract.

2. 1.22 + 0.34

3. 0.63 + 0.41

4. 2.73 − 0.94

5. $1.38 − $0.73

6. 0.47 − 0.21

7. 2.02 + 0.8

Independent Practice

In **8–11**, add or subtract. Use place-value blocks to help.

8. 0.1 + 0.73

9. $1.33 − $0.35

10. $0.37 + $0.47

11. 1.11 + 0.89

Problem Solving

12. **Construct Arguments** How is adding 4.56 + 2.31 similar to adding \$2.31 + \$4.56?

13. Write an expression that is represented by the model below.

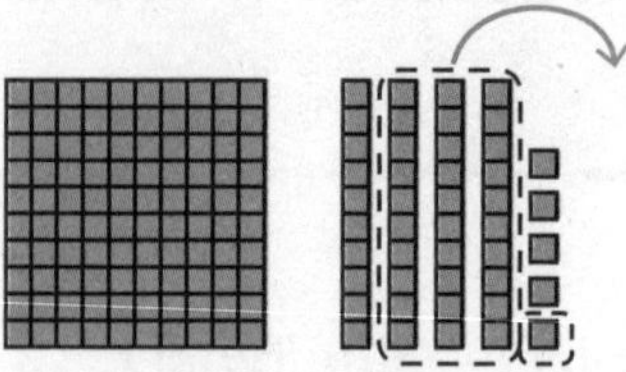

14. Without adding the decimals, tell if the sum of 0.46 + 0.25 is less than or greater than 1? Explain.

15. **Number Sense** Estimate to decide if the sum of 314 + 175 is more or less than 600.

16. **Higher Order Thinking** Do you think the difference of 1.4 – 0.95 is less than or greater than 1? Explain.

17. **Vocabulary** Estimate 53.8 – 27.6. Circle the **compatible numbers** to substitute.

54 – 28 53 – 28 55 – 27 55 – 25

18. **Algebra** Write an expression that can be used to find the perimeter of the pool shown to the right. Remember, perimeter is the distance around a figure.

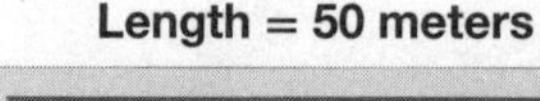

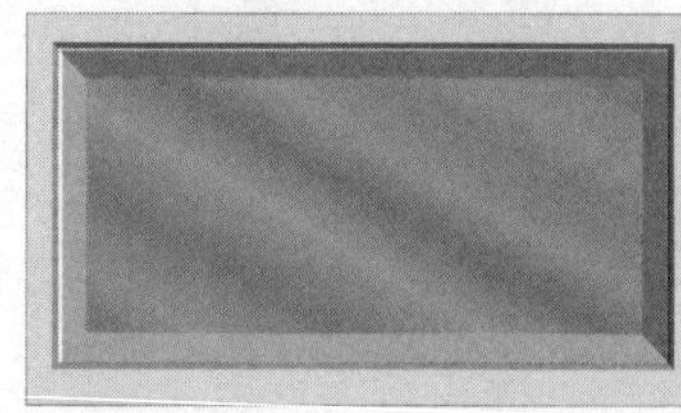

19. Each set of place-value blocks below represents a decimal.

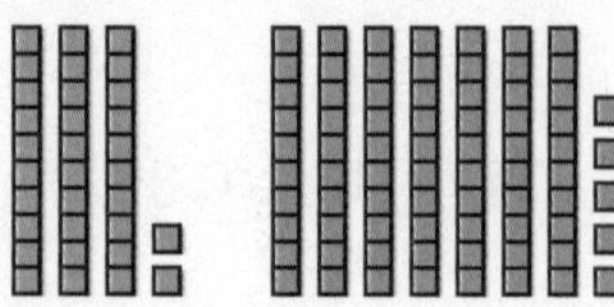

Part A

What is the sum of the decimals?

Part B

Explain how you found your answer.

Name ______________________________

Lesson 2-4

Use Strategies to Add Decimals

I can ...

add decimals using place value and properties of operations.

Content Standard 5.NBT.B.7
Mathematical Practices MP.3, MP.8

Solve & Share

Mr. Davidson has two sacks of potatoes. The first sack weighs 11.39 pounds. The second sack weighs 14.27 pounds. How many pounds of potatoes does Mr. Davidson have in all? ***Solve this problem any way you choose.***

You can generalize what you know about whole number addition to decimal addition.

Look Back! How is adding decimals similar to adding whole numbers?

How Can You Add Decimals?

A

A swim team participated in a relay race. The swimmers' times for each leg of the race were recorded in a table. What was the combined time for Caleb and Bradley's legs of the relay race?

DATA

Swimmers in Relay	Time in Seconds
Caleb	21.39
Bradley	21.59
Vick	20.35
Matthew	19.03

B

Step 1

Just like with whole numbers, line up the addends by place value. The decimal points will also line up.

tens	ones .	tenths	hundredths
2	1 .	3	9
+ 2	1 .	5	9

Adding decimals is just like adding whole numbers!

C

Step 2

Use what you know about partial sums to add the hundredths, tenths, ones, and tens.

tens	ones .	tenths	hundredths	
2	1 .	3	9	
+ 2	1 .	5	9	
	.	1	8	(0.09 + 0.09)
	.	8		(0.3 + 0.5)
	2 .			(1 + 1)
4	0 .			(20 + 20)
4	2 .	9	8	

The combined time for Caleb and Bradley was 42.98 seconds. The sum is close to the estimate.

Convince Me! **Critique Reasoning** André said the last two legs of the race took 3,938 seconds. What mistake did he make?

Name ______________________________

Practice Tools Assessment

Another Example

Carson ran 7.81 miles last week. He ran 14 miles this week. How many miles did he run in the two weeks?

Use properties and a number line to find the sum.

$7.81 + 14 = 14 + 7.81$ (Commutative Property)
$= 14 + (7 + 0.81)$
$= (14 + 7) + 0.81$ (Associative Property)
$= 21 + 0.81$
$= 21.81$

Carson ran 21.81 miles in all.

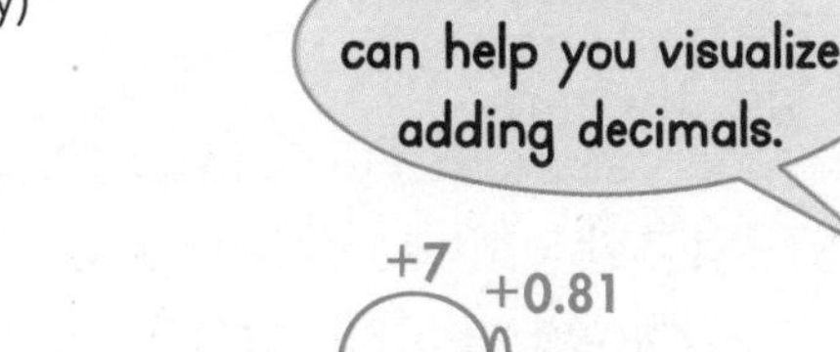

Guided Practice

Do You Understand?

1. How is adding 21.39 + 21.59 like adding 2,139 + 2,159?

Do You Know How?

In **2-5**, use place value and properties to find each sum.

2. 0.82 + 4.21
3. 9.1 + 7.21
4. 0.26 + 8.3
5. 4.98 + 3.02

Independent Practice

Leveled Practice In **6-12**, use place value and properties of operations to find each sum.

You can estimate first to be sure your answers are reasonable.

6. $\begin{array}{r} 1.03 \\ +\ 0.36 \\ \hline \end{array}$

7. $\begin{array}{r} 6.9 \\ +\ 2.8 \\ \hline \end{array}$

8. $\begin{array}{r} 45.08 \\ +\ 2.01 \\ \hline \end{array}$

9. $\begin{array}{r} 2.00 \\ +\ 0.78 \\ \hline \end{array}$

10. \$271.90 + \$34.22

11. 7.2 + 3.96 + 8.8

12. 16.62 + 4 + 2.38

Problem Solving

13. A farmer sold 53.2 pounds of carrots and 29.4 pounds of asparagus to a restaurant. How many pounds of these two vegetables did the restaurant buy?

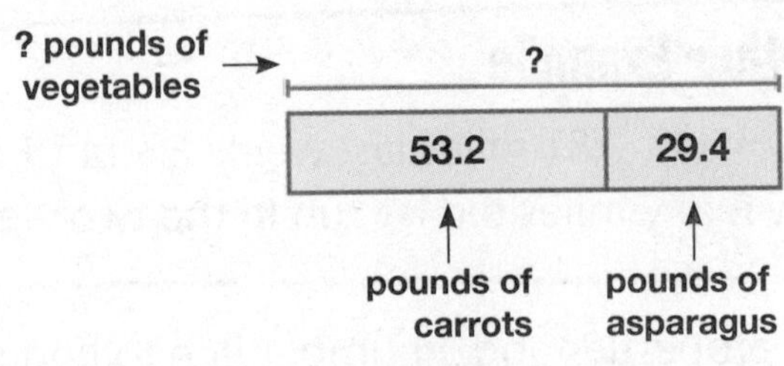

For **14** and **15**, use the table.

14. enVision® STEM Which two cities have the greatest combined rainfall for a typical year?

15. Number Sense Which location had less than 45 inches of rain but more than 40 inches of rain?

DATA

Location	Rainfall Amount in a Typical Year (in inches)
Macon, GA	45
Boise, ID	12.19
Caribou, ME	37.44
Springfield, MO	44.97

16. Higher Order Thinking Tim earned \$16 babysitting and \$17.50 mowing a lawn. He paid \$8.50 for a movie and bought a small popcorn for \$1.95. Write an expression to show how much money he has left.

17. Critique Reasoning Juan adds 3.8 + 4.6 and gets a sum of 84. Is his answer correct? Tell how you know.

Assessment Practice

18. Choose all expressions that are equal to 12.9.

- ☐ 0.02 + 12 + 0.88
- ☐ 0.06 + 12.03
- ☐ 11.9 + 1
- ☐ 6.2 + 3.4 + 2.3
- ☐ 3.01 + 2.01 + 7.7

19. Choose all expressions that are equal to 16.02.

- ☐ 16 + 0.02
- ☐ 3.42 + 8 + 4.6
- ☐ 16.01 + 1
- ☐ 12.06 + 3.14
- ☐ 7.36 + 8.66

Name ______________________

Activity

Solve & Share

Ms. Garcia is an electrician and has a length of wire that is 32.7 meters long. She has another length of wire that is 15.33 meters long. How much longer is one wire than the other? ***Solve this problem any way you choose.***

Lesson 2-5

Use Strategies to Subtract Decimals

I can ...

subtract decimals using place value and properties of operations.

Content Standard 5.NBT.B.7
Mathematical Practices MP.1, MP.6, MP.7

You can use what you know about whole number subtraction to subtract decimals.

Look Back! Use Structure How can you use the relationship between addition and subtraction to check your work above?

 Visual Learning 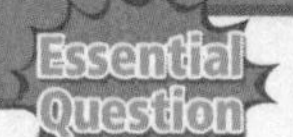 Glossary

Essential Question How Can You Subtract Decimals?

A

What is the difference in the wingspans of the two butterflies?

5.92 cm

4.37 cm

Estimate before you find the exact answer.
6 − 4 = 2

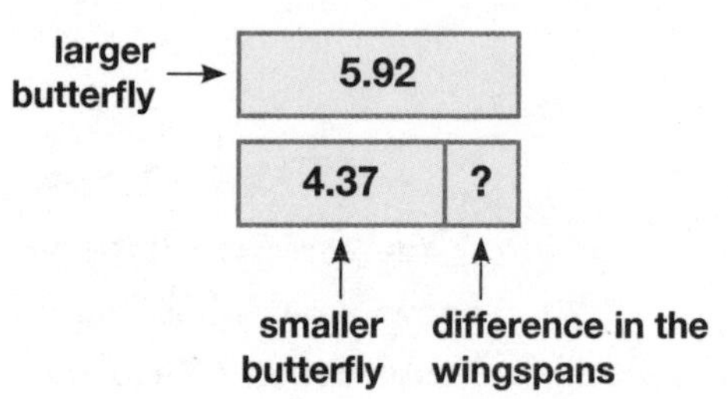

B You can use a number line to subtract.

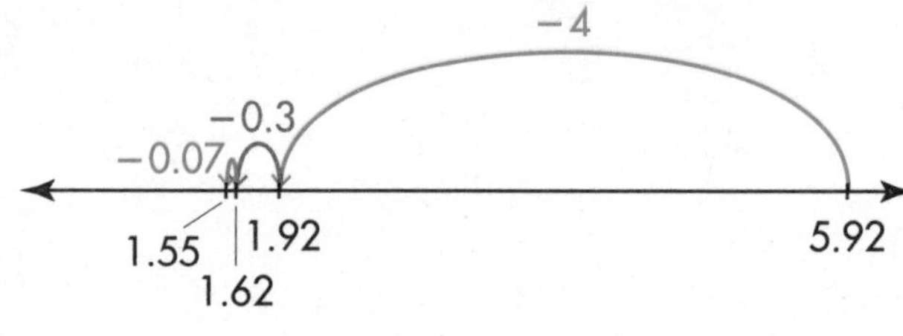

C Here's one way to subtract using partial differences.

Find 5.92 − 4.37

$$\begin{array}{rl} 5.92 & \\ -\ 4.00 & \text{subtract 4 ones} \\ \hline 1.92 & \\ -\ 0.30 & \text{subtract 3 tenths} \\ \hline 1.62 & \\ -\ 0.07 & \text{subtract 7 hundredths} \\ \hline 1.55 & \end{array}$$

5.92 − 4.37 = 1.55

Convince Me! **Be Precise** In the solution above, what strategies can you use to subtract the 7 hundredths?

Name

Practice Tools Assessment

Guided Practice

Do You Understand?

1. How can you use addition to check that 1.55 cm is the difference in the wingspans of the two butterflies?

2. Maria rewrote 45.59 − 7.9 as 45.59 − 7.90. Did she change the value of 7.9 by placing the zero after 7.9? Why or why not?

Do You Know How?

In **3–10**, subtract the decimals.

3. 16.82 − 5.21

4. 7.21 − 6.1

5. 23.06 − 8.24

6. $4.08 − $2.12

7. 56.8 − 2.76

8. $43.80 − $16.00

9. 22.4 − 10.7

10. $36.40 − $21.16

Independent Practice

Leveled Practice In **11–26**, find the difference.

11. 7.8 − 4.9

12. $20.60 − $14.35

13. 43.90 − 7.52

14. 65.90 − 28.38

15. 15.03 − 4.12

16. 13.9 − 3.8

17. 65.18 − 12.05

18. $52.02 − $0.83

19. 7.09 − 3.65

20. 34.49 − 12.61

21. 85.22 − 43.5

22. $10.05 − $4.50

23. 5.27 − 3.4

24. 23.6 − 8.27

25. 8.04 − 0.3

26. $21.37 − $10.95

Problem Solving

27. **Algebra** The Pyramid of Khafre measured 143.5 meters high. The Pyramid of Menkaure measured 65.5 meters high. Write and solve an equation to find d, the difference in the heights of these two pyramids.

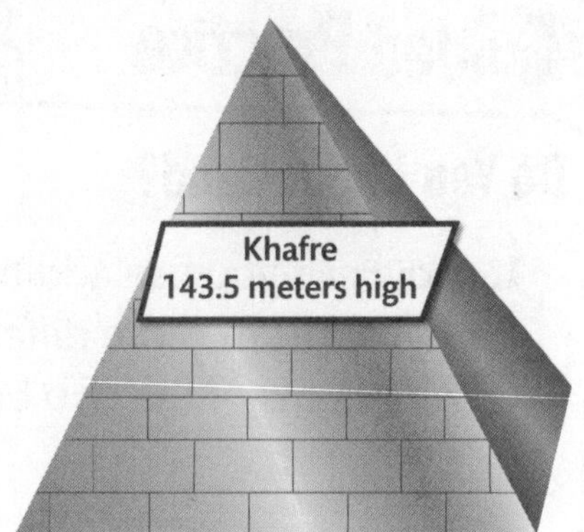

28. **Higher Order Thinking** Jonah bought a 1.5-liter bottle of seltzer. He used 0.8 liter of seltzer in some punch. Which is greater, the amount he used or the amount he has left? Explain how you decided.

29. Sue subtracted 2.9 from 20.9 and got 1.8. Explain why this is not reasonable.

30. **Make Sense and Persevere** Abe had $156.43 in his bank account at the beginning of the month. He made the two withdrawals shown in his check register. How much money does he have left in his bank account? He must have at least $100 in his account by the end of the month or he will be charged a fee. How much money does he need to deposit to avoid being charged a fee?

Date	Deposit	Withdrawal	Balance
9/1	17.85		156.43
9/8		24.97	
9/10		39.41	

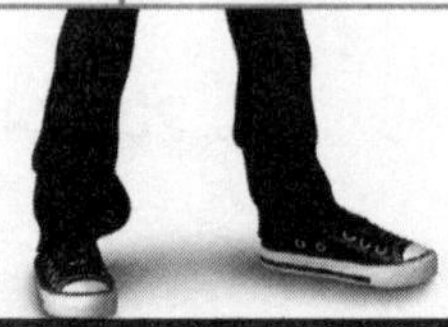

Assessment Practice

31. Circle all of the subtraction problems with a difference of 1.65.

27.30 – 16.65   12.68 – 2.03

11.23 – 9.58   21.74 – 20.09

40.4 – 23.9

Name ____________________

Activity

Solve & Share

At a baseball game, Sheena bought a sandwich for $6.95 and two pretzels for $2.75 each. She paid with a $20 bill. How much change did she receive? ***Solve this problem any way you choose. Use bar diagrams to help.***

Problem Solving

Lesson 2-6

Model with Math

I can ...

use the math I know to solve problems.

Mathematical Practices MP.4 Also MP.1, MP.3
Content Standard 5.NBT.B.7

Thinking Habits

Be a good thinker!
These questions can help you.

- How can I use math I know to help solve the problem?
- How can I use pictures, objects, or an equation to represent the problem?
- How can I use numbers, words, and symbols to solve the problem?

Look Back! Model with Math What other way can you represent this problem situation?

Visual Learning  Glossary

How Can You Represent a Problem with Bar Diagrams?

A

Monica wants to buy all of the art supplies shown on this sign. She has a coupon for $5.50 off the cost of her purchases. What will Monica's total cost be after the discount?

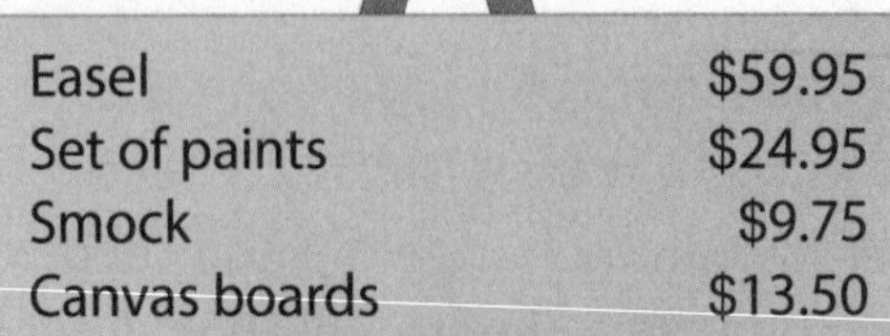

Easel $59.95
Set of paints $24.95
Smock $9.75
Canvas boards $13.50

Model with math means you apply math you have learned to solve problems.

What do I need to do to solve the problem?

I need to find Monica's cost for the art supplies.

B **How can I model with math?**

I can

- use the math I know to help solve the problem.
- find and answer any hidden questions.
- use bar diagrams and equations to represent and solve this problem.

C

Here's my thinking...

I will use bar diagrams to represent this situation.

? total cost

$59.95	$24.95	$9.75	$13.50

$\$59.95 + \$24.95 + \$9.75 + \$13.50 = \$108.15$

The total cost before the discount is $108.15.

$108.15 total before discount

$5.50	? total after discount

$\$108.15 - \$5.50 = \$102.65$

Monica's cost after the discount is $102.65.

Convince Me! Model with Math How could you decide if your answer makes sense?

Name ____________________

Guided Practice

Model with Math

Nate has $30.50. He wants to buy his dog a sweater that costs $15, a toy that costs $3.79, and a leash that costs $14.79. How much more money does he need?

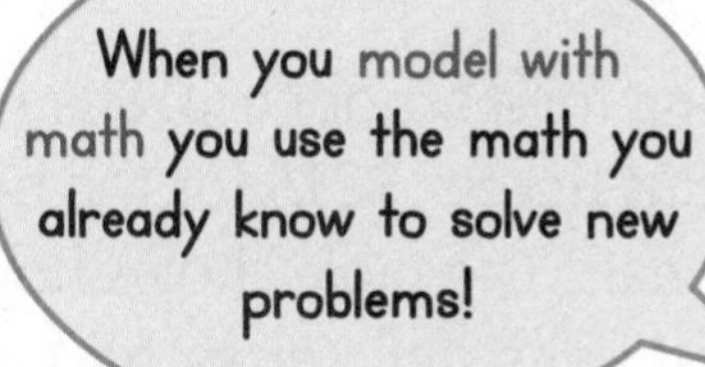

When you model with math you use the math you already know to solve new problems!

1. What do you need to find before you can solve the problem?

2. Draw bar diagrams to represent the problem and then solve the problem. Show the equations you used to solve the problem.

Independent Practice

Model with Math

Luz Maria has $15. She buys a ticket to a movie and a smoothie. How much money does she have left?

Ticket	$9.50
Popcorn	$4.50
Smoothie	$2.85

3. What do you need to find before you can solve the problem?

4. Draw two bar diagrams to represent the problem.

5. What is the solution to the problem? Show the equations you used to solve the problem.

Performance Task

School Trip
Audrey is saving for a school trip. She needs $180 for the bus tickets, $215 for the hotel, and $80 for meals. The table shows how much money she and her sister, Kelsey, have saved over a 4-month period. How much more money does Audrey need for the trip?

DATA

Monthly Savings		
Month	**Audrey's Savings**	**Kelsey's Savings**
September	$68	$28
October	$31.50	$42.50
November	$158	$90.25
December	$74.75	$89

6. **Make Sense and Persevere** What are you trying to find?

7. **Construct Arguments** Should you multiply Audrey's savings for September by 4 since there are 4 months? Explain.

8. **Model with Math** Draw bar diagrams to represent the total cost of Audrey's trip and the total she has saved. Then find the total cost and total savings.

You can model with math by using what you know about adding and subtracting whole numbers to add and subtract decimals.

9. **Model with Math** Write and solve an equation to determine how much more money Audrey needs for the trip.

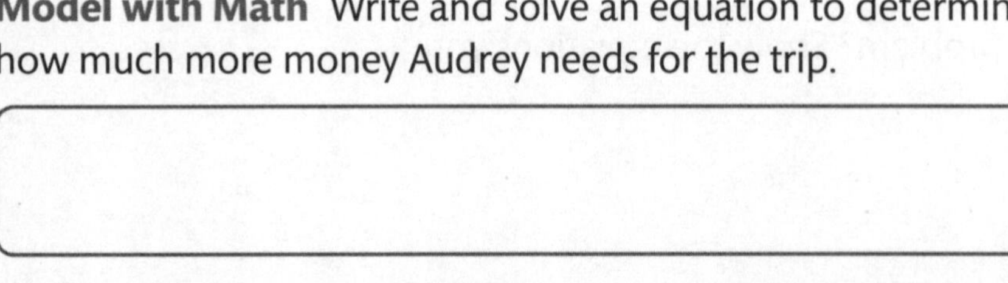

Name ______________________________

TOPIC 2 Fluency Review Activity

Find a partner. Get paper and a pencil. Each partner chooses either light blue or dark blue.

Partner 1 and Partner 2 each point to a black number at the same time. Each partner subtracts the lesser number from the greater number.

If the answer is on your color, you get a tally mark. Work until one partner has twelve tally marks.

I can ...

subtract multi-digit whole numbers.

Content Standard 4.NBT.B.4
Mathematical Practices MP.3, MP.6, MP.7, MP.8

Partner 1
500
750
961
1,945
5,520

383	1,705	721	1,517
260	733	5,280	1,891
1,928	907	483	322
696	5,503	5,092	72
5,153	446	944	594
133	533	5,466	1,578

Partner 2
17
54
240
367
428

Tally Marks for Partner 1	Tally Marks for Partner 2

TOPIC 2

Vocabulary Review

Glossary

Word List

- Associative Property of Addition
- Commutative Property of Addition
- compatible numbers
- compensation
- equivalent decimals
- inverse operations

Understand Vocabulary

Choose the best term from the Word List. Write it on the blank.

1. When you adjust one number and change another number in the problem to make a computation easier, you use ______________________.

2. You can replace the values in a problem with ______________________ so that it's easier to use mental math to complete the computation.

3. To align decimal points in a decimal addition problem, annex zeros to write ______________________ so that all addends have the same number of decimal places.

4. Because of the ______________________, I know that $477.75 + (76.89 + 196.25) = (76.89 + 196.25) + 477.75$ without adding.

5. Cross out the numbers below that are NOT equivalent to 500.0.

   500.00 5×10 5×10^2 50.05 500.500

6. Cross out the numbers below that are NOT equivalent to $53.2 + 16.8$.

   7×10^1 0.070 7.0 $7 \times \frac{1}{10}$ $(7 \times 10) + (0 \times 1)$

Circle the problem that uses compensation.

7. $32.7 + 15.6 = 32.6 + 15.7$ $45.7 + 26.2 = 45.7 + 26.3 - 0.1$

8. $14.24 - 11.8 = 14.24 - 12 + 0.2$ $168.3 - 53.8 = 168.3 - 53.4 - 0.4$

Use Vocabulary in Writing

9. Explain how the Commutative Property of Addition, the Associative Property of Addition and mental math can help you find $75.2 + (57.376 + 24.8)$. What is the sum?

Name ______________________

TOPIC 2

Reteaching

Set A pages 45–48

Add 15.3 + 1.1 + 1.7 using mental math.

15.3 and 1.7 are compatible numbers because they are easy to calculate mentally.

The Commutative Property of Addition enables us to add in any order.

15.3 + 1.1 + 1.7 = 15.3 + 1.7 + 1.1
= 17.0 + 1.1
= 18.1

Remember that you can use compatible numbers or compensation to find sums and differences.

Use mental math to add or subtract.

1. 8.6 + 23.4 + 1.4

2. 27 − 9.9

3. 13.5 + 5.7 + 36.5

4. 205.4 − 99.7

Set B pages 49–52

Estimate 22.4 − 16.2.

22.4	⟶	20	Use compatible
− 16.2	⟶	− 15	numbers.
		5	

22.4 − 16.2 is about 5.

Remember that compatible numbers can give a different estimate than rounding.

Estimate each sum or difference.

1. 358 + 293

2. 15.01 − 4.4

3. 80.01 + 2.89

4. 25,003 − 12,900

Set C pages 53–56

Use place-value blocks to subtract 1.86 − 0.95.

Show 1 flat, 8 longs, and 6 small squares to represent 1.86.

Remove 9 tenths and 5 hundredths, regrouping as needed.

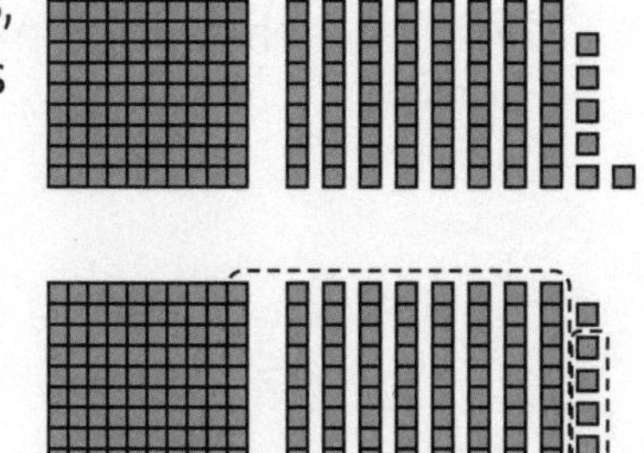

Count what is left.

1.86 − 0.95 = 0.91

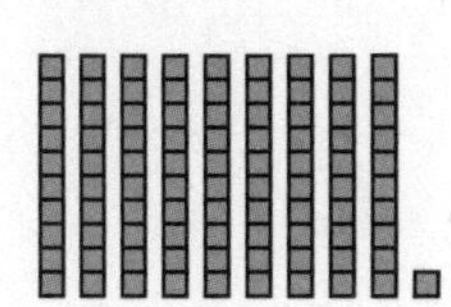

Add or subtract. Use place-value blocks for help.

1. 0.02 + 0.89

2. 0.67 − 0.31

3. 0.34 + 0.34

4. 0.81 − 0.78

Set D pages 57–60, 61–64

Lucy bought 2.12 pounds of pears and 3 pounds of apples. Find how many more pounds of apples than pears Lucy bought.

Use place-value blocks to help.

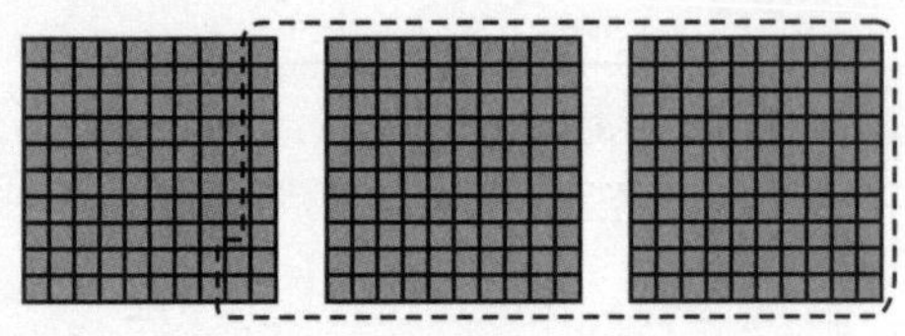

3.00 − 2.12 = 0.88

Add or subtract. Use place-value blocks to help.

1. 7.06 + 0.85
2. 24.07 − 5.31
3. 51.92 − 28.03
4. 8.71 − 0.4
5. 98 + 3.79
6. Talia measured two strings. The green string was 2.37 cm long. The blue string was 4 cm long. How many centimeters longer was the blue string than the green string?

Set E pages 65–68

Think about these questions to help you **model with math.**

Thinking Habits

- How can I use math I know to help solve the problem?
- How can I use pictures, objects, or an equation to represent the problem?
- How can I use numbers, words, and symbols to solve the problem?

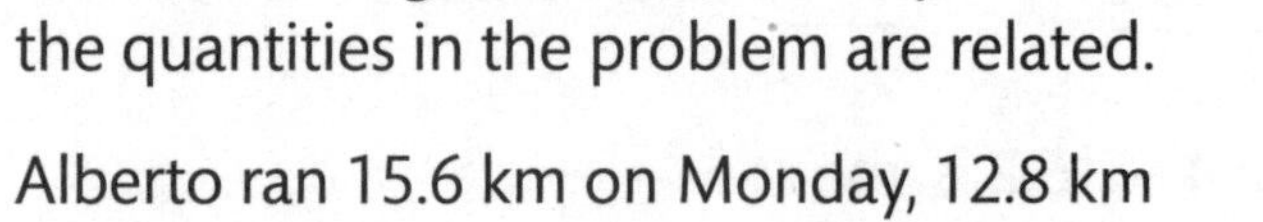

Remember a good model clearly shows how the quantities in the problem are related.

Alberto ran 15.6 km on Monday, 12.8 km on Tuesday, and 6.5 km on Wednesday. Dennis ran 11.25 km on Monday, 14.6 km on Tuesday, and 8 km on Wednesday. Who ran farther? How much farther?

1. What do you need to find before you can solve the problem?

2. Write equations to model this problem. Then solve the problem.

Name ____________________

TOPIC 2

Assessment Practice

1. Kayla's dollhouse has 15.15 square feet downstairs and 6.45 square feet upstairs. What is the estimated total area if you round the decimals to the nearest tenth?

Ⓐ 21.0

Ⓑ 21.6

Ⓒ 21.7

Ⓓ 22.0

2. Estimate the sum of $12.15, $16.85, and $1.74 by rounding each number to the nearest tenth.

Ⓐ $30.70 Ⓒ $31.00

Ⓑ $30.80 Ⓓ $30.00

3. What is the sum of 2.65 + 3.78?

Ⓐ 5.33

Ⓑ 5.43

Ⓒ 6.33

Ⓓ 6.43

4. Which decimal makes this equation true?
4.95 + □ = 12.1

Ⓐ 7.15

Ⓑ 7.85

Ⓒ 8.15

Ⓓ 8.85

5. Lawrence spent $1.89 on a bottle of paint and $0.45 on a brush.

A. What was the total amount he spent? Use the model to help you.

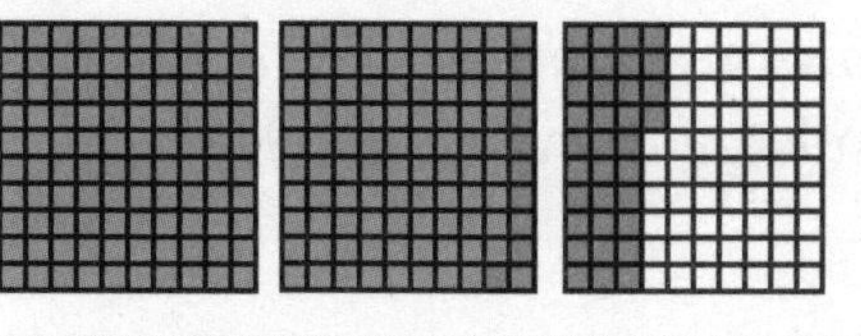

B. Explain how the model helps you find the sum.

6. Match each expression on the left with the equivalent decimal.

	4.8	5.8	4.7	3.7
3.05 + 1.65	❑	❑	❑	❑
8.5 − 4.8	❑	❑	❑	❑
4.25 + 1.55	❑	❑	❑	❑
11.4 − 6.6	❑	❑	❑	❑

7. Ed is training for a race. He ran 12.56 miles on one day, 12.98 miles the second, and 13.04 miles the third day.

A. What is his combined distance for the first three days?

B. How much farther did he run the second day than the first day?

---

8. The Thomas Jefferson Memorial is on 18.36 acres of land, the Franklin Delano Roosevelt Memorial is on 7.5 acres of land, the Vietnam Veterans Memorial is on 8.9 acres of land, and the World War I Memorial is on 9.6 acres of land. Which two memorials have the greatest difference in area?

What is the difference between the areas of these two memorials? Explain.

---

9. Amber bought a hardcover book for \$23.70 and a paperback for \$6.91. How much did she spend in all? If she paid with 2 twenty-dollar bills, how much change did she get?

10. Kassandra has a rectangular patio in her backyard. The patio is 12.74 meters long and 5.45 meters wide.

5.45 m

12.74 m

A. Round the length and width to the nearest whole number. Then estimate the perimeter of Kassandra's patio. Write an equation to model your work.

B. Round the length and width to the nearest tenth. Then estimate the perimeter of Kassandra's patio. Write an equation to model your work.

C. Find the exact perimeter. Which estimate is closer? Explain why you think that estimate is closer.

Name ____________________

Video Games

Four students are playing the same video game. Their scores for the first three levels are added together to see if the student has enough points to move on to Round 2.

1. The students' scores are shown in the table below.

Round 1				
Level	**Kim**	**Sally**	**Tina**	**Zoey**
1	7.18	5.49	8.02	8.64
2	6.55	6.18	7.94	8.32
3	6.45	5.72	8.38	8.13
Total Points				

Part A

A student must have at least 18 points to advance to Round 2. Use estimation to decide if any of the students did not get 18 points.

Part B

Use estimation to decide which student had the greatest number of points. Explain your reasoning.

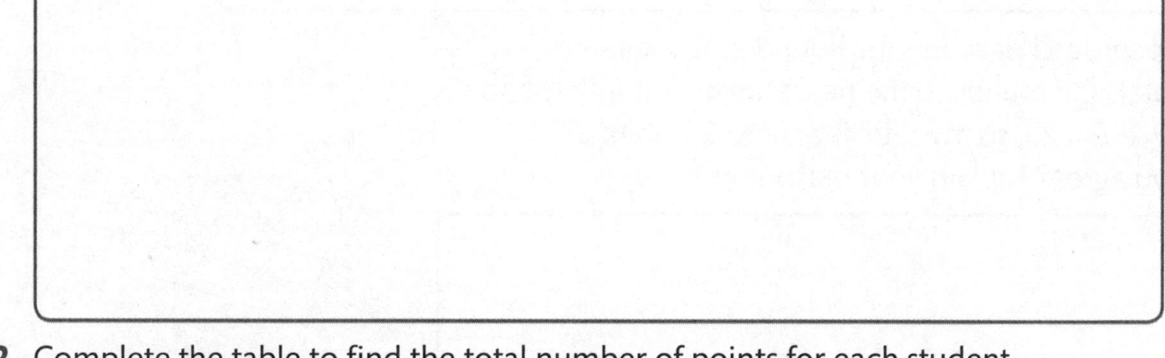

2. Complete the table to find the total number of points for each student.

3. How many more points did Zoey score than Sally? Write an equation to model your work.

4. Use the total points scored for each student.

Part A

About how many points did the four students score in Round 1? Estimate by rounding each point total to the nearest whole number.

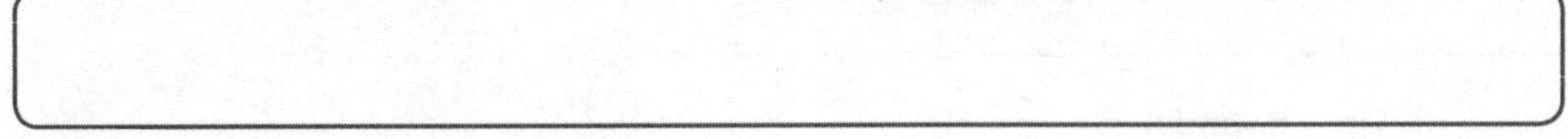

Part B

Complete the bar diagram to show the exact total number of points the students scored.

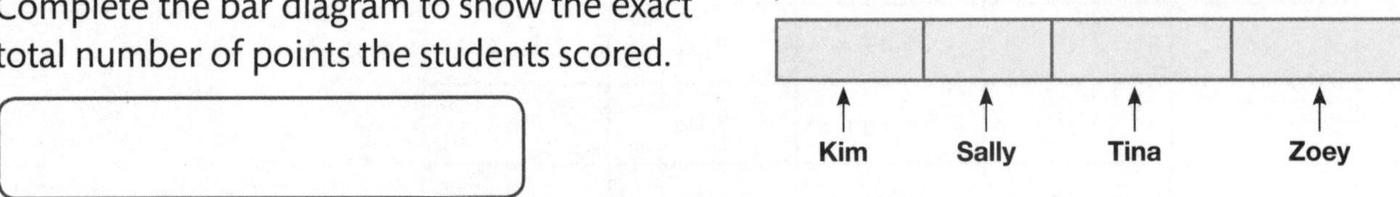

5. In Round 2, Zoey had a total of 23.43 points. She got a score of 7.96 in Level 2 and a score of 8.03 in Level 3.

Part A

What score did she receive in Level 1?

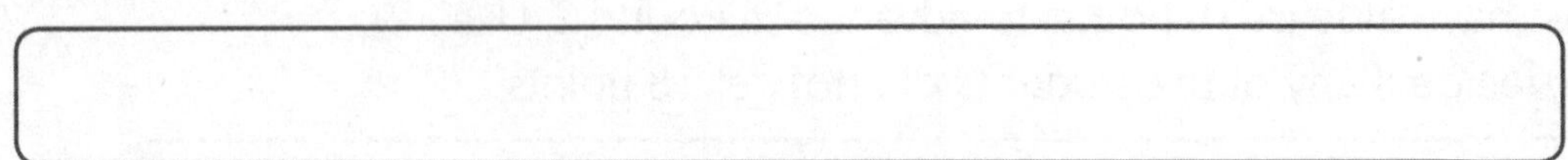

Part B

Explain how you found your answer.

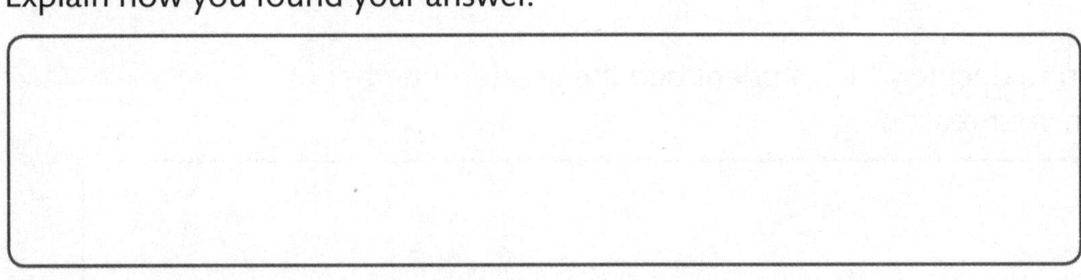

6. Kim recorded her scores for Round 2. To estimate her total, she rounds to the nearest whole number and says, "7 + 9 + 7 = 23, so my total is at least 23 points." Do you agree? Explain your reasoning.

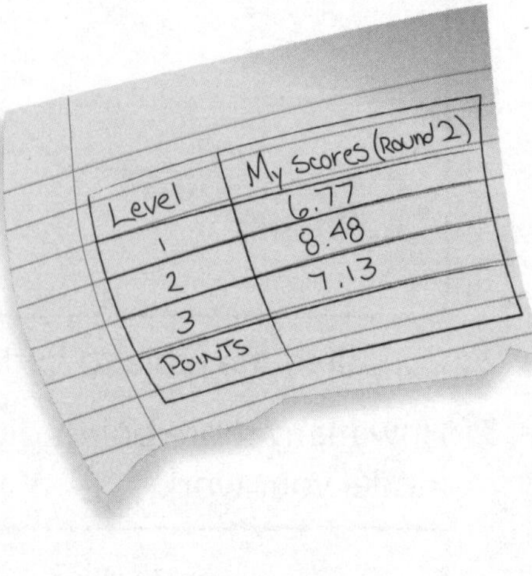

Level
My Scores (Round 2)
1
6.77
2
8.48
3
7.13
POINTS

TOPIC 3 Fluently Multiply Multi-Digit Whole Numbers

Essential Question: What are the standard procedures for estimating and finding products of multi-digit numbers?

Natural resources like water and coal come from Earth.

Water is a renewable resource because it can be used over and over again.

I'll get a giant straw! Here's a project on water usage and multiplication.

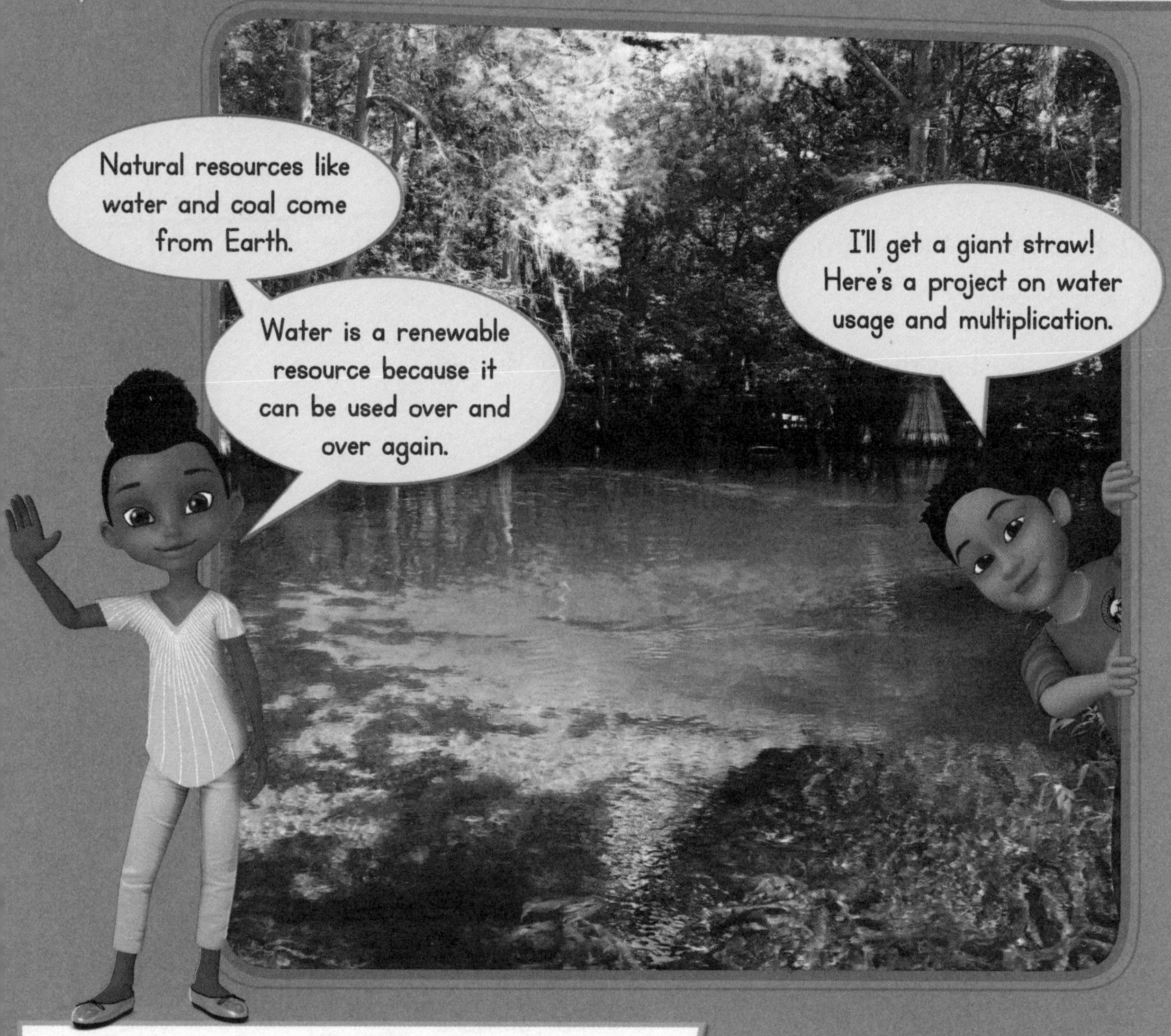

enVision STEM Project: Water Usage

Do Research Use the Internet or other sources to find how much water is used for household activities like taking a shower or bath, using a dishwasher, hand washing dishes, and using a washing machine.

Journal: Write a Report Include what you found. Also in your report:

- Choose 3 of the activities. Estimate how many times each activity is done each week in your household.
- Estimate the weekly water usage for each activity. Organize your results in a table.
- Make up and solve multiplication problems based on your data.

Name ____________________

Review What You Know

Vocabulary

Choose the best term from the box. Write it on the blank.

- equation
- exponent
- factor
- multiple
- power
- product

1. The answer to a multiplication problem is the __________.

2. A number sentence that shows two expressions with the same value is a(n) __________.

3. A(n) __________ tells the number of times the base is used as a(n) __________.

4. 50 is a(n) __________ of 10 because $5 \times 10 = 50$.

Operations

Find each sum or difference.

5. 9,007 + 3,128

6. 7,904 − 3,199

7. 27,924 − 13,868

8. 9.27 + 3.128

9. 119.04 − 86.5

10. 165.2 − 133.18

Round Whole Numbers and Decimals

Round each number to the place of the underlined digit.

11. $1\underline{4}.3$

12. $3\underline{8}5.7$

13. $0.\underline{5}45$

14. $49\underline{6}.533$

15. $49\underline{6}.353$

16. $1{,}857.2\underline{0}5$

Compare Decimals

17. Write the numbers in order from least to greatest. 8.062 8.26 8.026 8.6

18. Write the numbers in order from greatest to least. 0.115 0.15 0.005 0.5

Name ____________________

PROJECT 3A

What puts the bounce in a bouncy ball?

Project: Make a Business Plan

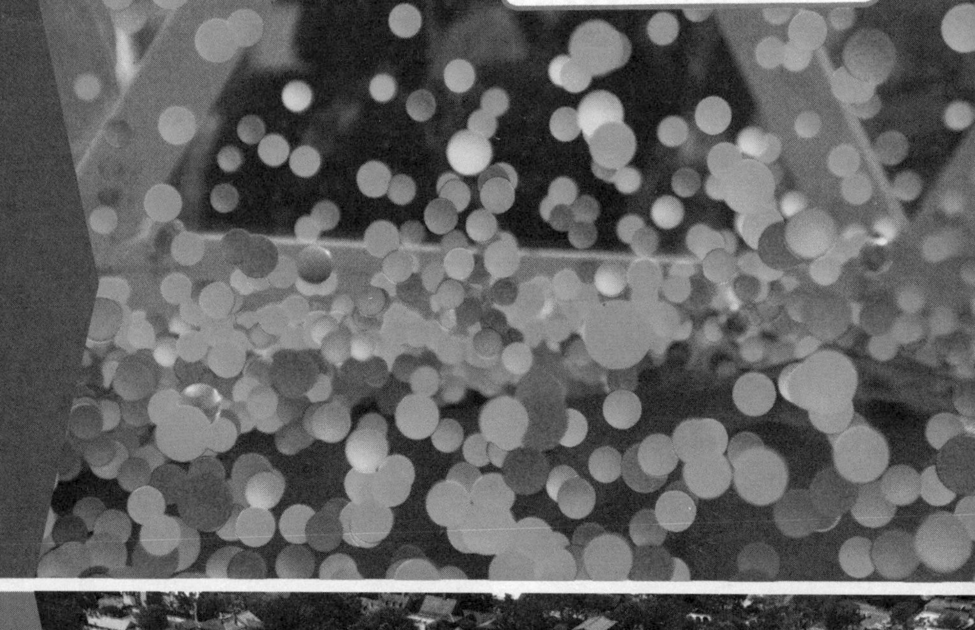

PROJECT 3B

How can you build a fort?

Project: Build a Model Fort

PROJECT 3C

How many people can a ferry carry?

Project: Design a Prototype Ferry

3-ACT MATH PREVIEW

Video

Math Modeling

Morning Commute

Before watching the video, think:

Train conductors don't wear this kind of hat anymore. Even paper tickets are less common now that some train lines use an app to purchase tickets. What are some other ways we have updated transportation as part of our modern society? All aboard!

I can ...

model with math to solve a problem that involves computing with whole numbers.

Mathematical Practices MP.4 Also MP.7, MP.8

Content Standards 5.NBT.B.5 Also 5.NBT.A.1, 5.NBT.A.2

Name ______________________

Activity

Lesson 3-1
Multiply Greater Numbers by Powers of 10

I can ...
use mental math to multiply a whole number by a power of 10.

Content Standards 5.NBT.A.2 Also 5.NBT.A.1
Mathematical Practices MP.3, MP.5

Solve & Share

At Izzy's Party Store, party invitations come in packages of 8. How many invitations are in 10 packages? 100 packages? 1,000 packages? ***Solve this problem any way you choose.***

You can use appropriate tools. Place-value blocks are useful for picturing problems that involve powers of 10.

Look Back! What patterns do you notice in your work above?

How Can You Use Patterns and Mental Math to Multiply a Whole Number by a Power of 10?

Visual Learning Bridge

A

The value of each place in a number is 10 times the value of the place to the right. The place-value chart shows this relationship for the number 4. Look for patterns.

1; 10; 100; 1,000; 10,000; and 100,000 are powers of 10.

Thousands			Ones			
Hundreds	Tens	Ones	Hundreds	Tens	Ones	
					4	
				4	0	10 times greater than 4
			4	0	0	10 times greater than 40
		4,	0	0	0	10 times greater than 400
	4	0,	0	0	0	10 times greater than 4,000
4	0	0,	0	0	0	10 times greater than 40,000

B

Find $32 \times 10{,}000$ by using place-value relationships.

Multiply 32 by 1; 10; 100; 1,000; and 10,000.

$32 \times 1 = 32$ ones $= 32$
$32 \times 10 = 32$ tens $= 320$
$32 \times 100 = 32$ hundreds $= 3{,}200$
$32 \times 1{,}000 = 32$ thousands $= 32{,}000$
$32 \times 10{,}000 = 32$ ten thousands $= 320{,}000$

Pattern
The product ends with the same number of zeros as the power of 10.

C

Instead of using the standard form, write each power of 10 using exponents.

$32 \times 1 = 32 \times 10^0 = 32$
$32 \times 10 = 32 \times 10^1 = 320$
$32 \times 100 = 32 \times 10^2 = 3{,}200$
$32 \times 1{,}000 = 32 \times 10^3 = 32{,}000$
$32 \times 10{,}000 = 32 \times 10^4 = 320{,}000$

Pattern
The exponent tells how many additional zeros the product will end with.

Convince Me! **Critique Reasoning** Nellie says that $60 \times 1{,}000$ is 6,000 because there are three zeros in 1,000. Kara says that $60 \times 1{,}000 = 60{,}000$. Whose thinking is correct? Explain.

Name ______________________________

Practice Tools Assessment

Guided Practice

Do You Understand?

1. How many zeros will there be in the product of $39 \times 1{,}000$? How many zeros will there be in the product of $50 \times 1{,}000$?

2. Explain how to find the product of 90×10^4.

Do You Know How?

In **3–5**, use reasoning to fill in the missing numbers.

3. $60 \times 1 =$ ____
$60 \times 100 =$ ______
$60 \times 10{,}000 =$ ________

4. $13 \times$ ______ $= 13{,}000$

5. ___ $\times 10^4 = 100{,}000$

Independent Practice

Leveled Practice In **6–13**, find each product.

6. 89×1
89×10
89×100
$89 \times 1{,}000$
$89 \times 10{,}000$

7. 30×1
30×10
30×100
$30 \times 1{,}000$
$30 \times 10{,}000$

8. 41×1
41×10^1
41×10^2
41×10^3
41×10^4

9. 90×1
90×10^1
90×10^2
90×10^3
90×10^4

10. 4×10^3

11. 85×100

12. 16×10^2

13. $10^3 \times 38$

In **14–19**, use reasoning to fill in the missing numbers.

14. $52 \times 10^{\_\_} = 520{,}000$

15. $68{,}637 = 10^1 \times$ ________

16. ________ $= 382 \times 10^4$

17. ________ $= 10^3 \times 80$

18. $10^{\_\_} \times 374 = 37{,}400$

19. $500{,}000 = 50 \times 10^{\_\_}$

Problem Solving

20. At a football championship game, the home team gave a football to each of the first 100 fans who arrived at the stadium. Each football cost the team $28. How much did the team pay for the footballs it gave away?

21. **Construct Arguments** Without multiplying, tell which expression is greater, 93×10^3 or 11×10^4? How do you know?

22. A truck is carrying 10^2 bushels of onions, 10^1 bushels of peaches, and 10^3 bushels of corn. What is the total weight of the crops?

DATA

Crop	Weight per bushel (pounds)
Apples	48
Onions	57
Peaches	50
Ears of corn	70

23. Norman bought a 16-pound bag of charcoal for $7.89 and a 10.4-pound bag of charcoal for $5.69. What was the total weight of the two bags of charcoal?

24. **Higher Order Thinking** There are 2,000 pounds in 1 ton. In the United States, the weight limit for a truck and its cargo is 40 tons. How many pounds is that? How did you find the answer?

Assessment Practice

25. Which is equivalent to multiplying a number by 10^4?

Ⓐ multiplying by 40
Ⓑ multiplying by 100
Ⓒ multiplying by 1,000
Ⓓ multiplying by 10,000

26. Select the statements that are equivalent to multiplying 20×10^4.

- ☐ Add 10 to 20 four times.
- ☐ Multiply 20 by 10 four times.
- ☐ Multiply 10 by 20 four times.
- ☐ Multiply 20 by 10,000.
- ☐ Multiply 20 by 100,000.

Name ______________________________

Lesson 3-2
Estimate Products

I can ...
estimate products using mental math.

Content Standard 5.NBT.B.5
Mathematical Practices MP.2, MP.3

Solve & Share

A school club wants to buy shirts for each of its 38 members. Each shirt costs $23. About how much money will all the shirts cost? ***Solve this problem any way you choose.***

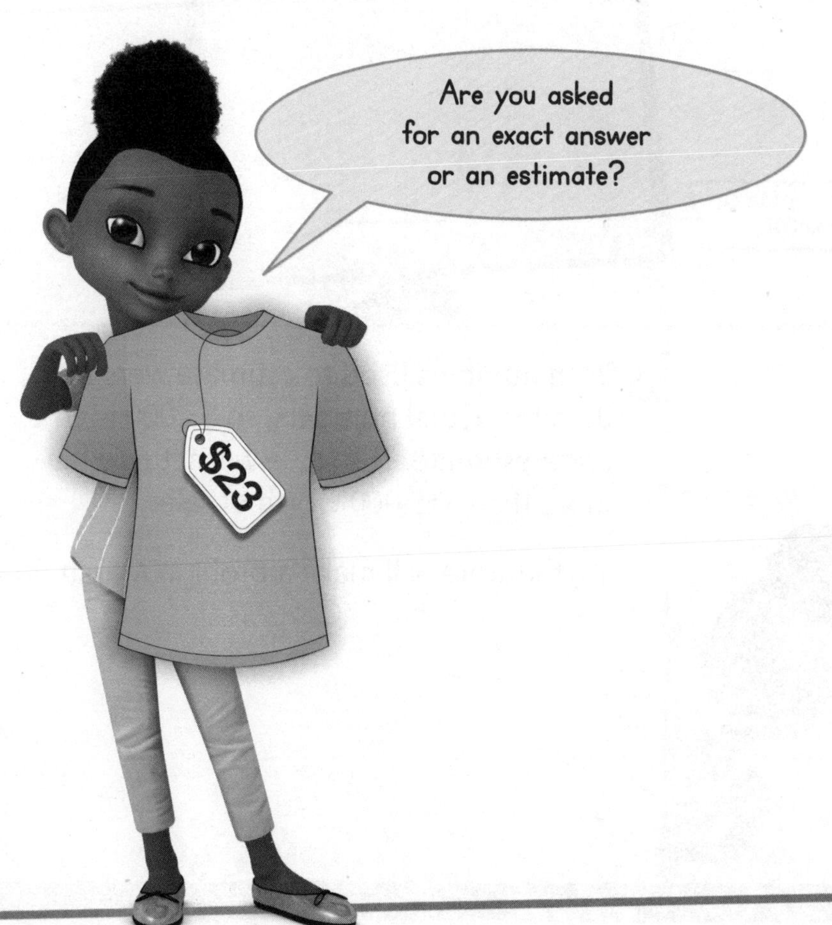

Are you asked for an exact answer or an estimate?
$23

Look Back! Construct Arguments How can you use number sense to tell that the exact answer has to be greater than $600? Explain how you know.

Visual Learning Bridge

Essential Question

How Can You Estimate Products?

A

A store needs at least $15,000 in sales per month to make a profit. If the store is open every day in March and sales average $525 per day, will the store make a profit in March?

You can use rounding to estimate.

Is the sales total for March at least $15,000?

B

Use Rounding to Estimate

$525 rounds to $500.

31 rounds to 30.

Find 30 × 500.

30 × 500 = 15,000

You know that 3 × 5 = 15.

C

Both numbers used to estimate were less than the actual numbers, so 15,000 is an underestimate. The store will actually have more than $15,000 worth of sales.

So, the store will make a profit in March.

 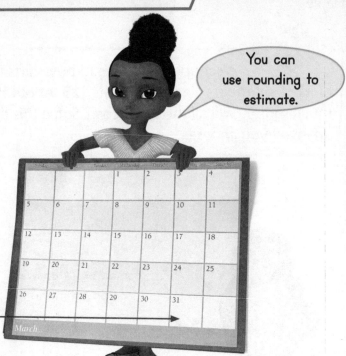

Convince Me! **Critique Reasoning** A different store needs to make at least $20,000 to make a profit in March. They average $685 a day for the month. James used rounding and estimation to say, "$685 is almost $700. $700 × 30 days is $21,000. I think it is going to be a close call!" What do you think?

Name

Another Example

Estimate 24 × 398.

25 and 4 are compatible numbers because their product is easy to compute mentally.

25 × 4 = 100

25 × 40 = 1,000

25 × 400 = 10,000

So, 10,000 is a good estimate for 24 × 398.

You can also use compatible numbers to estimate.

Both numbers used to estimate were greater than the actual numbers.

So, 10,000 is an overestimate.

Guided Practice

Do You Understand?

1. **Number Sense** Each egg carton holds one dozen eggs. Michael's chicken farm fills 121 egg cartons. He thinks that there were over 1,500 eggs. Is he correct? Use an estimate to find out.

Do You Know How?

In **2–5**, estimate. Then, tell if your estimate is an overestimate or underestimate.

2. 29 × 688
3. 210 × 733
4. 43 × 108
5. 380 × 690

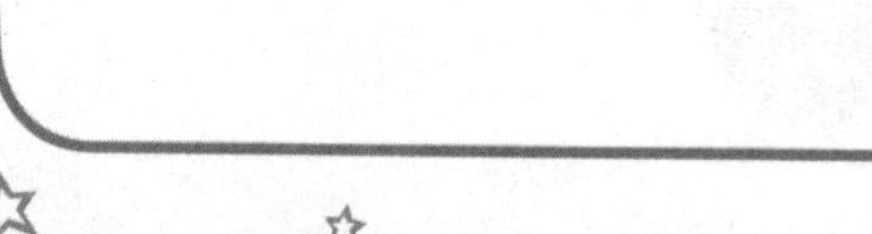

Independent Practice

Leveled Practice In **6–17**, estimate each product.

6. 180 × 586
7. 300 × 118
8. 19 × 513
9. 38 × 249
10. 11 × 803
11. 44 × 212
12. 790 × 397
13. 42 × 598
14. 25 × 191
15. 408 × 676
16. 290 × 12
17. 854 × 733

Problem Solving

18. Reasoning Estimate 530×375. Is the estimated product closer to 150,000 or 200,000? Explain.

19. **Vocabulary** Is 500 an **underestimate** or **overestimate** for the product of 12 and 53?

20. Samuel needs to estimate the product of 23×495. Explain two different methods Samuel can use to estimate.

21. Rebekah said that 10^3 is 30 because $10 + 10 + 10 = 30$. Do you agree? Explain.

22. Higher Order Thinking Abby counts 12 large boxes and 18 small boxes of pencils in the supply cabinet. Each large box contains 144 pencils. Each small box contains 24 pencils. Estimate the total number of pencils. Is your estimate an overestimate or an underestimate? Explain why it might be better to have an underestimate rather than an overestimate.

23. Susan used rounding to estimate 24×413 and found 20×400. Jeremy used compatible numbers and found 25×400. Whose method gives an estimate closer to the actual product? Explain.

Is your answer reasonable?

Assessment Practice

24. Lance has 102 packages of sports cards. Each package has 28 cards. Use rounding to estimate. About how many cards does Lance have?

Ⓐ 2,000
Ⓑ 2,500
Ⓒ 3,000
Ⓓ 3,500

25. Which does NOT show a reasonable estimate of 24×338?

Ⓐ 6,000
Ⓑ 7,000
Ⓒ 7,500
Ⓓ 10,000

Name ______________________________

Solve & Share

Suppose a school ordered 7 boxes of books. There are 25 books in each box. How can you use paper and pencil to find how many books were ordered? How can you check if your answer is reasonable? ***Solve these problems using any strategy you choose.***

Lesson 3-3
Multiply by 1-Digit Numbers

I can ...
use place-value strategies and algorithms to multiply by 1-digit numbers.

Content Standard 5.NBT.B.5
Mathematical Practices MP.1, MP.3, MP.4

You can make sense and persevere. Formulating a plan can help you solve problems. *Show your work!*

Look Back! Without finding the exact answer, how do you know that the answer to the problem above is less than 210?

What Is a Common Way to Record Multiplication?

A

Ms. Stockton ordered 6 boxes of T-shirts with the school name on them. Each box contains 26 T-shirts. How many T-shirts did Ms. Stockton order?

You can multiply using partial products. You can write and add the partial products in any order.

B

One Way to Record Multiplication

	20	6
6	$6 \times 20 = 120$	$6 \times 6 = 36$

$$\begin{array}{lrl} & 26 & \\ & \times\ \ 6 & \\ \hline \text{Partial product} & 36 & 6 \times 6 \text{ ones} = 6 \times 6 = 36 \\ \text{Partial product} & +\ 120 & 6 \times 2 \text{ tens} = 6 \times 20 = 120 \\ \hline & 156 & \end{array}$$

C

Another Way to Record Multiplication

You can multiply each place value in order, beginning with the ones. Regroup if needed. Add any regrouped values to each place value.

Step 1: Multiply by the ones.

$$\begin{array}{r} {}^{3} \\ 26 \\ \times\ \ 6 \\ \hline 6 \end{array}$$

6×6 ones = 36 ones = 3 tens 6 ones

Record the 6 ones.
Record the 3 tens.

Step 2: Multiply by the tens.

$$\begin{array}{r} {}^{3} \\ 26 \\ \times\ \ 6 \\ \hline 156 \end{array}$$

6×2 tens = 12 tens

12 tens + 3 tens = 15 tens

This method of multiplying is called the Standard Algorithm.

Mrs. Stockton ordered 156 T-shirts.

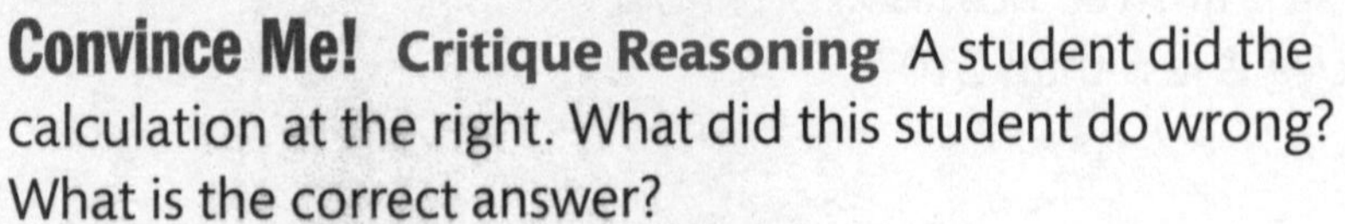

Convince Me! **Critique Reasoning** A student did the calculation at the right. What did this student do wrong? What is the correct answer?

Incorrect Answer

$$\begin{array}{r} {}^{1} \\ 26 \\ \times\ \ 3 \\ \hline 98 \end{array}$$

Name ____________________

Another Example!

Find 4 × 156.

```
  2 2
  1 5 6
×     4
  6 2 4
```

Think:

4 × 6 ones = 24; 24 is 2 tens 4 ones.

4 × 5 tens = 20 tens; 20 tens + 2 tens = 22 tens; 22 tens is 2 hundreds 2 tens.

4 × 1 hundred = 4 hundreds; 4 hundreds + 2 hundreds = 6 hundreds.

```
  2 1 1
  2,746
×     3
  8,238
```

The thinking and the process is the same when there are 3 or 4 digits.

Guided Practice

Do You Understand?

1. Use place value to explain each step in finding 3 × 2,746.

Do You Know How?

For **2-5**, find each product. Estimate to check if your answer is reasonable.

2. 23 × 4

3. 378 × 2

4. 157 × 5

5. 1,746 × 3

Independent Practice

For **6-13**, find each product. Estimate to check if your answer is reasonable.

6. 519 × 4

7. 28 × 3

8. 72 × 5

9. 138 × 5

10. 27 × 3

11. 123 × 9

12. 1,445 × 5

13. 2,204 × 6

Problem Solving

For **14–16**, use the information in the pictures below to find each mass.

14. Elephant Seal **15.** Sports Car **16.** Bison

Zebra: 435 kilograms

Bison: 2 times as much as a zebra

Sports Car: 4 times as much as a zebra

Elephant Seal: 8 times as much as a zebra

17. Model with Math Last year, Anthony's grandmother gave him 33 silver coins and 16 gold coins to start a coin collection. Now Anthony has six times as many coins in his collection. How many coins does Anthony have in his collection? Complete the bar diagram to show your work.

____ coins in all

coins now

coins to start

18.  **Vocabulary** Use *Distributive* or *Commutative* to complete the definition.

According to the ______________ Property of Multiplication, factors can be multiplied in any order and the product remains the same.

19. Higher Order Thinking Do you think you could use a multiplication algorithm to multiply a 4-digit number by a 1-digit number? Explain.

Assessment Practice

20. Find the product.

$$\begin{array}{r} 768 \\ \times \quad 8 \\ \hline \end{array}$$

21. Find the product.

$$\begin{array}{r} 1,945 \\ \times \quad 3 \\ \hline \end{array}$$

Name ____________________

Activity

Lesson 3-4
Multiply 2-Digit by 2-Digit Numbers

I can ...
use area models, place-value strategies, and properties of operations to help multiply 2-digit by 2-digit numbers.

Content Standard 5.NBT.B.5
Mathematical Practices MP.1, MP.3, MP.4

Solve & Share

Ms. Silva has 12 weeks to train for a race. Over the course of one week, she plans to run 15 miles. If she continues this training, how many miles will Ms. Silva run before the race? ***Solve this problem using any strategy you choose.***

You can use partial products to help make sense of and solve the problem. *Show your work in the space below!*

Look Back! Critique Reasoning Dwayne estimated 60 miles as an answer to the above problem. Is this estimate reasonable? If not, what mistake do you think Dwayne made?

Visual Learning

Glossary

What Is a Common Way to Record Multiplication?

Visual Learning Bridge

A

A ferry carried 37 cars per trip on the weekend. If the ferry made 11 trips on Saturday and 13 trips on Sunday, how many cars did it carry on the weekend?

You can add to find 24 trips were made on Saturday and Sunday. So the ferry carried 37 × 24 cars on the weekend.

	30	7
20	20×30	20×7
4	4×30	4×7

B

Use Partial Products

Use the area model to find the partial products for 24 × 37.

$$\begin{array}{r} 37 \\ \times\ 24 \\ \hline 28 \\ 120 \\ 140 \\ +\ 600 \\ \hline 888 \end{array}$$

The ferry carried 888 cars on the weekend.

C

Use the Standard Algorithm

Step 1: Multiply by the ones.

$$\begin{array}{r} {\scriptstyle 2} \\ 37 \\ \times\ 24 \\ \hline 148 \end{array}$$

Step 2: Multiply by the tens.

$$\begin{array}{r} {\scriptstyle 1} \\ {\scriptstyle 2} \\ 37 \\ \times\ 24 \\ \hline 148 \\ +\ 740 \\ \hline 888 \end{array}$$

Add the partial products.

The ferry carried 888 cars.

Convince Me! **Make Sense and Persevere** What are ways you can estimate to check the reasonableness of the answer?

Name

Practice Tools Assessment

Guided Practice

Do You Understand?

1. Janet said that the standard algorithm is just a shortcut for partial products. Do you agree? Explain.

Do You Know How?

For **2**, use an algorithm or partial products to find the product. Estimate to check if your answer is reasonable.

2.
```
      4 1
  ×   2 3
  -------
    1 2 □
  + □ 2 0
  -------
    9 □ □
```

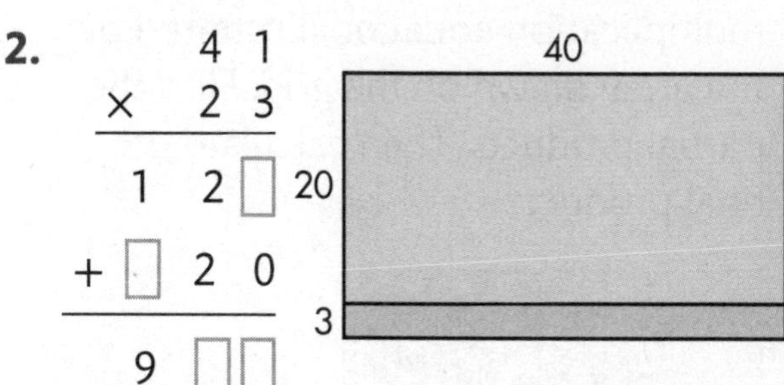

Independent Practice

Leveled Practice For **3–14**, use an algorithm or partial products to find the product. Use and draw area models as needed.

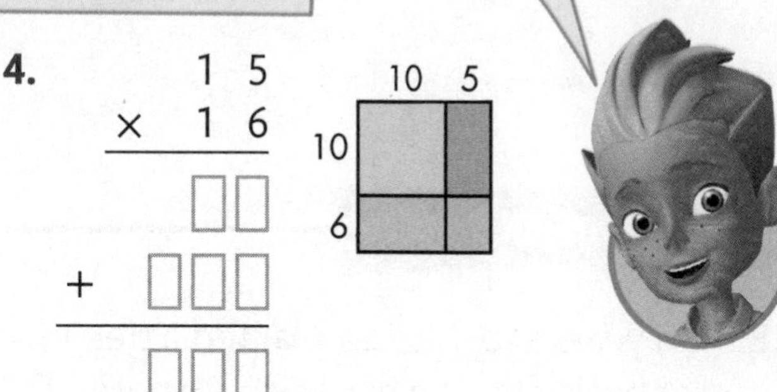

3.
```
      1 6
  ×   2 2
  -------
      □ 2
  + □ □ 0
  -------
    □ □ □
```

10 6 / 20 / 2

4.
```
      1 5
  ×   1 6
  -------
      □ □
  + □ □ □
  -------
    □ □ □
```

5.
```
   27
 × 12
```

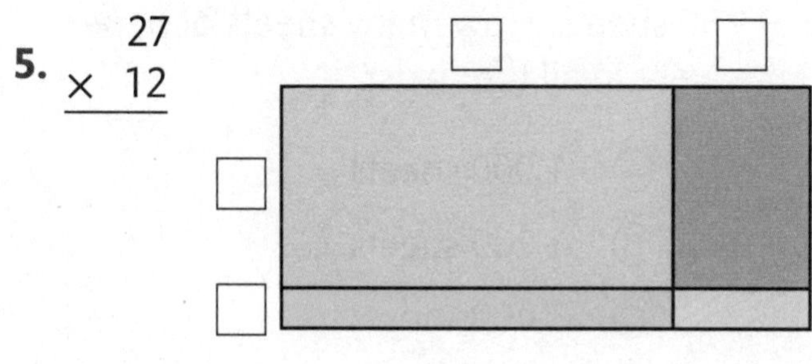

6.
```
   18
 × 15
```

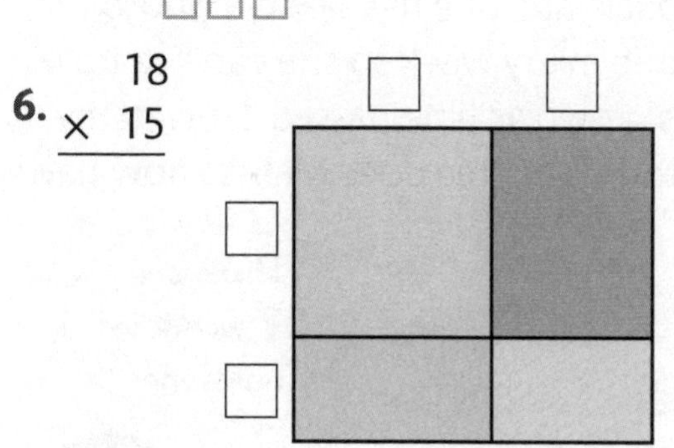

7. 53×17

8. 81×46

9. 15×16

10. 17×21

11. 12×22

12. 38×41

13. 42×52

14. 38×19

Problem Solving

15. **Number Sense** The *Queen Mary 2*'s height above water is about the same as a 14-story building. What is the *Queen Mary 2*'s height above water?

Each story is
12 feet tall.

16. **Model with Math** Write the multiplication equation illustrated by the array drawn on the grid. Find the partial products. Then calculate the final product.

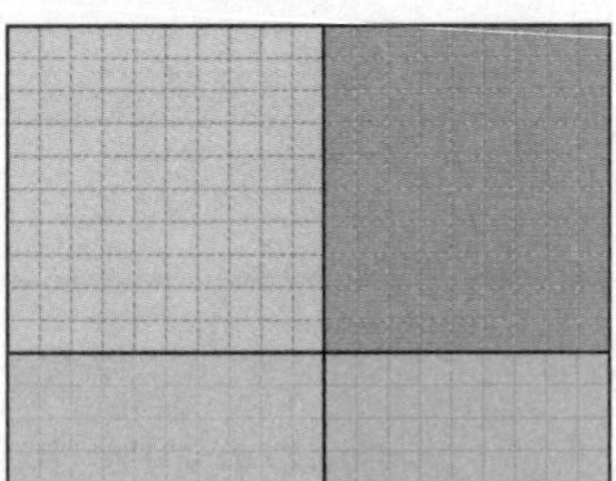

17. **Higher Order Thinking** An elevator can carry 15 adults or 20 children at one time. During the course of a day, the elevator carries a full passenger load 52 times. If all the passengers were children, how many more people would the elevator carry than if all the passengers were adults?

Assessment Practice

18. Ten years ago, Melissa planted a tree in her backyard. She has taken a photo of the tree every week so she can see how it has grown as time passed. How many photos of the tree does Melissa now have?

There are
52 weeks in
one year.

Ⓐ 62 photos
Ⓑ 120 photos
Ⓒ 520 photos
Ⓓ 620 photos

19. Mr. Morris bought sketchpads for 24 of his students. Each pad contained 50 sheets. How many sheets of paper were in all the pads?

Ⓐ 1,000 sheets
Ⓑ 1,200 sheets
Ⓒ 1,400 sheets
Ⓓ 1,600 sheets

Name ____________________

Activity

Solve & Share

A local charity collected 163 cans of food each day for 14 days. How many cans did they collect in all? Explain how you found your answer.

Lesson 3-5
Multiply 3-Digit by 2-Digit Numbers

I can ...
multiply 3-digit by 2-digit numbers.

Content Standard 5.NBT.B.5
Mathematical Practices MP.1, MP.3

You can use what you know about multiplying 2-digit numbers by 2-digit numbers to help solve the problem.
FOOD DRIVE

Look Back! Make Sense and Persevere How can you check that your answer is reasonable?

How Do You Multiply 3-Digit Numbers by 2-Digit Numbers?

Visual Learning Bridge

A

Last month a bakery sold 389 boxes of bagels. How many bagels did the store sell last month? Find 12 × 389.

You can show all partial products or you can use the standard algorithm.

$$\begin{array}{rl} 389 & \\ \times\ 12 & \\ \hline 18 & 2 \times 9 \\ 160 & 2 \times 80 \\ 600 & 2 \times 300 \\ 90 & 10 \times 9 \\ 800 & 10 \times 80 \\ +\ 3{,}000 & 10 \times 300 \\ \hline 4{,}668 & \end{array}$$

B

Step 1

To use the Standard Algorithm, first multiply by the ones. Regroup as needed.

$$\begin{array}{r} {}^{1\,1} \\ 389 \\ \times\ 12 \\ \hline 778 \end{array}$$

2 × 9 ones = 18 ones or 1 ten and 8 ones

2 × 8 tens = 16 tens

16 tens + 1 ten = 17 tens

17 tens = 1 hundred 7 tens

2 × 3 hundreds = 6 hundreds

6 hundreds + 1 hundred = 7 hundreds

C

Step 2

Multiply by the tens. Regroup as needed.

$$\begin{array}{r} 389 \\ \times\ 12 \\ \hline 778 \\ +\ 3890 \\ \hline \end{array}$$

10 × 9 ones = 90 ones

10 × 8 tens = 80 tens, or 8 hundreds

10 × 3 hundreds = 30 hundreds, or 3 thousands

D

Step 3

Add to get the final product.

$$\begin{array}{r} 389 \\ \times\ 12 \\ \hline 778 \\ +\ 3890 \\ \hline 4{,}668 \end{array}$$

The store sold 4,668 bagels last month.

Convince Me! **Construct Arguments** Is 300 × 10 a good estimate for the number of bagels sold at the bakery? Explain.

Name ____________________

Practice Tools Assessment

Guided Practice

Do You Understand?

1. A theater can seat 540 people at one time. How many tickets are sold if the theater sells out every seat for one 30-day month?

2. **Number Sense** Is 500 × 30 a good estimate for the number of tickets sold at the theater in one month? Explain.

Do You Know How?

In **3–6**, find each product. Estimate to check that your answer is reasonable.

3. 236×46

4. 61×25

5. 951×62

6. 185×5

Independent Practice

Leveled Practice In **7–18**, find each product. Estimate to check that your answer is reasonable.

7. 51×10

8. 892×18

9. 946×33

10. 735×41

11. 100×25

12. 81×11

13. 106×7

14. 90×59

15. 360×18

16. 222×75

17. 481×35

18. 659×17

Problem Solving

19. **enVision® STEM** How many times does a rabbit's heart beat in 1 hour?

Remember, there are 60 minutes in 1 hour.

20. In 1 hour, how many more times does a rabbit's heart beat than a dog's heart? Write an equation to show your work.

DATA

Animal	Heart Rate (beats per minute)
Dog	100
Gerbil	360
Rabbit	212

21. **Construct Arguments** Is 3,198 a reasonable product for 727 × 44? Why or why not?

22. **Higher Order Thinking** A garden store sells plants in flats. There are 6 plants in each tray. Each flat has 6 trays. The garden store sold 18 flats on Saturday and 21 flats on Sunday. How many plants did the garden store sell in all?

Assessment Practice

23. Tricia is building a rectangular patio. The patio will be 108 bricks wide and 19 bricks long. How many bricks does she need to build the patio?

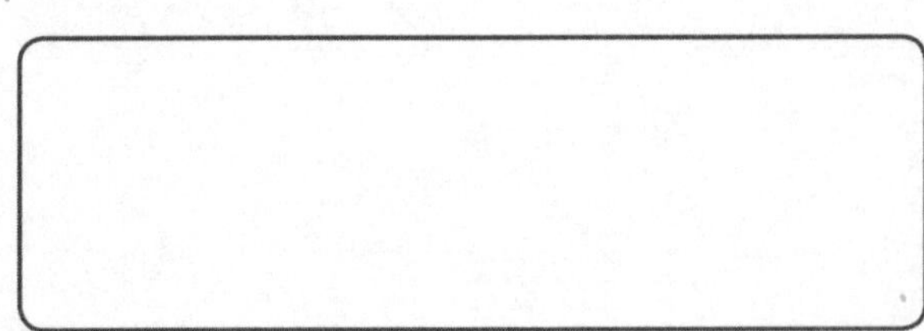

24. What is the product?

$$\begin{array}{r} 312 \\ \times\ 14 \\ \hline \end{array}$$

Ⓐ 1,560
Ⓑ 1,568
Ⓒ 4,268
Ⓓ 4,368

Name ______________________________

Activity

Lesson 3-6
Multiply Whole Numbers with Zeros

I can ...
multiply numbers that have a zero in them.

Content Standard 5.NBT.B.5
Mathematical Practices MP.1, MP.4, MP.7

Solve & Share A school district is replacing all of the desks in its classrooms. There are 103 classrooms and each classroom needs 24 new desks. How many desks will the school district need to buy? ***Solve this problem any way you choose!***

Use what you know about multiplying 3-digit and 2-digit numbers. Show your work!

Look Back! Make Sense and Persevere What is a good estimate for the problem above? Explain.

Visual Learning Bridge

Essential Question How Can You Multiply with Zeros?

A

An antique steam train makes one sight-seeing tour each day. If every seat is filled for each trip, how many passengers can it carry for 31 tours?

The standard algorithm does not change when there is a zero in a factor.

The train has a total of 208 seats.

B Step 1

Find 31 × 208.

Estimate:

$30 \times 200 = 6{,}000$

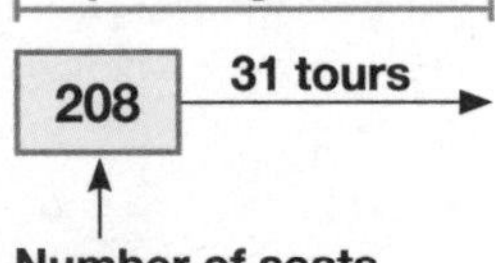

C Step 2

Multiply by the ones.

Regroup if necessary.

Remember that multiplying with a zero gives a product of zero.

$$\begin{array}{r} 208 \\ \times\ 31 \\ \hline 208 \end{array}$$

D Step 3

Multiply by the tens.

Regroup if necessary.

Add to get the final product.

$$\begin{array}{r} \scriptstyle 2 \\ 208 \\ \times\ 31 \\ \hline 208 \\ +\ 6240 \\ \hline 6{,}448 \end{array}$$

The train can carry 6,448 passengers.

Convince Me! **Model with Math** Suppose the train fills an average of 102 seats for each tour. What is a reasonable estimate for the number of passengers that the train can carry in 28 tours? Write an equation to show your work.

Name ____

Assessment

Guided Practice

Do You Understand?

1. In an auditorium, there are 104 rows with 24 seats in each row. How many seats are available?

2. Why is it important to “estimate to check for reasonableness”?

Do You Know How?

In **3–6**, multiply to find the product. Estimate to check for reasonableness.

3. $\begin{array}{r} 205 \\ \times\ \ 23 \\ \hline \end{array}$

4. $\begin{array}{r} 108 \\ \times\ \ 34 \\ \hline \end{array}$

5. $\begin{array}{r} 410 \\ \times\ \ 44 \\ \hline \end{array}$

6. $\begin{array}{r} 302 \\ \times\ \ 30 \\ \hline \end{array}$

Independent Practice

Leveled Practice In **7–18**, find each product. Estimate to check for reasonableness.

7. $\begin{array}{r} 302 \\ \times\ \ 17 \\ \hline \end{array}$

8. $\begin{array}{r} 608 \\ \times\ \ 23 \\ \hline \end{array}$

9. $\begin{array}{r} 109 \\ \times\ \ 47 \\ \hline \end{array}$

10. $\begin{array}{r} 510 \\ \times\ \ 72 \\ \hline \end{array}$

11. $\begin{array}{r} 902 \\ \times\ \ 35 \\ \hline \end{array}$

12. $\begin{array}{r} 207 \\ \times\ \ 61 \\ \hline \end{array}$

13. $\begin{array}{r} 108 \\ \times\ \ 58 \\ \hline \end{array}$

14. $\begin{array}{r} 505 \\ \times\ \ 77 \\ \hline \end{array}$

15. $\begin{array}{r} 407 \\ \times\ \ 39 \\ \hline \end{array}$

16. $\begin{array}{r} 280 \\ \times\ \ 66 \\ \hline \end{array}$

17. $\begin{array}{r} 105 \\ \times\ \ 24 \\ \hline \end{array}$

18. $\begin{array}{r} 360 \\ \times\ \ 48 \\ \hline \end{array}$

Problem Solving

19. There are 27 students in Mr. Mello's class. Find the total number of pages the students read by the end of November.

20. Each student read 41 pages in December. How many total pages did the students read by the end of December?

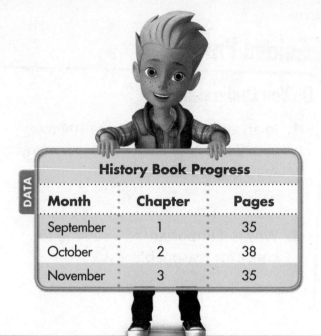

DATA

History Book Progress

Month	Chapter	Pages
September	1	35
October	2	38
November	3	35

21. Meredith says that 15.17 is greater than 15.8 because 17 is greater than 8. Do you agree? Explain your reasoning.

22. **Use Structure** Trudy wants to multiply 66×606. She says that all she has to do is find 6×606 and then double that number. Explain why Trudy's method will not give the correct answer. Then show how to find the correct product.

23. **Higher Order Thinking** Maria needs a trombone for only 12 months. Renting the trombone costs $34 per month. She can buy the trombone for $495. Should she buy or rent the trombone? Explain. How much does she pay?

24. Another music store rents trombones for $30 per month plus a yearly fee of $48. Which deal is better? Should Maria change her rental plan?

Assessment Practice

25. What is the product?

$$\begin{array}{r} 709 \\ \times\ 41 \\ \hline \end{array}$$

Name ___________________________ Activity

Lesson 3-7
Practice Multiplying Multi-Digit Numbers

I can ...
find the product of multi-digit factors.

Content Standard 5.NBT.B.5
Mathematical Practices MP.2, MP.4, MP.6

Solve & Share

Which of the two car payment options will cost less for 1 year? How much less? ***Solve this problem any way you choose!*** Show all of your work.

Car Payment Options	Monthly Amount	Quarterly
	$325	$952

You can use reasoning to connect mathematics to everyday life. Think about the situations multiplication describes.

Look Back! How can you estimate the total for the year when paying monthly? When paying quarterly?

How Can You Use Multiplication to Solve Problems?

A

What is the yearly total for water, gas, and electric?
What is the yearly total for cell phones?

Bills	Amount (frequency)
Water	$760 (quarterly)
Gas & Electric	$510 (quarterly)
Cell phones	$271 (monthly)

The standard algorithm for multiplying whole numbers involves breaking numbers apart using place value.

B What is the yearly total for water, gas, and electric?

Find $4 \times (760 + 510)$.

Estimate:
$4 \times (760 + 510)$ is about $4 \times 1{,}200 = 4{,}800$.
$4 \times (760 + 510) = 4 \times 1{,}270$

$$\begin{array}{r} {}^{1\,2} \\ 1{,}270 \\ \times \quad 4 \\ \hline 5{,}080 \end{array}$$

The yearly total for water, gas, and electric is $5,080.

C What is the yearly total for cell phones?

Find 12×271.

Estimate:
12×271 is about $10 \times 270 = 2{,}700$.

$$\begin{array}{r} {}^{1} \\ 271 \\ \times \quad 12 \\ \hline 542 \\ +\,2710 \\ \hline 3{,}252 \end{array}$$

The process for multiplying is the same regardless of the number of digits in the factors.

The yearly total for cell phones is $3,252.

Convince Me! **Be Precise** How are the processes for multiplying alike for the two calculations above? How are they different?

Name

Practice Tools Assessment

Guided Practice

Do You Understand?

1. Carlos saves 18 cents every day of the year. If there are 365 days this year, how many cents will he have saved by the end of the year? Write an equation that represents the problem. Then, solve the equation.

2. Lila drives 129 kilometers round trip to work. How many kilometers does she drive in 31 days? Write an equation that represents the problem. Then solve the equation.

Do You Know How?

In **3-6**, estimate each product. Then complete each calculation. Check that your answer is reasonable.

3. 134 × 11

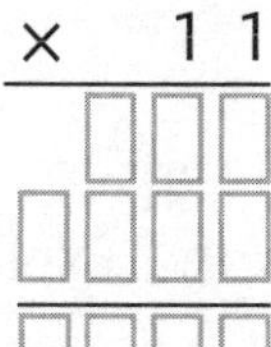

4. 208 × 26

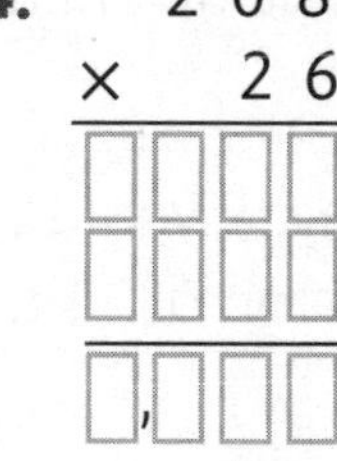

5. 428 × 35

6. 275 × 56

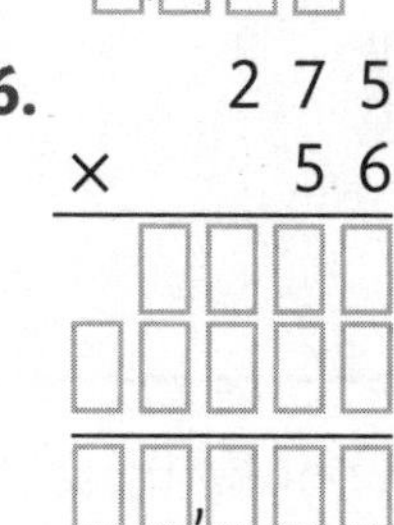

Independent Practice

Leveled Practice In **7-22**, estimate and then compute each product. Check that your answer is reasonable.

7. 531 × 47

8. 759 × 68

9. 367 × 92

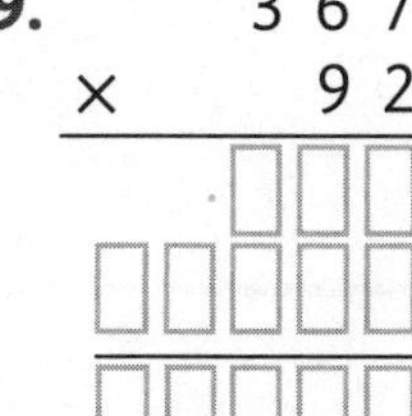

10. 817 × 45

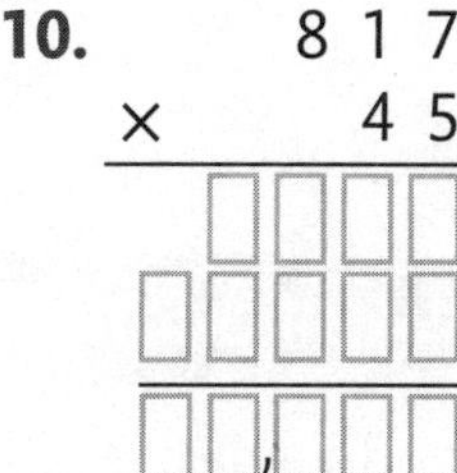

11. 1,206 × 77

12. 543 × 18

13. 908 × 62

14. 750 × 81

15. 6,755 × 9

16. 869 × 46

17. 922 × 81

18. 783 × 14

19. 684 × 15

20. 650 × 22

21. 2,525 × 37

22. 615 × 41

Problem Solving

For **23** and **24**, use the table.

23. Model with Math Jason frequently travels for work. This year he plans to make 15 trips to Chicago. What is the total cost for the airfare? Write an equation that represents the problem. Then, solve the equation.

24. Which would cost more: 15 trips to Boston or 11 trips to New York? Explain.

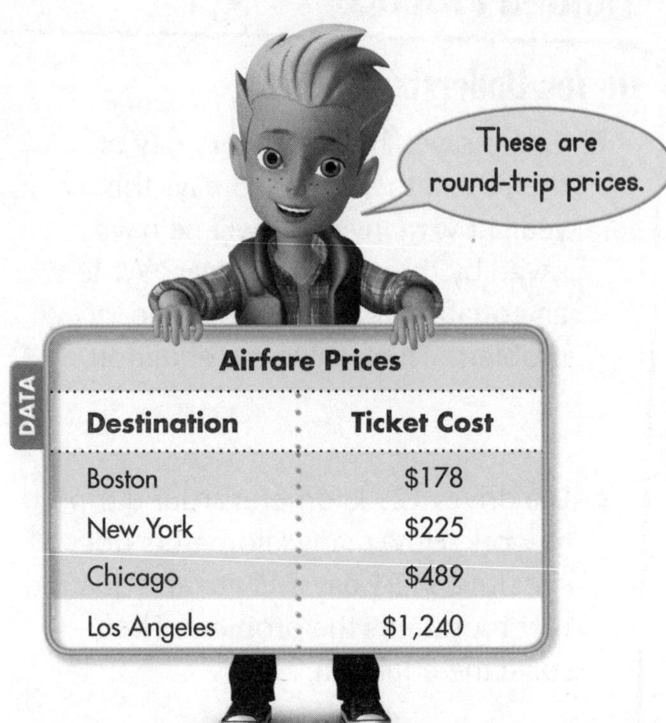

These are round-trip prices.
DATA

Airfare Prices

Destination	Ticket Cost
Boston	$178
New York	$225
Chicago	$489
Los Angeles	$1,240

25. A cook at a restaurant is planning her food order. She expects to use 115 pounds of potatoes each day for 12 days. How many pounds of potatoes will she order?

? number of pounds

115	115	115	115	115	115	115	115	115	115	115	115

12 days

26. Higher Order Thinking Carolyn bought a gallon of paint that covers 250 square feet. She wants to paint a wall that is 16 feet wide and 12 feet high. Explain whether or not she will need more than one gallon of paint.

Assessment Practice

27. The product of the following expression is 7,453.

$$\begin{array}{r} 2\ 5\ 7 \\ \times\ \square\ 9 \\ \hline \end{array}$$

What is the missing digit?

Ⓐ 1

Ⓑ 2

Ⓒ 4

Ⓓ 7

28. When you multiply a 3-digit number by a 2-digit number, what is the greatest number of digits the product can have?

Name ______________________________

Activity

Lesson 3-8
Solve Word Problems Using Multiplication

I can ...
solve word problems involving multiplication.

Content Standard 5.NBT.B.5
Mathematical Practices MP.1, MP.3, MP.4

Solve & Share

Kevin's family took 239 photos on their summer vacation. Marco and his family took 12 times as many photos on their vacation. How many photos did Marco's family take? ***Solve this problem any way you choose.***

How can you use an equation to model the situation with math?

Look Back! How can you use estimation to tell if your answer is reasonable? Explain.

How Can You Use a Bar Diagram to Solve a Multiplication Problem?

Visual Learning Bridge

A

In 1980, a painting sold for $1,575. In 2015, the same painting sold for 5 times as much. What was the price of the painting in 2015?

You can draw a bar diagram and use a variable to find the new price of the painting.

B

What am I asked to find?

The price of the painting in 2015.

Let p = the price of the painting in 2015.

Draw a bar diagram to represent the problem.

price in 2015 (p)

2015	$1,575	$1,575	$1,575	$1,575	$1,575	5 times as much
1980	$1,575					

C

Write and solve an equation using the variable.

$\$1{,}575 \times 5 = p$

$\$1{,}575 \times 5 = \$7{,}875.$

So, $p = \$7{,}875$.

In 2015, the painting sold for $7,875.

You can use repeated addition or division to check your answer!

Convince Me! **Construct Arguments** How can you use estimation to justify that the answer $7,875 is reasonable?

Name ______________________________

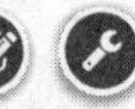

Guided Practice

Do You Understand?

1. Write a real-world problem that uses multiplication. Then, draw a bar diagram and write an equation to solve your problem.

Do You Know How?

In **2**, write and solve an equation.

2. Sharon's Stationery Store has 1,219 boxes of cards. May's Market has 3 times as many boxes of cards. How many boxes of cards does May's Market have?

b boxes of cards

May's	1,219	1,219	1,219	3 times as many
Sharon's	1,219			

Independent Practice

In **3–5**, draw a bar diagram to model the situation. Then, write and solve an equation.

3. There are 14 theaters at the mall. Each theater has 175 seats. How many seats are there in all?

? seats → ?

14 theaters →	175	175	175	175	175	175	175	175	175	175	175	175	175	175

175 seats for each theater

4. Brad lives 12 times as far away from the ocean as Jennie. If Jennie lives 48 miles from the ocean, how many miles from the ocean does Brad live?

5. A hardware store ordered 13 packs of nails from a supplier. Each pack contains 155 nails. How many nails did the store order?

Problem Solving

6. **Algebra** Sandi's school has 1,030 students. Karla's school has 3 times as many students as Sandi's school. Write an equation to find *s*, the number of students in Karla's school. Then, solve your equation.

	s			
Karla's school	**1,030**	**1,030**	**1,030**	**3 times as many**
Sandi's school	**1,030**			

7. **enVision® STEM** Jupiter is about 5 times the distance Earth is from the Sun. Earth is about 93,000,000 miles from the Sun. About how far is Jupiter from the Sun?

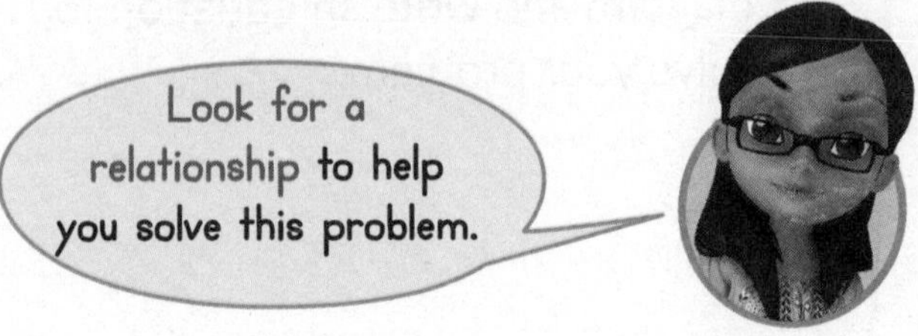

Look for a relationship to help you solve this problem.

8. **Higher Order Thinking** William travels only on Saturdays and Sundays and has flown 1,020 miles this month. Jason travels every weekday and has flown 1,200 miles this month. If each man travels about the same number of miles each day, who travels more miles per day for this month? Explain.

9. **Make Sense and Persevere** Hwong can fit 12 packets of coffee in a small box and 50 packets of coffee in a large box. He has 10 small boxes of coffee and would like to reorganize the packets into large boxes. How many large boxes could he fill? Explain.

Assessment Practice

10. Martin ran 108 miles last year. Katrina ran 13 times as many miles as Martin last year. How many miles did Katrina run last year?

    Ⓐ 1,008 miles

    Ⓑ 1,404 miles

    Ⓒ 1,806 miles

    Ⓓ 2,000 miles

11. The Erie shoe factory makes 245 pairs of shoes a day. The Columbus shoe factory makes 34 times as many pairs of shoes a day as the Erie shoe factory. How many pairs of shoes does the Columbus shoe factory make a day?

    Ⓐ 7,545 pairs of shoes

    Ⓑ 8,010 pairs of shoes

    Ⓒ 8,330 pairs of shoes

    Ⓓ 8,750 pairs of shoes

Name ______________________

Activity

Solve & Share

A group of 44 students is planning a train trip to Washington, D.C. They held many fundraisers and raised $10,880. Nathan said, "We should have enough money to pay for the train tickets. There are about 50 students going on the trip and one round trip ticket costs about $200. That makes the total cost of the tickets less than $10,000."

Does Nathan's reasoning make sense?

Train Travel	
April 14 Clorisville to Washington, D.C.	$92
April 18 Washington, D.C., to Clorisville	$92
Total Ticket Price	**$184**

Problem Solving

Lesson 3-9

Critique Reasoning

I can ...

critique the reasoning of others by using what I know about estimating products.

Mathematical Practices MP.3 Also MP.1, MP.2, MP.6
Content Standard 5.NBT.B.5

Thinking Habits

Be a good thinker! These questions can help you.

- What questions can I ask to understand people's thinking?
- Are there mistakes in other people's thinking?
- Can I improve other people's thinking?

Look Back! **Critique Reasoning** What argument would you make to support Nathan's estimate?

How Can You Critique Reasoning of Others?

A

Ms. Lynch needs to ship 89 boxes. 47 boxes weigh 150 pounds each. Each of the other boxes weighs 210 pounds.

Mia says that all 89 boxes can fit into one container. She reasons that 47 × 150 is less than 7,500 and 42 × 210 is a little more than 8,000, so the sum of their weights should be less than 15,400.

What is Mia's reasoning to support her estimate?

Mia estimates the total weight of the lighter boxes and the total weight of the heavier boxes, then adds the two estimates.

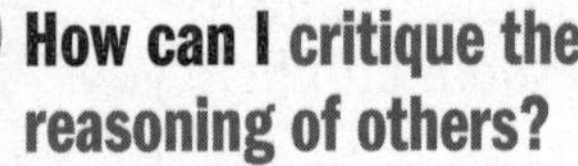

B

How can I critique the reasoning of others?

I can

- ask questions for clarification.
- decide if the strategy used makes sense.
- look for flaws in estimates or calculations.

C

Here's my thinking...

Mia's reasoning has flaws. She estimated that 42 × 210 is a little more than 8,000, but a better estimate is 9,000.

She underestimated the products so her conclusion is not valid.

The weight of the heavier boxes is 8,820 pounds. The weight of the lighter boxes is 7,050 pounds.

The total weight is 15,870 pounds. The sum is greater than 15,400. Mia's reasoning does not make sense.

Convince Me! **Critique Reasoning** Raul states that one way to get the cargo under the weight limit is to remove two of the heavier boxes and one of the lighter boxes. How can you decide if Raul's reasoning makes sense?

Name ______

Guided Practice

Critique Reasoning

A stadium has 58 sections of seats. There are 288 seats in each section. Mary estimated the total number of seats by multiplying 60×300. She concluded that the stadium has fewer than 18,000 seats.

1. What is Mary's argument? How does she support it?

2. Describe at least one thing you would do to critique Mary's reasoning.

3. Does Mary's conclusion make sense? Explain.

Independent Practice

Critique Reasoning

An office manager has \$10,000 to spend on new equipment. He planned to purchase 300 lamps for \$72 each. He completed the calculations at the right and concluded that there would be plenty of money left to buy additional equipment.

$300 \times 72 =$

$(300 \times 7) + (300 \times 2) =$

$2{,}100 + 600 = 2{,}700$

4. What does the office manager do to support his thinking?

5. Describe how you could decide if the office manager's calculation is reasonable.

When you critique reasoning, you need to explain if the method used by another makes sense.

6. Does the office manager's conclusion make sense? Explain.

Problem Solving

Performance Task

Buying a Piano

Over the summer Kathleen sold 1,092 jars of jam at outdoor markets. She made a $12 profit on each one. She wants to use the profits to buy the Ivory-5K piano. She said, "Since $1{,}000 \times 12 = 12{,}000$, and 1,092 is greater than 1,000, I know my profits add up to more than $12,000. So, I can buy the piano."

Piano Model	Price with tax
Harmony-2L	$8,675
Ivory-5K	$11,500
Goldtone-TX	$14,250

7. **Make Sense and Persevere** Does it make sense for Kathleen to find an overestimate or an underestimate to decide if she has earned enough money? Why?

8. **Reasoning** Should Kathleen use multiplication to estimate her total profits? Explain your reasoning.

9. **Be Precise** Is Kathleen's estimate appropriate? Is her calculation correct? Explain.

10. **Critique Reasoning** Explain whether Kathleen's conclusion is logical. How did you decide? If it is not logical, what can you do to improve her reasoning?

When you critique reasoning, ask questions to help understand someone's thinking.

Name ______________________________

TOPIC 3 Fluency Practice Activity

Solve each problem. Then follow multiples of 10 to shade a path from **START** to **FINISH**. You can only move up, down, right, or left.

I can ...

multiply multi-digit numbers fluently.

Content Standard 5.NBT.B.5
Mathematical Practices MP.2, MP.6, MP.7

Start

53 × 20	70 × 89	84 × 40	35 × 63	241 × 62
19 × 83	55 × 17	30 × 80	77 × 24	57 × 32
60 × 90	10 × 57	80 × 14	526 × 47	64 × 32
50 × 30	73 × 73	45 × 35	47 × 85	17 × 13
70 × 12	15 × 90	20 × 14	20 × 17	100 × 100

Finish

TOPIC 3 Vocabulary Review

Glossary

Word List

- expression
- multiple
- overestimate
- partial products
- power
- underestimate
- variable

For each of these terms, give an example and a non-example.

	Example	Non-example
1. Power of 10	________	________
2. Multiple of 10^2	________	________
3. An expression with a variable	________	________
4. An underestimate of 532×11	________	________

Write *always*, *sometimes*, or *never*.

5. The sum of partial products is equal to the final product.

6. A multiple of a number is a power of the number.

7. An underestimate results from rounding each factor to a greater number.

8. A power of a number is a multiple of the number.

Write T for *true* or F for *false*.

9. $642 \times 12 = 642$ tens $+ 1{,}284$ ones

10. $41 \times 10^6 = 41{,}000{,}000$

11. $80 \times 10^3 = 8{,}000$

12. Suppose both factors in a multiplication problem are multiples of 10. Explain why the number of zeros in the product may be different than the total number of zeros in the factors. Include an example.

Name ____________________

TOPIC 3

Reteaching

Set A pages 81–84

Find 65×10^3.

Look at the exponent for the power of 10. Annex that number of zeros to the other factor to find the product.

65000

Remember to look at the number of zeros or the exponent for the power of 10.

1. 12×10^4
2. 100×815
3. $10^2 \times 39$
4. $6{,}471 \times 10^1$

Set B pages 85–88

Estimate 37×88.

Step 1

Round both factors. 37 is about 40 and 88 is about 90.

Step 2

Multiply the rounded factors. $40 \times 90 = 3{,}600$

Remember to either round the factors or use compatible numbers.

Estimate each product.

1. 7×396
2. 17×63
3. 91×51
4. 45×806

Set C pages 89–92

$$\begin{array}{r} {\scriptstyle 1\ 3\ \ } \\ 249 \\ \times \quad 4 \\ \hline 996 \end{array}$$

Think:

4 × 9 ones = 36; 36 is 3 tens 6 ones.

4 × 4 tens = 16 tens; 16 tens + 3 tens = 19 tens; 19 tens is 1 hundred 9 tens.

4 × 2 hundreds = 8 hundreds; 8 hundreds + 1 hundred = 9 hundreds

Remember to keep track of the place values.

Find each product.

1. 133×3
2. 343×5
3. 893×7
4. $1{,}278 \times 4$

Set D pages 93–96

Find 17×35.

$$\begin{array}{r} {\scriptstyle 2} \\ {\scriptstyle 3} \\ 17 \\ \times\ 35 \\ \hline 85 \\ +\ 510 \\ \hline 595 \end{array}$$

85 ← Multiply 17 by 5 ones.

+ 510 ← Multiply 17 by 3 tens.

Remember that you can draw arrays or area models to represent multiplication.

Find each product.

1. 21×13
2. 34×52
3. 89×27
4. 78×47

Set E pages 97–100, 101–104, 105–108

Find 53 × 406.
Estimate: 50 × 400 = 20,000

```
     3
     1
   406
×   53
  1218  ← 3 × 406
+ 20300 ← 50 × 406
 21,518
```

Remember to regroup if necessary. Estimate to check that your answer is reasonable.

Find each product.

1. 54 × 9
2. 76 × 59
3. 47 × 302
4. 32 × 871
5. 604 × 55
6. 7,133 × 4

Set F pages 109–112

Draw a picture and write an equation. Solve.

The length of James's pool is 16 feet. The length of the pool at Wing Park is 4 times as long. How long is the pool at Wing Park?

ℓ = length of Wing Park Pool

16	16	16	16

↑ length of James's pool

$16 \times 4 = \ell$
$\ell = 64$ feet

The length of Wing Park pool is 64 feet.

Remember that pictures and equations can help you model and solve problems.

Draw a picture and write an equation. Solve.

1. Alexandria has a collection of 34 dolls. A toy store has 15 times as many dolls as Alexandria. How many dolls are in the store?
2. A store received a shipment of 37 TVs valued at $625 each. What is the total value of the shipment?

Set G pages 113–116

Think about these questions to help you **critique the reasoning of others.**

Thinking Habits

- What questions can I ask to understand other people's thinking?
- Are there mistakes in other people's thinking?

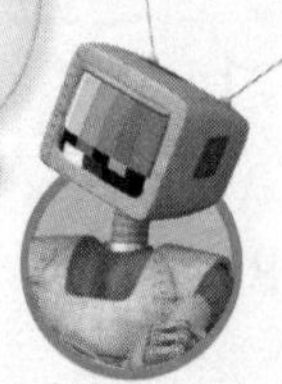

Remember you need to carefully consider all parts of an argument.

Sarah has 214 bags of beads. Each bag has enough beads for 22 bracelets. She estimates that since 200 × 20 = 4,000, there are enough beads for at least 4,000 bracelets.

Tell how you can critique Sarah's reasoning.

Name ______________________________

1. Dr. Peterson works 178 hours each month. How many hours does she work in a year?

   Ⓐ 2,000

   Ⓑ 2,136

   Ⓒ 3,000

   Ⓓ 2,200

2. A banana contains 105 calories. Last week, Brendan and Lea ate a total of 14 bananas. How many calories does this represent?

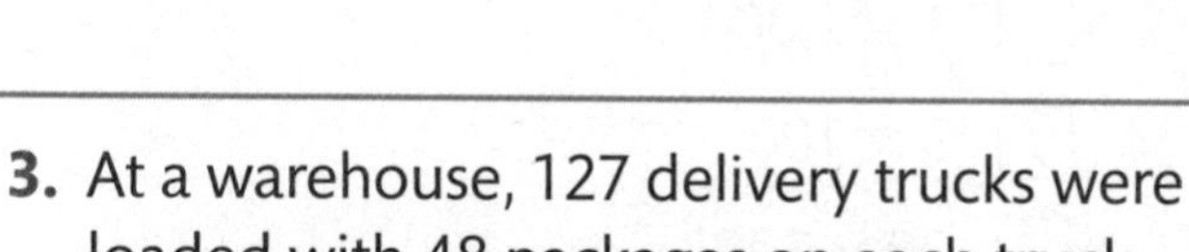

3. At a warehouse, 127 delivery trucks were loaded with 48 packages on each truck.

   A. Estimate the total number of packages on the trucks. Write an equation to model your work.

   B. Did you calculate an overestimate or an underestimate? Explain how you know.

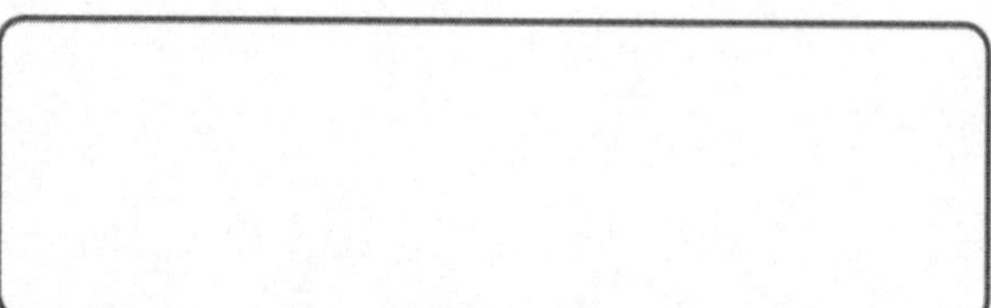

4. Is the equation below correct? Explain.

   $5.6 \times 10^3 = 560$

   Ⓐ The equation is incorrect. The product should have 3 zeros.

   Ⓑ The equation is correct. The product should have 1 zero.

   Ⓒ The equation is incorrect. The product should have 0 zeros.

   Ⓓ The equation is incorrect. The product should have 2 zeros.

5. The latest mystery novel costs $24. The table shows the sales of this novel by a bookstore.

DATA

Day	Books Sold
Thursday	98
Friday	103
Saturday	157
Sunday	116

   A. What was the dollar amount of sales of the mystery novel on Saturday? Write an equation to model your work.

   B. What was the dollar amount of sales of the mystery novel on Friday? Write an equation to model your work.

6. There are 45 cans of mixed nuts. Each can has 338 nuts. Below is Mary's work to find the total number of nuts. What is the missing number? Enter your answer in the box.

$$\begin{array}{r} 3\ 3\ 8 \\ \times\ \ 4\ 5 \\ \hline 1\ 6\ 9\ 0 \\ 1\ 3\ \square\ 2\ 0 \\ \hline 1\ 5\ 2\ 1\ 0 \end{array}$$

7. There are 36 large fish tanks at the zoo. Each tank holds 205 gallons of water. How many gallons of water would it take to fill all of the tanks?

8. Kai ordered 1,012 baseball cards. Sharon ordered 5 times as many cards as Kai. Write and solve an equation to find *b*, the number of baseball cards Sharon ordered.

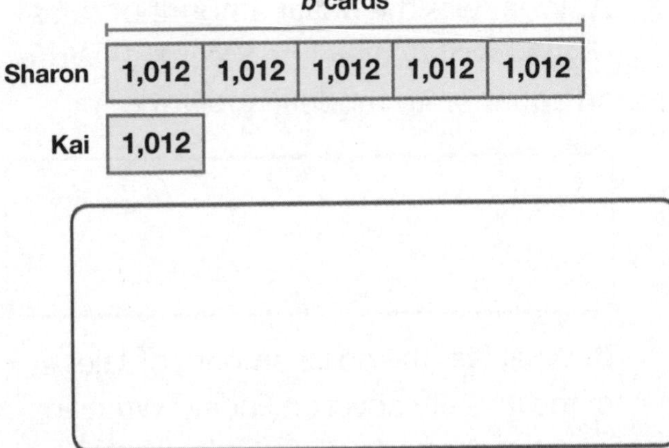

9. Multiply.

$$\begin{array}{r} 289 \\ \times\ \ 16 \\ \hline \end{array}$$

10. Match each number on the left with an equivalent expression.

	12×10^0	12×100	12×10^3	12×10^1
1,200	❑	❑	❑	❑
120	❑	❑	❑	❑
12	❑	❑	❑	❑
12,000	❑	❑	❑	❑

11. Select all the expressions that are equal to 3×10^3.

- ☐ $3 \times 1{,}000$
- ☐ 3×100
- ☐ 30×100
- ☐ 300×100
- ☐ 300×10

12. Rosanne has 142 songs on her MP3 player. Teresa has 11 times as many songs as Rosanne. How many songs does Teresa have?

Name ____________________

TOPIC 3

Performance Task

Baseball Apparel

Coach Sandberg wants to buy items for the baseball league. The league already has caps with the league logo on them, but the coach would like to offer the option of purchasing a T-shirt, sweatshirt, sweatpants, or jacket with the logo. Use the information in the table to answer the questions.

Jackie's Sports Store

Item	Item Price
jacket	$53
sweatshirt	$32
T-shirt	$14
sweatpants	$24

1. The players asked their families and friends if they want to buy T-shirts with the league logo. If 254 people want T-shirts, what would be the total cost? Write an equation to model your work.

2. Coach Sandberg wants to order 127 sweatshirts.

Part A

Will the total cost of the sweatshirts be greater than or less than $3,000? Use estimation to decide. Explain your reasoning.

Part B

What is the total cost of 127 sweatshirts?

3. Which would cost more, 32 T-shirts or 14 sweatshirts? How can you tell without multiplying?

4. There are 18×10^1 players in the league.

Part A

The league raised $1,560 through fundraisers. Trenton estimates the cost of buying jackets for each player in the league. He concludes that the league has raised enough money. Do you agree with Trenton? Explain.

180 rounds to 200.

53 rounds to 50.

200 × $50 = $1,000

Part B

How much would it cost to order sweatpants for each player? Write and solve an equation with a variable to show your work.

5. Which costs more: 136 sweatpants or 103 sweatshirts? How much more?

6. Coach Sandberg wants to order 115 jackets and 27 caps for $12 each.

Part A

Estimate the total cost for his order. Show your work.

Part B

What is his total cost? Compare your answer to your estimate.

TOPIC 4 Use Models and Strategies to Multiply Decimals

Essential Question: What are some common procedures for estimating and finding products involving decimals?

In one hour, the Sun provides enough energy to power everything on Earth for a whole year.

We can use solar energy for heat and electricity without polluting the air.

Let's see if we can use the Sun to charge my music player. Here's a project about solar energy.

enVision STEM Project: Solar Energy

Do Research Use the Internet or other sources to learn about solar energy. Find at least five ways that we use the Sun's energy today.

Journal: Write a Report Include what you found. Also in your report:

- Describe at least one way that you could use solar energy. Could it save you money?
- Estimate how much your family pays for energy costs such as lights, gasoline, heating, and cooling.
- Make up and solve problems by multiplying whole numbers and decimals.

Name ______________________________

Review What You Know

Vocabulary

Choose the best term from the box. Write it on the blank.

- exponent
- hundredths
- overestimate
- partial products
- power
- round
- tenths
- thousandths
- underestimate

1. One way to estimate a number is to ____________ the number.

2. Using 50 for the number of weeks in a year is a(n) ____________ .

3. In the number 3.072, the digit 7 is in the ____________ place and the digit 2 is in the ____________ place.

4. 10,000 is a(n) ____________ of 10 because $10 \times 10 \times 10 \times 10 = 10{,}000$.

Whole Number Multiplication

Find each product.

5. 64×100

6. $7{,}823 \times 10^3$

7. $10 \times 1{,}405$

8. 53×413

9. 906×57

10. $1{,}037 \times 80$

Round Decimals

Round each number to the nearest tenth.

11. 842.121

12. 10,386.145

13. 585.055

Properties of Multiplication

Use the Commutative and Associative Properties of Multiplication to complete each multiplication.

14. $96 \times 42 = 4{,}032$ so $42 \times 96 =$ ____________

15. $4 \times (58 \times 25) = 4 \times (25 \times$ ____ $) = ($ ____ $\times$ ____ $) \times 58 =$ ____________

16. $(293 \times 50) \times 20 = 293 \times (50 \times$ ____ $) =$ ____________

Name ____________________

Pick a Project

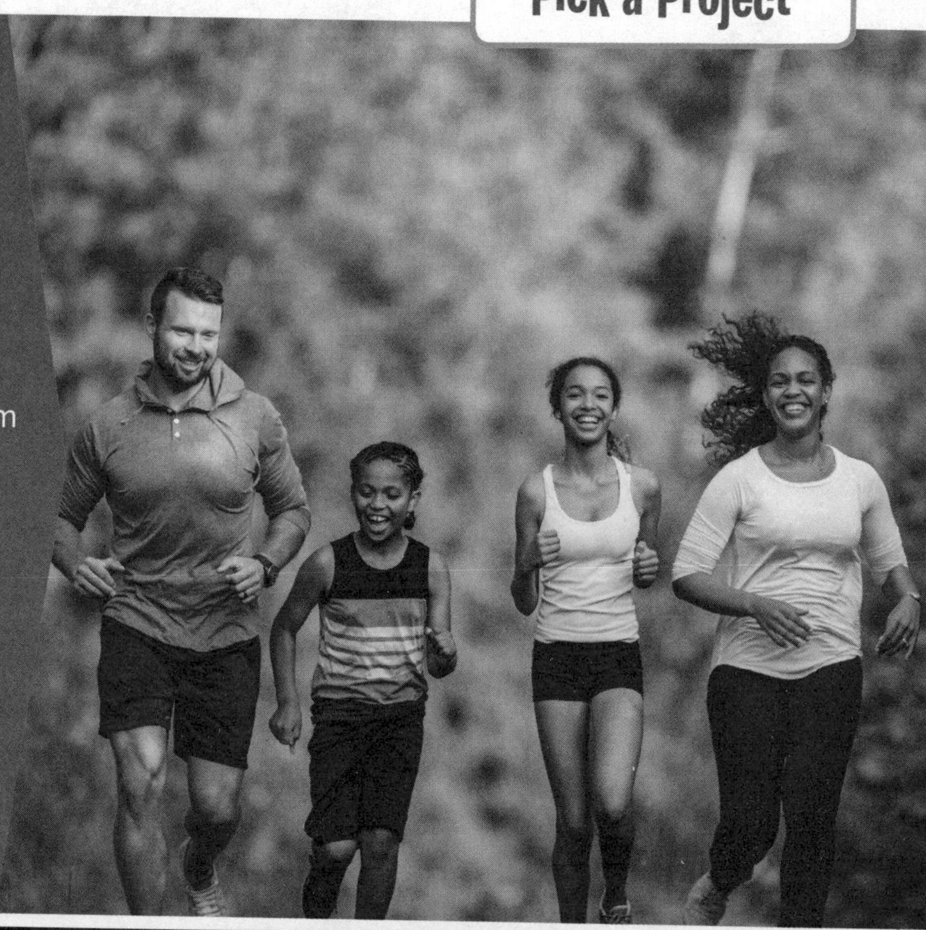

PROJECT 4A

How can you set up an exercise plan?

Project: Plan an Exercise Program

PROJECT 4B

How much does it cost to dress a team?

Project: Budget a Team

PROJECT 4C

How far can a rocket go in 100 seconds?

Project: Make a Poster

PROJECT 4D

How much extra do you have to pay?

Project: Make a Data Display

Name ________________________________

Activity

Solve & Share Javier is helping his parents put up posters in their movie theater. Each poster has a thickness of 0.012 inch. How thick is a stack of 10 posters? 100 posters? 1,000 posters? ***Solve this problem any way you choose.***

Lesson 4-1
Multiply Decimals by Powers of 10

I can ...
find the product of a decimal number and a power of 10.

Content Standards 5.NBT.A.2
Also 5.NBT.B.7
Mathematical Practices MP.3, MP.7

You can use the structure of our number system and mental math to help you.

Look Back! Use Structure How is your answer for 1,000 posters similar to 0.012? How is it different?

Essential Question

What Patterns Can Help You Multiply Decimals by Powers of 10?

Visual Learning Bridge

A

You can use place value and what you know about whole numbers to multiply decimals by powers of 10. What patterns can you find?

We already know what happens when a whole number is multiplied by powers of 10.

	Hundred Thousands	Ten Thousands	Thousands	Hundreds	Tens	Ones
$363 \times 1 =$				3	6	3
$363 \times 10^1 =$			3	6	3	0
$363 \times 10^2 =$		3	6	3	0	0
$363 \times 10^3 =$	3	6	3	0	0	0

B In a place-value chart, the same pattern appears when a decimal is multiplied by powers of 10.

	Thousands	Hundreds	Tens	Ones	Tenths	Hundredths
$3.63 \times 1 =$				3.	6	3
$3.63 \times 10^1 =$			3	6.	3	0
$3.63 \times 10^2 =$		3	6	3.	0	0
$3.63 \times 10^3 =$	3	6	3	0.	0	0

A digit in one place is worth 10 times more when moved to the place on its left.
Every time a number is multiplied by 10, the digits of the number shift to the left.

C Holding the numbers still, another pattern appears.

$3.63 \times 1 = 3.63$

$3.63 \times 10^1 = 36.3$

$3.63 \times 10^2 = 363.0$

$3.63 \times 10^3 = 3630.0$

It looks like the decimal point moves to the right each time.

Convince Me! **Use Structure** Complete the chart. What patterns can you use to place the decimal point?

	$\times 10^1$	$\times 10^2$	$\times 10^3$
1.275			
26.014			
0.4			

Name ____

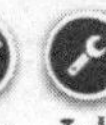

Guided Practice

Do You Understand?

1. When multiplying by a power of 10, like 4.58×10^3, how do you know you are moving the decimal in the correct direction?

Do You Know How?

In **2–5**, find each product.

2. 0.009×10
3. 3.1×10^3
4. 0.062×10^2
5. 1.24×10^4

Independent Practice

Place-value patterns can help you solve these problems.

Leveled Practice In **6** and **7**, find each product.

6. $42.3 \times 1 =$ ________
   $42.3 \times 10 =$ ________
   $42.3 \times 10^2 =$ ________

7. ________ $= 0.086 \times 10^1$
   ________ $= 0.086 \times 100$
   ________ $= 0.086 \times 1{,}000$

In **8–15**, find each product.

8. 63.7×10
9. 563.7×10^2
10. 0.365×10^4
11. 5.02×100
12. 94.6×10^3
13. 0.9463×10^2
14. 0.678×100
15. 681.7×10^4

In **16–18**, find the missing exponent.

16. $0.629 \times 10^{\square} = 62.9$
17. $10^{\square} \times 0.056 = 560$
18. $1.23 = 10^{\square} \times 0.123$

Problem Solving

In **19–21**, use the table to find the answers.

19. Monroe uses a microscope to observe specimens in science class. The microscope enlarges objects to 100 times their actual size. Find the size of each specimen as seen in the microscope.

20. Monroe's teacher wants each student to draw a sketch of the longest specimen. Which specimen is the longest?

21. Seen through the microscope, a specimen is 0.75 cm long. What is its actual length?

Specimen	Actual Length (cm)	Size Seen in the Microscope (cm)
A	0.008	
B	0.011	
C	0.0025	
D	0.004	

22. Jon's binoculars enlarge objects to 10 times their actual size. If the length of an ant is 0.43 inch, what is the length as seen up close through his binoculars?

23. Higher Order Thinking Jefferson drew a line 9.5 inches long. Brittany drew a line 10 times as long. What is the difference in length between the two lines?

24. Construct Arguments José ran 2.6 miles. Pavel ran 2.60 miles. Who ran farther? Explain your reasoning.

Assessment Practice

25. Choose all equations that are true.

- ☐ $4.82 \times 1{,}000 = 482{,}000$
- ☐ $4.82 \times 10^2 = 482$
- ☐ $0.482 \times 10^1 = 48.2$
- ☐ $0.482 \times 10^3 = 482$
- ☐ $48.2 \times 10^4 = 4{,}820$

26. Choose all equations that are true when 10^2 is placed in the box.

- ☐ $37 = \square \times 0.37$
- ☐ $0.37 = \square \times 0.037$
- ☐ $370 = \square \times 3.7$
- ☐ $0.37 = \square \times 3.7$
- ☐ $3.7 = \square \times 0.037$

Name ____________________

Activity

Lesson 4-2
Estimate the Product of a Decimal and a Whole Number

Solve & Share

Renee needs 32 strands of twine for an art project. Each strand must be 1.25 centimeters long. About how many centimeters of twine does she need? ***Solve this problem any way you choose!***

I can ...
use rounding and compatible numbers to estimate the product of a decimal and a whole number.

Content Standard 5.NBT.B.7
Mathematical Practices MP.2, MP.6, MP.8

Generalize
How can you relate what you know about estimating with whole numbers to estimating with decimals? Show your work!

Look Back! Is your estimate an overestimate or an underestimate? How can you tell?

 Visual Learning  Glossary

What Are Some Ways to Estimate Products of Decimals and Whole Numbers?

Visual Learning Bridge

A

A wedding planner needs to buy 16 pounds of sliced cheddar cheese. About how much will the cheese cost?

The words about how much mean you only need an estimate.
$2.15 per pound
You can use different strategies to estimate a product.

B

One Way

Round each number to the nearest dollar and nearest ten.

$$\begin{array}{ccc} \$2.15 & \times & 16 \\ \downarrow & & \downarrow \\ \$2 & \times & 20 \end{array}$$

$\$2 \times 20 = \$40$

The cheese will cost about $40.

C

Another Way

Use compatible numbers that you can multiply mentally.

$$\begin{array}{ccc} \$2.15 & \times & 16 \\ \downarrow & & \downarrow \\ \$2 & \times & 15 \end{array}$$

$\$2 \times 15 = \$30$

The cheese will cost about $30.

Convince Me! Reasoning About how much money would 18 pounds of cheese cost if the price is $3.95 per pound? Use two different ways to estimate the product. Are your estimates overestimates or underestimates? Explain.

Name ______________________________

Practice Tools Assessment

Another Example

Manuel walks a total of 0.75 mile to and from school each day. If there have been 105 school days so far this year, about how many miles has he walked in all?

Round to the nearest whole number.

105×0.75

$\downarrow \quad \downarrow$

$105 \times 1 = 105$

Use compatible numbers.

105×0.75

$\downarrow \quad \downarrow$

$100 \times 0.8 = 80$

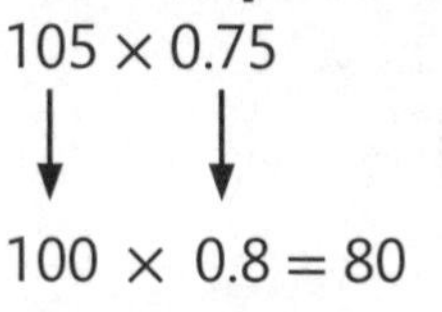

Be sure to place the decimal point correctly.

Both methods provide reasonable estimates of how far Manuel has walked.

Guided Practice

Do You Understand?

1. **Number Sense** There are about 20 school days in a month. In the problem above, about how many miles does Manuel walk each month? Write an equation to show your work.

2. Without multiplying, which estimate in the Another Example do you think is closer to the exact answer? Explain your reasoning.

Do You Know How?

In **3–8**, estimate each product using rounding or compatible numbers.

3. 0.87×112
4. 104×0.33
5. 9.02×80
6. 0.54×24
7. 33.05×200
8. 0.79×51

Independent Practice

In **9–16**, estimate each product.

9. 0.12×105
10. 45.3×4
11. 99.2×82
12. 37×0.93
13. 1.67×4
14. 3.2×184
15. 12×0.37
16. 0.904×75

Problem Solving

17. About how much money does Stan need to buy 5 T-shirts and 10 buttons?

18. Joseph buys a pair of shorts for $17.95 and 4 T-shirts. About how much money does he spend?

DATA

Souvenir	Cost
Button	$1.95
T-Shirt	$12.50

19. Marcy picked 18.8 pounds of peaches at the pick-your-own orchard. Each pound costs $1.28. About how much did Marcy pay for the peaches? Write an equation to model your work.

20. **Be Precise** Joshua had $20. He spent $4.58 on Friday, $7.43 on Saturday, and $3.50 on Sunday. How much money does he have left? Show how you found the answer.

21. **Higher Order Thinking** Ms. Webster works 4 days a week at her office and 1 day a week at home. The route to Ms. Webster's office is 23.7 miles. The route home is 21.8 miles. About how many miles does she drive for work each week? Explain how you found your answer.

Assessment Practice

22. Rounding to the nearest tenth, which of the following give an **underestimate**?

- ☐ 39.45×1.7
- ☐ 27.54×0.74
- ☐ 9.91×8.74
- ☐ 78.95×1.26
- ☐ 18.19×2.28

23. Rounding to the nearest whole number, which of the following give an **overestimate**?

- ☐ 11.6×9.5
- ☐ 4.49×8.3
- ☐ 12.9×0.9
- ☐ 0.62×1.5
- ☐ 8.46×7.38

Name ______________________

Activity

Lesson 4-3

Use Models to Multiply a Decimal and a Whole Number

I can ...

use models to represent multiplying a decimal and a whole number.

Content Standard 5.NBT.B.7
Mathematical Practices MP.1, MP.3

Solve & Share Mara has 4 garden plots. Each is 0.7 acre in area. What is the total area of the garden plots? Use objects or the grids below to show your work.

How can you represent multiplying a decimal and a whole number?

Look Back! Critique Reasoning Ed says a decimal grid shows 10 tenths. Monica says a decimal grid shows 100 hundredths. Who is correct? Explain.

Essential Question: How Can You Model Multiplying a Decimal by a Whole Number?

A

How can you use models to find 4 × 0.36?

When showing decimals, it is important to establish which type of block represents 1.

You can use place-value blocks to show multiplication of a decimal by a whole number.

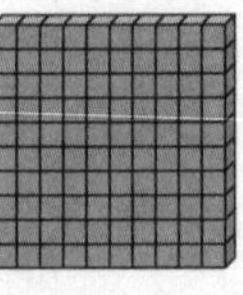

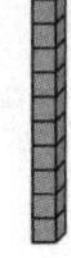

B

Multiplying 4 × 0.36 is like combining 4 groups each containing 0.36.

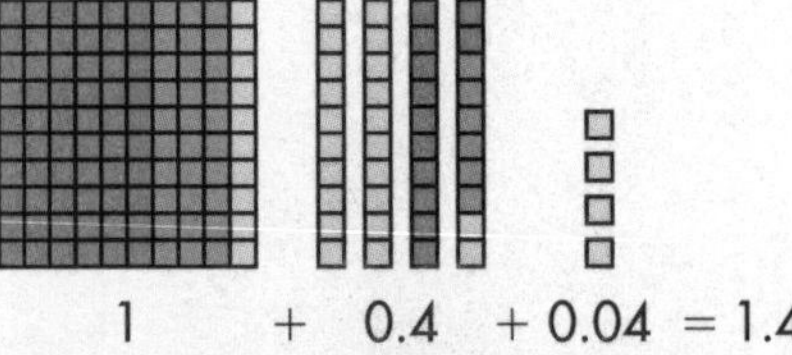

Regrouping after combining the blocks gives:

1 + 0.4 + 0.04 = 1.44

Convince Me! **Make Sense and Persevere** Bari made a train with 5 cars that are each 1.27 meter long. What is the total length of the train? Use place-value blocks to model the problem. Then find the product using an equation and compare the answers.

Name ______________________

Practice Tools Assessment

Guided Practice

Do You Understand?

1. Without multiplying, is 4×0.36 less than or greater than 4? Explain.

Do You Know How?

In **2–5**, find the product. You may use place-value blocks to help.

2. 0.8×4

3. 0.7×3

4. 0.5×6

5. 0.6×5

Independent Practice

In **6** and **7**, find the product. Use place-value blocks to help.

Use or draw place-value blocks to help you model the problem.

6. $0.55 \times 3 =$ ____

7. ____ $= 0.45 \times 2$

In **8–19**, find the product. Use place-value blocks to help.

8. 5×0.5

9. 4×0.27

10. 6×0.13

11. 0.78×5

12. 10×0.32

13. 6×2.03

14. 1.35×5

15. 100×0.12

16. 4×0.15

17. 3×2.5

18. 0.9×7

19. 0.35×3

Problem Solving

20. A city is building 3 parks in a new subdivision. Each park will be 1.25 acres. How many total acres will the 3 parks be? Use place-value blocks to model the problem if you need help.

How is multiplying with decimals like multiplying whole numbers?

21. **Higher Order Thinking** The city acquired more land next to the subdivision. If it decides to make each park 12.5 acres, how many additional acres would the parks occupy?

22. Write a multiplication equation that matches the shading on the grid.

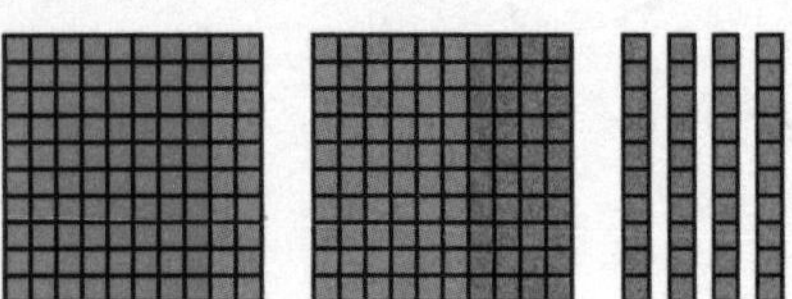

23. **Critique Reasoning** Jen multiplied 9 by 0.989 and got an answer of 89.01. How can you use estimation to show that Jen's answer is wrong? What mistake do you think she made?

Assessment Practice

24. Anita needs 5 pounds of bananas to make banana bread for a bake sale. Each pound of bananas costs $0.50.

Part A

How can Anita use place-value blocks to find the total cost of the bananas? What is the total cost?

Part B

How can Anita use what she knows about whole-number multiplication to check her answer?

Name ____________________

Lesson 4-4

Multiply a Decimal and a Whole Number

I can ...
multiply a decimal by a whole number.

Content Standard 5.NBT.B.7
Mathematical Practices MP.3, MP.8

A car travels 1.15 kilometers in 1 minute. If it travels at a constant speed, how far will it travel in 3 minutes? in 5 minutes? ***Solve this problem any way you choose!***

Generalize
You can connect what you know about whole-number multiplication to multiplying a decimal by a whole number.

Look Back! How can addition be used to answer the questions above?

How Do You Multiply a Decimal by a Whole Number?

Visual Learning Bridge

A

To raise money for a charity, $0.15 was collected from every ticket sold to a Lions baseball game. If you bought 12 tickets, how much money would go to the charity?

You can multiply 0.15 × 12 by thinking about 15 × 12 and using place-value patterns.

B

One Way

Add 0.15 twelve times.

$$\begin{array}{r} 0.15 \\ 0.15 \\ 0.15 \\ 0.15 \\ 0.15 \\ 0.15 \\ 0.15 \\ 0.15 \\ 0.15 \\ 0.15 \\ 0.15 \\ +\ 0.15 \\ \hline 1.80 \end{array}$$

C

Another Way

First, multiply as you would with whole numbers.

$$\begin{array}{r} \overset{1}{1}2 \\ \times\ 15 \\ \hline 60 \\ 120 \\ \hline 180 \end{array}$$

Use number sense to place the decimal point.

$$\begin{array}{r} \overset{1}{1}2 \\ \times\ 0.15 \\ \hline 60 \\ 120 \\ \hline 1.80 \end{array}$$

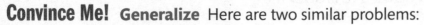

Convince Me! **Generalize** Here are two similar problems:

$\begin{array}{r} 33 \\ \times\ 19 \\ \hline 297 \\ +\ 330 \\ \hline 627 \end{array}$	$\begin{array}{r} 0.33 \\ \times\ 19 \\ \hline 297 \\ +\ 330 \\ \hline 627 \end{array}$

Place the decimal point correctly in each answer. Explain your thinking.

Name

Guided Practice

Do You Understand?

1. What is the difference between multiplying a whole number by a decimal and multiplying two whole numbers?

2. If a group bought 24 tickets, how much money would go to charity? Explain how you found your answer.

Do You Know How?

For **3–8**, find each product.

3. 9.8×2

4. 0.67×8

5. 34×5.3

6. 4.6×21

7. 0.6×15

8. 55×1.1

Independent Practice

For **9–20**, find each product.

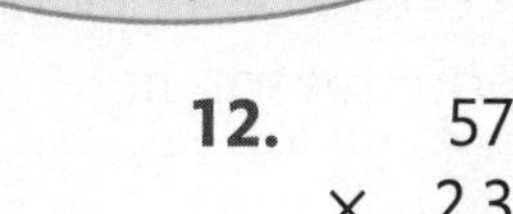

Use what you know about whole-number multiplication and place value to help you!

9. 34.6×9

10. 64.2×20

11. 40×0.22

12. 57×2.3

13. 5.8×11

14. 56×0.4

15. 170×0.003

16. 0.3×99

17. 26×1.61

18. 50×0.914

19. 10.76×100

20. 2.54×12

Problem Solving

21. enVision® STEM To meet peak energy demand, an electric power cooperative buys back electricity generated locally. They pay $0.07 per solar-powered kWh (kilowatt-hour). How much money does a school make when it sells back 956 kWh to the cooperative?

Round and estimate to check for reasonableness.

22. The airline that Vince is using has a baggage weight limit of 41 pounds. He has two green bags, each weighing 18.4 pounds, and one blue bag weighing 3.7 pounds. Are his bags within the weight limit? Explain.

23. Michael keeps track of how much time he uses his family's computer each week for 10 weeks. He created the frequency table with the data he collected. How many hours did Michael spend on the computer?

DATA

Number of Hours	Frequency
$3\frac{1}{2}$	2
4	4
$4\frac{1}{2}$	3
5	1

24. Critique Reasoning Sara is multiplying two factors, one is a whole number and one has two decimal places. She says the product could have one decimal place. Is she correct? Give an example and explain your reasoning.

25. Higher Order Thinking Heather clears a rectangular region in her yard for a garden. If the length is a one-digit whole number and the width is 5.5 meters, what is the least possible area? What is the greatest possible area? Explain how you found your answers.

Assessment Practice

26. Which of the following equations is **NOT** true?

Ⓐ $75 \times 3 = 225$

Ⓑ $75 \times 0.3 = 22.5$

Ⓒ $7.5 \times 3 = 2.25$

Ⓓ $75 \times 0.03 = 2.25$

27. Which of the following equations is **NOT** true?

Ⓐ $50 \times 12 = 600$

Ⓑ $50 \times 0.12 = 6$

Ⓒ $0.5 \times 12 = 60$

Ⓓ $50 \times 1.2 = 60$

Name ____________________ Activity

Solve & Share

A rectangle has an area of 0.24 square meter. What are some possibilities for the length and width of the rectangle? Tell why. ***Solve this problem any way you choose. You may use hundredths grids if you like.***

Lesson 4-5
Use Models to Multiply a Decimal and a Decimal

I can ...
use grids to multiply decimals.

Content Standard 5.NBT.B.7
Mathematical Practices MP.4, MP.6, MP.8

Can both dimensions be greater than 1 meter? Can both dimensions be less than 1 meter? *Show your work in the space below.*

Look Back! Generalize How did you use what you know about whole numbers and place value to find the dimensions that worked?

A-Z Glossary

How Can You Model Decimal Multiplication?

Visual Learning Bridge

A

A farmer has a square field that is 1 mile wide by 1 mile long. Her irrigation system can water the northern 0.5 mile of her field. If her tomatoes are planted in a strip 0.3 mile wide, what is the area of her watered tomatoes?

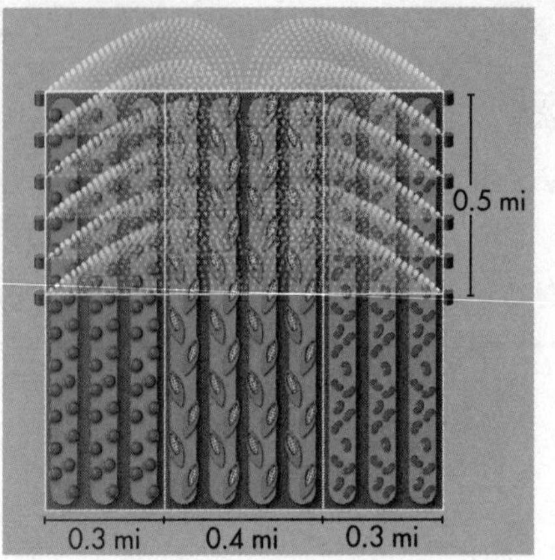

B This problem can be shown on a hundredths grid with each side representing 1 mile. The tomato area is 0.3 mile wide, so shade the first 3 columns red. The watered area is the top 0.5 miles, so shade the top 5 rows blue.

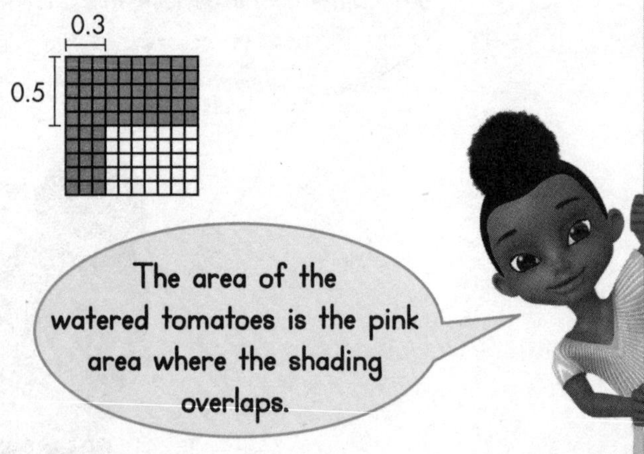

0.3
0.5
The area of the watered tomatoes is the pink area where the shading overlaps.

C This area can be written as a product of decimals.

$0.3 \times 0.5 = 0.15$

There is 0.15 square mile of watered tomatoes.

Because both factors are less than 1, the product is less than either factor.

Convince Me! **Be Precise** Use the double hundredths grid to model 0.7×1.6. What does the length of each side of a hundredths grid represent? Explain how to find the product.

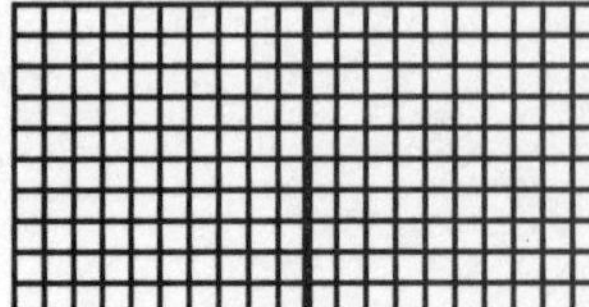

Name ___

Practice Tools Assessment

Guided Practice

Do You Understand?

1. Write a multiplication equation to match the model.

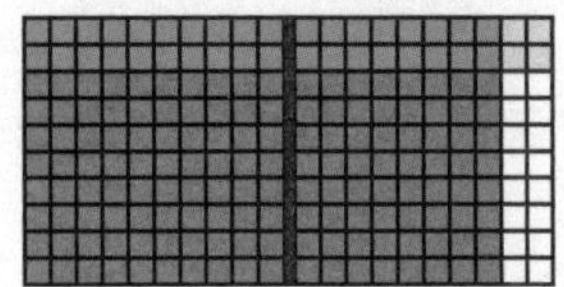

2. Explain why 2.7 is not a reasonable answer for 0.3 × 0.9. What is the correct answer?

Do You Know How?

In **3** and **4**, shade the hundredths grids to find the product.

3. 0.7 × 0.8

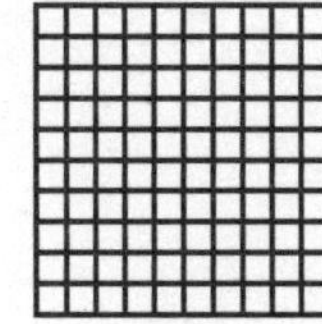

4. 0.1 × 2.1

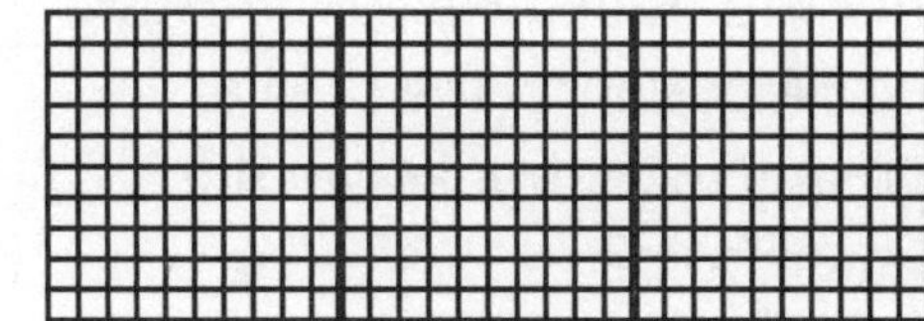

Independent Practice

In **5–8**, shade the hundredths grids to find the product.

Remember that the area where the shading overlaps represents the product.

5. 0.4 × 0.5

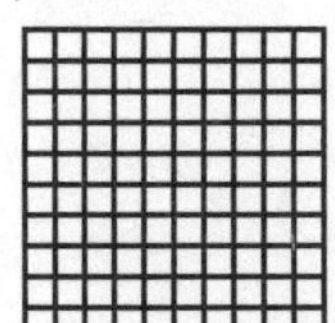

6. 0.3 × 0.7

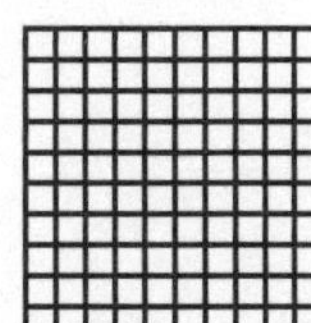

7. 0.5 × 1.7

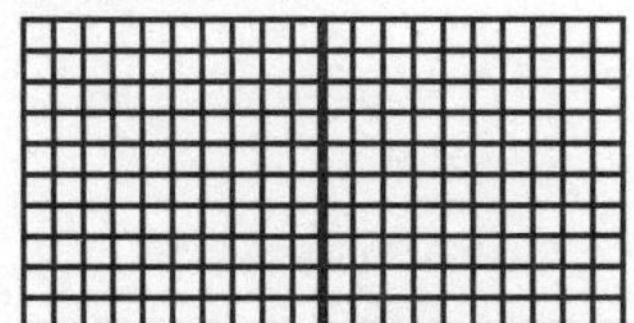

8. 0.6 × 1.2

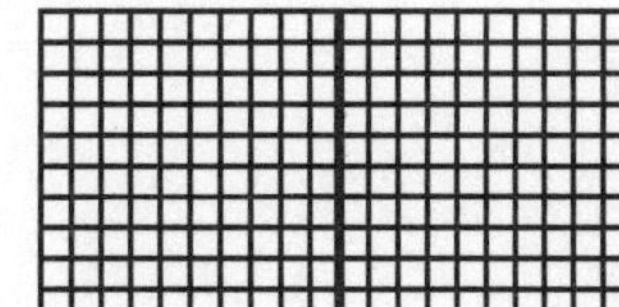

In **9–16**, find the product. You may use grids to help.

9. 0.2 × 0.8

10. 2.4 × 0.7

11. 3.9 × 0.4

12. 0.5 × 0.7

13. 0.9 × 0.1

14. 0.2 × 1.5

15. 0.6 × 0.6

16. 2.8 × 0.3

Problem Solving

17. **Model with Math** Write a multiplication equation to represent this decimal model.

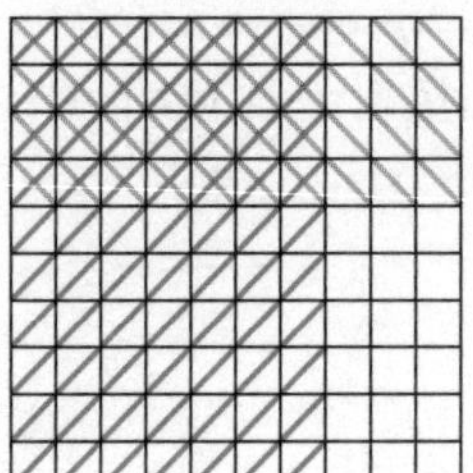

18. **Higher Order Thinking** Explain why 3.4 × 0.5 has only one decimal place in the product.

19. Jack's bookshelf has 6 shelves. Each shelf can hold 12 books. He has already placed 54 books on the shelves. How many more books can the bookshelf hold?

20. **Number Sense** Write a number that has a 6 in the thousandths place, a 5 in the hundredths place, and a 0 in the tenths place. Then write a number less than your number and a number greater than your number.

21. If you multiply two decimals less than 1, can you predict whether the product will be less than or greater than either of the factors? Explain.

22. Judy claims that she can find 0.5 × 2.4 by dividing 2.4 into two equal parts. Is she correct? Draw a decimal model to explain your answer.

Assessment Practice

23. Find two numbers that you can multiply to get a product of 0.54. Write the numbers in the box.

Product = 0.54
6 0.7 0.9 0.8 7 8 0.6 9

Name ______________________

Activity

Lesson 4-6
Multiply Decimals Using Partial Products

I can ...
multiply two decimals using what I know about place value and partial products with whole numbers.

Content Standard 5.NBT.B.7
Mathematical Practices MP.1, MP.5

Solve & Share

Julie has 0.5 of her backyard set up for growing vegetables. Of the vegetable area, 0.4 has bell peppers in it. What part of the backyard contains bell peppers?

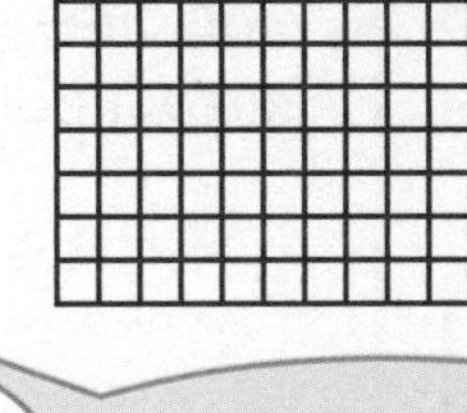

You can use appropriate tools, such as a grid, to model decimal multiplication.

Look Back! What do you notice about the factors and their product in the above problem?

Essential Question

How Can You Multiply Decimals Using Partial Products?

Visual Learning Bridge

A

June walked 1.7 miles in 1 hour. If she walks at the same rate, how far will she walk in 1.5 hours?

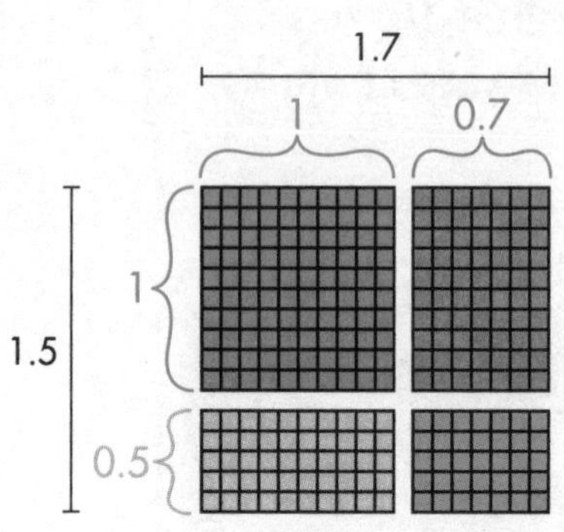

You can use what you know about partial products and whole numbers to model multiplication with decimals.

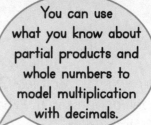

B Estimate first.

1.7 × 1.5
↓ ↓
2 × 2 = 4

Since 2 is greater than 1.7 and 1.5, 4 is an overestimate.

C Like with whole numbers, you can use an area model to help break the problem into parts.

	1.0	0.7
1.0	1.0 × 1.0 = 1.00	1.0 × 0.7 = 0.7
0.5	0.5 × 1.0 = 0.5	0.5 × 0.7 = 0.35

D The partial products make up the different pieces of the area model.

$$\begin{array}{r} 1.7 \\ \times\ 1.5 \\ \hline 0.35 \\ 0.50 \\ 0.70 \\ 1.00 \\ \hline 2.55 \end{array}$$

1.7 × 1.5 = 2.55, which is close to the estimate. June will walk 2.55 miles.

Convince Me! **Make Sense and Persevere** In the example above, how many miles will June walk in 2.8 hours? Estimate first, then compare your answer to the estimate.

Name ____________________

Practice Tools Assessment

Guided Practice

Do You Understand?

1. Carter is filling 6.5-ounce bottles with salsa. He was able to fill 7.5 bottles. How many ounces of salsa did he have? Draw an area model to show the partial products.

Do You Know How?

In **2–5**, estimate first. Then find each product. Check that your answer is reasonable.

2. $\begin{array}{r} 9.3 \\ \times \ 4.1 \\ \hline \end{array}$

3. $\begin{array}{r} 3.2 \\ \times \ 0.6 \\ \hline \end{array}$

4. 0.7×1.9

5. 12.6×0.2

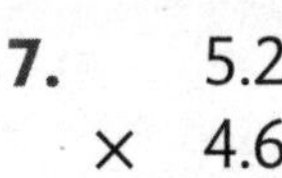

Independent Practice

6. Find 7.5×1.8 using partial products. Draw an area model to show the partial products.

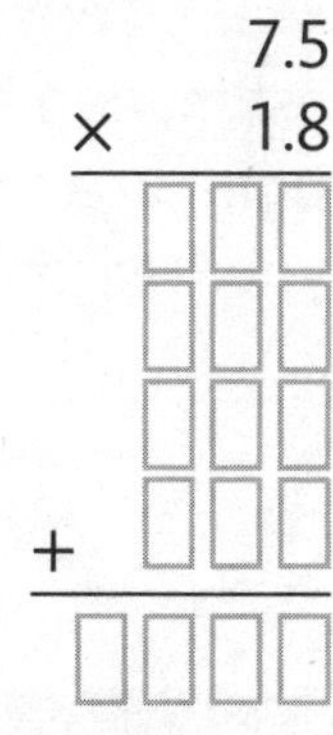

In **7–14**, estimate first. Then multiply using partial products. Then check that your answer is reasonable.

7. $\begin{array}{r} 5.2 \\ \times \ 4.6 \\ \hline \end{array}$

8. $\begin{array}{r} 19.1 \\ \times \ 8.5 \\ \hline \end{array}$

9. $\begin{array}{r} 0.5 \\ \times \ 4.5 \\ \hline \end{array}$

10. $\begin{array}{r} 8.6 \\ \times \ 0.8 \\ \hline \end{array}$

11. 5.5×0.6

12. 3.5×0.4

13. 6.8×7.2

14. 8.3×6.4

Problem Solving

15. **enVision® STEM** The gravity of Venus is 0.35 times that of Jupiter. What is the gravity of Venus in relation to Earth's gravity?

16. About how many times as great is Jupiter's relative surface gravity as Neptune's relative surface gravity?

DATA

Relative (to Earth) Surface Gravity

Planet	Gravity
Mercury	0.39
Neptune	1.22
Jupiter	2.6

17. One quart of water weighs about 2.1 pounds. There are 4 quarts in a gallon. How much does a gallon of water weigh?

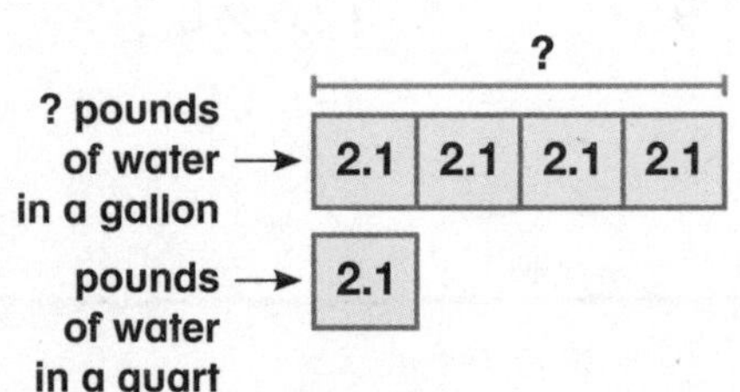

18. Isaac bought three packages of nuts. He bought one package of peanuts that weighed 3.07 pounds. He also bought two packages of pecans that weighed 1.46 pounds and 1.5 pounds. Did the peanuts or the pecans weigh more? How much more?

19. **Make Sense and Persevere** How does estimation help you place the decimal point in a product correctly? Explain your reasoning.

20. **Higher Order Thinking** The area of Dimitri's table top is a whole number of square feet. Could the length and width be decimal numbers each with one decimal place? Explain your answer.

Assessment Practice

21. Joy drinks 4.5 bottles of water per day. Each bottle contains 16.5 fluid ounces. How many fluid ounces of water does she drink per day?

Ⓐ 20.10 fluid ounces

Ⓑ 64.00 fluid ounces

Ⓒ 74.25 fluid ounces

Ⓓ 82.50 fluid ounces

22. One square mile equals 2.6 square kilometers. How many square kilometers are in 14.4 square miles?

Ⓐ 11.52 square kilometers

Ⓑ 17.00 square kilometers

Ⓒ 37.44 square kilometers

Ⓓ 86.40 square kilometers

Name ______________________________

Lesson 4-7

Use Properties to Multiply Decimals

I can ...

use properties to multiply decimals.

Content Standard 5.NBT.B.7
Mathematical Practices MP.1, MP.7

Solve & Share The weight of a small bag of raisins is 0.3 times the weight of a large bag. The large bag weighs 0.8 pound. What is the weight of the small bag? ***Solve this problem any way you choose.***

You can estimate whether the answer is greater than or less than 0.5 pound.

Look Back! Look for Relationships How is solving this problem like finding the product of 3 and 8? How is it different?

How Can You Use Properties to Multiply Decimals?

Visual Learning Bridge

A

Entries for a poster contest must be $0.5\ m^2$ or smaller. Can Jemelle enter her poster?

Jemelle's poster

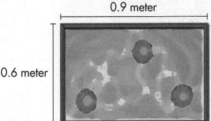

0.9 meter

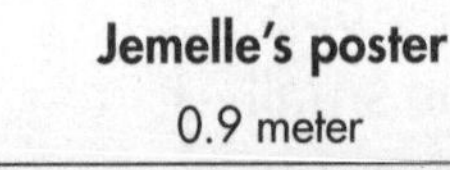

0.6 meter

Use what you know about decimals and properties to multiply 0.6 × 0.9.

B

Step 1

Rewrite the multiplication expression.

$0.6 \times 0.9 = (6 \times 0.1) \times (9 \times 0.1)$

Rearrange the factors using the Associative and Commutative Properties.

$(6 \times 0.1) \times (9 \times 0.1) = (6 \times 9) \times (0.1 \times 0.1)$

C

Step 2

Multiply the whole numbers. Multiply the decimals. Write the product.

$(6 \times 9) \times (0.1 \times 0.1) =$

$54 \times 0.01 = 0.54$

One tenth of one tenth is one hundredth. $0.1 \times 0.1 = 0.01$

$0.54 > 0.5$, so Jemelle cannot enter her poster.

Convince Me! **Use Structure** Tyler explained how he multiplies 0.7×0.2. "I multiply $7 \times 2 = 14$. I know that a tenth times a tenth is a hundredth, so I use hundredths to write the product. The product is 0.14." Use properties to show that Tyler is correct.

Name ______________________________

Another Example

A slice of bread has 1.25 grams of fat. How many grams of fat are in 1.5 slices?

$1.25 \times 1.5 =$

$= (125 \times 0.01) \times (15 \times 0.1)$

$= (125 \times 15) \times (0.01 \times 0.1)$

$= 1{,}875 \times 0.001$

$= 1.875$

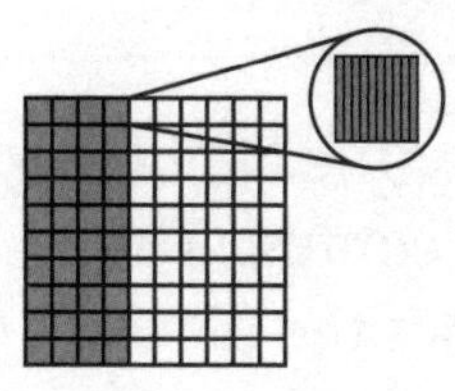

The picture shows that one tenth of one hundredth is one thousandth.
$0.1 \times 0.01 = 0.001$

There are 1.875 grams of fat in 1.5 slices of bread.

Guided Practice

Do You Understand?

1. Mason is multiplying $(3 \times 5) \times (0.1 \times 0.1)$. What decimal multiplication problem is he solving?

2. Complete Mason's work to find the product.

Do You Know How?

In **3-6**, use properties to find each product.

3. 0.3×0.7
4. 0.63×2.8
5. 2.6×1.4
6. 4.5×0.08

Independent Practice

In **7-15**, find each product.

7. 0.6×0.2
8. 0.33×0.8
9. 1.7×0.22
10. 1.8×0.9
11. 0.03×1.6
12. 4.2×4.2
13. 11.1×0.8
14. 1.16×0.4
15. 1.6×0.01

Problem Solving

16. The total rainfall in March was 3.6 inches. In April, the total rainfall was 1.4 times as much. What was the total rainfall in April?

17. A newly hatched alligator is 0.5 foot long. An adult alligator is 16.4 times as long. How many feet longer is the adult alligator than the newborn alligator?

18. **Make Sense and Persevere** The Nature Club held a grasshopper jumping contest. The distance Bugmaster jumped is 1.2 times the distance Green Lightning jumped. The distance Top Hopper jumped is 1.5 times the distance Bugmaster jumped. Complete the table to show the distances Bugmaster and Top Hopper jumped.

Grasshopper	Distance
Green Lightning	1.4 feet
Bugmaster	
Top Hopper	

19. Amanda bought a 6-cup bag of shredded cheese for $6.89. She used 2.25 cups to make lasagna and 1.25 cups to make pizza. How much cheese is left?

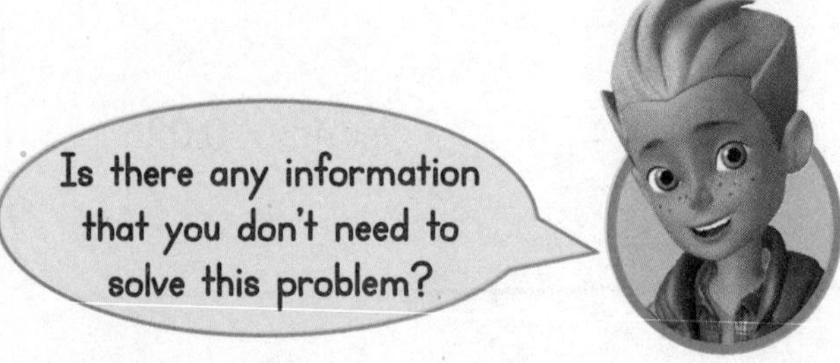

Is there any information that you don't need to solve this problem?

20. **Higher Order Thinking** Jodi drew the Eiffel Tower 6.5 inches tall. She thought it was too tall, so she multiplied its height by 0.8. The second drawing was too short, so she multiplied its height by 1.2. Predict whether her last drawing was shorter, the same as, or taller than her first drawing. Check your prediction by finding the height of the last drawing.

Assessment Practice

21. Which expression is equivalent to 0.4×0.3?

Ⓐ $(4 \times 0.01) \times (3 \times 0.01)$
Ⓑ $(4 \times 10) \times (3 \times 10)$
Ⓒ $(4 \times 0.1) \times (3 \times 0.1)$
Ⓓ $(4 \times 0.1) \times (3 \times 0.01)$

22. Which expression is equivalent to 0.71×2.8?

Ⓐ $(71 \times 28) \times (0.01 \times 0.1)$
Ⓑ $(71 \times 28) \times (0.1 \times 0.1)$
Ⓒ $(0.71 \times 2.8) \times (0.01 \times 0.1)$
Ⓓ $(71 \times 28) \times (100 \times 10)$

Name ______________________________  Activity

Lesson 4-8
Use Number Sense to Multiply Decimals

I can ...
use number sense to place the decimal point in a product.

Content Standard 5.NBT.B.7
Mathematical Practices MP.2, MP.3, MP.8

Three students in Ms. Cho's class wrote the following problems on the board. The correct digits in the products are given, but the decimal point isn't placed yet. Where should the decimal point go in each product?

1. $7.85 \times 16 = 1256$

2. $0.98 \times 0.5 = 49$

3. $1.06 \times 1.5 = 159$

You can use reasoning to consider the size of each factor when placing the decimal point. *Show your work!*

Look Back! Generalize If both factors are less than 1, what do you know about their product?

Visual Learning A-Z Glossary

Visual Learning Bridge

Essential Question

How Can You Use Number Sense to Multiply Decimals?

A

You have learned how to estimate when multiplying with decimals. You can also use number sense to reason about the relative size of factors and the product.

You can use number sense to put the decimal point in the correct place.

49.20 × 0.55 = 2706

B Think about the relative size of the factors.

Multiplying a number by a decimal less than 1 gives a product less than the other factor.

Since 0.55 is less than 1, the product is less than 49.2.

Since 0.55 is about one half, the product is about half of 49.2, or about half of 50. So, the decimal point should be between the 7 and 0.

49.2 × 0.55 = 27.06

C Use number sense to reason about the product.

How can you place the decimal point in the product of the equation below?

6.2 × 5.1 is 3162.

Notice that the smallest unit in both factors is a tenth (0.1). Since the product of 0.1 and 0.1 is 0.01, the product of 6.2 and 5.1 will have two decimal places.

So, 6.2 × 5.1 = 31.62.

This makes sense because 6 times 5 equals 30.

Convince Me! **Construct Arguments** The decimal point is missing in the answer for each of these problems. Use number sense to decide where the decimal point should be placed. Explain your thinking.

54.7 × 0.53 = 28991

54.7 × 5.3 = 28991

Name ________________

Practice Tools Assessment

Guided Practice

Do You Understand?

1. Describe the unknown factor.

   _____ × 5.1 is about 300.

2. **Number Sense** Janelle wrote 23.4 for the product of 7.8 × 0.3. Use number sense to decide if Janelle placed the decimal point in the correct place in the product. If it is incorrect, give the correct product.

Do You Know How?

Use number sense to decide where the decimal point belongs in the product.

3. 5 × 3.4 = 17

4. 1922 = 3.1 × 6.2

5. 0.6 × 0.4 = 24

Independent Practice

In **6-9**, the product is shown without the decimal point. Use number sense to place the decimal point correctly.

6. 5.01 × 3 = 1503

7. 6.22 × 3 = 1866

8. 81 = 0.9 × 0.9

9. 1.8 × 1.9 = 342

In **10-15**, tell whether or not the decimal point has been placed correctly in the product. If not, rewrite the product with the decimal point correctly placed.

10. 12 × 4.8 = 57.6

11. 5.2 × 6.4 = 3.328

12. 6.99 × 21 = 14.679

13. 6.2 = 0.05 × 12.4

14. 60.84 = 18 × 3.38

15. 9.01 × 91 = 81.991

Use number sense or estimation to help you!

Problem Solving

16. A pig farmer needs 60 square feet to house a sow. Is the pen pictured to the right large enough? Explain your reasoning.

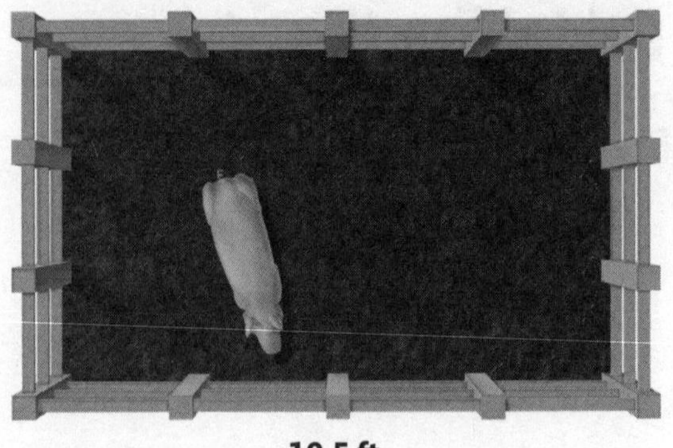

17. **Critique Reasoning** Quincey says that 3 is a good estimate for 3.4×0.09. Is he correct? Why?

18. Ron bought 2 DVDs for $12.95 each. He spent $25 on magazines. Did he spend more on DVDs or magazines? How much more? Write equations to show your work.

19. You can convert gallons to liters by using a factor of 3.79. That is, 1 gallon is about 3.79 liters. About how many liters are in 37 gallons? Is your answer an underestimate or overestimate? Explain.

20. **Higher Order Thinking** Find two factors that would give a product of 0.22.

Assessment Practice

21. Which of the following is the missing factor?

$\_\_\_\_ \times 2.3 = 34.73$

Ⓐ 0.151
Ⓑ 1.51
Ⓒ 15.1
Ⓓ 151

22. Which two factors would give a product of 7.5?

Ⓐ 0.3 and 0.25
Ⓑ 0.3 and 2.5
Ⓒ 3 and 0.25
Ⓓ 3 and 2.5

Name ______________________________

Activity

Problem Solving

Lesson 4-9
Model with Math

Solve & Share

Susan is making sandwiches for a picnic. She needs 1.2 pounds of ham, 1.5 pounds of bologna, and 2 pounds of cheese. How much will she spend in all? ***Solve this problem any way you choose. Use models to help.***

I can ...
apply the math I know to solve problems.

Mathematical Practices MP.4
Also MP.1, MP.3, MP.6
Content Standard 5.NBT.B.7

	price per pound
Ham	$3.40
Bologna	$2.90
Cheese	$4.99

Thinking Habits

Be a good thinker! These questions can help you.

- How can I use math I know to help solve this problem?
- How can I use pictures, objects, or an equation to represent the problem?
- How can I use numbers, words, and symbols to solve the problem?

Look Back! What math did you use to solve this problem?

How Can You Model a Problem with an Equation?

A

Alex is buying vegetables for dinner. He buys 6 ears of corn, 1.4 pounds of green beans, and 2.5 pounds of potatoes. How much money does he spend?

Green Beans	\$1.80/lb
Potatoes	\$0.70/lb
Corn	\$0.35/ear

What do I need to do to solve the problem?

I need to find how much money Alex spends on vegetables.

B **How can I model with math?**

I can

- use previously learned concepts and skills.
- decide what steps need to be completed to find the final answer.
- use an equation to represent and solve this problem.

C

I will use an equation to represent this situation.

Let t be the total cost.

$t = (6 \times \$0.35) + (1.4 \times \$1.80) + (2.5 \times \$0.70)$

Multiply with money as you would multiply with decimals.

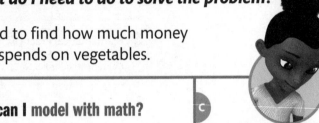

Corn	Green beans	Potatoes
0.35	1.8	0.7
× 6	× 1.4	× 2.5
.30	.32	.35
1.80	.40	1.40
2.10	.80	1.75
	1.00	
	2.52	

Now add the subtotals.

$\$2.10 + \$2.52 + \$1.75 = \$6.37$

So, Alex spends \$6.37 on vegetables.

Convince Me! Model with Math Beth buys 3.2 pounds of potatoes and gives the clerk a \$5 bill. Write an equation that shows how much change she will get back. Explain how your equation represents this problem.

Name ____________________

Guided Practice

Model with Math

Jackie downloaded 14 songs priced at $0.99 each and 1 song for $1.29. She had a coupon for $2.50. What was the total amount Jackie paid?

You can model with math by writing an equation to show how the quantities in the problem are related.

1. What do you need to find first?

2. Write an equation to represent the problem.

3. What is the solution to the problem?

Independent Practice

Model with Math

George bought 2.5 pounds of each type of fruit shown on the sign. What was the total cost of the fruit he bought?

Apples	$1.30/lb
Grapes	$1.65/lb
Bananas	$0.49/lb

4. What do you need to find?

5. Write an equation to represent the problem.

6. What is the solution to the problem?

Problem Solving

Performance Task

Coin Collection

Tina and Shannon counted the coins in their coin collections. Tina discovered that she had 538 more coins than Shannon. Whose collection is worth more? How much more?

Type of Coin	Number Saved	
	Tina	**Shannon**
	917	488
	100	23
	45	10
	19	22

7. Make Sense and Persevere Do you need all of the information given to solve the problem? Explain.

8. Reasoning How is finding the total value of the coins in Tina's collection similar to finding the total value of coins in Shannon's collection?

Deciding what steps need to be completed to find the final answer can help you model with math.

9. Model with Math Write and solve an equation to represent the total value of the coins in Tina's collection. Then write and solve an equation to represent the total value of the coins in Shannon's collection.

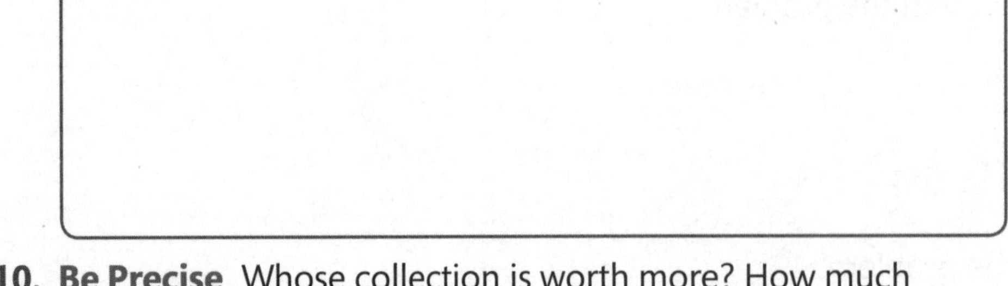

10. Be Precise Whose collection is worth more? How much more? Show your work.

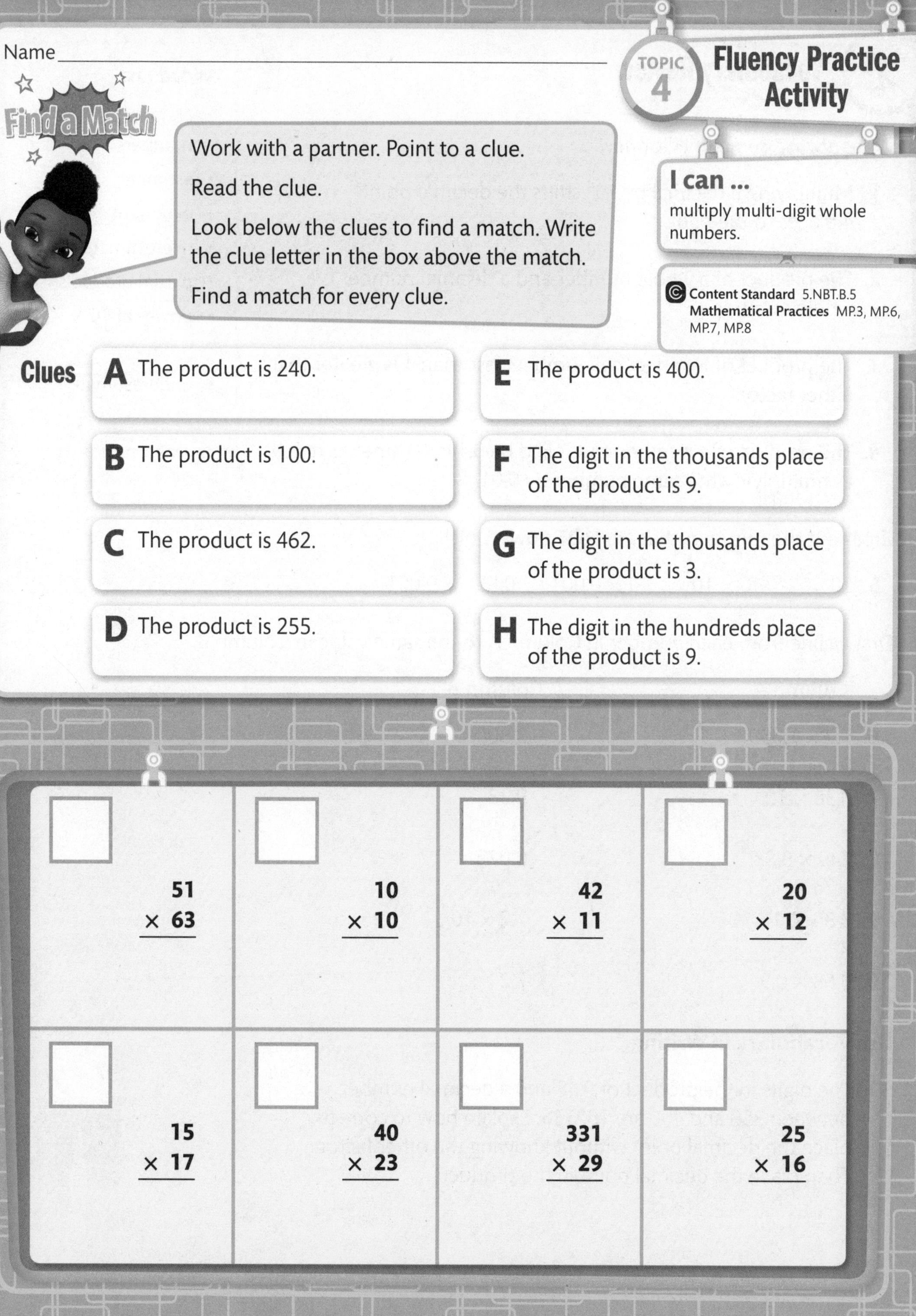

Name

Find a Match

TOPIC 4 Fluency Practice Activity

Work with a partner. Point to a clue.

Read the clue.

Look below the clues to find a match. Write the clue letter in the box above the match.

Find a match for every clue.

I can ...
multiply multi-digit whole numbers.

Content Standard 5.NBT.B.5
Mathematical Practices MP.3, MP.6, MP.7, MP.8

Clues

A The product is 240.

B The product is 100.

C The product is 462.

D The product is 255.

E The product is 400.

F The digit in the thousands place of the product is 9.

G The digit in the thousands place of the product is 3.

H The digit in the hundreds place of the product is 9.

$\begin{array}{r} 51 \\ \times\ 63 \\ \hline \end{array}$	$\begin{array}{r} 10 \\ \times\ 10 \\ \hline \end{array}$	$\begin{array}{r} 42 \\ \times\ 11 \\ \hline \end{array}$	$\begin{array}{r} 20 \\ \times\ 12 \\ \hline \end{array}$
$\begin{array}{r} 15 \\ \times\ 17 \\ \hline \end{array}$	$\begin{array}{r} 40 \\ \times\ 23 \\ \hline \end{array}$	$\begin{array}{r} 331 \\ \times\ 29 \\ \hline \end{array}$	$\begin{array}{r} 25 \\ \times\ 16 \\ \hline \end{array}$

TOPIC 4 Vocabulary Review

Glossary

Word List

- compatible numbers
- estimate
- exponent
- overestimate
- partial products
- power of 10
- product
- underestimate

Write *always*, *sometimes*, or *never*.

1. Multiplying a decimal by 10^4 shifts the decimal point 4 places to the right.

2. The product of a whole number and a decimal number is a whole number.

3. The product of two decimal numbers less than 1 is greater than either factor.

4. The product of a number multiplied by 0.1 is 10 times as much as multiplying the same number by 0.01.

Cross out the numbers that are **NOT** powers of 10.

5. 10^6 40×10^3 1×0.001 0.55   0.001

Draw a line from each number in Column A to the same value in Column B.

Column A	Column B
6. $7.2 \times 1{,}000$	3,800
7. 0.38×10^4	0.38
8. 240×0.03	0.072
9. 3.8×0.1	7.2×10^3
10. 0.08×0.9	7.2

Use Vocabulary in Writing

11. The digits in the product of 0.48 and a decimal number between 350 and 400 are 182136. Explain how to correctly place the decimal point without knowing the other factor. Then place the decimal point in the product.

Name ___

Set A pages 129–132, 133–136

Use the patterns in this table to find 8.56×10 and 0.36×100.

Multiply by	Move the decimal point to the right
10	1 place
100	2 places
1,000	3 places

$8.56 \times 10 = 85.6 = 85.6$

$0.36 \times 100 = 36.0 = 36$

Remember you can use rounding or compatible numbers to estimate.

Find each product.

1. 10×4.5
2. $10^3 \times 3.67$
3. 100×4.5
4. 0.008×10^2

Estimate each product.

5. 0.38×99
6. 8×56.7
7. 11×4.89
8. 24×3.9

Set B pages 137–140, 141–144

Find 3×0.15.

Model the multiplication as repeated addition with place-value blocks.

So, $3 \times 0.15 = 0.45$.

Remember to estimate by rounding or using compatible numbers to check the reasonableness of the answer.

Find each product. Use place-value blocks as necessary.

1. 50×3.67
2. 5.86×5
3. 14×9.67
4. 8×56.7
5. 11×0.06
6. 2.03×6
7. 25×1.63
8. 5.62×75

Set C pages 145–148, 149–152

Find 0.2 × 1.7.

Model using hundredths grids.

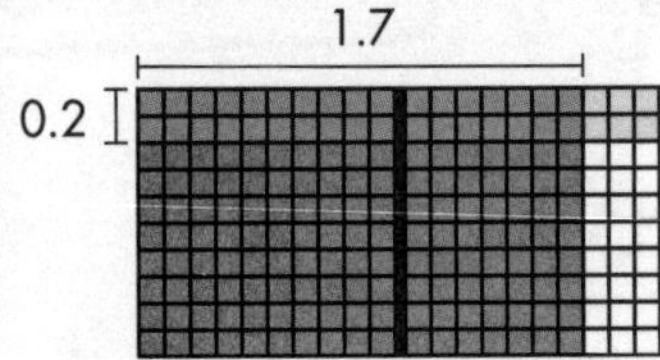

The product is where the shading overlaps.
So, 0.2 × 1.7 = 0.34.

Find each product.

1. 1.3 × 0.4
2. 5.8 × 5.2
3. 8.3 × 10.7
4. 3.4 × 0.7
5. 2.4 × 3.6
6. 9.7 × 11.2
7. 1.5 × 0.6
8. 67.5 × 9.2

Set D pages 153–156

Use properties to find 0.8 × 0.4.

Rewrite each decimal as a product of a whole number and a decimal. Next, use the Associative and Commutative Properties to rearrange the factors.

$$
\begin{aligned}
0.8 \times 0.4 &= \\
&= (8 \times 0.1) \times (4 \times 0.1) \\
&= (8 \times 4) \times (0.1 \times 0.1) \\
&= 32 \times 0.01 \\
&= 0.32
\end{aligned}
$$

So, 0.8 × 0.4 = 0.32.

Remember if two factors less than one are multiplied, their product is less than either factor.

Use properties to find each product.

1. 0.6 × 0.3
2. 2.5 × 0.7
3. 0.04 × 1.9
4. 0.23 × 0.8
5. 0.1 × 8.2
6. 5.7 × 3.6
7. 4.2 × 6.5
8. 9.11 × 0.3

Name ______________________

Set E pages 157–160

Reteaching
Continued

The decimal is missing in the product below. Use number sense to place the decimal point correctly.

$43.5 \times 1.7 = 7395$

Since 1.7 is greater than 1, the product will be greater than 43.5. Since 43.5 is about 40 and 1.7 is about 2, the answer will be about 80. The decimal point should be between the 3 and the 9.

$$\begin{array}{r} 43.5 \\ \times\ 1.7 \\ \hline 73.95 \\ \uparrow \end{array}$$

So, $43.5 \times 1.7 = 73.95$.

Remember that it may be helpful to compare each factor to 1 in order to determine the relative size of the product.

The decimal point is missing in each product. Use number sense to place the decimal point correctly.

1. $4 \times 0.21 = 84$

2. $4.5 \times 6.2 = 279$

3. $7 \times 21.6 = 1512$

4. $6.4 \times 3.2 = 2048$

5. $31.5 \times 0.01 = 315$

6. $1.4 \times 52.3 = 7322$

7. $0.12 \times 0.9 = 108$

8. $12.5 \times 163.2 = 2040$

Set F pages 161–164

Think about these questions to help you **model with math**.

Thinking Habits

- How can I use math I know to help solve this problem?
- How can I use pictures, objects, or an equation to represent the problem?
- How can I use numbers, words, and symbols to solve the problem?

Remember that you can write an equation to show how the quantities in a problem are related.

Mr. Jennings made the stained glass window below with the dimensions shown. What is the total area of the window?

1.8 ft by 1.25 ft	1.5 ft by 0.75 ft
	1.5 ft by 0.5 ft

1. What do you need to find first?

2. Write an equation to model the problem. Then solve the problem.

Patti went to the bakery. She bought a loaf of bread for \$3.49, 6 muffins that cost \$1.25 each, and a bottle of juice for \$1.79. She gave the cashier a \$20 bill. How much change should Patti receive?

3. What do you need to find first?

4. Answer the question. Write equations to show your work.

Name ____________________

1. A credit card is 0.76 mm thick. How thick is a stack of 10^3 credit cards? Explain.

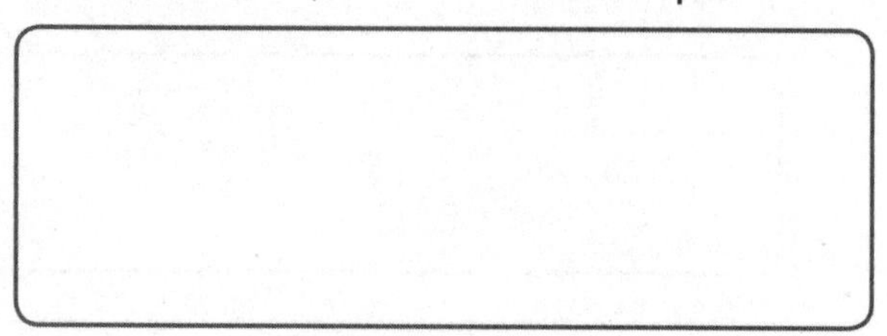

2. Leo has 59 bricks each measuring 0.19 m long. He lines up the bricks to make a row.

A. Estimate the length of Leo's row of bricks. Write an equation to model your work.

B. Find the actual length of the row of bricks.

3. Susan colored in the decimal grid shown below. Write an expression that shows the area she colored. Then evaluate the expression.

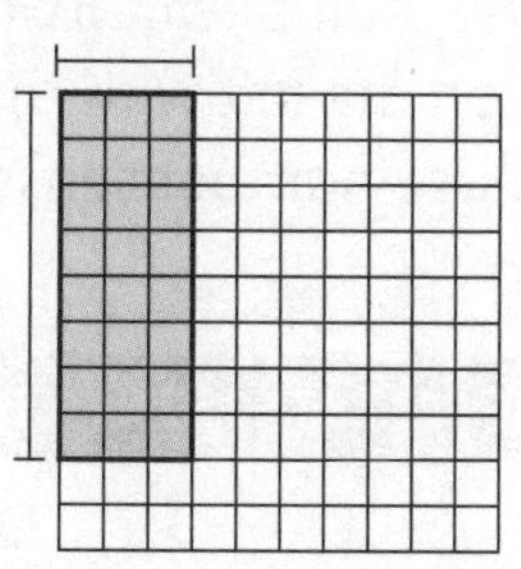

4. Match each expression on the left with its product.

	4	40	0.4	0.04
5×0.08	☐	☐	☐	☐
0.5×0.08	☐	☐	☐	☐
50×0.8	☐	☐	☐	☐
5×0.8	☐	☐	☐	☐

5. Michelle bought 4.6 yards of fabric. Each yard of fabric cost $4.95. How much did Michelle spend on fabric? Enter your answer in the box.

6. Choose all the expressions that are equal to 0.75×0.5.

☐ $\frac{5}{10} \times \frac{75}{10}$
☐ $\frac{5}{10} \times \frac{75}{100}$
☐ $\frac{5}{100} \times \frac{75}{100}$
☐ $\frac{50}{100} \times \frac{75}{100}$
☐ $\frac{75}{100} \times \frac{5}{10}$

7. Select each equation that the number 10^2 makes true.

☐ $0.031 \times \square = 31$
☐ $0.501 \times \square = 501$
☐ $4.08 \times \square = 408$
☐ $0.97 \times \square = 97$
☐ $0.55 \times \square = 550$

8. Nadia drew a square in her notebook. Each side measured 2.5 centimeters.

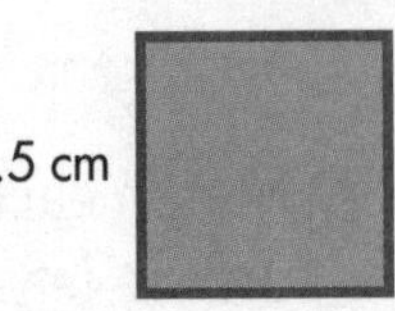

A. What is the perimeter of Nadia's square? Write an equation to model your work.

B. What is the area of Nadia's square? Write an equation to model your work.

9. Match each expression on the left with its product.

	3.04	30.4	304	3,040
3.04×10^2	☐	☐	☐	☐
0.304×10^4	☐	☐	☐	☐
3.04×10	☐	☐	☐	☐
0.304×10	☐	☐	☐	☐

10. Select all the expressions that are equal to 0.09×0.4.

☐ $\frac{9}{100} \times \frac{4}{10}$

☐ $\frac{4}{10} \times \frac{9}{100}$

☐ $\frac{4}{100} \times \frac{9}{100}$

☐ $\frac{40}{100} \times \frac{9}{100}$

☐ $\frac{9}{10} \times \frac{4}{10}$

11. One glass of lemonade has 115 calories. How many calories are in 3.5 glasses of lemonade? Write an equation to model your work.

12. Natalie likes to mail lots of postcards when she goes on vacation. In 2014, the cost of a postcard stamp was $0.34.

A. Natalie buys 10 postcard stamps. What is the total cost of the stamps? Explain.

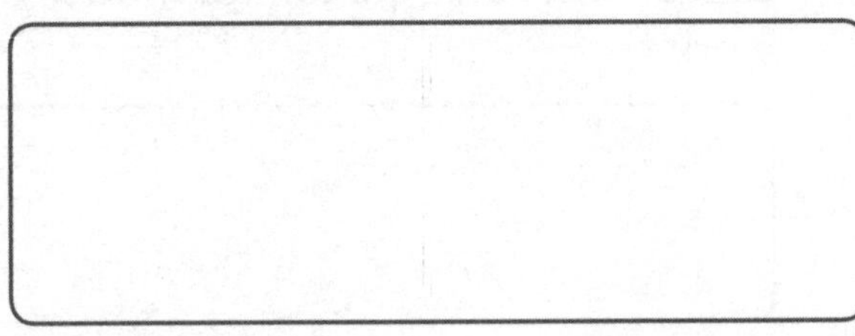

B. Natalie and her friends decide to buy 100 postcard stamps. What will be the total cost of the stamps? Explain.

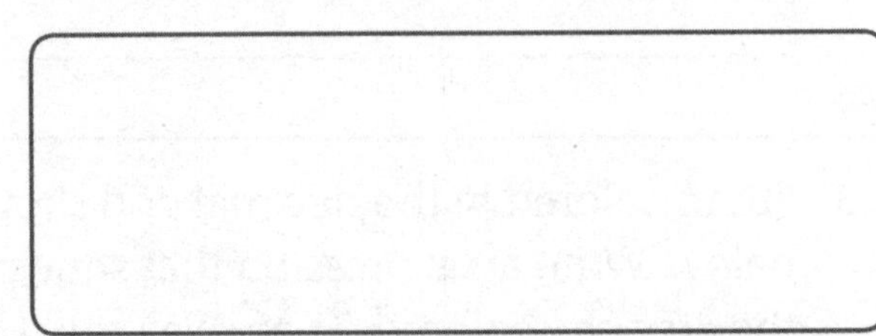

13. Without doing the multiplication, match each expression on the left with the correct product. Use number sense to help you.

	19.716	29.682	2.023	9.568
8.32×1.15	☐	☐	☐	☐
5.78×0.35	☐	☐	☐	☐
6.12×4.85	☐	☐	☐	☐
7.95×2.48	☐	☐	☐	☐

Name ______________________________

14. Derrick runs 2.25 miles each day. How many total miles will he have run after 10 days? Explain.

15. Select each equation that the decimal 0.65 makes true.

- ☐ $10^2 \times \square = 65$
- ☐ $10^4 \times \square = 650$
- ☐ $10^1 \times \square = 6.5$
- ☐ $10^3 \times \square = 65$
- ☐ $10^1 \times \square = 65$

16. A farmer plants 0.4 of a field with wheat. The field is 2.3 acres.

A. Shade the grids to model the multiplication.

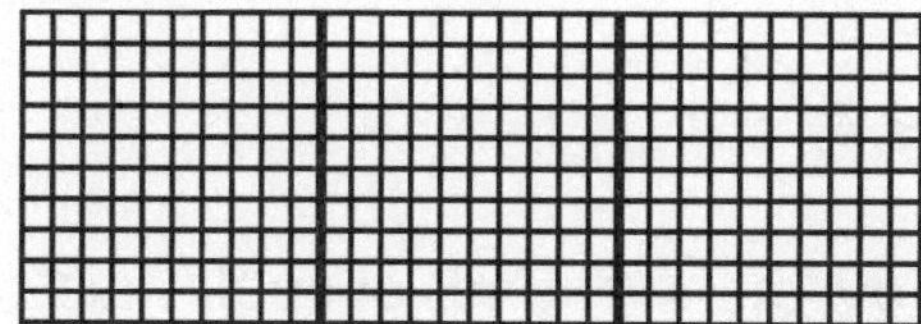

B. How many acres are planted with wheat? Use an equation and the model to explain.

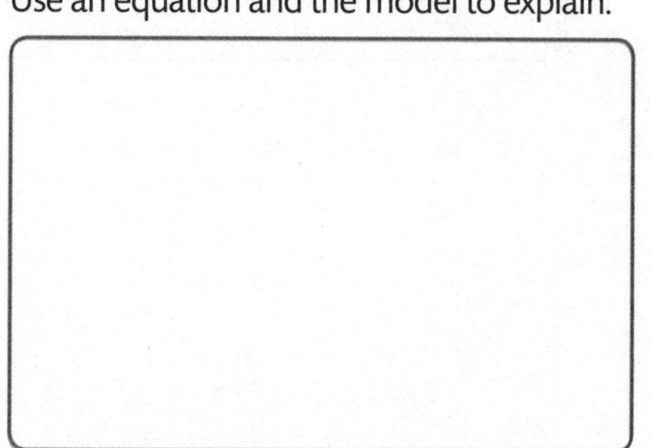

17. Bradley walks 0.65 mile each Friday to his friend's house. He takes a different route home that is 1.2 miles. How many miles will Bradley walk to his friend's house and back in a year? Show your work. Reminder: there are 52 weeks in a year.

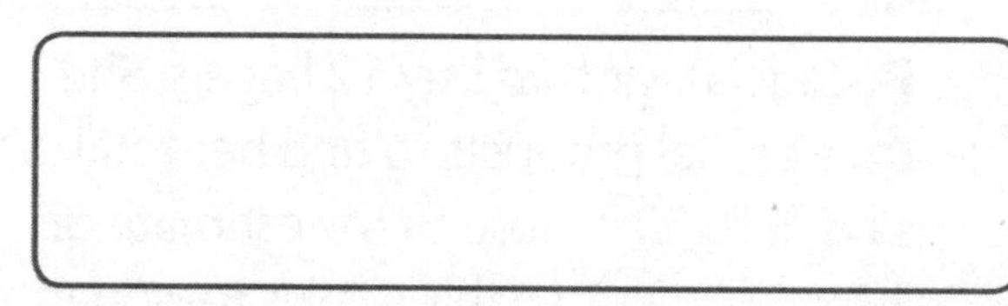

18. Alyssa paints 3 walls blue. Each of the walls is 8.3 feet tall and 7.5 feet wide.

A. Round the length and width to the nearest whole number. Then estimate the area that Alyssa will paint. Write equations to model your work.

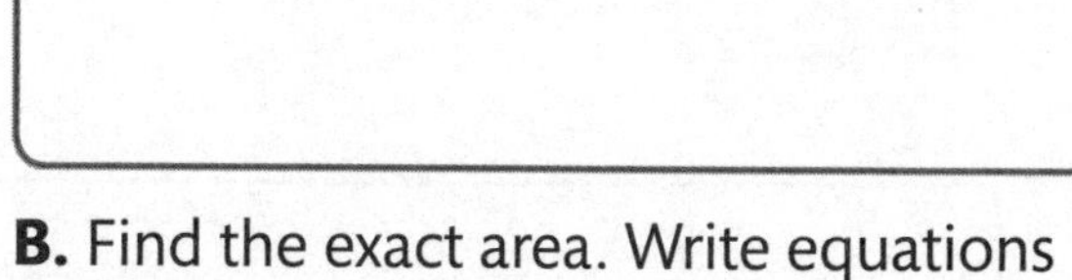

B. Find the exact area. Write equations to model your work.

C. Compare your estimate to the exact answer. Why is your answer reasonable?

19. Leticia and Jamal go to a bakery.

Bagel	\$0.95
Muffin	\$1.99
Fruit Pie	\$3.29

A. Jamal wants to buy 6 muffins. How much will this cost? Write an equation to model your work.

B. Leticia wants to buy 12 bagels. She uses partial products to find her total. She says "\$16.80 is close to my estimate of $12 \times \$1 = \$12$, so this total is reasonable." Do you agree with her? Explain your reasoning.

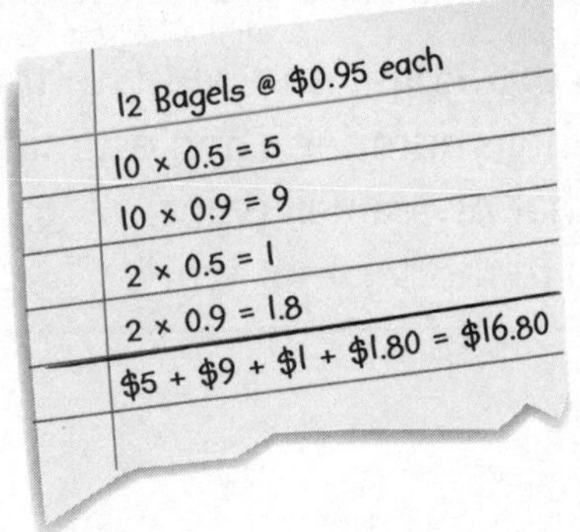

12 Bagels @ \$0.95 each
10 × 0.5 = 5
10 × 0.9 = 9
2 × 0.5 = 1
2 × 0.9 = 1.8
\$5 + \$9 + \$1 + \$1.80 = \$16.80

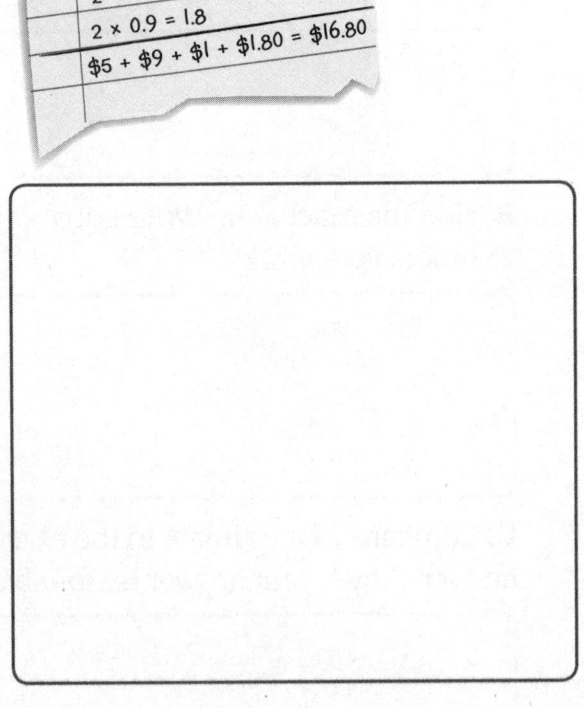

20. The area of one fabric square is 4.85 square inches. What is the area of a quilt made with 10^2 fabric squares? Explain.

21. Jen bought 3.72 pounds of apples at a farmer's market. Andrea bought 4 times as much as Jen.

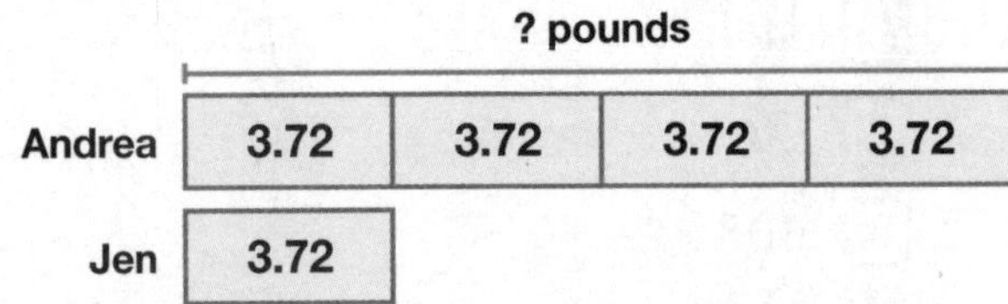

A. Which expression represents the problem? Use the bar diagram to help.

Ⓐ 3.72×4

Ⓑ 3.72×1

Ⓒ $3.72 \div 4$

Ⓓ $3.72 \div 1$

B. How many pounds of apples did Andrea buy?

Name ____________________

TOPIC 4

Performance Task

An *exchange rate* is how much of one country's currency (money) you would get for another country's currency. The table below shows the recent exchange rate between the U.S. dollar and the currency of some other countries.

For example, if you had \$2 (U.S.) dollars, you could exchange that for 26.48 Mexican pesos:

$2 \times 13.24 = 26.48$.

U.S. \$1.00 =
6.29 Venezuelan bolívares
6.45 Swedish Krona
61.92 Indian rupees
101.82 Japanese yen
86.4 Kenyan shillings
13.24 Mexican pesos

1. Jade has \$10, Julio has \$100, and Anna has \$1,000. How many Japanese yen would each person get in exchange for their dollars?

2. Ivana has \$5.50. Luc has 1.4 times as much money as Ivana.

Part A

How many Indian rupees would Ivana get?

Part B

How many dollars does Luc have? How many rupees can he exchange for that? Round your answer to the nearest hundredth.

3. Use estimation to solve. Marcus has \$250. About how many Venezuelan bolívares could he obtain? Is your estimate an overestimate or an underestimate? Explain.

4. Jorge is traveling to Kenya to photograph wildlife. How many Kenyan shillings will he receive for $500? His friends give him a $50 gift certificate right before he leaves. How many Kenyan shillings can he exchange for that amount?

5. Kofi is taking a trip to Mexico to see Mayan and Aztec pyramids. He wants to exchange $300 before arriving there. How many Mexican pesos can he receive? Write and solve an equation to show your work.

6. Mary is planning a vacation to Europe. The exchange rate for the U.S. dollar to the Euro is 0.73.

Part A

Sketch place-value blocks to model how many Euros Mary will get for 3 U.S. dollars.

Part B

How many Euros can Mary get for $3? Write an equation to show your work.

Part C

How does the model help you find the product?

TOPIC 5 Use Models and Strategies to Divide Whole Numbers

Essential Question: What are some common procedures for division and why do they work?

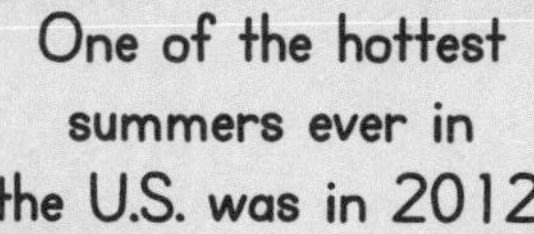

One of the hottest summers ever in the U.S. was in 2012.

More iced tea, anybody? Here's a project on finding the average temperature using division.

enVision® STEM Project: Average Temperature

Do Research Use a weather site from the Internet or another source of daily weather reports to find the average daily temperature for your city or town for every day of one month. The average daily temperature is the average temperature for a whole 24-hour period.

Journal: Write a Report Include what you found about daily temperatures. Also in your report:

- Find the average daily high temperature for the month. Which day had the greatest high temperature?
- Find the average daily low temperature for the month. Which day had the least low temperature?
- Make up and solve division problems based on your data.

Name ______________________________

Review What You Know

Vocabulary

Choose the best term from the box. Write it on the blank.

- dividend
- quotient
- divisor
- remainder

1. In the equation $80 \div 10 = 8$, the number 80 is the __________.

2. The number used to divide another number is the __________.

3. The result of dividing two numbers is the __________.

Multiplication and Division

Multiply or divide.

4. $630 \div 9$ **5.** $480 \div 6$ **6.** $755 \div 5$

7. $657 \div 9$ **8.** 57×13 **9.** 71×109

10. For the state fair next month, 132 people volunteered to plan the fair's activities. The volunteers formed 12 equal groups. How many volunteers were in each group?

11. A town is holding a competition for various athletic games. Each community has 14 players. There are 112 communities competing in the games. How many players are competing?

Ⓐ 1,676 Ⓑ 1,568 Ⓒ 126 Ⓓ 98

Estimate

12. A county has a goal to build 12,000 bus stop shelters in 48 months. If the county builds 215 bus shelters each month, will it reach its goal? Explain one way to estimate the answer.

Name ____________________

Pick a Project

PROJECT 5A

How much does a field trip cost?

Project: Plan an Educational Field Trip

PROJECT 5B

How does an assembly line work?

Project: Design an Assembly Line for Toy Vehicles

PROJECT 5C

How do marathon runners get enough water?

Project: Position Water Stations

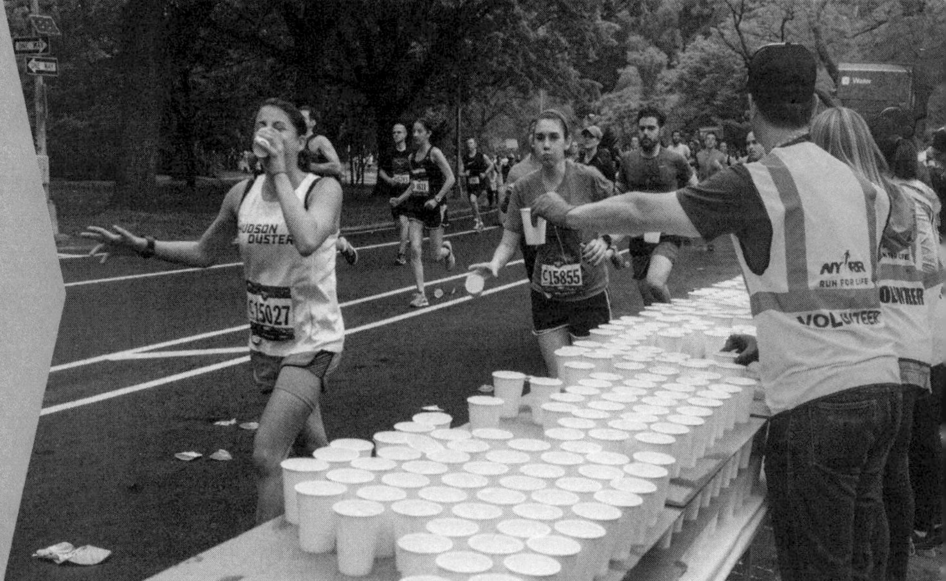

Math Modeling

Flapjack Stack

Video

Before watching the video, think:

Pancakes have been around for thousands of years and are popular all over the world. Some pancakes are made from potatoes and served with applesauce and sour cream. Other pancakes are sweet and served with blueberries and maple syrup.

Maybe I should plant a maple tree.

I can ...

model with math to solve a problem that involves computing with whole numbers and estimating.

Mathematical Practices MP.4 Also MP.1, MP.2
Content Standard 5.NBT.B

Name ______________________

Lesson 5-1
Use Patterns and Mental Math to Divide

I can ...
use patterns to find quotients.

Content Standard 5.NBT.B.6
Mathematical Practices MP.6, MP.7

Solve & Share A bakery sells muffins to local grocery stores in boxes that hold 20 muffins each. How many boxes are used if 60 muffins are sold? 600 muffins? 6,000 muffins? ***Solve this problem any way you choose.***

Find the answer for 60 muffins. Then you can look for relationships to help find the answers for 600 and 6,000 muffins. *Show your work!*

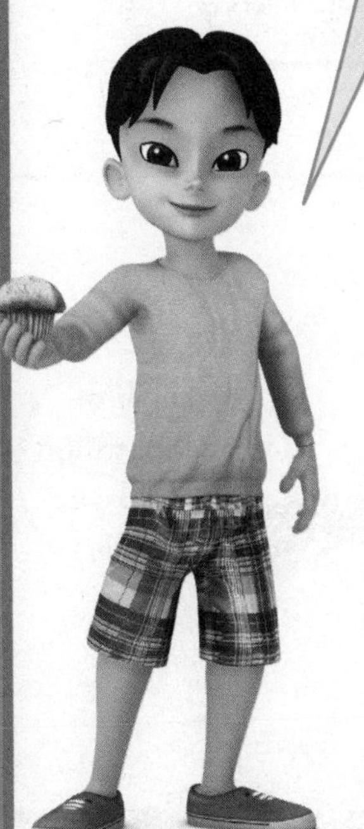

Number of Muffins Sold	Number of Muffins per Box	Number of Boxes
60	20	
600	20	
6,000	20	

Look Back! How can you use multiplication to help you divide 6,000 by 20?

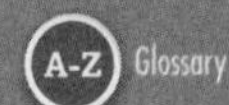

How Can Patterns Help You Divide Multiples of 10?

Visual Learning Bridge

A

A jet carries 18,000 passengers in 90 trips. The plane is full for each trip. How many passengers does the plane hold?

Find 18,000 ÷ 90, the number of passengers on each trip.

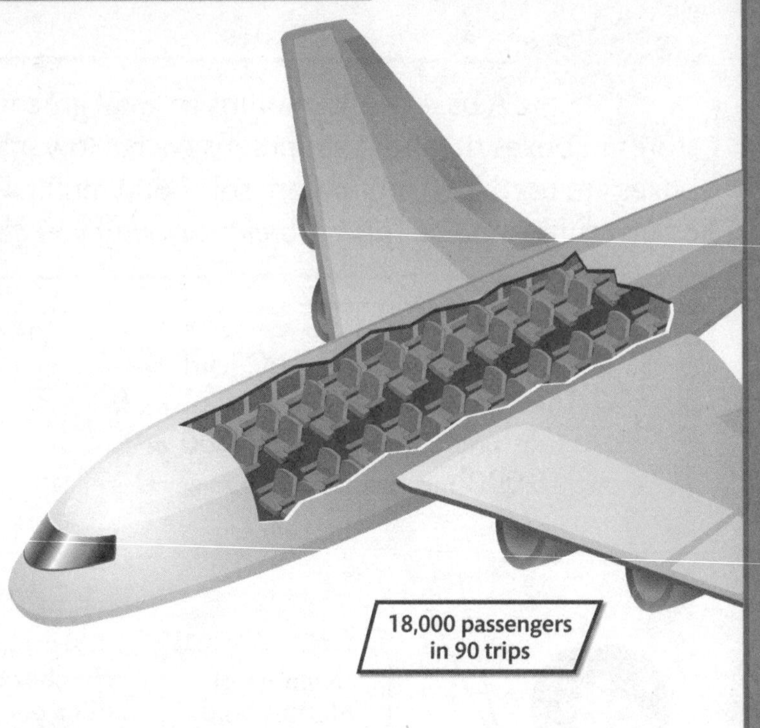

18,000 passengers in 90 trips

B

Think of a basic fact to help you.
$18 \div 9 = 2$

Think about patterns in place value and multiples of 10:

$180 \div 90 = 18$ tens $\div 9$ tens $= 2$

$1{,}800 \div 90 = 180$ tens $\div 9$ tens $= 20$

$18{,}000 \div 90 = 1{,}800$ tens $\div 9$ tens $= 200$

So, the jet can hold 200 passengers.

C

Or, use multiplication.
$90 \times 2 = 180$

$90 \times 20 = 1{,}800$

$90 \times 200 = 18{,}000$

So $18{,}000 \div 90 = 200$

The jet can hold 200 passengers.

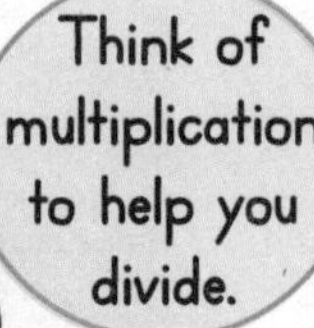

Think of multiplication to help you divide.

Convince Me! **Look for Relationships** If the jet above carried 10,000 people in 50 trips, how many people did it carry each trip? The jet carried the same number of people each trip.

What basic fact helped you find the answer?

Name ______________________

Guided Practice

Do You Understand?

1. Why is 210 ÷ 30 the same as 21 tens ÷ 3 tens?

2. A jet carried 12,000 people in 40 trips. If the jet was full each trip, how many people did it carry for each trip?

Use a basic fact to help you.

Do You Know How?

In **3–9**, find each quotient. Use mental math.

3. 210 ÷ 30 = 21 tens ÷ 3 tens = ____

4. 480 ÷ 60 = 48 tens ÷ 6 tens = ____

5. 15,000 ÷ 30 = 1,500 tens ÷ 3 tens = ____

6. ____ = 8,100 ÷ 90

7. 2,800 ÷ 70 = ____

8. 30,000 ÷ 50 = ____

9. ____ = 1,800 ÷ 60

Independent Practice

Leveled Practice In **10–25**, use mental math to find the missing numbers.

10. 560 ÷ 70 = 56 tens ÷ 7 tens = ____

11. 360 ÷ 60 = 36 tens ÷ 6 tens = ____

12. 6,000 ÷ 50 = 600 tens ÷ 5 tens = ____

13. 24,000 ÷ 60 = 2,400 tens ÷ 6 tens = ____

14. ____ = 2,000 ÷ 20

15. 6,300 ÷ 90 = ____

16. ____ ÷ 10 = 24

17. 21,000 ÷ ____ = 700

18. 2,500 ÷ 50 = ____

19. 72,000 ÷ ____ = 800

20. 56,000 ÷ ____ = 800

21. ____ ÷ 10 = 100

22. 45,000 ÷ 90 = ____

23. ____ = 42,000 ÷ 70

24. 64,000 ÷ ____ = 800

25. 32,000 ÷ ____ = 400

Problem Solving

26. The table shows the number of passengers who flew on airplane flights in or out of one airport. Each flight had the same number of passengers. How many passengers were on each flight?

DATA	
Total passengers	27,000
Number of flights	90
Crew members	900

27. Algebra A truck delivers 478 dozen eggs to stores in one day. Write and solve an equation to find *n*, the number of eggs the truck delivers in one day.

28. Paula wants to divide 480 tomatoes equally among 80 baskets. How many tomatoes will Paula put in each basket?

29. Be Precise Ernesto measured the width of each of the three coins shown below.

0.7 inch | 0.84 inch | 0.74 inch

What is the difference in width between the widest coin and the least wide coin?

30. Higher Order Thinking A baker uses 30 grams of sea salt for each batch of bread. Sea salt comes in an 18-kilogram package or an 800-gram package. Which size package should the baker buy so that no sea salt is left after all of the batches are made? Explain.

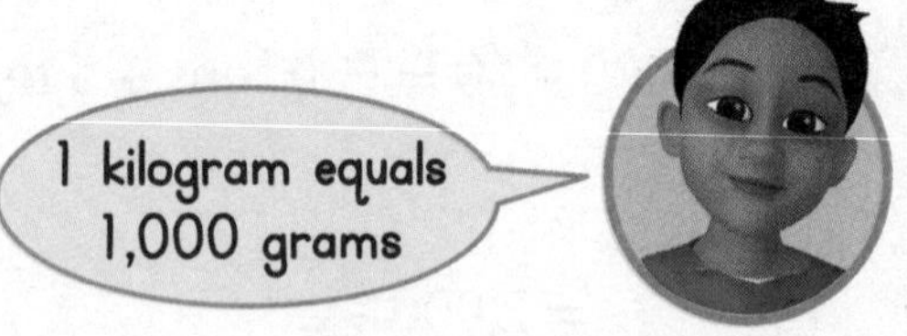
1 kilogram equals
1,000 grams

Assessment Practice

31. Which is 2,400 divided by 80?

Ⓐ 3

Ⓑ 4

Ⓒ 30

Ⓓ 40

32. Which expression has a quotient of 70?

Ⓐ $420 \div 60$

Ⓑ $4{,}200 \div 6$

Ⓒ $4{,}200 \div 60$

Ⓓ $4{,}200 \div 600$

Name ______________________________ Activity

Lesson 5-2
Estimate Quotients with 2-Digit Divisors

I can ...
estimate quotients.

Content Standard 5.NBT.B.6
Mathematical Practices MP.1, MP.4

Solve & Share Kyle's school needs to buy posters for a fundraiser. The school has a budget of $147. Each poster costs $13. About how many posters can his school buy? ***Solve this problem any way you choose.***

You can find compatible numbers to estimate quotients. *Show your work!*

Look Back! **Make Sense and Persevere** What numbers are close to 147 and 13 that would be easy to divide using mental math?

 Visual Learning (A-Z) Glossary

How Can You Use Compatible Numbers to Estimate Quotients?

Visual Learning Bridge

A

Ella earned $159 by selling bracelets. Each bracelet was the same price. About how much did each bracelet cost?

You can use division to find the price.
$159 for 75 bracelets

You know the total amount earned and the number of bracelets.

B The question asks, "About how much?" So, an estimate is enough.

Use compatible numbers to estimate $159 \div 75$.

Think: 159 is close to 160. Is there a number close to 75 that divides 160 evenly? Try 80.

$160 \div 80 = 2$

So, 160 and 80 are compatible numbers.

16 can be divided evenly by 8.

C Since $160 \div 80 = 2$, $159 \div 75$ is about 2.

Ella charged *about* $2 for each bracelet.

Use multiplication to check for reasonableness:

$2 \times 80 = 160$.

Convince Me! **Make Sense and Persevere** Suppose Ella earned $230 selling the 75 bracelets. Estimate the price of each bracelet. What compatible numbers did you use?

Name ______________________________

Practice Tools Assessment

Guided Practice

Do You Understand?

1. Ella has 425 more bracelets to sell. She wants to store these in bags that hold 20 bracelets each. She estimates she will need about 25 bags. Do you agree? Why or why not?

Do You Know How?

In **2-7**, estimate using compatible numbers.

2. 287 ÷ 42

3. 320 ÷ 11

4. 208 ÷ 72

5. 554 ÷ 62

6. 815 ÷ 23

7. 2,491 ÷ 48

Independent Practice

Leveled Practice In **8-10**, fill in the blanks to find each estimate.

8. 412 ÷ 84
400 ÷ ☐ = ☐

9. 288 ÷ 37
280 ÷ ☐ = ☐

10. 2,964 ÷ 73
2,800 ÷ ☐ = ☐

In **11-22**, estimate using compatible numbers.

11. 228 ÷ 19

12. 1,784 ÷ 64

13. 7,260 ÷ 83

14. 2,280 ÷ 12

15. 485 ÷ 92

16. 540 ÷ 61

17. 1,710 ÷ 32

18. 2,740 ÷ 67

19. 4,322 ÷ 81

20. 5,700 ÷ 58

21. 7,810 ÷ 44

22. 6,395 ÷ 84

Problem Solving

23. **Model with Math** The sign shows the price of baseball caps for different pack sizes. Coach Lewis will buy the medium-size pack of caps. About how much will each cap cost? Write an equation to model the problem.

Packs of Baseball Caps

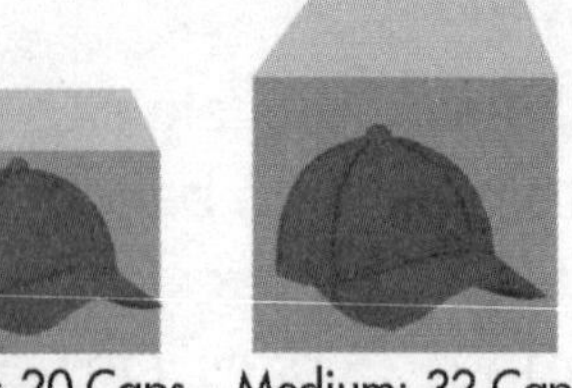
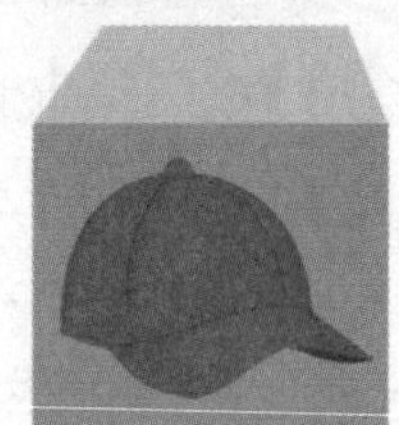

Small: 20 Caps $180.00 | Medium: 32 Caps $270.00 | Large: 50 Caps $360.00

24. There are 91 days until the craft sale. Autumn needs to make 817 rings before the sale. She wants to make about the same number of rings each day. About how many rings should she make each day? Explain how Autumn can use compatible numbers to estimate.

25. **Higher Order Thinking** A company purchased 3,128 bottles of water. Each department needs 55 bottles. Find compatible numbers to estimate the number of departments that can get the bottles they need. Explain.

26. Rita had $20. Then, she saved $5.85 each week for 8 weeks. How much money does she have now? Use the bar diagram to solve the problem. Show your work.

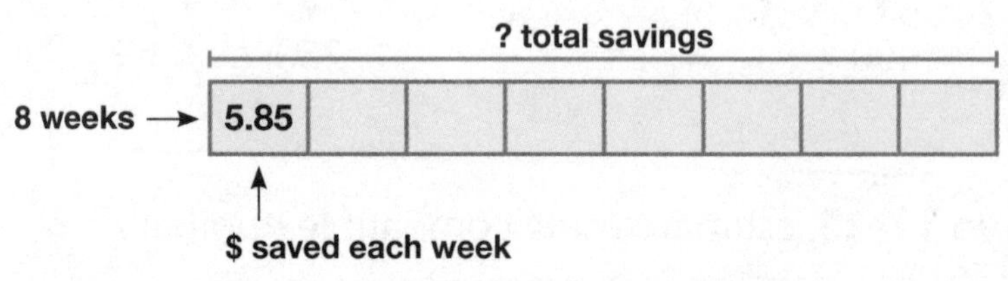

Assessment Practice

27. Lea bought 225 flowers and 12 vases. She put about the same number of flowers in each vase. Which is the best estimate for the number of flowers in each vase?

Ⓐ 40 flowers
Ⓑ 30 flowers
Ⓒ 20 flowers
Ⓓ 10 flowers

28. A school has 617 students. Each class has between 28 and 32 students. Which is the best estimate of the number of classes in the school?

Ⓐ 14 classes
Ⓑ 20 classes
Ⓒ 30 classes
Ⓓ 60 classes

Name ____________________

Activity

Lesson 5-3
Use Models and Properties to Divide with 2-Digit Divisors

I can ...
use models to help find quotients.

Content Standard 5.NBT.B.6
Mathematical Practices MP.1, MP.5

Solve & Share

A parking lot has 270 parking spaces. Each row has 18 parking spaces. How many rows are in this parking lot? ***Solve this problem any way you choose.***

You can use appropriate tools, such as grid paper, to solve the problem. *Show your work!*

Look Back! How can you use estimation to check that your answer to the problem above is reasonable?

How Can You Use Area Models and Properties to Find Quotients?

Visual Learning Bridge

A

Emily has a rectangular garden with an area of 360 square feet. The length of her garden measures 20 feet. How many feet wide is her garden?

Think: $20 \times w = 360$ or $360 \div 20 = w$.

You can have w stand for the unknown side. Use place value and the Distributive Property to find the unknown side length.

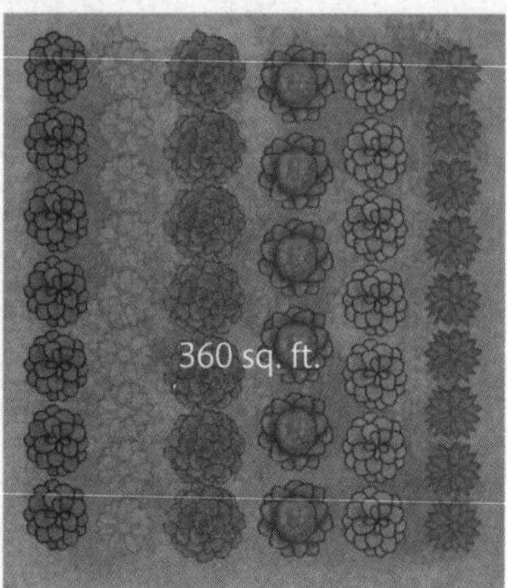

B $20 \times 10 = 200$ and $20 \times 20 = 400$,

so w is between 10 and 20.

That is, $w = 10 + ?$

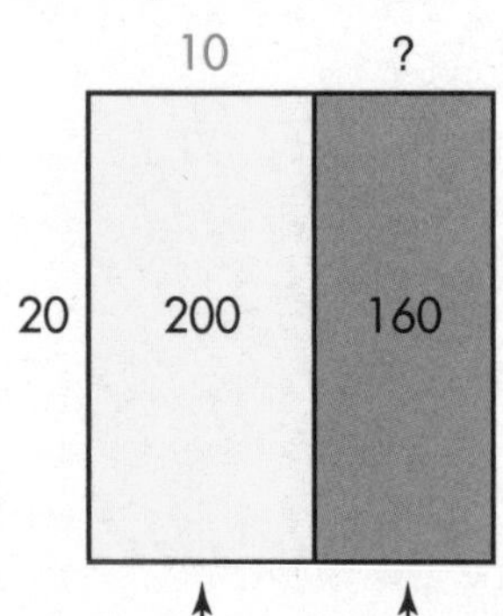

$20 \times ? = 160$

C $20 \times 8 = 160$

So $w = 10 + 8 = 18$.

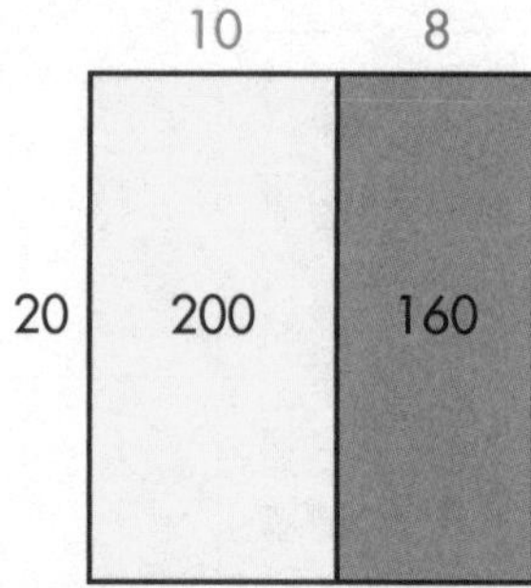

Multiply to check:

$20 \times 18 = 20 \times (10 + 8) = 200 + 160 = 360$

So $360 \div 20 = 18$.

The garden is 18 feet wide.

Convince Me! **Make Sense and Persevere** Use the diagram, place value, and the Distributive Property to find the quotient $408 \div 12$. Hint: Find the value of x and solve.

Name ____________________

Guided Practice

Do You Understand?

1. Write the missing numbers to find 154 ÷ 11.

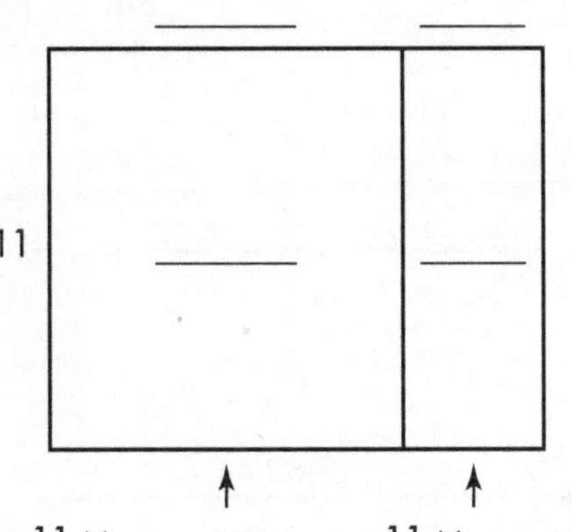

11 × ____ = ____ 11 × ____ = ____

154 = 11 × ___ + 11 × ___

= 11 × (___ + ___)

= 11 × ___

So, 154 ÷ 11 = ___.

Do You Know How?

2. Use the diagram to find 156 ÷ 12.

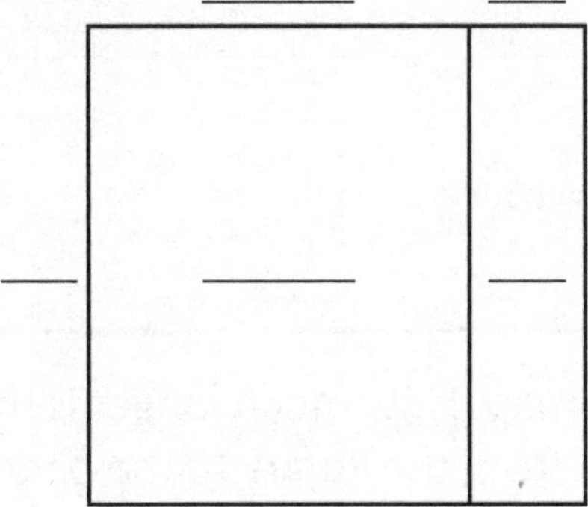

So, 156 ÷ 12 = ___.

In **3** and **4**, use grid paper or draw a picture to find each quotient.

3. 682 ÷ 22

4. 143 ÷ 11

Start by estimating how many tens will be in the quotient.

Independent Practice

Leveled Practice In **5–11**, use grid paper or draw a picture to find each quotient.

5. Use the diagram to find 182 ÷ 13.

So, 182 ÷ 13 = ___.

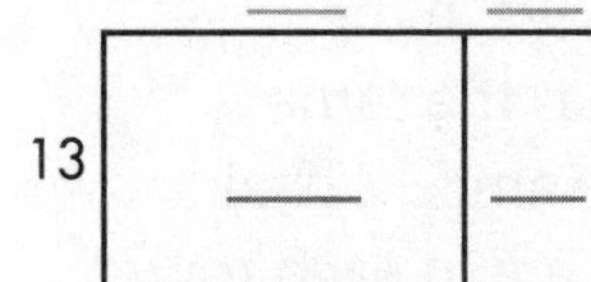

6. 342 ÷ 38

7. 720 ÷ 16

8. 608 ÷ 19

9. 752 ÷ 47

10. 375 ÷ 25

11. 576 ÷ 24

Problem Solving

12. Angelo is training for a long-distance bicycle ride. He travels 15 miles each hour. How many hours will it take him to ride 210 miles?

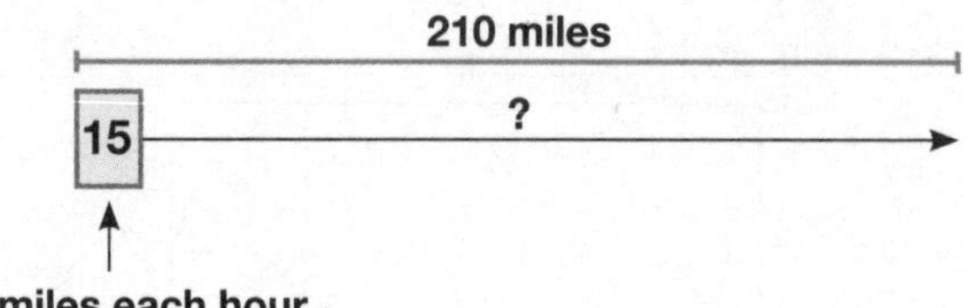

13. **Higher Order Thinking** A rectangular doormat is 21 inches long and has an area of 714 square inches. Find its width. Will the doormat fit in an entryway that is 36 inches wide? Show your work.

14. Use the map. How much longer is the distance from the library to the park to the train station than the distance from the library straight to the train station?

15. **Algebra** If you walk from the train station to the library, then to the park, and then back to the train station, how many miles would you walk in all? Write an equation to model your work.

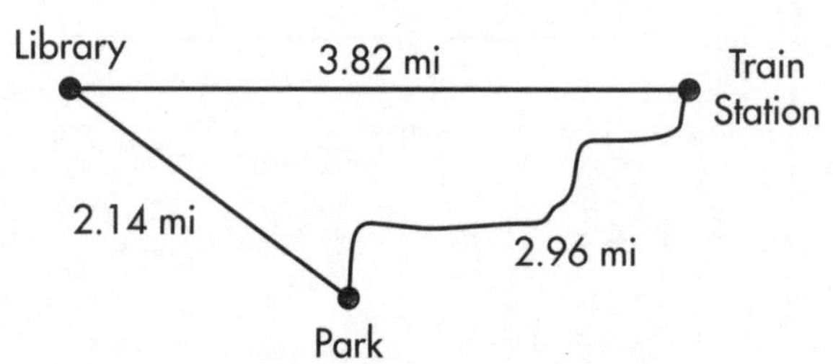

16. **Make Sense and Persevere** Explain how you can use the picture to show that $391 \div 23 = 17$.

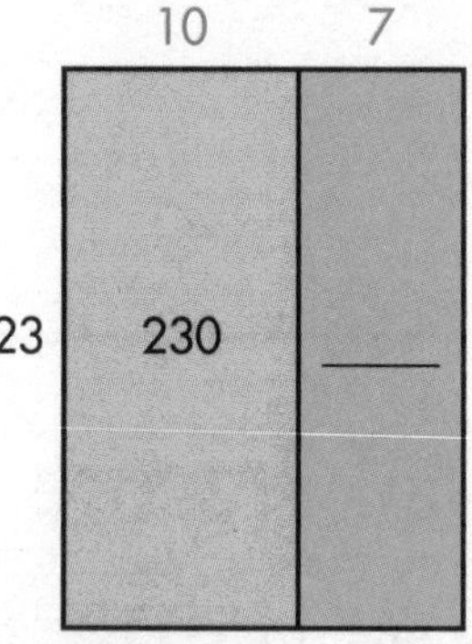

Assessment Practice

17. There are 16 rows of chairs in the auditorium. Each row has the same number of chairs. There are 512 chairs in all. How many chairs are in each row?

Ⓐ 22 chairs
Ⓑ 30 chairs
Ⓒ 32 chairs
Ⓓ 33 chairs

18. A patio has an area of 286 square feet. If the length of the patio is 22 feet, what is the width?

Ⓐ 10 feet
Ⓑ 13 feet
Ⓒ 14 feet
Ⓓ 144 feet

Name ______________________________ Activity

Lesson 5-4
Use Partial Quotients to Divide

I can ...
find quotients of whole numbers.

Content Standard 5.NBT.B.6
Mathematical Practices MP.1, MP.3, MP.4

Solve & Share A hotel sets up tables for a conference for 156 people. If each table seats 12 people, how many tables will be needed? ***Solve this problem any way you choose.***

You can use estimation to help solve this problem. Think about how many groups of 12 you can take away from 156. *Show your work!*

Look Back! Make Sense and Persevere How can you check that the answer to a division problem is correct?

Essential Question

How Can You Use Partial Quotients to Solve Division Problems?

Visual Learning Bridge

A

A theater has 375 seats arranged in rows with 15 seats in each row. How many rows are in this theater? Let r equal the number of rows.
Think: $15 \times r = 375$ or $375 \div 15 = r$.

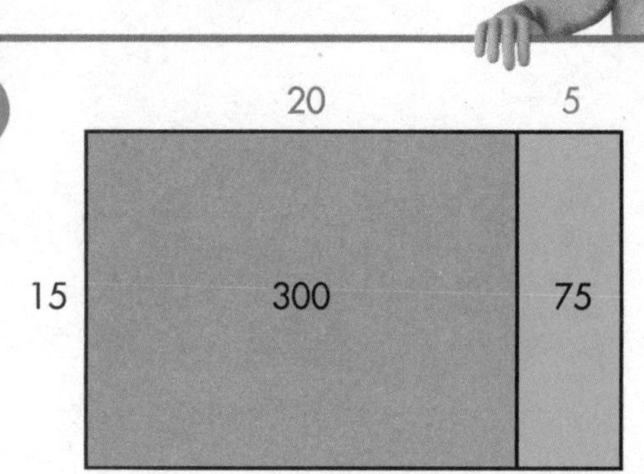

An area model can help you find how many 15s are in 375.

B

Area model: width 15; sections 20 and 5; areas 300 and 75.

$20 \times 15 = 300$ $375 - 300 = 75$
$5 \times 15 = 75$

$300 + 75 = 375$ with 0 left over.
So $375 \div 15 = 25$.

$$\begin{array}{r} 5 \\ 20 \\ 15\overline{)375} \\ -\underline{300} \\ 75 \\ -\underline{75} \\ 0 \end{array}$$

How many 15s are in 375? Try 20.
20 groups of 15 = 300
How many 15s are in 75? Try 5.
5 groups of 15 = 75

$375 \div 15 = 25$ because $15 \times 25 = 375$.

So, there are 25 rows and 0 additional seats in the theater.

Convince Me! **Critique Reasoning** Yimil's solution to the problem above is shown at the right. Is his solution correct? Explain.

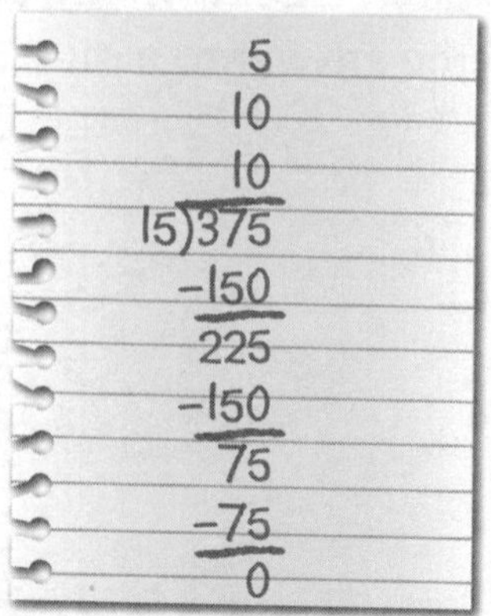

Name ____________________

Practice Tools Assessment

Guided Practice

Do You Understand?

1. Show one way of using partial quotients to find 233 ÷ 11.

2. How can you use estimation to check that your answer to Problem 1 is correct?

Do You Know How?

In **3–6**, use partial quotients to divide. Show your work.

3. 15)210 **4.** 13)286

5. 25)575 **6.** 32)960

Independent Practice

Leveled Practice In **7–16**, use partial quotients to divide. Show your work.

7. 19)247
 − 190 ☐ groups of 19 = 190
 57
 − 38 ☐ groups of 19 = 38
 19
 − 19 ☐ group of 19 = 19
 0

Add the partial quotients:
☐ + ☐ + ☐ = ☐

8. 14)631
 − 280 ☐ groups of 14 = 280
 351
 − 280 ☐ groups of 14 = 280
 71
 − 70 ☐ groups of 14 = 70
 1
There is 1 left over.

Add the partial quotients:
☐ + ☐ + ☐ = ☐ and ☐ left over

9. 11)132 **10.** 21)845 **11.** 16)304 **12.** 32)480

13. 23)715 **14.** 30)660 **15.** 43)731 **16.** 16)610

Problem Solving

17. A 969-acre wildlife preserve has 19 cheetahs. About how many acres does each cheetah have to itself, if each cheetah roams the same number of acres?

18. A factory produces 272 chairs in an 8-hour shift. If the factory produces the same number of chairs each hour, how many chairs does it produce in 30 minutes?

19. A cafeteria can seat 5×10^2 students. Each table has 2×10^1 seats. How many tables are in the cafeteria?

20. Model with Math Peter is driving 992 miles from Chicago to Dallas. His sister Anna is driving 1,068 miles from Phoenix to Dallas. Write and solve an equation to find how much farther Anna drives than Peter drives.

21. Write a multiplication equation and a division equation that represent the model shown below.

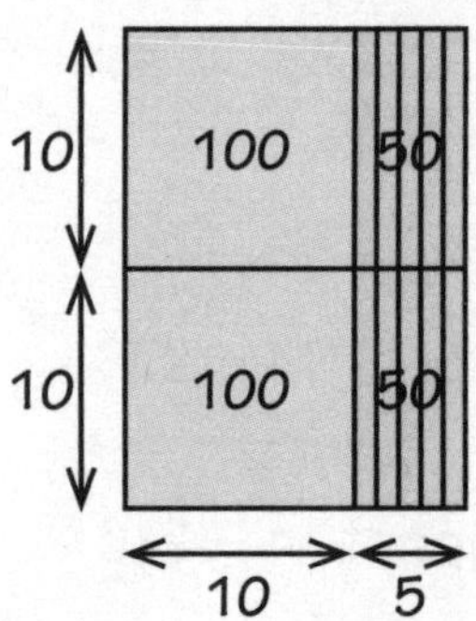

22. Higher Order Thinking How can you use partial quotients to find 325 ÷ 13? Explain.

Assessment Practice

23. Which expressions are equivalent to 35?

- ☐ 1,400 ÷ 4
- ☐ 420 ÷ 12
- ☐ 875 ÷ 25
- ☐ 7,700 ÷ 22
- ☐ 14,000 ÷ 40

24. Which expressions are equivalent to 22?

- ☐ 704 ÷ 32
- ☐ 1,078 ÷ 49
- ☐ 1,890 ÷ 30
- ☐ 1,430 ÷ 65
- ☐ 4,500 ÷ 50

Name ______________________

Activity

Lesson 5-5
Use Sharing to Divide: Two-Digit Divisors

I can ...
use place value and sharing to divide.

Content Standard 5.NBT.B.6
Mathematical Practices MP.2, MP.4, MP.5

Solve & Share

The Recycling Club has $294 to purchase one set of recycling bins for each of the 14 members. Each of the 14 sets of bins will be identical to the others and cost the same amount. What is the greatest amount they can spend on one set of bins? Use objects or draw pictures to help solve this problem. Explain how you found your answer.

Using appropriate tools like play money or place-value blocks can help you divide.

Look Back! Why can you use division to answer this question?

Visual Learning

Glossary

How Can You Record Division with a Two-Digit Divisor?

A

Orchard workers have 258 grapefruit seedlings to plant in 12 equal rows. How many seedlings will be in each row?

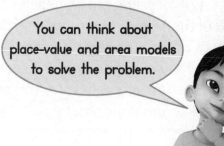

You can think about place-value and area models to solve the problem.

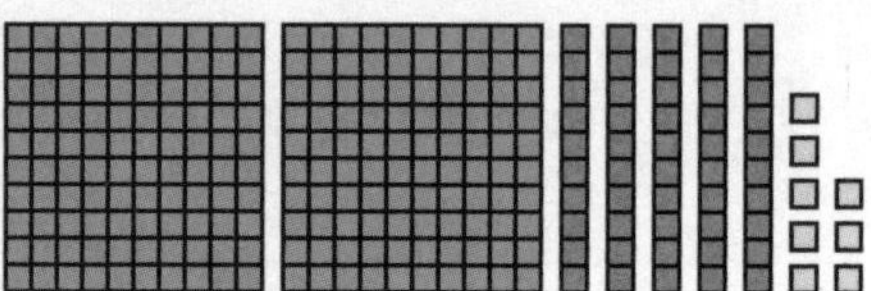

Estimate: $258 \div 12$ is close to $250 \div 10 = 25$.

B

Regroup the blocks to fill the 12 rows.

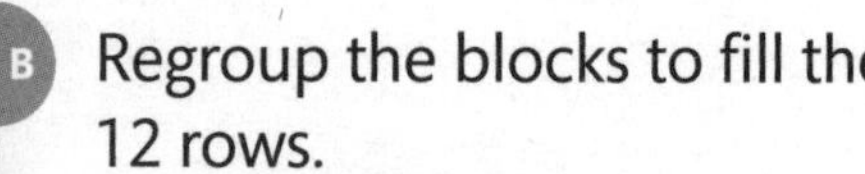

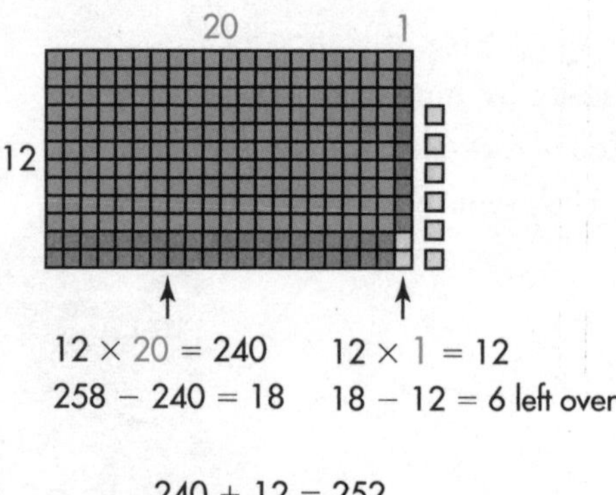

$12 \times 20 = 240$
$258 - 240 = 18$

$12 \times 1 = 12$
$18 - 12 = 6$ left over

$240 + 12 = 252$
So $258 \div 12 = 21R6$

$$\begin{array}{r} 21 \\ 12\overline{)258} \\ -\underline{240} \\ 18 \\ -\underline{12} \\ 6 \end{array}$$

25 tens divided into 12 equal groups is 2 tens in each group
12 groups of 20 = 240
18 ones divided into 12 equal groups is 1 one in each group
12 groups of 1 = 12
plants left over

$258 \div 12 = 21$ R6 because $12 \times 21 + 6 = 258$.

There will be 21 seedlings in each row with 6 seedlings left over.

Convince Me! **Reasoning** What does the remainder mean in the problem above?

Name ____

Guided Practice

Do You Understand?

1. If the orchard has 200 seedlings and 12 are planted in each row, how many rows will be filled? Draw place-value blocks to show your answer.

2. In Problem 1, what does the remainder represent?

Do You Know How?

In **3** and **4**, divide. Write the missing numbers.

3. 14)196

4. 80)766 = ☐ R46

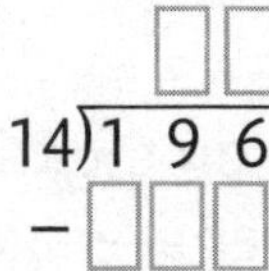

An estimate can help you decide if your answer is reasonable.

Independent Practice

Leveled Practice In **5–13**, divide. Write the missing numbers.

5. 19)304

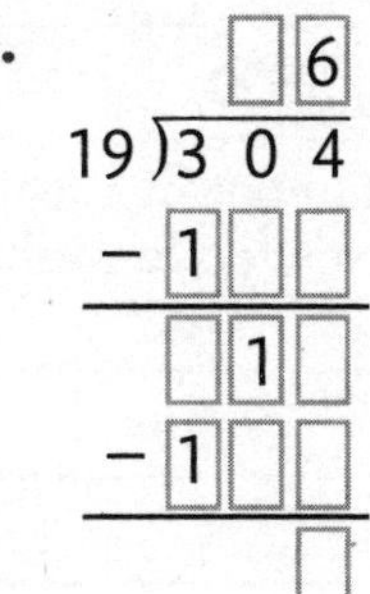

6. 61)593 = ☐ R ☐

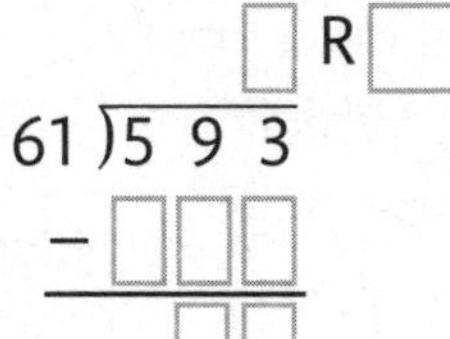

7. 11)360 = ☐☐ R ☐

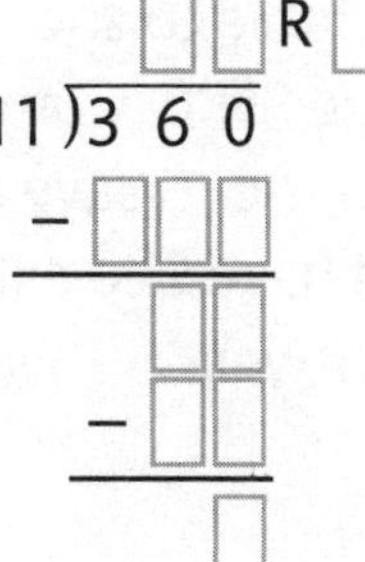

8. 17)544

9. 50)250

10. 68)867

11. 23)966

12. 79)492

13. 40)375

Problem Solving

14. Rita's family is moving from Grand Junction to Dallas. The moving van averages 60 miles each hour. About how many hours does the van take to reach Dallas? Explain your work.

DATA

Dallas, TX, to Grand Junction, CO	980 miles
Nashville, TN, to Norfolk, VA	670 miles
Charleston, SC, to Atlanta, GA	290 miles
Denver, CO, to Minneapolis, MN	920 miles
Little Rock, AR, to Chicago, IL	660 miles

15. Due to construction delays on the trip from Little Rock to Chicago, a van driver averaged 48 miles each hour. About how long did that trip take?

16. **Higher Order Thinking** A scientist needs 72 milliliters of distilled water for each of 15 experiments. She has a bottle that contains 975 milliliters of distilled water. Is there enough water in the bottle for all 15 experiments? Explain.

17. **Model with Math** The Port Lavaca fishing pier is 3,200 feet long. There is one person fishing for each ten feet of length. Write and solve an equation to find how many people are fishing from the pier.

18. Todd made a table to show different plans he can use to save $500. Complete the table. Which plan can Todd use to save $500 in less than 16 weeks and have $20 extra? Explain how you found your answer.

Plans for Saving $500

Plan	Amount to Save Each Week	Number of Weeks Needed to Make Goal
A	$20	25
B	$30	
C	$40	
D	$50	

Assessment Practice

19. Find an expression that produces a quotient of 9 R15. Write the expression in the box.

Quotient: 9 R15

335 ÷ 40   360 ÷ 40   365 ÷ 40
375 ÷ 40   409 ÷ 40   415 ÷ 40

Name ____

Activity

Lesson 5-6

Use Sharing to Divide: Greater Dividends

I can ...
use place value and sharing to divide.

Content Standard 5.NBT.B.6
Mathematical Practices MP.2, MP.7

Solve & Share
To make sense of the problem, you need to read carefully to find all the important information.

The city built a skate park that cost $3,240 and will be paid for over two years in equal monthly payments. How much is each monthly payment? Use objects or draw pictures to help solve this problem. Explain how you found your answer.

Look Back! **Use Structure** How did you use what you know about place value to find the answer to the problem?

How Can You Record Division with a Two-Digit Divisor and a Four-Digit Dividend?

A

Jake works at a flower shop. The shop just received a delivery of 1,830 roses. If the roses are distributed evenly among 15 coolers, how many roses should Jake put in each cooler?

You can use place-value and area models to solve the problem.

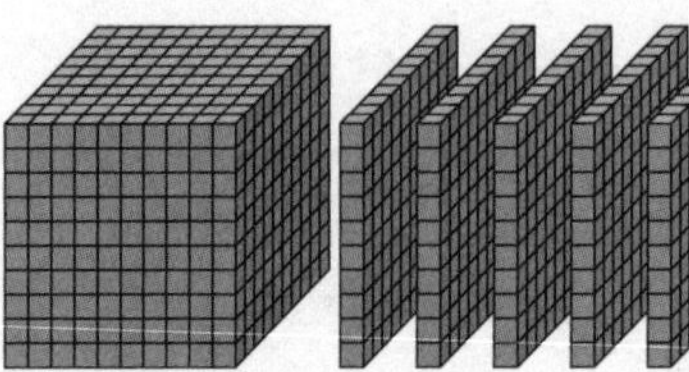

B

There are not enough thousands to put one thousand in each group, so regroup the thousands into hundreds.

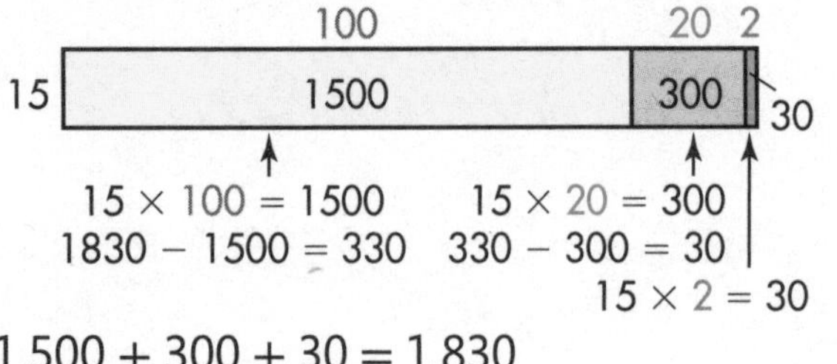

$1{,}500 + 300 + 30 = 1{,}830$

So $1{,}830 \div 15 = 122$.

122	
15)1,830	18 hundreds divided into 15 equal groups is 1 hundred in each group
− 1,500	15 groups of 100 = 1500
330	33 tens divided into 15 equal groups is 2 tens in each group
− 300	15 groups of 20 = 300
30	30 ones divided into 15 equal groups is 2 ones in each group
− 30	15 groups of 2 = 30
0	nothing left over

$1{,}830 \div 15 = 122$ because $15 \times 122 = 1{,}830$.

There should be 122 roses in each cooler with no roses left over.

Convince Me! Reasoning Why is 122 a reasonable answer for the problem?

Name ___

Practice
Tools
Assessment

Another Example

Divide 4,108 ÷ 82.

$$\begin{array}{r} 50 \\ 82\overline{)4108} \\ -\ \underline{4100} \\ 8 \end{array}$$

41 hundreds divided into 82 equal groups is 5 tens in each group
82 groups of 50 = 4,100
left over

Think 41 hundreds divided into 82 equal groups.

4,108 ÷ 82 = 50 R8 because 82 × 50 + 8 = 4,108.

Guided Practice

Do You Understand?

1. Use place-value blocks to model 3,710 ÷ 18.

Do You Know How?

In **2–5**, divide. Use place-value blocks to help.

2. 4,632 ÷ 15
3. 3,332 ÷ 30
4. $25\overline{)1,013}$
5. $40\overline{)916}$

Independent Practice

In **6**, draw an area model for the division problem.

6. $16\overline{)3,418}$

In **7–12**, divide. Use place-value blocks or area models to help.

7. 7,905 ÷ 35
8. 5,500 ÷ 90
9. 2,838 ÷ 11
10. $46\overline{)875}$
11. $28\overline{)1,240}$
12. $18\overline{)6,020}$

Problem Solving

13. **Number Sense** The booster club picked 1,370 apples. They plan to sell bags of apples with 15 apples in each bag. How many bags can they make? Explain.

14. Mason teaches ice skating. He earns $24.50 per lesson. How much does he earn in 5 days if he gives 6 lessons per day?

15. **Reasoning** A delivery to the flower shop is recorded at the right. The shop makes centerpiece arrangements using 36 flowers that are all the same type. Will they be able to make at least 10 arrangements using each type of flower? At least 100 arrangements? Explain.

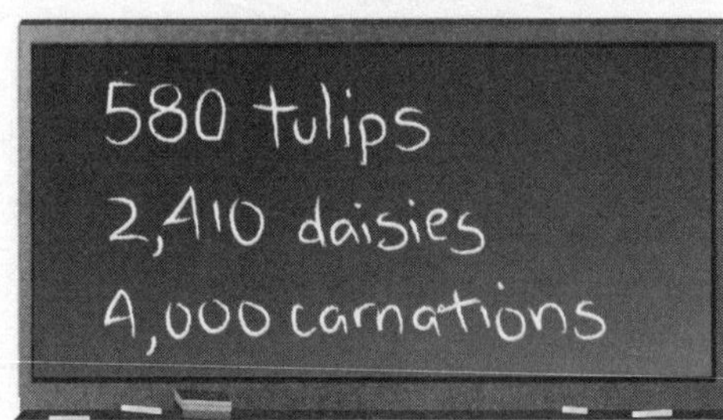

16. Amelia and Ben have two different answers for $1,955 \div 85$. Without dividing, how can you tell who might be correct?

Amelia: $1,955 \div 85 = 23$
Ben: $1,955 \div 85 = 203$

17. **Higher Order Thinking** Estimate the quotient of $4,839 \div 15$ to the nearest hundred. Explain how you found the estimate.

Assessment Practice

18. Find $5,092 \div 38$. How can you check the reasonableness of your answer?

Name ____________________ Activity

Solve & Share

Choose a strategy to solve each problem. Explain your solutions.

Problem 1: Bob's Citrus and Nursery sells cartons of citrus fruits. There are 24 oranges in each carton. They have 5,643 oranges to pack into cartons. How many cartons can they fill?

Problem 2: This year, 4,338 grapefruits have been harvested so far. Bob's has 18 storage bins for grapefruits. If the grapefruits are distributed evenly among the 18 bins, how many grapefruits are in each bin?

Lesson 5-7

Choose a Strategy to Divide

I can ...

select from different strategies to divide

Content Standard 5.NBT.B.6
Mathematical Practices MP.1, MP.2

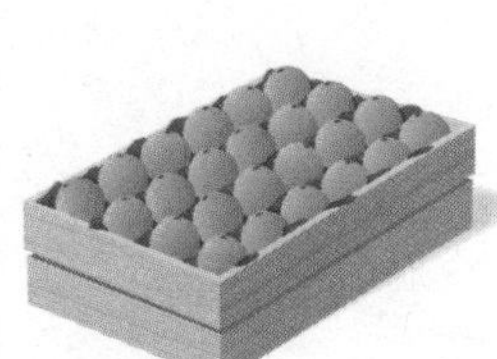

The numbers and the situations in the problems can help you choose strategies. *Show your work!*

Look Back! Make Sense and Persevere How are your two strategies alike? How are they different?

 Visual Learning  Glossary

What Are Some Different Strategies I Can Use to Solve a Division Problem?

Visual Learning Bridge

A

A company has three printers. The printer in Room 102 is for all of their 15 employees to use. If the available pages are distributed evenly among the employees, how many pages can each employee use?

Printer	Number of Pages Available to Print
Room 101	4,618
Room 102	3,720
Room 103	5,075

B

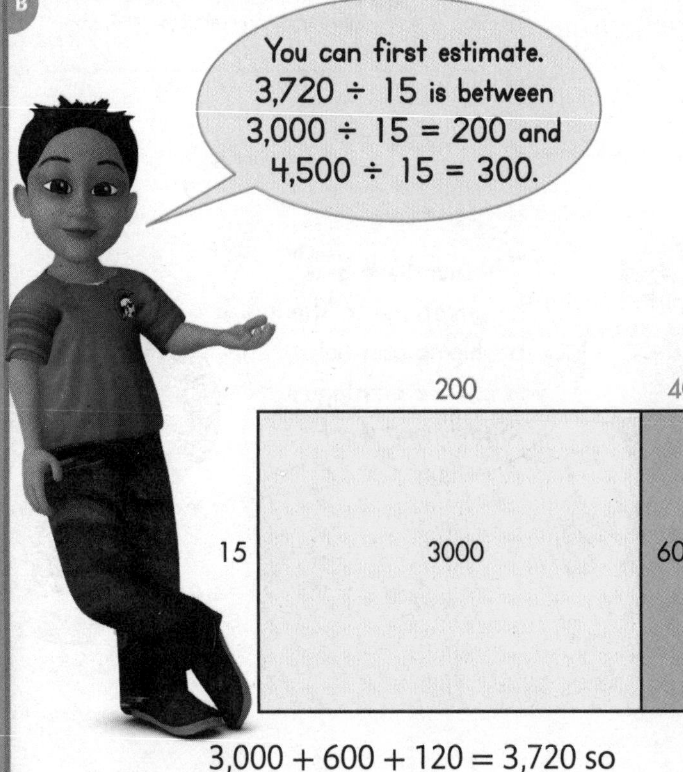

	200	40	8
15	3000	600	120

$3{,}000 + 600 + 120 = 3{,}720$ so
$3{,}720 \div 15 = 248$.

$$
\begin{array}{r l}
248 & \\
15\overline{)3720} & \\
-\underline{3000} & \text{15 groups of 200 = 3,000.} \\
720 & \\
-\underline{600} & \text{15 groups of 40 = 600.} \\
120 & \\
-\underline{120} & \text{15 groups of 8 = 120.} \\
0 &
\end{array}
$$

Each employee can print 248 pages.

Convince Me! Reasoning How can you check your answer?

Name ______________________

Practice
Tools
Assessment

Another Example

How many 32-page brochures can the printer in Room 101 print?

```
     4 ⎫
    40 ⎬ 144
   100 ⎭
32)4618
 − 3200   100 groups of 32
   1418
 − 1280   40 groups of 32
    138
 −  128   4 groups of 32
     10   10 pages are left over.
```

The printer in Room 101 can print 144 brochures.

You need to find how many 32s are in 4,618. You can use division and show partial quotients. You can estimate 4,618 ÷ 32 using 4,500 ÷ 30 = 150.

Guided Practice

Do You Understand?

1. Can the remainder be greater than the divisor? Why or why not?

Do You Know How?

2. Estimate 452 ÷ 21.

3. Divide.
21)452

Remember to check that your answer is reasonable.

Independent Practice

In **4–11**, estimate and then find the quotient. Use your estimate to check for reasonableness.

4. 54)378 **5.** 83)664 **6.** 761 ÷ 5 **7.** 510 ÷ 30

8. 7,704 ÷ 24 **9.** 7,830 ÷ 33 **10.** 3,136 ÷ 64 **11.** 6,253 ÷ 71

Problem Solving

For **12**, use the table at right.

12. Make Sense and Persevere Bob's sells tangelo gift cartons each December. Last year, they shipped a total of 3,300 tangelos. If each carton sells for $28, how much money did Bob's earn from the tangelo gift cartons sold?

DATA

Bob's Citrus Gift Cartons

Citrus Fruit	Number per Carton
Grapefruits	18
Oranges	24
Tangelos	12

13. Higher Order Thinking A *score* is a group of 20 things. For example, a period of 20 years is called a score of years. The Statue of Liberty was dedicated in 1886. About how many scores of years ago was that?

14. At an automobile plant, each car is inspected by 34 different workers before it is shipped to a dealer. One day, workers performed 9,690 inspections. How many cars were shipped? Explain.

9,690

?

Assessment Practice

15. For which division problems is 46 the quotient? Write those division problems in the box.

Quotient = 46

10)4,600 21)966 53)2,385
43)946 46)2,116

Name ____________________

Activity

Write a word problem for the equation:

$2{,}530 \div 23 = q$

Solve your problem any way you choose.

Problem Solving

Lesson 5-8

Make Sense and Persevere

I can ...

make sense of problems and keep working if I get stuck.

Mathematical Practices MP.1
Also MP.2, MP.3
Content Standard 5.NBT.B.6

Thinking Habits

Be a good thinker! These questions can help you.

- What information is provided?
- How are the quantities related to each other?
- What strategies do I know for solving this type of problem?
- What tools might help me?
- How can I check that my solution makes sense?

Look Back! Make Sense and Persevere Does your word problem ask you to find the equal number in each group, or the number of equal groups?

How Can You Make Sense of Problems and Persevere in Solving Them?

Visual Learning Bridge

A

For 3 months, a fifth-grade class raised money for charities. If the class divides the money equally among 32 different organizations, how many dollars will each organization receive and how many dollars will be left over?

DATA

Funds Raised	
September	\$1,104
October	\$2,117
November	\$3,275

You can make sense of the problem by answering these questions. How much money was raised in all? How much should each organization get?

B

How can I make sense of and solve the problem?

I can

- identify the quantities given.
- understand how the quantities are related.
- choose and implement an appropriate strategy.
- check to be sure my work and answer make sense.

C

Here's my thinking...

First, I can write an addition equation to find the total amount raised:

$1{,}104 + 2{,}117 + 3{,}275 = 6{,}496$

Next, I can write a division equation to model equal sharing:

$6{,}496 \div 32 =$
$(6400 + 96) \div 32 =$
$(6400 \div 32) + (96 \div 32) =$
$200 + 3 = 203$

So, each organization will receive \$203.

Convince Me! Critique Reasoning Julio says that you can solve this problem by dividing each month's total by 32 and then adding the three quotients together. Do you agree? Do you think his approach is easier or harder? Justify your answer.

Stuck? Try solving a simpler problem.

Name

Practice Tools Assessment

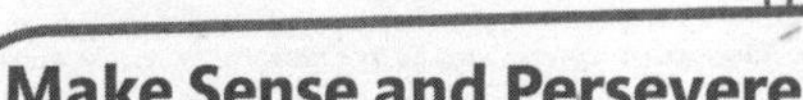

Guided Practice

Make Sense and Persevere

Dana starts with 875 stamps in her stamp collection. Her grandparents give her 332 stamps. Then, she buys 72 more. How many pages in her scrapbook can she fill?

1. What do you know?

2. What are you trying to find?

3. How are the quantities related? What is the answer to the problem? Write equations to model your work.

Independent Practice

Make Sense and Persevere

Tanya is saving for a vacation. She wants to have at least $75 for each of the 12 days of her trip. If she saves $85 each month for 10 months, will she save enough money?

4. Use the strategy of mental math to find the total amount she will save. Then, write a division equation to see if she will save enough.

5. Jorge says he can solve this problem a different way. He says that he can compare 85 × 10 and 75 × 12. Do you agree? Explain your thinking.

Problem Solving

Performance Task

Pumpkin Patch Farms
The table shows the number of seeds the owners of Pumpkin Patch Farms received from different seed suppliers. Each of the pumpkins they harvest usually weighs between 10 and 12 pounds. There are 60 rows, and the farmers will plant the same number of seeds in each row. How many seeds will they plant in each row?

DATA

Seed Supplier	Number of Seeds
Sid's Seeds	1,220
Vicki's Seed Supply	750
Seeds and More	1,450

6. **Make Sense and Persevere** What do you know? What are you trying to find?

7. **Reasoning** How are the quantities in the problem related? What steps are needed to solve the problem?

8. **Model with Math** Write equations with variables to represent the steps needed to solve the problem.

9. **Be Precise** Solve the equations and answer the question.

10. **Reasoning** What strategy can you use to check that your answer makes sense?

Think about the problem-solving strategies to help you!

Name ______________________________

Fluency Practice Activity

Work with a partner. Get paper and a pencil. Each partner chooses light blue or dark blue.

At the same time, Partner 1 and Partner 2 each point to one of their black numbers. Both partners find the product of the two numbers.

The partner who chose the color where the product appears gets a tally mark. Work until one partner has seven tally marks.

I can ...
multiply multi-digit whole numbers.

Content Standard 5.NBT.B.5
Mathematical Practices MP.3, MP.6, MP.7, MP.8

Partner 1: 52, 68, 97, 451, 213

884	5,238	3,672	5,964
24,354	11,502	7,668	2,808
1,649	1,156	2,448	20,746
12,628	2,716	1,456	4,462
1,872	2,392	7,667	9,798
16,236	3,128	3,621	1,904

Partner 2: 17, 54, 46, 36, 28

Tally Marks for Partner 1	Tally Marks for Partner 2

Vocabulary Review

Word List

- compatible numbers
- dividend
- divisor
- estimate
- multiple
- product
- quotient
- remainder

Understand Vocabulary

Choose the best term from the Word List. Write it on the blank.

1. One way to estimate the answer to a division problem is to replace the divisor and dividend with ________________.

2. The part that is left when you divide into equal groups is called the ________________.

3. To decide where to place the first digit of a quotient, ________________ the number of digits in the answer.

4. The answer to a division problem is the ________________.

For each of these terms, give an example and a non-example.

	Example	Non-example
5. Multiple of 10	________	________
6. Product of 10	________	________
7. Quotient of 10	________	________

Use Vocabulary in Writing

8. Write a division problem with a 3-digit dividend, a divisor of 20, and remainder of 10. Use at least three of the terms in the Word List to explain how you chose the numbers for your example.

Name ____

Reteaching

Set A pages 181–184

Find 32,000 ÷ 80 using mental math.

Use basic facts and place-value patterns to help.

32 ÷ 8 = 4
320 ÷ 80 = 4
3,200 ÷ 80 = 40
32,000 ÷ 80 = 400

Remember to look for a basic division fact in the numbers. Check your answer by multiplying.

Find each quotient. Use mental math.

1. 360 ÷ 40 **2.** 270 ÷ 90

3. 2,100 ÷ 30 **4.** 4,800 ÷ 80

5. 72,000 ÷ 80 **6.** 81,000 ÷ 90

Set B pages 185–188

Estimate 364 ÷ 57.

Use compatible numbers and patterns to divide.

364 ÷ 57
↓ ↓
360 ÷ 60 = 6

So, 364 ÷ 57 is about 6.

Remember that compatible numbers are numbers that are easy to compute mentally.

Estimate using compatible numbers.

1. 168 ÷ 45 **2.** 525 ÷ 96

3. 379 ÷ 63 **4.** 234 ÷ 72

5. \$613 ÷ 93 **6.** \$748 ÷ 92

Set C pages 189–192

Find 195 ÷ 13.

Draw a model to help you find the number of tens and ones in the quotient.

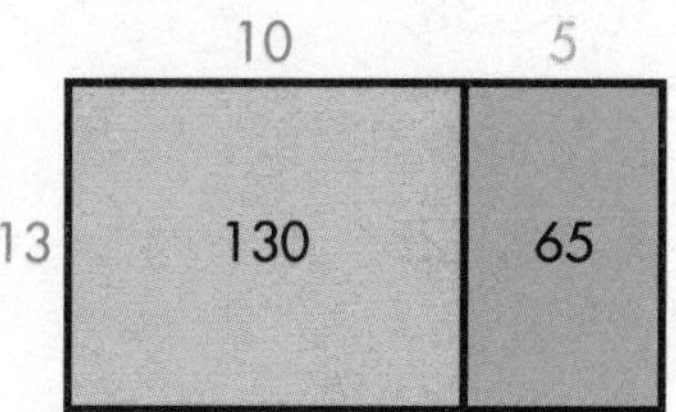

1 ten + 5 ones = 15.

So, 195 ÷ 13 = 15.

Remember to find the number of tens first, then find the number of ones.

Use a model to find each quotient.

1. 180 ÷ 15 **2.** 154 ÷ 14

3. 351 ÷ 27 **4.** 192 ÷ 16

5. 143 ÷ 11 **6.** 217 ÷ 31

7. 130 ÷ 26 **8.** 270 ÷ 18

Set D pages 193–196

Find 336 ÷ 21 using partial quotients.

$$\begin{array}{r} 6 \\ 10 \\ 21\overline{)336} \\ -210 \\ \hline 126 \\ -126 \\ \hline 0 \end{array}$$

10 groups of 21 = 210

6 groups of 21 = 126

Add the partial quotients: 10 + 6 = 16.

So, 336 ÷ 21 = 16.

Remember to add the partial quotients to find the actual quotient.

Use partial quotients to divide.

1. $30\overline{)570}$ **2.** $17\overline{)714}$

3. $24\overline{)984}$ **4.** $40\overline{)920}$

5. $13\overline{)858}$ **6.** $29\overline{)986}$

7. $35\overline{)980}$ **8.** $73\overline{)803}$

Set E pages 197–200

Find 461 ÷ 50.

$$\begin{array}{r} 9 \\ 50\overline{)461} \\ -450 \\ \hline 11 \end{array}$$

50 groups of 9 = 450

11 left over

Remember that you can check your answer by multiplying the quotient by the divisor, and then adding any remainder.

1. $20\overline{)420}$ **2.** $31\overline{)558}$

3. $45\overline{)387}$ **4.** $58\overline{)653}$

5. $59\overline{)826}$ **6.** $70\overline{)910}$

7. $78\overline{)698}$ **8.** $27\overline{)849}$

9. Ivan uses 30 craft sticks to make each toy cabin. He has a box of 342 craft sticks. How many toy cabins can Ivan make? How many sticks will be left?

Name ____

Set F pages 201–204

Find 3,657 ÷ 23.

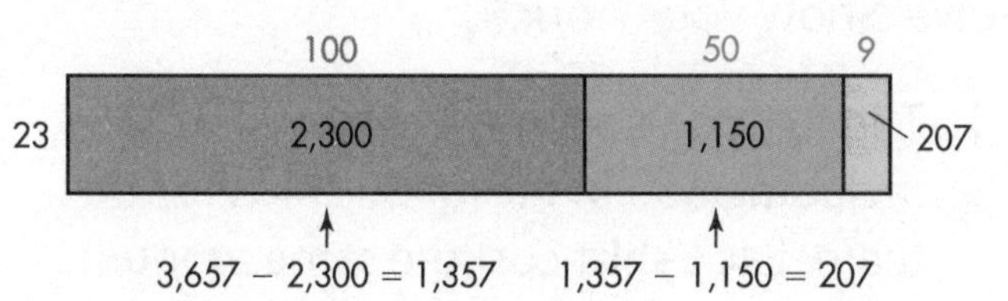


```
     159
23)3,657   36 hundreds divided into 23 equal groups is
           1 hundred in each group
  −2,300   23 groups of 100 = 2,300
   1,357   135 tens divided into 23 equal groups is 5 tens
           in each group
  −1,150   23 groups of 50 = 1,150
     207   207 ones divided into 23 equal groups is
           9 ones in each group
    −207   23 groups of 9 = 207
       0   nothing left over
```

Remember you can multiply the divisor by powers of 10 to estimate the quotient.

Divide. Use place-value blocks to help.

1. 14)966
2. 53)6,519
3. 91)728
4. 72)2,376
5. 26)8,168
6. 66)612
7. 40)5,520
8. 39)3,871

Set G pages 205–208

Find 789 ÷ 19.

```
     41
19)789   78 tens divided into 19 equal groups is
         4 tens in each group
  −760   19 groups of 40 = 760
    29   29 ones divided into 19 equal groups is
         1 one in each group
   −19   19 groups of 1 = 19
    10   left over
```

Remember that you can check your answer by multiplying the quotient by the divisor, and then adding any remainder.

1. 16)224
2. 38)792
3. 42)504
4. 47)5,170
5. 58)7,211
6. 12)3,549
7. 25)1,352
8. 33)1,500
9. 42)5,825
10. 28)2,941

Set H pages 209–212

Think about these questions to help you **make sense and persevere** in solving problems.

Thinking Habits

- What do I know?
- What do I need to find?
- What's my plan for solving the problem?
- What else can I try if I get stuck?
- How can I check that my solution makes sense?

Selena is planning to visit her aunt in 5 weeks. She has saved \$365 but thinks the trip will cost \$500. She plans to save the same amount each week so she has \$500 for the trip. How much does she need to save each week?

I can write an equation to find how much more money Selena needs:

$500 - 365 = 135$

Then divide the amount she needs by 5 weeks: $135 \div 5 = 27$

Selena needs to save \$27 each week.

My answer is reasonable because $365 + 27 + 27 + 27 + 27 + 27 = 500$.

Remember to think about what steps are needed to solve each problem.

Solve. Show your work.

1. The football coach spent a total of \$890 including \$50 in tax for 35 shirts for the team. Each shirt cost the same amount. What was the price of one shirt before tax was added?

2. A gymnast practices 6 days each week. She practices the same number of hours each day. If she practices a total of 120 hours in a 4-week period, how many hours each day does she practice?

3. Nathan works the same number of hours each day, 5 days each week. He earns \$12 per hour. Last week he earned \$420. How many hours did he work each day last week? Write equations to model your work.

4. A high-rise apartment building has 15 floors with 26 apartments on each floor. There are 3 kinds of apartments in the building: 1-, 2-, and 3-bedroom. The building has the same number of each kind of apartment. How many of each kind of apartment are in the building? Show your work.

Name ______________________________

1. Select all of the following equations the number 60 will make true.

- ☐ 420 ÷ ☐ = 70
- ☐ 1,800 ÷ ☐ = 300
- ☐ 5,400 ÷ ☐ = 90
- ☐ 2,400 ÷ ☐ = 40
- ☐ 500 ÷ ☐ = 10

2. Which of the following is the best estimate of 487 ÷ 67?

Ⓐ 80
Ⓑ 70
Ⓒ 10
Ⓓ 7

3. The carnival committee has purchased 985 small prizes. The prizes are to be divided equally among the 20 game booths.

A. In what place will the first digit of the quotient be?

☐

B. How many prizes will each booth have?

☐

C. How many prizes will be left?

☐

4. A rectangular living room has an area of 425 square feet. The width of the room is 17 feet.

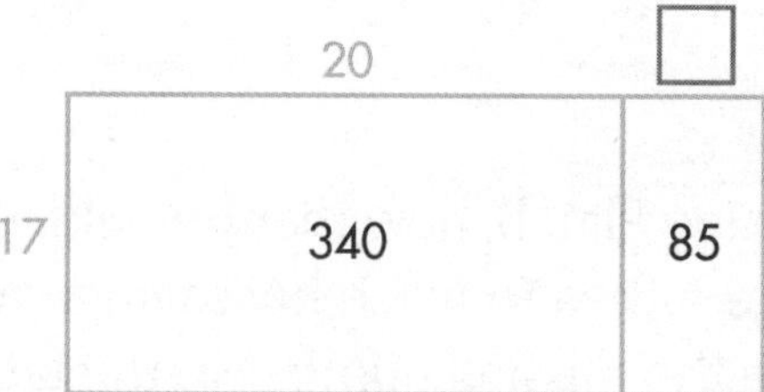

Write a number in the box to show the missing dimension.

What is the length of the room?

___ feet

5. **A.** Divide.

2,700 ÷ 30 = _____

B. Select all the expressions that are equal to 2,700 ÷ 30.

- ☐ 270 ÷ 3
- ☐ 270 tens ÷ 3 tens
- ☐ 2,700 ÷ 3 tens
- ☐ 2,700 ÷ 3
- ☐ 2,700 tens ÷ 30

6. Select the quotient for each expression.

	700	7	60	70
420 ÷ 6	☐	☐	☐	☐
420 ÷ 60	☐	☐	☐	☐
4,200 ÷ 6	☐	☐	☐	☐
4,200 ÷ 70	☐	☐	☐	☐

7. Use the table.

Althea's Plans for Saving $384		
Plan	Amount to Save Each Week	Number of Weeks Needed
A	$20	20
B	$30	
C	$50	8

A. Using Plan B, how many weeks will it take Althea to reach her savings goal? Write the missing number in the table.

B. Show how you found your answer to **A.**

8. Five Star Farm purchased 2,400 apple trees. If 80 trees can be planted on each acre of land, how many acres will be needed to plant all the trees?

A. Identify which expression represents the problem.

Ⓐ 2,400 × 80
Ⓑ 80 ÷ 2,400
Ⓒ 80 × 2,400
Ⓓ 2,400 ÷ 80

B. How many acres will be needed to plant all the trees?

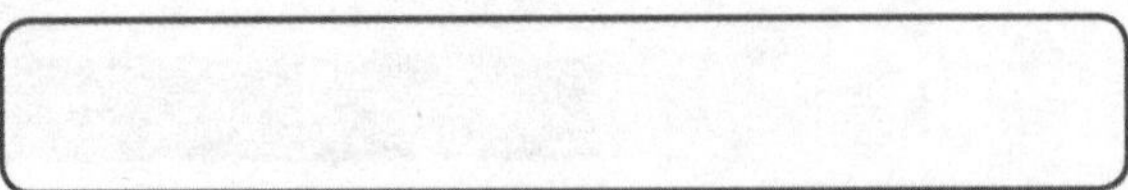

9. Mrs. Reiss has 264 crayons for her art class of 22 students. How many crayons will each student get if the crayons are divided equally? Use the model.

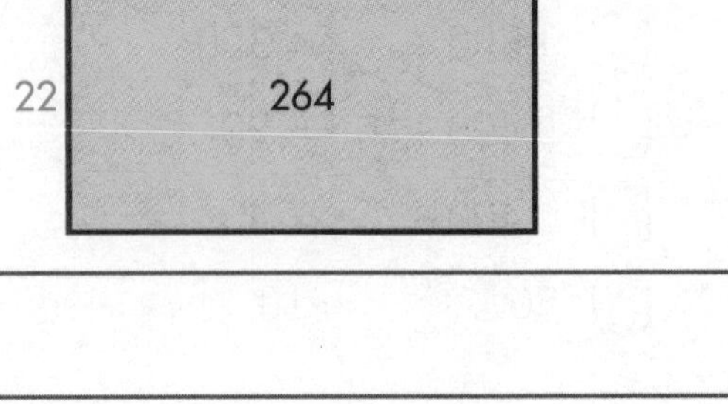

10. Select all the expressions that have the value of 9.

- ☐ 270 ÷ 3
- ☐ 250 ÷ 25
- ☐ 270 ÷ 30
- ☐ 207 ÷ 23
- ☐ 189 ÷ 21

11. Kari wants to find 3,277 ÷ 29.

A. Without doing the division, which number will the quotient be closest to?

Ⓐ 1
Ⓑ 10
Ⓒ 100
Ⓓ 1,000

B. What is the exact quotient?

Name ____________________

12. The cost to rent a lodge for a family reunion is $975. If 65 people attend and pay the same price, how much does each person pay?

A. Which of the following expressions represents the problem?

Ⓐ $975 + 65$ Ⓒ 975×65

Ⓑ $975 \div 65$ Ⓓ $975 \div 2$

B. How much does each person pay?

Ⓐ $16 Ⓒ $14

Ⓑ $15 Ⓓ $13

13. Shady Rivers summer camp has 188 campers this week. If there are 22 campers to each cabin, what is the least number of cabins needed?

Ⓐ 7 cabins Ⓒ 9 cabins

Ⓑ 8 cabins Ⓓ 10 cabins

14. The area of a rectangular banquet hall is 7,400 square feet. The length of one side of the hall is 82 feet. Explain how you can use compatible numbers to estimate the width of the hall.

15. The cost of renting a bus is $1,344. Tony wants to find how much each person will pay if 32 people ride the bus and share the cost equally. Fill in the partial quotients that are missing from Tony's work below.

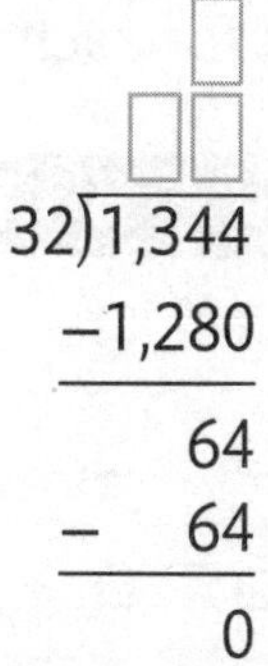

16. Jessie made 312 mini energy bars. She puts 24 bars in each bag. She plans to sell each bag for $6.

A. Write two equations with variables that Jessie can use to find the amount of money she will earn if she sells all of the bags.

B. How much will she earn if she sells all of the bags?

17. Select all of the following equations the number 40 will make true.

- ☐ 280 ÷ ☐ = 7
- ☐ 800 ÷ ☐ = 20
- ☐ 4,000 ÷ ☐ = 10
- ☐ 3,200 ÷ ☐ = 80
- ☐ 800 ÷ ☐ = 200

18. Select the quotient for each expression.

	9	80	90	8
2,700 ÷ 30	☐	☐	☐	☐
270 ÷ 30	☐	☐	☐	☐
2,400 ÷ 30	☐	☐	☐	☐
240 ÷ 30	☐	☐	☐	☐

19. Charles burns 4,350 calories hiking 15 miles of the Appalachian Trail. How many calories does he burn each mile?

A. Identify which expression represents the problem.

Ⓐ 4,350 ÷ 15

Ⓑ 4,350 × 15

Ⓒ 4,350 – 15

Ⓓ 4,350 ÷ 10

B. How many calories does he burn each mile?

20. Find the quotient 432 ÷ 48.

21. Which partial quotients could be added to find 465 ÷ 15?

Ⓐ 20 and 1

Ⓑ 30 and 1

Ⓒ 30 and 9

Ⓓ 30 and 10

22. The table shows the number of students going on field trips. For each trip, one adult is needed for every 15 students.

DATA

Grade	Number of Students
Fifth Grade	310
Sixth Grade	305
Seventh Grade	225

How many adults are needed to go on the seventh grade trip?

Name ____________________

School Supplies

A store had a sale on school supplies in August. The store manager recorded how many of several types of items were sold. Each of the same type of item cost the same amount. Use the information in the table to answer the questions.

School Supply	Backpacks	Paper	Notebooks	Pens	Pencils
Number Sold	60	616	432	568	784

1. Backpack sales totaled $1,200. How much did each backpack cost? Write an equation to model your work.

2. The store sold 71 packages of pens. Use compatible numbers to estimate how many pens were in each package. Show your work.

3. There were 16 pencils in each box. Olivia wants to find how many boxes of pencils were sold.

Part A

When Olivia divides 784 by 16, in which place should she write the first digit of the quotient? Tell how you know without dividing.

Part B

How many boxes of pencils were sold?

4. The store manager has ordered the calculators shown, but the shipment has been delayed.

$19 for each calculator

Part A

If all the calculators ordered are sold, the total sales would be $2,014. Was the number of calculators ordered less than or greater than 100? How do you know without dividing?

Part B

How many calculators were ordered? Write an equation to model your work.

5. The manager wants to order 408 more notebooks. The notebooks are shipped in packages of 12. He used partial quotients to find the number of packages to order. His work is shown at the right. Is his solution correct? Explain.

```
  40
  30
12)408
  -360
    48
   -48
     0
```

6. An additional 40 packages of paper were ordered at a total cost of $520. How much did each package of paper cost? Write an equation to model your work.

Use Models and Strategies to Divide Decimals

Essential Question: What are some common procedures for estimating and finding quotients involving decimals?

Digital Resources

Interactive Student Edition | Activity | Visual Learning | Video | Practice

Assessment | Games | Tools | Glossary

Water is the only substance on Earth that exists in nature as a solid, as a liquid, and as a gas.

Solid water is ice. Water as a gas is water vapor. The same water molecules that we find in liquid water are also in water vapor and ice: H_2O.

Cool! I can skate on water – solid water, not liquid water! Here's a project on states of water.

ënVision STEM Project: States of Water

Do Research Use the Internet or other sources to learn about the states of water. Find at least 5 examples of water in nature as a solid, as a liquid, and as a gas. At what temperature does liquid water change to ice? At what temperature does liquid water change to water vapor?

Journal: Write a Report Include what you found. Also in your report:

- Explain how liquid water changes to ice and to water vapor.
- At 23°F, 1 inch of rain equals 10 inches of snow. Convert 2 inches of rainfall to snowfall.
- Make up and solve division problems that involve decimals.

Name ____________________

Review What You Know

Vocabulary

Choose the best term from the box. Write it on the blank.

- decimal
- divisor
- dividend
- quotient

1. __________ is the name for the answer to a division problem.

2. A number that is being divided by another number is called the __________.

Whole Number Operations

Find each value.

3. 9,007 − 3,128 **4.** 725,864 + 39,798 **5.** 35 × 17

6. 181 × 42 **7.** 768 ÷ 6 **8.** 506 ÷ 22

9. 6,357 ÷ 60 **10.** 3,320 ÷ 89 **11.** 88,888 ÷ 20

Rounding Decimals

Round each number to the place of the underlined digit.

12. $0.\underline{3}4$ **13.** $9\underline{6}.5$ **14.** $81.\underline{2}7$ **15.** $\underline{2}05.3$

Decimals

16. An insect measured 1.25 cm long. Which number is less than 1.25?

Ⓐ 1.35 Ⓑ 1.3 Ⓒ 1.26 Ⓓ 1.2

17. Explain The grid in this model represents 1. What decimal does the shaded part represent? Explain.

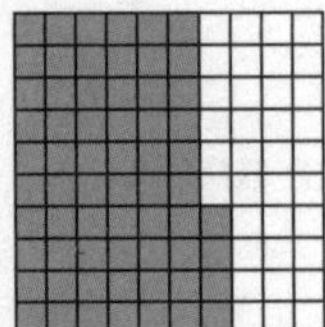

Decimal Operations

Find each value.

18. 23.7 − 11.82 **19.** 66.8 + 3.64 **20.** 9 × 1.4 **21.** 3.2 × 7.6

Name

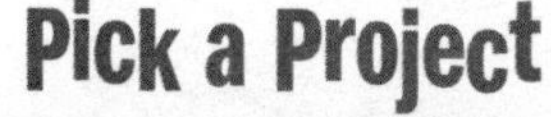

Can you throw a dinner party?

Project: Plan a Party

How much does it cost to run a company?

Project: Build a Company

PROJECT
6C

How do you organize food?

Project: Open Your Own Fruit Stand

PROJECT
6D

Would you like to build a house?

Project: Draw Plans for a Doll House

Name ____________________ Activity

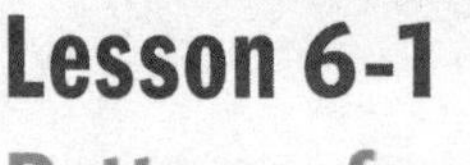

Lesson 6-1
Patterns for Dividing with Decimals

I can ...
use patterns to solve decimal division problems.

Content Standards 5.NBT.A.2 Also 5.NBT.B.7
Mathematical Practices MP.2, MP.7

Solve & Share

An object is 279.4 centimeters wide. If you divide the object into 10 equal parts, how wide will each part be? ***Solve this problem any way you choose.***

How can you use structure and the relationship between multiplication and division to help you?

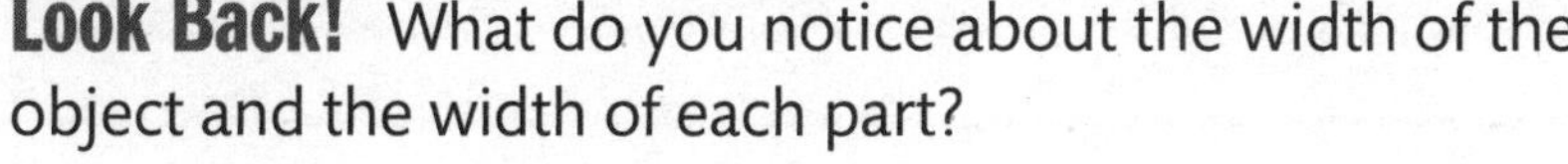

Look Back! What do you notice about the width of the object and the width of each part?

Essential Question How Can You Divide Decimals by Powers of 10?

A

Shondra wants to cut a cloth into 10 strips. All the strips should be exactly the same size. You can use place value and what you know about whole numbers to divide decimals by powers of 10. How long will each strip be?

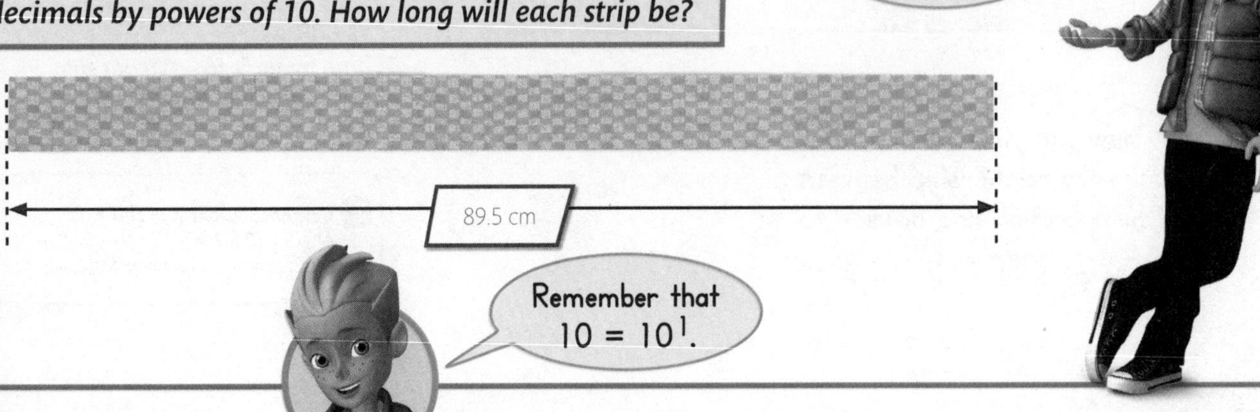

You can divide to find equal parts of a whole.
89.5 cm
Remember that $10 = 10^1$.

B Find 89.5 ÷ 10.

Place value is based on 10. The value of each place is $\frac{1}{10}$ the value of the place to the left. Dividing by 10 results in moving each digit one place to the right. This looks the same as moving the decimal point one place to the left.

	Thousands	Hundreds	Tens	Ones		Tenths	Hundredths	Thousandths
	8	9	5	0	.			
$8{,}950 \div 10^1 =$		8	9	5	.	0		
$895.0 \div 10^1 =$			8	9	.	5	0	
$89.50 \div 10^1 =$				8	.	9	5	0

$89.5 \div 10^1 = 8.95$

Each cloth strip will be 8.95 cm long.

Convince Me! **Use Structure** Celinda thought of 89.5 in parts, $80 + 9 + 0.5$, and divided each part: $80 \div 10 = 8$; $9 \div 10 = \frac{9}{10}$ or 0.9; $0.5 \div 10 = 0.05$. Then she added the parts to get 8.95. What do you notice?

Name

Practice Tools Assessment

Guided Practice

Do You Understand?

1. Suppose Shondra wanted to cut the cloth into 10^2 strips. How long would each strip be?

2. Krista divides a number by 10. Then she divides the same number by 50. Which quotient is greater? How can you tell?

Do You Know How?

In **3–10**, use mental math to find each quotient.

3. $370.2 \div 10^2$
4. $126.4 \div 10^1$
5. $7.25 \div 10$
6. $72.5 \div 10^3$
7. $281.4 \div 10^0$
8. $2{,}810 \div 10^4$
9. $3{,}642.4 \div 10^2$
10. $364.24 \div 10^1$

Independent Practice

Leveled Practice In **11–25**, find each quotient. Use mental math.

11. $4{,}600 \div 10$
$460 \div 10$
$46 \div 10$
$4.6 \div 10$
12. $134.4 \div 10^3$
$134.4 \div 10^2$
$134.4 \div 10^1$
$134.4 \div 10^0$
13. $98.6 \div 1$
$98.6 \div 100$
$98.6 \div 10$
$98.6 \div 1{,}000$
14. $136.5 \div 10$
15. $753 \div 100$
16. $890.1 \div 10^0$
17. $3.71 \div 10^2$
18. $8{,}100 \div 10^4$
19. $864 \div 10^3$
20. $0.52 \div 10^1$
21. $15.7 \div 1{,}000$
22. $7{,}700 \div 10^2$
23. $770 \div 10^2$
24. $77 \div 10^1$
25. $7.7 \div 10^1$

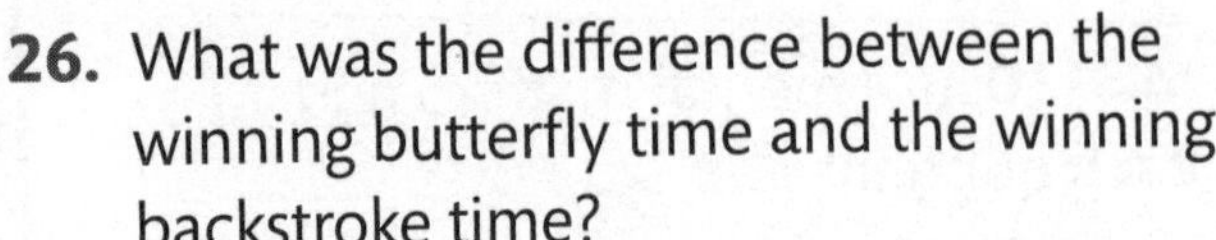

For **26–28**, use the table that shows the winning times at the Pacific Middle School swim meet.

DATA

50-yard freestyle	22.17 seconds
100-yard backstroke	53.83 seconds
100-yard butterfly	58.49 seconds

26. What was the difference between the winning butterfly time and the winning backstroke time?

27. The winning time for the 100-yard freestyle was twice the time for the 50-yard freestyle. What was the winning time for the 100-yard freestyle?

28. What was the difference between the winning 100-yard freestyle time and the winning butterfly time?

29. Reasoning A pickup truck carrying 10^3 identical bricks weighs 6,755 pounds. If the empty truck weighs 6,240 pounds, what is the weight of each brick? Explain how to solve the problem.

30. Higher Order Thinking Katie noticed a pattern in the answers for each of the expressions below. What do you notice?

14.6×0.1 $\quad$ $14.6 \div 10$

146×0.01 $\quad$ $146 \div 100$

146×0.001 $\quad$ $146 \div 1{,}000$

Assessment Practice

31. Choose the equations in which $n = 1{,}000$ makes the equation true.

- ☐ $2.5 \div n = 0.025$
- ☐ $947.5 \div n = 0.9475$
- ☐ $8{,}350 \div n = 8.35$
- ☐ $16.4 \div n = 0.0164$
- ☐ $0.57 \div n = 0.0057$

32. Choose the equations in which $d = 10^2$ makes the equation true.

- ☐ $386.2 \div d = 3.862$
- ☐ $4{,}963.6 \div d = 4.9636$
- ☐ $0.6 \div d = 0.006$
- ☐ $5.8 \div d = 0.58$
- ☐ $15.3 \div d = 0.153$

Name ______________________________

Activity

Solve & Share

A 135.8-foot piece of construction material needs to be cut into pieces that are each 16 feet long. About how many pieces can be cut? ***Solve this problem any way you choose.***

135.8 is about __________.

16 is about __________.

Lesson 6-2
Estimate Decimal Quotients

I can ...
estimate quotients in problems involving decimals.

Content Standard 5.NBT.B.7
Mathematical Practices MP.2, MP.3

You can use reasoning to estimate decimal quotients.

Look Back! **Reasoning** Can you find a different way to estimate the answer for the problem above? Explain.

 Visual Learning  Glossary

How Can You Use Estimation to Find Quotients?

Visual Learning Bridge

A

Diego borrowed money from his parents to purchase a video gaming system for $473.89 (including tax). About how much are his monthly payments to his parents if he wants to pay this off in one year?

You can use division to find equal groups.

B

One Way

Estimate $473.89 ÷ 12. Use rounding.

Round to the nearest ten:
473.89 rounds to 470;
12 rounds to 10.

$473.89 ÷ 12 is about
$470 ÷ 10 = $47.

Each monthly payment will be about $47.

C

Another Way

Estimate $473.89 ÷ 12.
Use compatible numbers.

Look for compatible numbers.

$473.89 ÷ 12 is close to
$480 ÷ 12 = $40.

You know
48 ÷ 12 = 4.

Each monthly payment will be about $40.

Convince Me! **Construct Arguments** In the example above, which estimate is closer to the exact answer? Tell how you decided.

Name ____________________

Practice Tools Assessment

Guided Practice

Do You Understand?

1. **Number Sense** Leo is estimating 53.1 ÷ 8.4. Do you think he should use 53 ÷ 8 or 54 ÷ 9 to estimate? Why?

2. Is each quotient greater than or less than 1? How do you know?

   A 0.2 ÷ 4

   B 1.35 ÷ 0.6

Do You Know How?

In **3–8**, estimate each quotient. Use rounding or compatible numbers.

3. 42 ÷ 6.8
4. 102 ÷ 9.6
5. 48.9 ÷ 4
6. 72.59 ÷ 7
7. 15.4 ÷ 1.9
8. 44.07 ÷ 6.3

Independent Practice

Leveled Practice In **9** and **10**, complete the work to estimate each quotient.

9. Estimate 64.5 ÷ 12.3 using rounding.

   ↓ ↓

   65 ÷ 10 = ____

10. Estimate 64.5 ÷ 12.3 using compatible numbers.

    60 ÷ 12 = ____

In **11–19**, estimate each quotient.

11. 7 ÷ 0.85
12. 9.6 ÷ 0.91
13. 17.7 ÷ 3.2
14. 91.02 ÷ 4.9
15. 45.64 ÷ 6.87
16. 821.22 ÷ 79.4
17. 22.5 ÷ 3
18. 15.66 ÷ 9.3
19. 156.3 ÷ 14.5

Problem Solving

20. Luci's mother gave her $7.50 to buy 8 spiral notebooks. With tax, the cost of each notebook is $1.05. Does Luci have enough money? Use compatible numbers and estimation to help you decide.

21. **Critique Reasoning** Kerri said that the quotient of 4.2 ÷ 5 is about 8 tenths because 4.2 ÷ 5 is close to 40 tenths ÷ 5. Do you agree with Kerri's reasoning? Explain.

22. **Higher Order Thinking** Write a decimal division problem that has an estimated quotient of 4. Explain how to get that estimate.

23. Lia's car averages 14.5 miles per gallon while Roman's car averages 28.5 miles per gallon. Use estimation to find how many times as many miles per gallon Roman's car gets compared to Lia's car.

In **24–26**, use the table.

DATA

Sample	Mass	Temperature
1	0.98 g	37.57°C
2	0.58 g	57.37°C
3	0.058 g	75.50°C
4	0.098 g	73.57°C

24. **enVision® STEM** Which sample from the experiment had the least mass? Which had the lowest temperature?

25. Sample 3 was used in another experiment. A temperature of 82.14°C was recorded. How many degrees did the temperature change?

26. What is the difference in mass between Sample 1 and Sample 2?

Assessment Practice

27. Mauricio scored a total of 34.42 points in five gymnastic events. Which equation shows the best way to estimate Mauricio's score for each event?

Ⓐ 35 ÷ 5 = 7

Ⓑ 35 ÷ 7 = 5

Ⓒ 30 ÷ 10 = 3

Ⓓ 40 ÷ 10 = 4

28. Terry paid $117.50 for 18 identical flash drives. Which is the best estimate for the cost of each flash drive?

Ⓐ $6

Ⓑ $10

Ⓒ $12

Ⓓ $60

Name ___________________________

Activity

Solve & Share

Chris paid $3.60 for 3 colored pens. Each pen costs the same amount. How much did each pen cost? ***Solve this problem any way you choose.***

Lesson 6-3

Use Models to Divide by a 1-Digit Whole Number

I can ...

use models to help find quotients in problems involving decimals.

Content Standard 5.NBT.B.7
Mathematical Practices MP.2, MP.5

You can use appropriate tools such as drawings, money, or place-value blocks to help you divide. *Show your work!*

Look Back! Without dividing, how do you know that the answer to the problem above must be greater than 1?

How Can You Use Models to Find a Decimal Quotient?

Visual Learning Bridge

A

Three friends received $2.58 for aluminum cans they recycled. They decided to share the money equally. How much will each friend get?

You can use place value blocks. Let a 100 square = $1.00, a tenth bar = $0.10, and a hundredth cube = $0.01.

Find 2.58 ÷ 3.

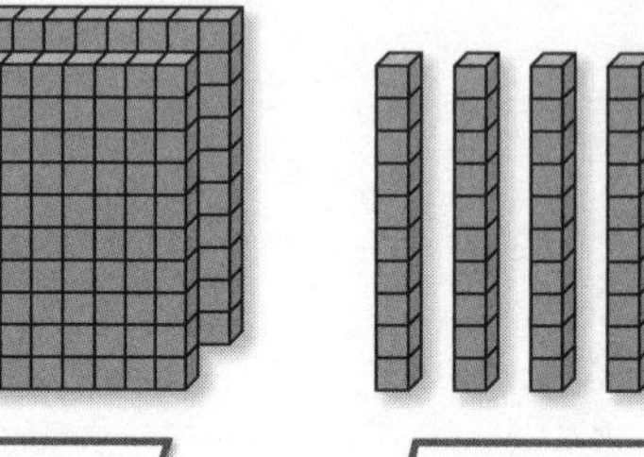
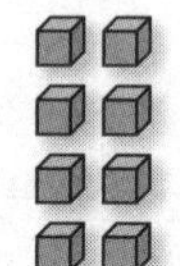

2 ones | 5 tenths | 8 hundredths

B There are not enough ones to put 1 in each group, so regroup the 2 ones into 20 tenths. You can see that there are 25 tenths in 2.58. Divide the 25 tenths into 3 equal groups.

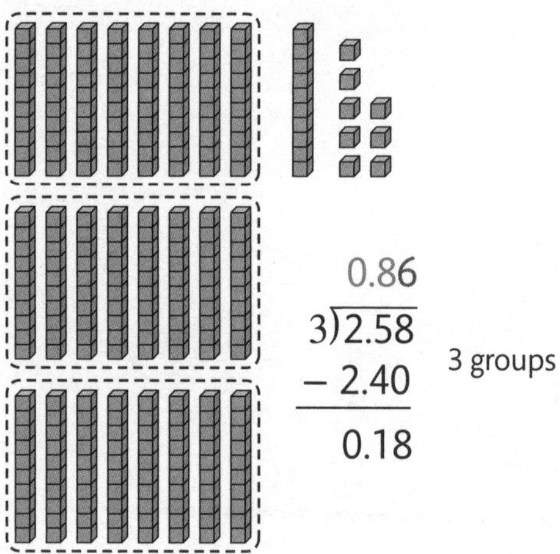

$$\begin{array}{r} 0.86 \\ 3\overline{)2.58} \\ -\,2.40 \\ \hline 0.18 \end{array}$$

3 groups of 0.8 = 2.40.

C Trade the one extra tenth for 10 hundredths to get 18 hundredths. Divide the 18 hundredths into 3 equal groups. Each group gets 6 hundredths.

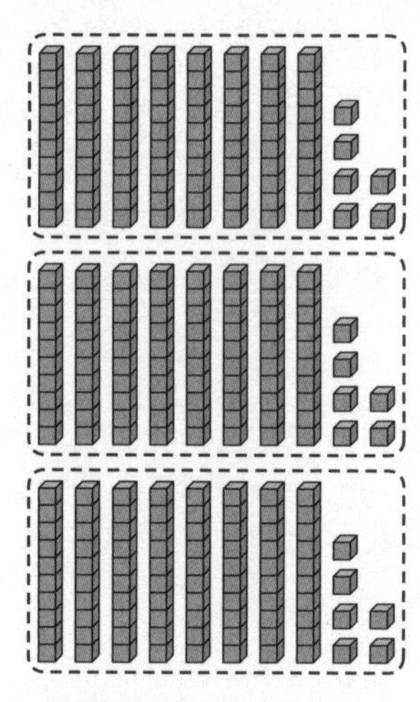

$$\begin{array}{r} 0.86 \\ 3\overline{)2.58} \\ -\,2.40 \\ \hline 0.18 \\ -\,0.18 \\ \hline 0 \end{array}$$

3 groups of 0.8 = 2.40.

3 groups of 0.06 = 0.18.

2.58 ÷ 3 = 0.86

Each of the 3 friends will get $0.86.

Convince Me! **Reasoning** The next week, 4 friends got $8.24 for the cans they collected. How much money will each friend get? Estimate using compatible numbers and then use a strategy to find the answer.

Name

Practice Tools Assessment

Guided Practice

Do You Understand?

1. What is a reasonable estimate for 8.24 ÷ 4? Explain.

2. How is dividing a decimal by a whole number similar to dividing a whole number by a whole number? Explain.

Do You Know How?

3. Use models to help you divide 2.16 ÷ 4. Complete the division calculation.

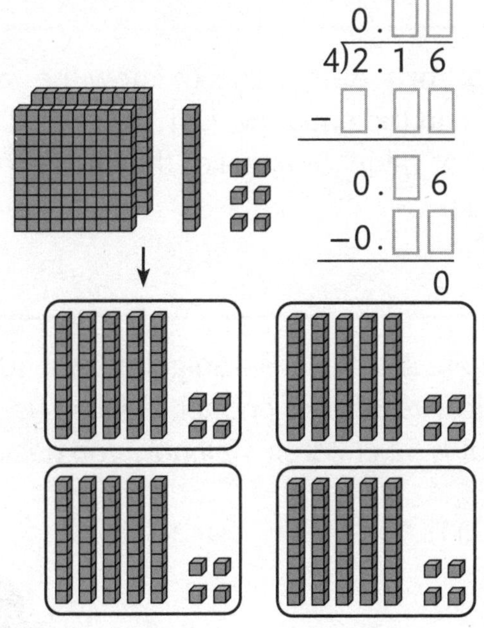

Independent Practice

Leveled Practice In **4–9**, divide. Use or draw models to help.

4.

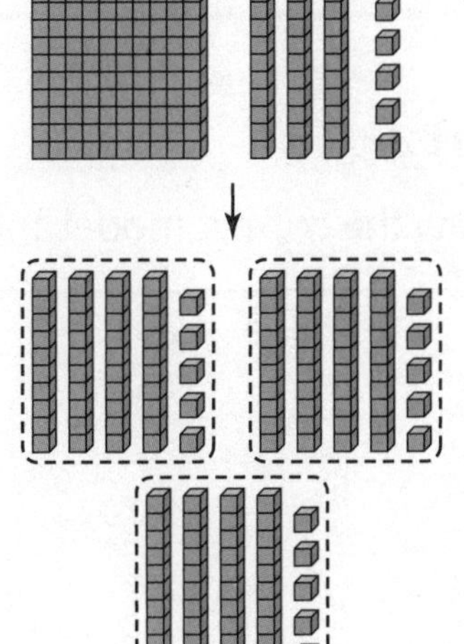

5.

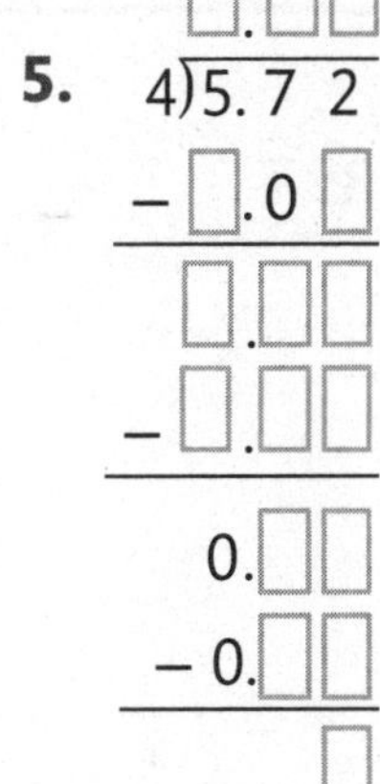

6. 2.38 ÷ 7

7. 4.71 ÷ 3

8. 1.76 ÷ 8

9. 5.36 ÷ 2

Problem Solving

10. **Reasoning** Alan is modeling 2.65 ÷ 5. How should he exchange the place-value blocks so he can make 5 equal shares?

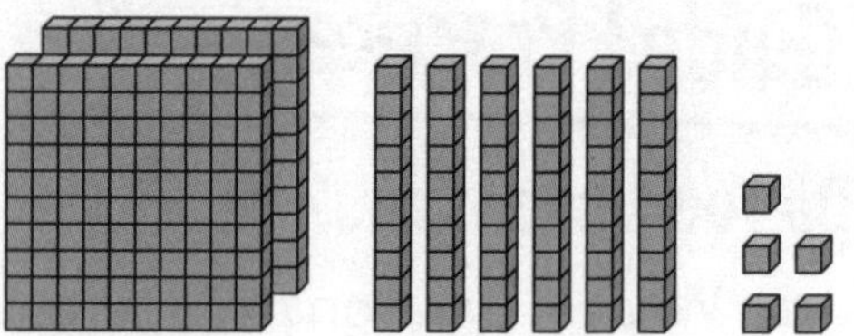

11. **Algebra** Abby wants to know the value of n in the equation $7.913 \times n = 791.3$. What value for n makes the equation true?

12. To find 5.16 ÷ 6, should you divide the ones first or the tenths first? Why?

13. There are 264 children going on a field trip. Are 5 buses enough if each bus holds 52 children? Tell how you decided.

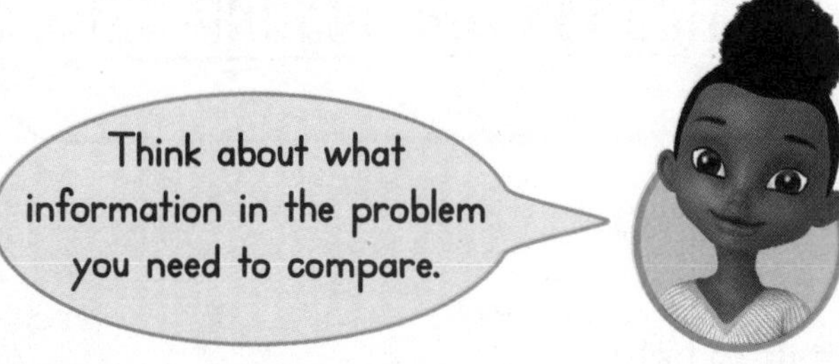

Think about what information in the problem you need to compare.

14. **Higher Order Thinking** Ginny earned \$49.50 for 6 hours of gardening and \$38.60 for 4 hours of babysitting. For which job did she earn more money per hour? How much more per hour did she earn? Explain how you found the answers.

Assessment Practice

15. Tia drew the model below for 1.35 ÷ 3.

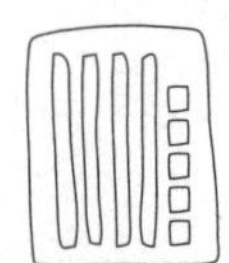 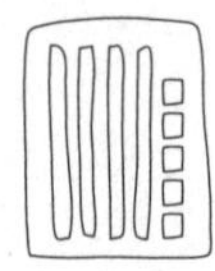 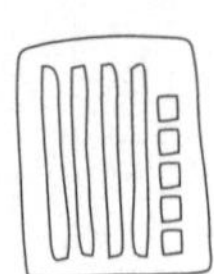 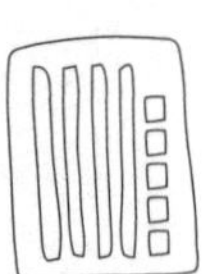

Part A

Explain the mistake Tia made.

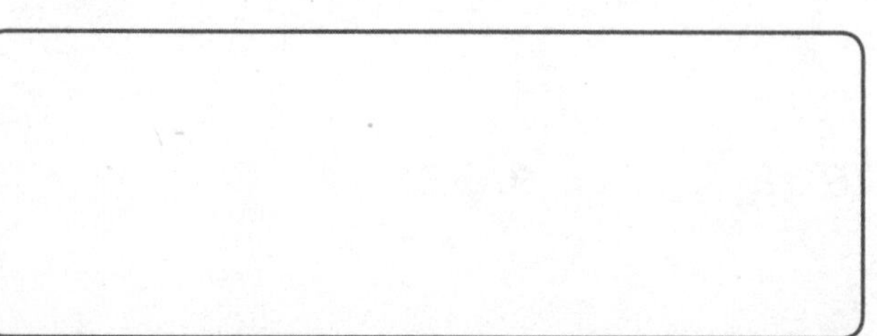

Part B

Draw the correct model and find the quotient.

Name ____________________ Activity

Solve & Share

Stan has a rectangular piece of carpet with an area of 23.4 square meters. The piece of carpet is 13 meters long. What is the width of the piece of carpet? ***Solve this problem any way you choose.***

Lesson 6-4
Divide by a 2-Digit Whole Number

I can ...
divide decimals by a two-digit whole number.

Content Standard 5.NBT.B.7
Mathematical Practices MP.1, MP.2, MP.4

Model with Math
You can write an equation to model the problem.

Look Back! How could you estimate the width of the piece of carpet?

How Do You Divide Decimals by 2-Digit Numbers?

A

Erin's garden has an area of 84.8 square feet. She knows the length is 16 feet. What is the width of Erin's garden? How can you solve $84.8 \div 16 = w$?

You can use what you know about dividing whole numbers to help.

w
16 ft

B

The total area is 84.8. The pieces of the model represent the areas for the partial quotients.

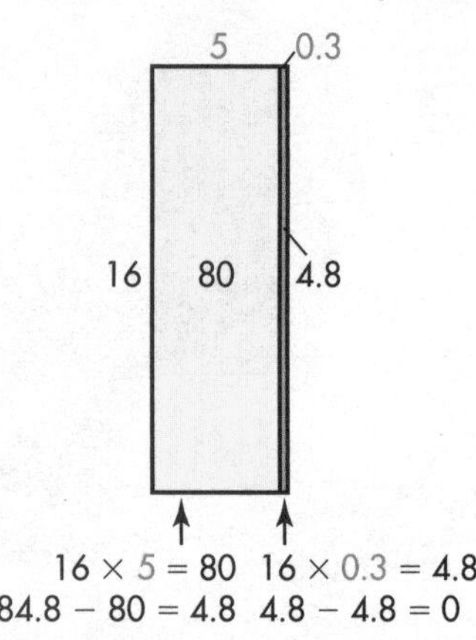

$16 \times 5 = 80$ $\quad 16 \times 0.3 = 4.8$
$84.8 - 80 = 4.8$ $\quad 4.8 - 4.8 = 0$

$5 + 0.3 = 5.3$

So $84.8 \div 16 = 5.3$.

$$\begin{array}{r} 5.3 \\ 16\overline{)84.8} \\ -\ 80.0 \\ \hline 4.8 \\ -\ 4.8 \\ \hline 0 \end{array}$$

$-\ 80.0$: The tan piece of the model has an area of 16×5.

$-\ 4.8$: The blue piece has an area of 16×0.3.

$84.8 \div 16 = 5.3$ because $16 \times 5.3 = 84.8$.

The width is 5.3 feet.

Convince Me! **Reasoning** How could Amy use estimation to make sure the decimal point is in the correct place in the quotient?

Name ____________________

Practice Tools Assessment

Guided Practice

Do You Understand?

In **1** and **2**, use the example on the previous page.

1. Where is 5.3 shown in the diagram?

2. How can you check that the quotient 5.3 is reasonable? Explain.

Do You Know How?

In **3** and **4**, complete the division problem.

3. $49\overline{)306.25}$, quotient □.2□; − □9□.00; 1□.□□; − 9.8□; □.□□; − 2.45; □

4. $15\overline{)28.5}$, quotient 1.□; − □□.□; □□.5; − □□.□; □

Independent Practice

Leveled Practice In **5–6**, find each quotient and label the model.

5. $17\overline{)78.2}$, quotient □□; − □□.0; □□.□; − □□.□; 0

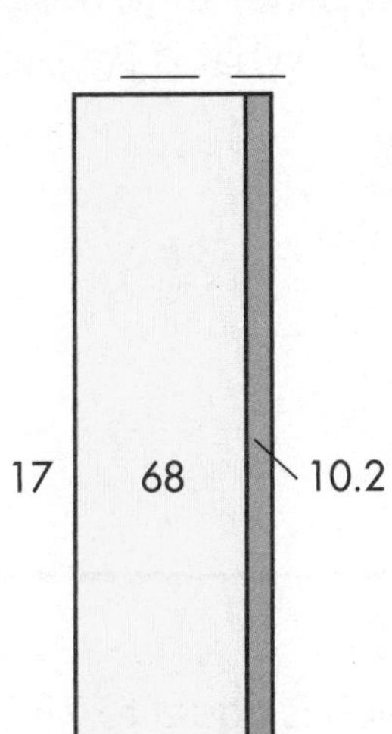

6. $53\overline{)304.75}$, quotient □.7□; − □6□.00; 3□.□5; −37.10; □.□□; − 2.65; □

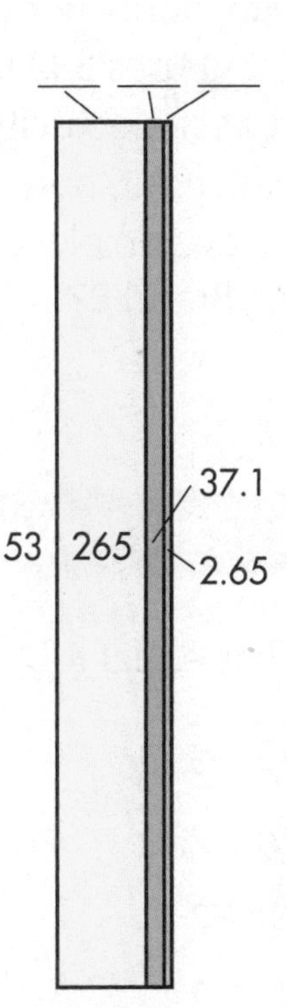

In **7–10**, find each quotient.

7. $27\overline{)91.8}$

8. $15\overline{)3.9}$

9. $12\overline{)39.6}$

10. $50\overline{)247.5}$

Problem Solving

11. Sharon pays $98.75 for twenty-five 14-ounce boxes of Yummy Flakes cereal. How much does one box of cereal cost?

12. Javier bought a new TV for $479.76. He will make equal payments each month for 2 years. How can Javier use compatible numbers to estimate each payment?

13. **Higher Order Thinking** The area of the rectangular flower bed shown is 20.4 square meters. How many meters of edging are needed to go around the flower bed? Explain.

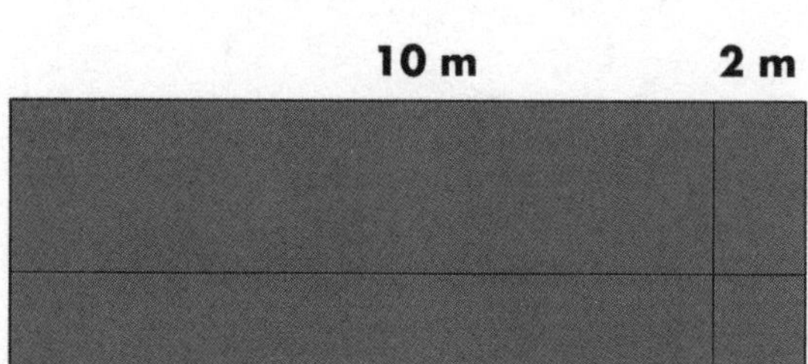

14. **Make Sense and Persevere** Ms. Wang is shopping for a new refrigerator. Brand A costs $569 and uses 635 kilowatt-hours per year. Brand B costs $647 and uses 582 kilowatt-hours per year. If electricity costs $0.18 per kilowatt-hour, how much would Ms. Wang save on electricity per year by buying Brand B?

15. Pat is driving from Seattle to Los Angeles. The distance is 1,135 miles. For the first 250 miles, it costs Pat $0.29 a mile to drive. After that, her driving cost is $0.16 a mile. What is Pat's total driving cost?

Assessment Practice

16. Which is equal to 27.3 divided by 13?

Ⓐ 0.21
Ⓑ 2.01
Ⓒ 2.1
Ⓓ 21

17. Which is equal to 73.5 divided by 21?

Ⓐ 0.35
Ⓑ 3.05
Ⓒ 3.5
Ⓓ 30.5

Name ____________________ Activity

Solve & Share

Aaron buys erasers for his pencils. Each eraser costs $0.20. The total cost is $1.20. How many erasers does Aaron buy? ***Solve this problem any way you choose.***

Lesson 6-5
Divide by a Decimal

I can ...
divide a decimal by another decimal.

Content Standard 5.NBT.B.7
Mathematical Practices MP.2, MP.3, MP.7

You can model the problem using hundredth grids or other drawings. *Show your work!*

Look Back! Reasoning How do you know your answer makes sense?

 Visual Learning  Glossary

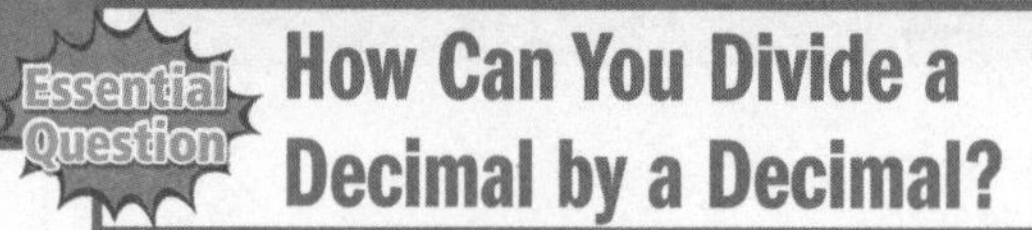

Essential Question: How Can You Divide a Decimal by a Decimal?

Visual Learning Bridge

A

Michelle purchases several bottles of water. Before tax is added, the total cost is \$3.60 and the cost of each bottle is \$1.20. How many bottles did she buy?

Divide \$3.60 by \$1.20.

You can use what you know about division with whole numbers to find how many groups of \$1.20 are in \$3.60.

B

One Way

Think:
\$3.60 is the same as 36 dimes.
\$1.20 is the same as 12 dimes.

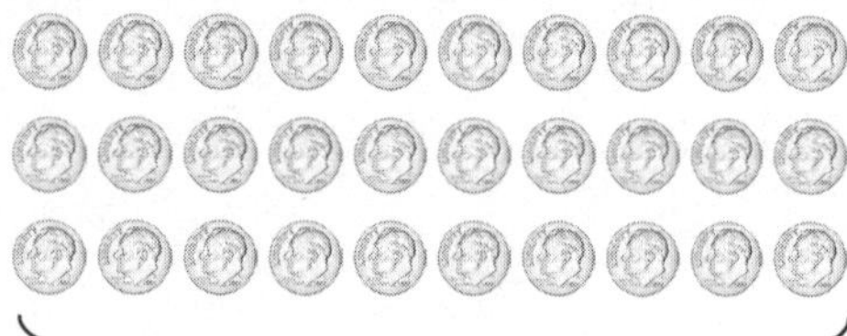

How many 12s are in 36?

$$\begin{array}{r} 3 \\ 12\overline{)36} \\ -\,36 \\ \hline 0 \end{array}$$

3 groups of 12 = 36

She bought 3 bottles.

C

Another Way

Think multiplication:

To find $3.60 \div 1.20$, use the relationship between multiplication and division.

$$1.20 \times ? = 3.60$$

Writing this another way:

120 hundredths × ? = 360 hundredths

? = 3

She bought 3 bottles.

Convince Me! **Construct Arguments** Is $3.6 \div 1.2$ equal to, less than, or greater than $36 \div 12$? Explain.

Name ____

Practice Tools Assessment

Guided Practice

Do You Understand?

1. How is dividing by a decimal like dividing by a whole number?

2. How can you use multiplication to find $2.8 \div 0.7$?

Do You Know How?

In **3–6**, use what you know about decimal division and mental math to find each quotient.

3. $2 \div 0.5$

4. $1.25 \div 0.25$

5. $2.1 \div 0.7$

6. $6.6 \div 0.3$

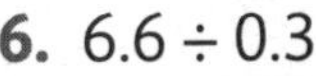

Think about how the dividend, divisor, and quotient are related.

Independent Practice

In **7–10**, use what you know about multiplication, division, place value, and partial quotients to divide.

7. $2.56 \div 0.04$

8. $25.6 \div 0.4$

9. $256 \div 4$

10. Describe the relationship among Problems 7, 8, and 9.

In **11–18**, find each quotient.

11. $0.25\overline{)4.75}$

12. $0.04\overline{)4.56}$

13. $0.05\overline{)1.05}$

14. $0.1\overline{)182.8}$

15. $0.03\overline{)17.25}$

16. $0.8\overline{)56.8}$

17. $0.06\overline{)6.24}$

18. $2.5\overline{)27.5}$

Problem Solving

19. Make up a money story for the equation $3.75 \div 0.25 = 15$.

20. Carol bought 5 pork chops and 3 steaks. Each pork chop weighed 0.32 pound and each steak weighed 0.8 pound. How many pounds of meat did Carol buy in all?

21. Tim estimates that $60 \div 5.7$ is about 10. Will the actual quotient be greater than or less than 10? Explain.

22. Dex estimates that $4,989 \div 0.89$ is about 500. Is his estimate reasonable? Why or why not?

23. **Higher Order Thinking** Susan solves $1.4 \div 0.2$ using the diagram at the right. Is her reasoning correct? Explain her thinking.

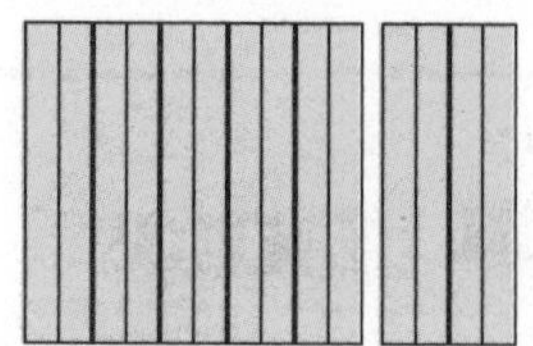

24. **Use Structure** The same dividend is divided by 0.1 and 0.01. How do the quotients compare? Explain your thinking.

25. **Vocabulary** Give three examples of a **power** of 10. Explain why one of your examples is a power of 10.

Assessment Practice

26. Select the expressions that have a quotient of 4.

- ☐ $2.8 \div 0.7$
- ☐ $0.28 \div 7$
- ☐ $2.8 \div 0.07$
- ☐ $0.28 \div 0.07$

27. Select the expressions that have a quotient of 9.

- ☐ $1.35 \div 1.5$
- ☐ $1.35 \div 0.15$
- ☐ $13.5 \div 1.5$
- ☐ $13.5 \div 0.15$

Name ____________________

Activity

Solve & Share

Aaron has three slabs of beeswax. He plans to melt them and use all of the wax to form 36 candles. If all the candles are the same size and weight, how much will each candle weigh? Use reasoning to decide.

BEESWAX 8.2 lb

BEESWAX 8.1 lb

BEESWAX 8.9 lb

Problem Solving

Lesson 6-6
Reasoning

I can ...

make sense of quantities and relationships in problem situations.

Mathematical Practices MP.2 Also MP.4, MP.6
Content Standard 5.NBT.B.7

Thinking Habits

Be a good thinker!
These questions can help you.

- What do the numbers and symbols in the problem mean?
- How are the numbers or quantities related?
- How can I represent a word problem using pictures, numbers, or equations?

Look Back! **Reasoning** Suppose Aaron wants each candle to weigh 0.5 pound. How many candles could he make with the beeswax?

How Can You Use Reasoning to Solve Problems?

A

Ms. Watson is mixing mint green paint for her art class. She combines full bottles of blue, yellow, and white paint. How many 8-fluid ounce jars can she fill? Use reasoning to decide.

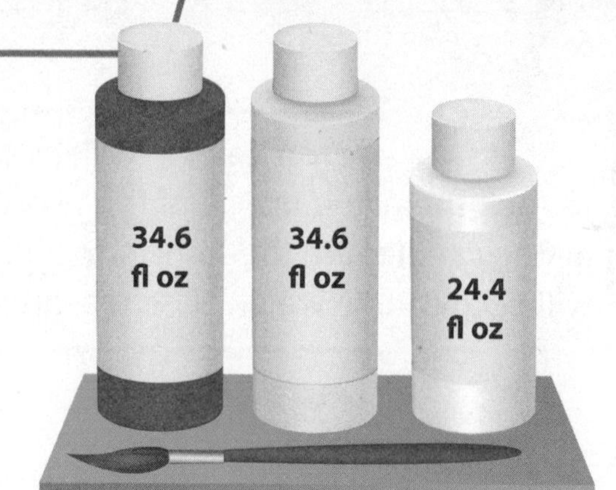

What do I need to do to solve this problem?

I need to add the three quantities of paint. Then I need to divide the sum by the capacity of a jar.

B

How can I use reasoning to solve this problem?

I can

- identify the quantities I know.
- draw a bar diagram to show relationships.
- give the answer using the correct unit.

C

Here's my thinking...

Use bar diagrams to show how the quantities are related.

First, find the sum of the three quantities of paint in the mixture.

? total number of fluid ounces

34.6	34.6	24.4

$$\begin{array}{r} 34.6 \\ 34.6 \\ +\ 24.4 \\ \hline 93.6 \end{array}$$

Then, divide 93.6 by 8 to find the number of jars that can be filled.

93.6

8 → ?

$$\begin{array}{rl} 11.7 & \\ 8\overline{)93.6} & \\ -\ 80.0 & \text{10 groups of } 8 = 80 \\ \hline 13.6 & \\ -\ 8.0 & \text{1 group of } 8 = 8.0 \\ \hline 5.6 & \\ -\ 5.6 & \text{0.7 groups of } 8 = 5.6 \\ \hline 0 & \end{array}$$

Ms. Watson can fill 11 jars. The 12th jar will be only partially filled.

Convince Me! **Reasoning** Ms. Watson is mixing 34.6 fluid ounces of red paint and 18.2 fluid ounces of yellow paint to make orange paint. How many 12-fluid ounce jars can she fill? Use reasoning to decide.

Name ______________________________

Practice
Tools
Assessment

Guided Practice

Reasoning

Miranda mixed 34.5 fluid ounces of blue paint, 40.5 fluid ounces of red paint, and 2 fluid ounces of black paint to make purple paint. She poured the same amount of the purple paint into each of 14 jars. How much paint did she pour in each jar?

Use reasoning to decide how the quantities in the problem are related.

1. Explain what each of the quantities in the problem means.

2. Describe one way to solve the problem.

3. What is the solution to the problem? Explain.

Independent Practice

Reasoning

Sue made chicken soup by combining the entire can of soup shown with a full can of water. How many 10-fluid ounce bowls can she fill with the soup? How much soup will be left over?

SOUP

18.6 fl oz

4. Explain what each of the quantities in the problem means.

5. Describe one way to solve the problem.

6. What is the solution to the problem? Explain.

Performance Task

Cooking Competition

Lucas's cooking class is having a cooking competition. There are 6 teams. Each student brought supplies that will be shared equally among the teams. The table shows the supplies Lucas brought. If the supplies are shared equally among the teams, how much of each supply will each team get?

DATA

Competition Supplies	Price
2 sacks of flour, 4.5 pounds per sack	\$2.67 per sack
3 boxes of rice, 3.5 cups per box	\$1.89 per box
15 pounds of ground turkey	\$2.36 per pound

7. **Make Sense and Persevere** Do you need all of the information given above to solve the problem? Explain.

8. **Reasoning** Describe how to solve the problem.

Use reasoning to think about what the quantities in the table represent.

9. **Model with Math** Write equations to represent how much of each supply each team will get.

10. **Be Precise** What is the solution to the problem? Explain.

11. **Critique Reasoning** Lucas says that to find the total cost of the rice, you should multiply 3.5 by \$1.89. Do you agree? Explain.

Name ______________________________

Fluency Practice Activity

Solve each problem. Follow products that are multiples of 20 to shade a path from **START** to **FINISH**. You can only move up, down, right, or left.

I can ...
multiply multi-digit whole numbers.

Content Standard 5.NBT.B.5
Mathematical Practices MP.3, MP.6, MP.7, MP.8

Start				
120 × 35	745 × 30	123 × 37	350 × 63	241 × 67
312 × 40	300 × 80	486 × 40	860 × 36	523 × 28
526 × 45	101 × 57	670 × 35	606 × 90	647 × 27
105 × 50	273 × 73	475 × 85	464 × 65	173 × 23
710 × 71	157 × 86	243 × 42	660 × 16	12,345 × 76
				Finish

Vocabulary Review

Glossary

Word List

- estimate
- exponent
- hundredths
- power
- quotient
- rounding
- tenths
- thousandths

Understand Vocabulary

Write *always*, *sometimes*, or *never*.

1. A digit in the hundredths place has $\frac{1}{10}$ the value of the same digit in the tenths place. ______
2. The answer to a division problem is less than the divisor. ______
3. A whole number divided by a decimal number is a whole number. ______
4. Dividing by 10^3 moves the decimal point in the dividend three places to the left. ______
5. Multiplying the dividend and the divisor by the same power of 10 changes the quotient. ______
6. The answer to a division problem is greater than the divisor. ______

Write T for true or F for false.

______ 7. $3.65 \div 5.2 < 1$

______ 8. $48 \div 0.6 = 0.8$

______ 9. $2.42 \div 2.1 > 1$

______ 10. $4.9 \div 0.8 < 4.9$

Use Vocabulary in Writing

11. Mary says the digits in the quotient of $381.109 \div 0.86$ are 4 4 3 1 5, but she doesn't know where to place the decimal point. How can Mary use number sense to place the decimal point? Use at least three terms from the Word List in your answer.

Name ______________________________

TOPIC 6

Reteaching

Set A pages 229–232

Find 340.5 ÷ 100.

Dividing by 10, or 10^1, means moving the decimal point one place to the left.

Dividing by 100, or 10^2, means moving the decimal point two places to the left.

Dividing by 1,000, or 10^3, means moving the decimal point three places to the left.

$340.5 \div 10^2 = 3.405 = 3.405$

Remember that when dividing decimals by a power of 10, you may need to use one or more zeros as placeholders.

Use mental math to find each quotient.

1. $34.6 \div 10^1$
2. $6{,}483 \div 10^2$
3. 148.3 ÷ 100
4. $29.9 \div 10^1$
5. 70.7 ÷ 10
6. $5{,}913 \div 10^3$

Set B pages 233–236

Estimate 27.3 ÷ 7.1. Use compatible numbers.

27.3 ÷ 7.1
↓ ↓
28 ÷ 7 = 4

So, 27.3 ÷ 7.1 is about 4.

Estimate 42.5 ÷ 11. Use rounding.

42.5 ÷ 11
↓ ↓
40 ÷ 10 = 4

So, 42.5 ÷ 11 is about 4.

Remember that compatible numbers are numbers that are easy to compute in your head.

Write a number sentence that shows a way to estimate each quotient.

1. 26.2 ÷ 5
2. 49.6 ÷ 7.8
3. 121 ÷ 12.75
4. 32.41 ÷ 10.9
5. 82.4 ÷ 3.7
6. 28.5 ÷ 0.94

Set C pages 237–240

Find 1.14 ÷ 3.

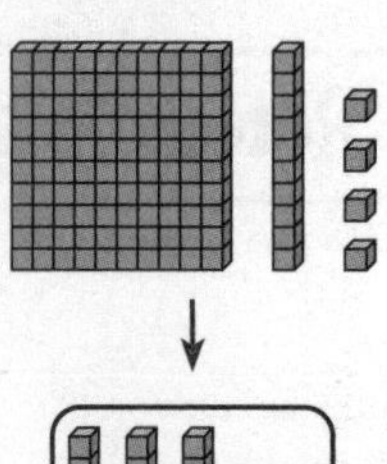

Estimate first.
1.14 ÷ 3 is less than 1, so start dividing in the tenths place.

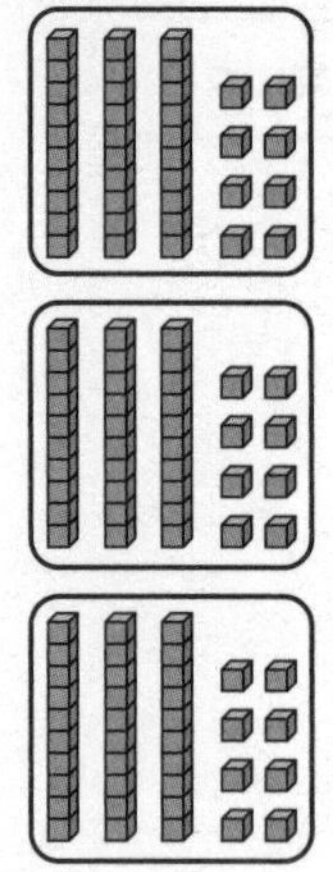

$$\begin{array}{r} 0.38 \\ 3\overline{)1.14} \\ -\ .90 \\ \hline .24 \\ -\ .24 \\ \hline 0 \end{array}$$

Remember to use estimation to check the placement of the decimal point in the quotient.

Divide. Use models to help.

1. 6.58 ÷ 7

2. 156 ÷ 8

3. 34.2 ÷ 3

4. 5.84 ÷ 4

5. Michelle pays $66.85 for a costume pattern and 8 yards of fabric. The costume pattern costs $4.85. How much does each yard of the fabric cost?

Set D pages 241–244

Find 94.5 ÷ 15.

Estimate first.

94.5 ÷ 15 is close to 100 ÷ 20 = 5, so start dividing with the ones place.

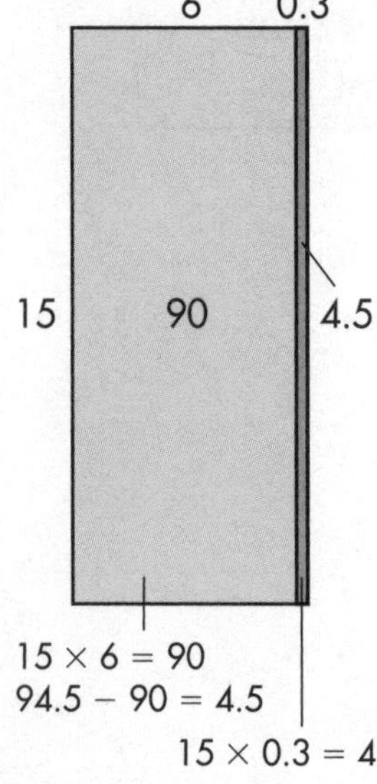

$$\begin{array}{r} 6.3 \\ 15\overline{)94.5} \\ -90.0 \\ \hline 4.5 \\ -\ 4.5 \\ \hline 0 \end{array}$$

So, 94.5 ÷ 15 = 6.3.

Remember that you can check your calculation by multiplying the quotient by the divisor.

Find each quotient.

1. 91.2 ÷ 16

2. 361.5 ÷ 15

3. 29.04 ÷ 22

4. 144 ÷ 45

5. A 12-ounce bottle of shampoo costs $4.20. A 16-ounce bottle costs $6.88. Which shampoo costs less per ounce? How do you know?

Name ______________________________

Set E pages 245–248

Reteaching Continued

Find $4.8 \div 0.6$.

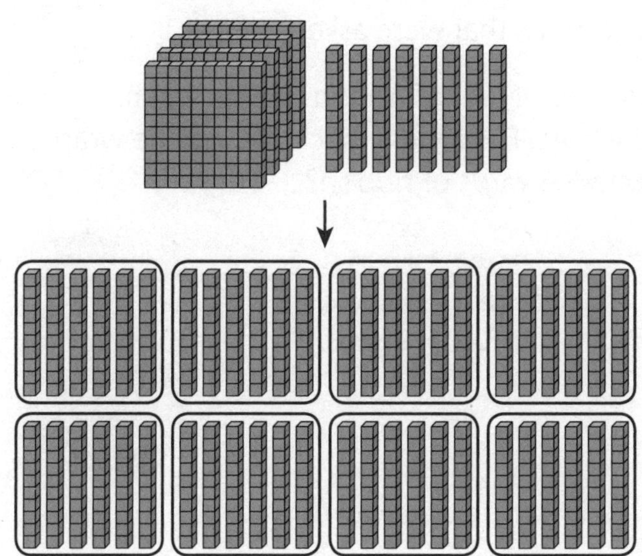

48 tenths ÷ 6 tenths

6 tenths × ? = 48 tenths

? = 8

So, $4.8 \div 0.6 = 8$.

Remember to use estimation to check the quotient for reasonableness.

1. $6.4 \div 3.2$

2. $6.4 \div 0.32$

3. $9.6 \div 0.8$

4. $0.96 \div 0.08$

5. $41.8 \div 2.2$

6. $4.18 \div 0.22$

7. $81.4 \div 7.4$

8. $814 \div 74$

9. $9.6 \div 0.03$

10. $9.6 \div 0.3$

Set F pages 249–252

Think about these questions to help you **reason abstractly and quantitatively**.

Thinking Habits

- What do the numbers and symbols in the problem mean?
- How are the numbers or quantities related?
- How can I represent a word problem using pictures, numbers, or equations?

Zoey has a goal of saving $750 for a vacation. Her vacation will last 6 days. She wants to save the same amount each week for 12 weeks to reach her goal. How much should she save each week?

Which quantities do you need to solve the problem?

The savings goal is $750; Zoey will save for 12 weeks.

Will Zoey need to save more than or less than $80 each week? Explain your reasoning.

Less than; $12 \times \$80 = \$960$, but she only needs to save $750.

How much should she save each week? Write an equation to represent the problem.

$62.50; $\$750 \div 12 = \$62.50$

Remember to check the reasonableness of a solution by making sure your calculations are correct, and that you answered all of the questions that were asked.

Ian uses 4 feet of ribbon to wrap each package. How many packages can he wrap with 5.6 yards of ribbon?

Remember there are
3 feet in a yard.

1. Describe one way to solve the problem.

2. What is the solution to the problem? Show your work.

A bushel of apples weighs about 42 pounds. There are 4 pecks in a bushel. It takes 2 pounds of apples to make one pie. How many pies can you make with one peck of apples?

3. How are the numbers in the problem related?

4. Describe one way to solve the problem.

5. Solve the problem. Show your work.

Name ______________________________

1. Mr. Dodd filled the gas tank on his lawn mower with 3.8 gallons of gas. He mowed his yard 10 times on the same tank of gas. He used the same amount of gas each time. How much gas did he use each time? Write an equation to show your work. Explain how the decimal point moves.

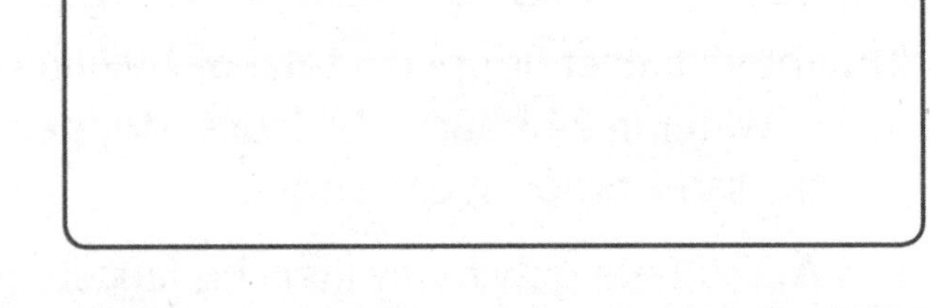

2. Kimberly scored a total of 35.08 points in four events for her gymnastic competition. If she scored the same number of points in each event, how many points did she score in each? Write an equation to show your work.

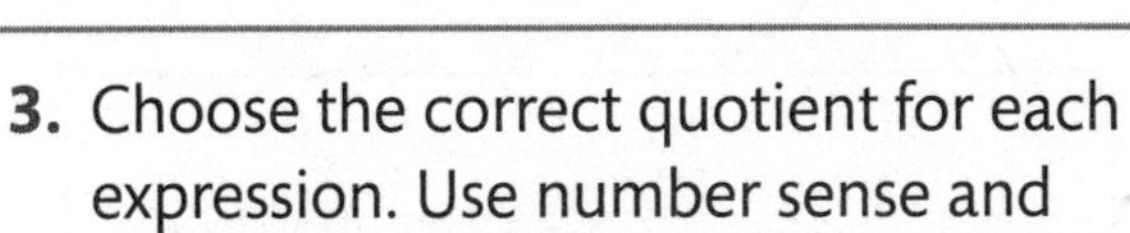

3. Choose the correct quotient for each expression. Use number sense and estimation to help.

	22.5	12	6.45	18.6
21.6 ÷ 1.8	❑	❑	❑	❑
10.23 ÷ 0.55	❑	❑	❑	❑
78.75 ÷ 3.5	❑	❑	❑	❑
29.67 ÷ 4.6	❑	❑	❑	❑

4. What is the value of the missing exponent in the equation?

$80.5 \div 10^{\square} = 0.805$

Ⓐ 1
Ⓑ 2
Ⓒ 3
Ⓓ 4

5. The chef at a restaurant bought 37 pounds of salad for $46.25. How much did she pay for each pound of salad?

Ⓐ $0.125
Ⓑ $1.25
Ⓒ $1.30
Ⓓ $12.50

6. Kathleen spent $231 on concert tickets for herself and 11 friends. Each ticket cost the same amount.

A. Estimate the cost of each ticket. Write an equation to show your work.

B. Find the exact cost of each ticket. Compare your answer to your estimate to check for reasonableness.

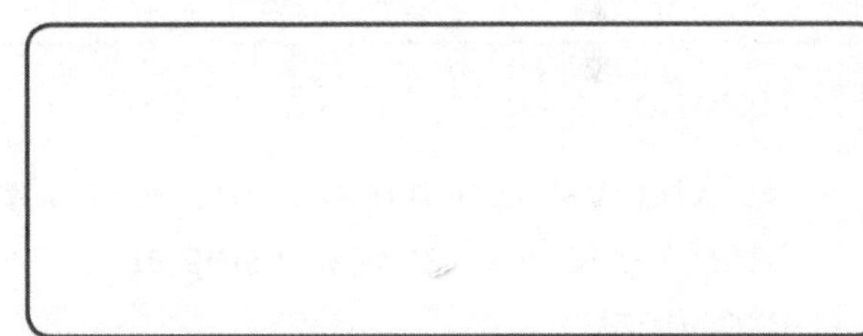

7. Select all of the following equations that are true when 12.5 is used. Use number sense to help.

☐ $\square \div 10 = 1.25$
☐ $\square \div 1 = 1.25$
☐ $\square \div 1 = 12.5$
☐ $\square \div 100 = 1.25$
☐ $\square \div 100 = 0.125$

8. Which division problem does the model Tess made represent?

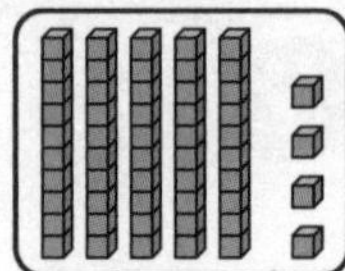 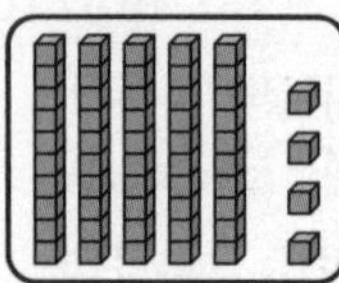 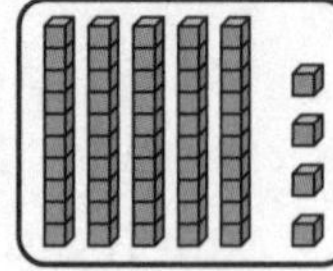

Ⓐ $1.35 \div 3 = 0.45$

Ⓑ $1.35 \div 3 = 0.54$

Ⓒ $1.62 \div 3 = 0.45$

Ⓓ $1.62 \div 3 = 0.54$

9. If 8 ounces of canned pumpkin has 82 calories, how many calories are in 1 ounce? Use your answer to find how many calories are in 6 ounces of pumpkin.

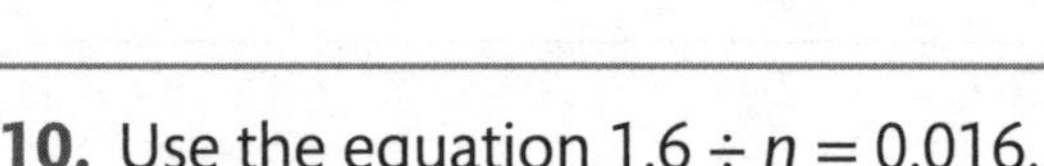

10. Use the equation $1.6 \div n = 0.016$.

A. What value of *n* makes the equation true? Write your answer using an exponent.

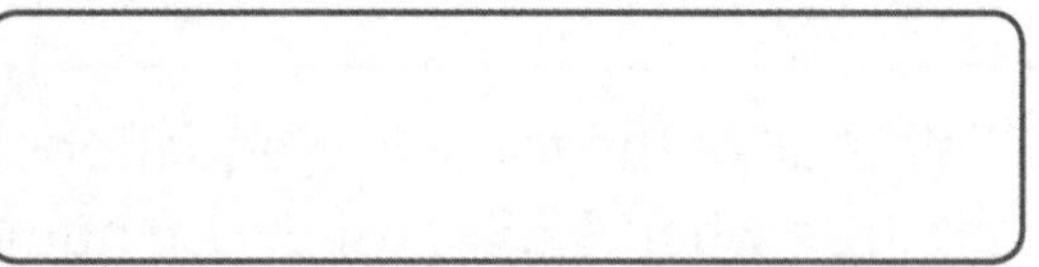

B. Explain how you know your answer is correct.

11. Eileen bought 8 roses for \$45.50. Which is the best way to estimate the cost of one rose?

Ⓐ \$45 ÷ 5 = \$9.00

Ⓑ \$48 ÷ 8 = \$6.00

Ⓒ \$45 ÷ 10 = \$0.45

Ⓓ \$40 ÷ 8 = \$0.50

12. Toby's faucet dripped a total of 1.92 liters of water in 24 hours. The faucet dripped the same amount each hour.

A. Estimate how many liters his faucet dripped each hour. Write an equation to model your work.

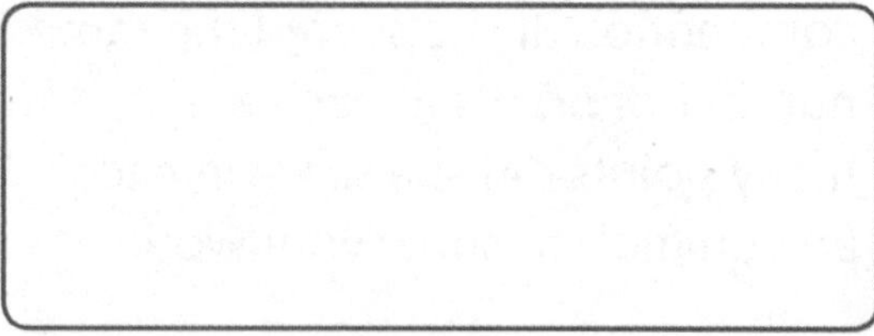

B. Find the exact amount of water that dripped each hour.

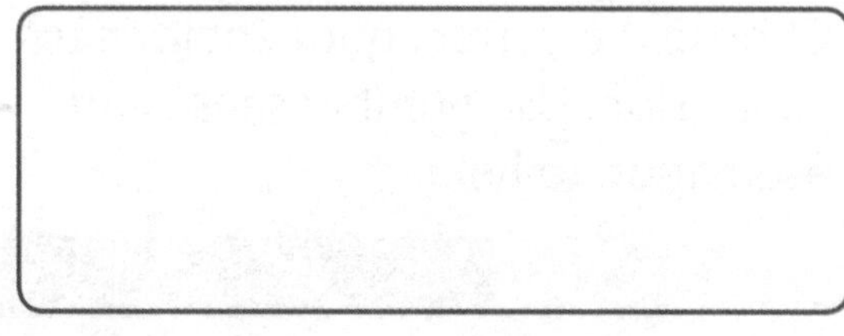

C. Compare your estimate to your answer. Is your answer reasonable? Explain.

Name ______________________

13. Choose the correct quotient for each expression.

	0.708	7.08	0.078	0.78
$0.78 \div 10$	❑	❑	❑	❑
$7{,}080 \div 10^3$	❑	❑	❑	❑
$70.8 \div 10^2$	❑	❑	❑	❑
$780 \div 10^3$	❑	❑	❑	❑

14. Diego is making a large mural. He draws a hexagon with a perimeter of 10.5 meters. Each side of the hexagon is the same length.

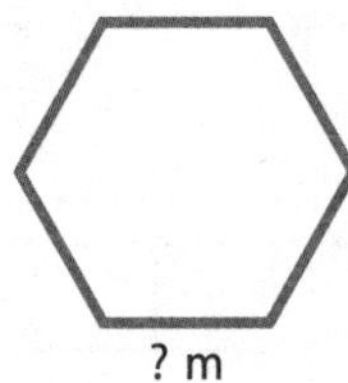

A. How many meters long is each side of Diego's hexagon? Write an equation to model your work.

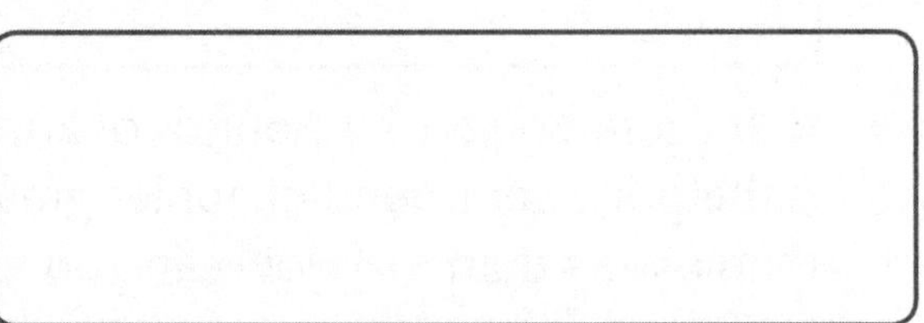

B. The total cost of the supplies to paint the mural is $38.70. Diego and 9 friends divide the total cost equally. How much does each person pay?

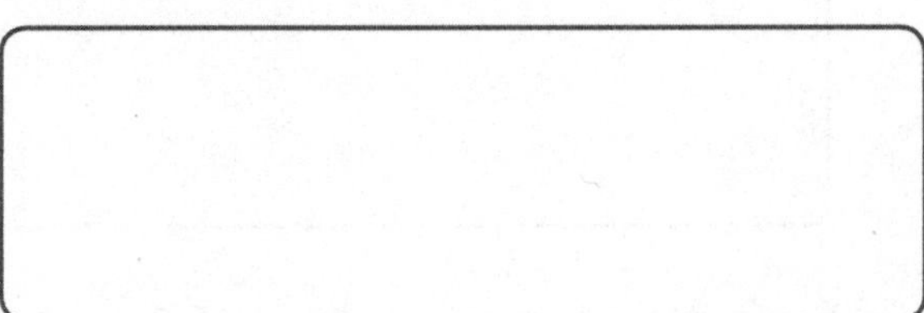

15. Select all of the following equations that are true when 40.3 is used. Use number sense to help.

- ▢ $\square \div 10^1 = 403$
- ▢ $\square \div 10^2 = 0.403$
- ▢ $\square \div 10^0 = 40.3$
- ▢ $\square \div 10^3 = 4.03$
- ▢ $\square \div 10^2 = 4.03$

16. Lou's Diner spent $12.80 on 8 pounds of potatoes. What was the cost of one pound of potatoes? What would be the total cost if the cost per pound remained the same and the diner bought 7 pounds? Show your work.

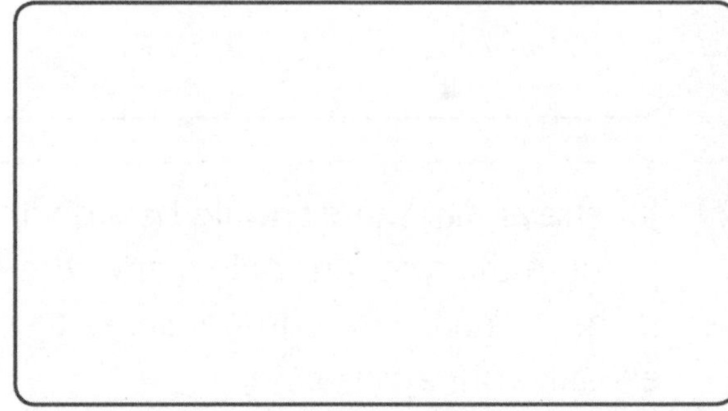

17. How many quarters are there in $30? Solve the equation $30 \div 0.25$ to help you.

Ⓐ 12 quarters
Ⓑ 20 quarters
Ⓒ 120 quarters
Ⓓ 200 quarters

18. When solving $6.1 \div 10^2$, how is the decimal point moved?

Ⓐ 1 place to the right
Ⓑ 1 place to the left
Ⓒ 2 places to the right
Ⓓ 2 places to the left

19. A group of 5 friends bought a bag of grapes to share equally. If the bag of grapes weighs 11.25 pounds, how much is each person's share? How many friends could share the grapes if each person's share was 1.25 pounds? Write an equation to model your work.

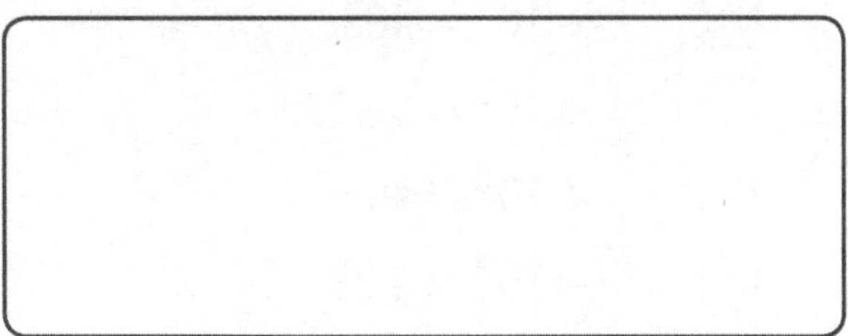

20. When dividing 560.9 by 100, how should the decimal point be moved?

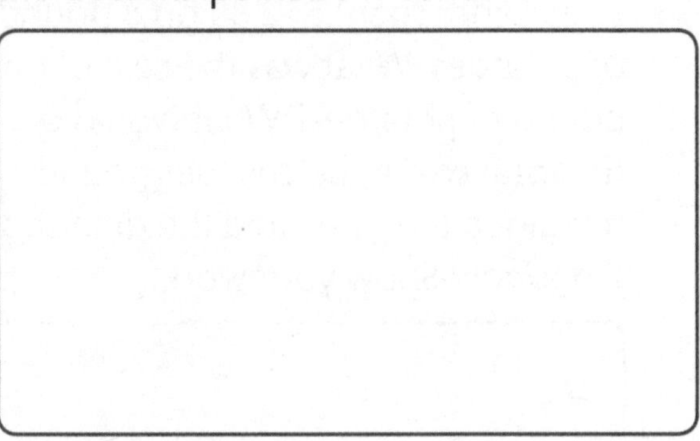

21. June says that there should be a decimal point in the quotient below after the 4. Is she correct? Use number sense to explain your answer.

$43.94 \div 5.2 = 845$

22. Three coworkers decided to buy fruit to share at lunchtime. Antonio spent \$1.47 on bananas. Laura spent \$2.88 on apples. Suzanne spent \$2.85 on oranges.

A. Complete the bar diagram to find out how much they spent in all on fruit.

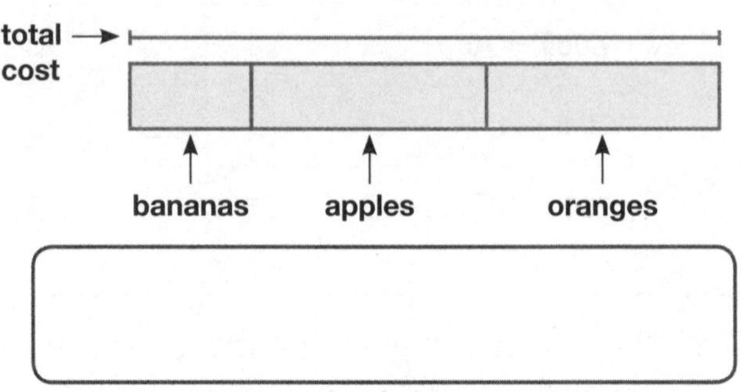

B. They evenly divided the cost of the 3 types of fruit. How much did each person pay? Complete the bar diagram to help you.

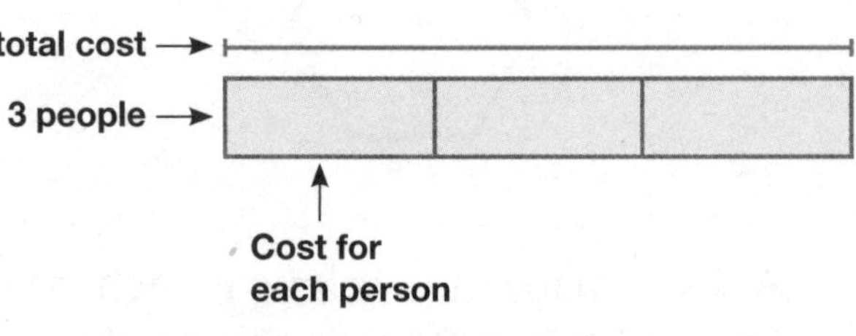

C. If Laura bought 2.1 pounds of apples, is the price per pound of apples greater than or less than \$1? How can you tell?

Name ______________________

Cooking Competition

Lydia is organizing a cooking competition at her school. She ordered some basic supplies to share among the teams that are competing. The teams will be bringing other ingredients as well.

Use the list at the right to answer the questions.

Cooking Supplies

- 738.4 grams, flour
- 8.25 liters, milk
- 5.4 liters, olive oil
- 87.6 grams, salt
- 36 eggs

1. If 10 of the teams divide the olive oil equally, how much will each team receive? Write an equation to model your work.

2. Eight teams agree to share the flour equally.

Part A

About how many grams of flour will each team get? Use compatible numbers to estimate. Write an equation to show how you estimated.

Part B

Find the actual amount of flour each team will receive. Show your work.

3. Several teams agree to share the salt equally. Each team will be given 7.3 grams of salt. How many teams agree to share the salt? Write a division equation to model the problem. Then write an equivalent equation using whole numbers.

4. Malcolm calculated how many liters of milk each team would get if 6 teams shared the milk equally. His work is shown at the right, but he forgot to place the decimal point in the quotient. Where should he place the decimal point? Explain.

$8.25 \div 6 = 1375$

5. Lydia decides to provide cheddar cheese for the competition. She buys 4.2 kilograms for $39.90.

Part A

She estimates the cost of 1 kilogram of cheese to be $1. Is her estimate reasonable? Explain.

Part B

To find the actual cost of 1 kilogram of cheese, Lydia needs to divide $39.90 by 4.2. How can she change the division problem to an equivalent problem using whole numbers? Write and solve the equivalent problem.

Part C

If 7 teams share the cheese equally, how much cheese will each team get?

Use Equivalent Fractions to Add and Subtract Fractions

Essential Questions: How can sums and differences of fractions and mixed numbers be estimated? What are common procedures for adding and subtracting fractions and mixed numbers?

Did you know that the fossil of the oldest bat was found in Wyoming?

Fossil evidence shows that around 50 million years ago, Earth's climate was warm, and land and oceans were filled with life.

Make no bones about it! You can find fossils of ancient animals today! Here's a project about fossils!

enVision® STEM Project: Fossils Tell Story

Do Research Use the Internet or other sources to find out more about fossils. What are fossils? How and where do we find them? What do they tell us about the past? What can they tell us about the future? Pay particular attention to fossils from the Eocene epoch.

Journal: Write a Report Include what you found. Also in your report:

- Describe a fossil that you have seen or would like to find.
- Tell if there are any fossils where you live.
- Make up and solve addition and subtraction problems about fossils. Use fractions and mixed numbers in your problems.

Name ________________

Review What You Know

Vocabulary

Choose the best term from the box. Write it on the blank.

- denominator
- numerator
- fraction
- unit fraction
- mixed number

1. A ______________ has a whole number part and a fraction part.

2. A ______________ represents the number of equal parts in one whole.

3. A ______________ has a numerator of 1.

4. A symbol used to name one or more parts of a whole or a set, or a location on the number line, is a ______________.

Compare Fractions

Compare. Write >, <, or = for each ◯.

5. $\frac{1}{5}$ ◯ $\frac{1}{15}$

6. $\frac{17}{10}$ ◯ $\frac{17}{5}$

7. $\frac{5}{25}$ ◯ $\frac{2}{5}$

8. $\frac{12}{27}$ ◯ $\frac{6}{9}$

9. $\frac{11}{16}$ ◯ $\frac{2}{8}$

10. $\frac{2}{7}$ ◯ $\frac{1}{5}$

11. Liam bought $\frac{5}{8}$ pound of cherries. Harrison bought more cherries than Liam. Which could be the amount of cherries that Harrison bought?

Ⓐ $\frac{1}{2}$ pound Ⓑ $\frac{2}{5}$ pound Ⓒ $\frac{2}{3}$ pound Ⓓ $\frac{3}{5}$ pound

12. Jamie has read $\frac{1}{4}$ of a book. Raul has read $\frac{3}{4}$ of the same book. Who is closer to reading the whole book? Explain.

Equivalent Fractions

Write a fraction equivalent to each fraction.

13. $\frac{6}{18}$

14. $\frac{12}{22}$

15. $\frac{15}{25}$

16. $\frac{8}{26}$

17. $\frac{14}{35}$

18. $\frac{4}{18}$

19. $\frac{1}{7}$

20. $\frac{4}{11}$

Name ______________________________

What's in your gumbo?

Project: Record a Cooking Show

PROJECT
7B

Does this story sound fishy?

Project: Write a Tall Tale about Fishing Friends

PROJECT
7C

How many cups of juice can you get from 5 oranges?

Project: Get the Juice from Oranges

3-ACT MATH PREVIEW

Math Modeling

The Gif Recipe

Video

Before watching the video, think:

Some recipes are easier to follow than others. I've never made this one before. Maybe I should read the entire recipe before starting to cook.

I can ...

model with math to solve a problem that involves estimating and computing with fractions.

Mathematical Practices MP.4 Also MP.5, MP.6
Content Standards 5.NF.A.1
Also 5.NBT.A.2, 5.NBT.B.7, 5.NF.A.2

Name ______________________________

Activity

Lesson 7-1
Estimate Sums and Differences of Fractions

I can ...
estimate sums and differences of fractions.

Content Standards 5.NF.A.2 Also 5.NF.A.1
Mathematical Practices MP.2, MP.3

Solve & Share

Jack needs about $1\frac{1}{2}$ yards of string. He has three pieces of string that are different lengths. Without finding the exact amount, which two pieces should he choose to get closest to $1\frac{1}{2}$ yards of string? ***Solve this problem any way you choose.***

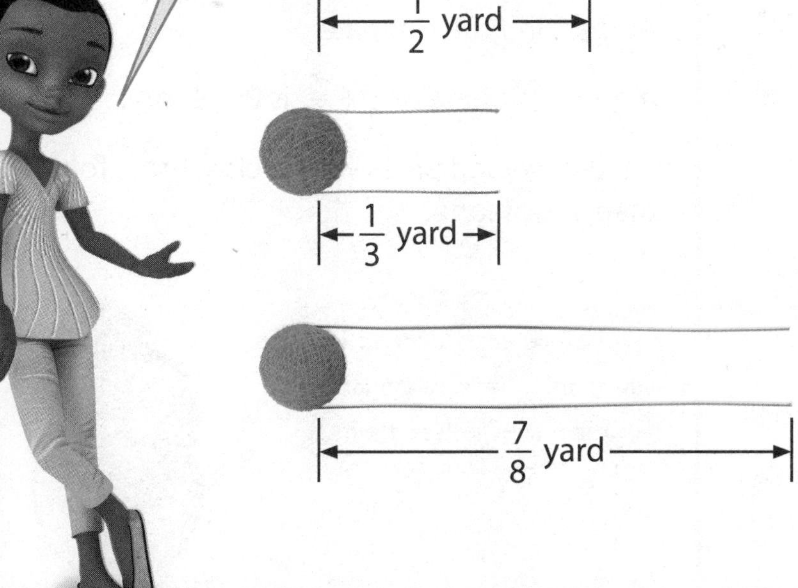

Reasoning You can use number sense to estimate the answer. *Show your work!*
1/2 yard
1/3 yard
7/8 yard

Look Back! How can a number line help you estimate?

 Visual Learning  Glossary

How Can You Estimate the Sum of Two Fractions?

Visual Learning Bridge

A

Mr. Fish is welding together two copper pipes to repair a leak. He will use the pipes shown. Is the new pipe closer to $\frac{1}{2}$ foot or 1 foot long? Explain.

Estimate the sum $\frac{1}{6} + \frac{5}{12}$ to find about how long the combined pipes will be.

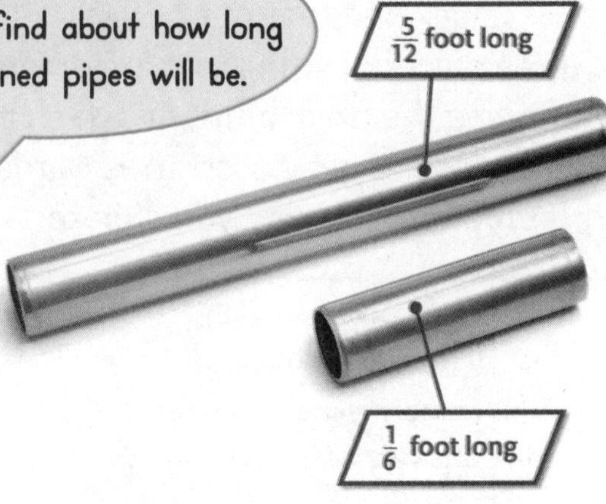

You can add to find the sum.

B

Step 1

Replace each fraction with the nearest half or whole. A number line can make it easy to decide if each fraction is closest to 0, $\frac{1}{2}$, or 1.

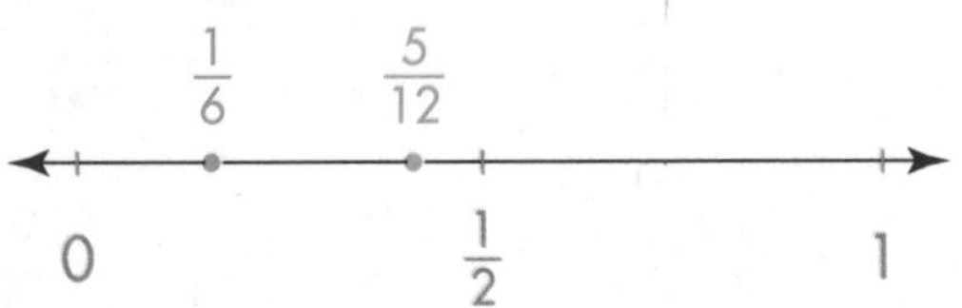

$\frac{1}{6}$ is between 0 and $\frac{1}{2}$, but is closer to 0.

$\frac{5}{12}$ is also between 0 and $\frac{1}{2}$, but is closer to the benchmark fraction $\frac{1}{2}$.

C

Step 2

Add to find the estimate.

A good estimate of $\frac{1}{6} + \frac{5}{12}$ is $0 + \frac{1}{2}$, or $\frac{1}{2}$.

So, the welded pipes will be closer to $\frac{1}{2}$ foot than 1 foot long.

Since each addend is less than $\frac{1}{2}$, it is reasonable that their sum is less than 1.

Convince Me! **Critique Reasoning** Nolini says that if the denominator is more than twice the numerator, the fraction can always be replaced with 0. Is she correct? Give an example in your explanation.

Name ______________________

Practice Tools Assessment

Guided Practice

Do You Understand?

1. In the problem at the top of page 270, would you get the same estimate if Mr. Fish's pipes measured $\frac{2}{6}$ foot and $\frac{7}{12}$ foot?

2. Number Sense If a fraction has a 1 in the numerator and a number greater than 2 in the denominator, will the fraction be closer to 0, $\frac{1}{2}$, or 1? Explain.

Do You Know How?

In **3** and **4**, use a number line to tell if each fraction is closest to 0, $\frac{1}{2}$, or 1. Then estimate the sum or difference.

3. 0 $\frac{1}{2}$ 1

a $\frac{11}{12}$ Closest to: _____

b $\frac{1}{6}$ Closest to: _____

Estimate the sum $\frac{11}{12} + \frac{1}{6}$.

c 1 + _____ = _____

4.

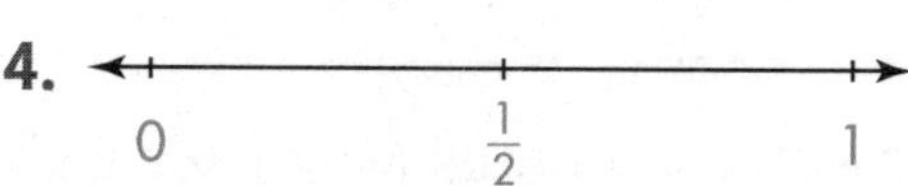

0 $\frac{1}{2}$ 1

a $\frac{14}{16}$ Closest to: _____

b $\frac{5}{8}$ Closest to: _____

Estimate the difference $\frac{14}{16} - \frac{5}{8}$.

c _____ − _____ = _____

Independent Practice

Leveled Practice In **5**, use a number line to tell if each fraction is closest to 0, $\frac{1}{2}$, or 1. In **6–11**, estimate the sum or difference by replacing each fraction with 0, $\frac{1}{2}$, or 1.

5. 0 $\frac{1}{2}$ 1

a $\frac{7}{8}$ Closest to: _____

b $\frac{5}{12}$ Closest to: _____

Estimate the difference $\frac{7}{8} - \frac{5}{12}$.

c _____ − _____ = _____

6. $\frac{9}{10} + \frac{5}{6}$

7. $\frac{11}{18} - \frac{2}{9}$

8. $\frac{1}{16} + \frac{2}{15}$

9. $\frac{24}{25} - \frac{1}{9}$

10. $\frac{3}{36} + \frac{1}{10}$

11. $\frac{37}{40} - \frac{26}{50}$

Problem Solving

12. Number Sense Name two fractions that are closer to 1 than to $\frac{1}{2}$. Then, name two fractions that are closer to $\frac{1}{2}$ than to 0 or 1 and two other fractions that are closer to 0 than to $\frac{1}{2}$. Find two of your fractions that have a sum of about $1\frac{1}{2}$.

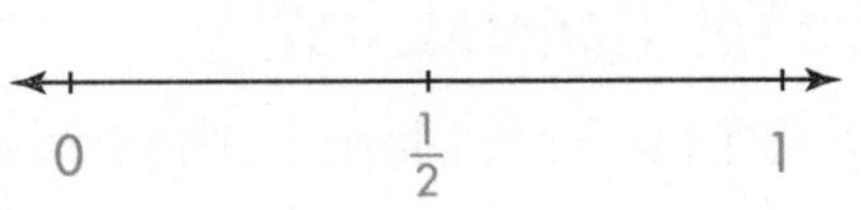

13. Higher Order Thinking How would you estimate whether $\frac{27}{50}$ is closer to $\frac{1}{2}$ or 1 without using a number line? Explain.

14. Katie made a bag of trail mix with $\frac{1}{2}$ cup of raisins, $\frac{3}{5}$ cup of banana chips, and $\frac{3}{8}$ cup of peanuts. About how much trail mix did Katie make?

15. Reasoning The Annual Mug Race is the longest river sailboat race in the world. The event is run along the St. Johns River, which is 310 miles long. About how many times as long as the race is the river?

Do you need an exact answer or an estimate? How do you know?

Assessment Practice

16. Part A

Steve is making breakfast. The recipes call for $\frac{7}{8}$ cup of milk for grits and $\frac{3}{4}$ cup for biscuits. He only has 2 cups of milk. Does he have enough to make his breakfast? Explain.

Part B

If he has enough milk, about how much milk will he have left? If he doesn't have enough milk, about how much will he need?

Name ______________________

Activity

Lesson 7-2
Find Common Denominators

I can ...

find common denominators for fractions with unlike denominators.

Content Standards 5.NF.A.1 Also 5.NF.A.2
Mathematical Practices MP.3, MP.5

Solve & Share

Sue wants $\frac{1}{2}$ of a rectangular pan of cornbread. Dena wants $\frac{1}{3}$ of the same pan of cornbread. How should you cut the cornbread so that each girl gets the size portion she wants? ***Solve this problem any way you choose.***

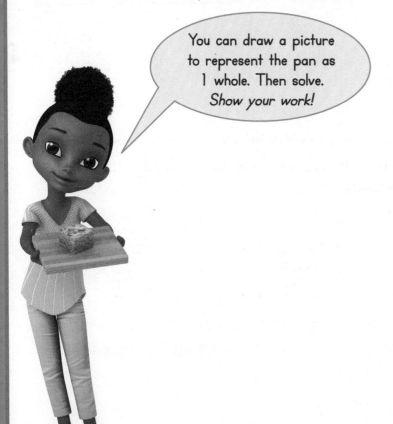

You can draw a picture to represent the pan as 1 whole. Then solve. *Show your work!*

Look Back! Construct Arguments Is there more than one way to divide the pan of cornbread into equal-sized parts? Explain how you know.

Visual Learning | A-Z Glossary

How Can You Find Common Denominators?

Visual Learning Bridge

A

Tyrone partitioned a rectangle into thirds. Sally partitioned a rectangle of the same size into fourths. How could you partition a rectangle of the same size so that you see both thirds and fourths?

You can partition a rectangle to show thirds or fourths.

Thirds

Fourths

B This rectangle is partitioned into thirds and fourths.

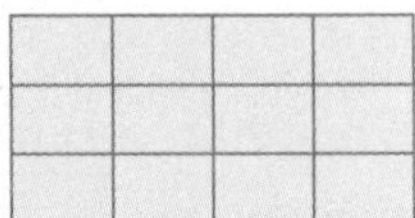

Twelfths

The rectangle is partitioned into 12 equal parts.
Each part is $\frac{1}{12}$.

C The fractions $\frac{1}{3}$ and $\frac{1}{4}$ can be renamed with equivalent fractions.

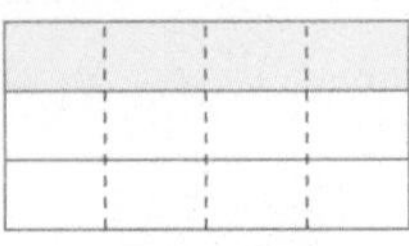

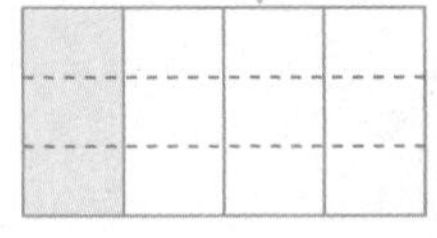

$\frac{1}{3} = \frac{4}{12}$ $\frac{1}{4} = \frac{3}{12}$

Fractions that have the same denominators, such as $\frac{4}{12}$ and $\frac{3}{12}$, are said to have common denominators.

Convince Me! **Use Appropriate Tools** Draw rectangles such as the ones above to find fractions equivalent to $\frac{2}{5}$ and $\frac{1}{3}$ that have the same denominator.

Name ____________________

Practice Tools Assessment

Another Example

Find a common denominator for $\frac{2}{3}$ and $\frac{5}{6}$. Then rename each fraction with an equivalent fraction.

Any common denominator for $\frac{2}{3}$ and $\frac{5}{6}$ is a multiple of both 3 and 6.

One Way

Multiply the denominators to find a common denominator: $3 \times 6 = 18$.

Write equivalent fractions with denominators of 18.

$$\frac{2}{3} = \frac{2 \times 6}{3 \times 6} = \frac{12}{18} \qquad \frac{5}{6} = \frac{5 \times 3}{6 \times 3} = \frac{15}{18}$$

So, $\frac{12}{18}$ and $\frac{15}{18}$ is one way to rename $\frac{2}{3}$ and $\frac{5}{6}$ with a common denominator.

Another Way

Use the fact that one denominator is a multiple of the other.

You know that 6 is a multiple of 3.

$$\frac{2}{3} = \frac{2 \times 2}{3 \times 2} = \frac{4}{6}$$

So, $\frac{4}{6}$ and $\frac{5}{6}$ is another way to rename $\frac{2}{3}$ and $\frac{5}{6}$ with a common denominator.

Guided Practice

Do You Understand?

1. In the example on the previous page, how many twelfths are in each $\frac{1}{3}$ section of Tyrone's rectangle? How many twelfths are in each $\frac{1}{4}$ section of Sally's rectangle?

Do You Know How?

In **2** and **3**, find a common denominator for each pair of fractions.

2. $\frac{3}{8}$ and $\frac{2}{3}$

3. $\frac{1}{6}$ and $\frac{4}{3}$

Independent Practice

In **4–11**, find a common denominator for each pair of fractions. Then write equivalent fractions with the common denominator.

4. $\frac{2}{5}$ and $\frac{1}{6}$

5. $\frac{1}{3}$ and $\frac{4}{5}$

6. $\frac{5}{8}$ and $\frac{3}{4}$

7. $\frac{3}{10}$ and $\frac{9}{8}$

8. $\frac{3}{7}$ and $\frac{1}{2}$

9. $\frac{5}{12}$ and $\frac{3}{5}$

10. $\frac{7}{9}$ and $\frac{2}{3}$

11. $\frac{3}{8}$ and $\frac{9}{20}$

Problem Solving

12. **Critique Reasoning** Explain any mistakes in the renaming of the fractions below. Show the correct renaming.

$\frac{3}{4} = \frac{9}{12}$ $\frac{2}{3} = \frac{6}{12}$

13. **Higher Order Thinking** For keeping business records, every three months of a year is called a quarter. How many months are equal to three-quarters of a year? Explain how you found your answer.

14. Nelda baked two kinds of pasta in pans. Each pan was the same size. She sliced one pan of pasta into 6 equal pieces. She sliced the other pan into 8 equal pieces. How can the pans of pasta now be sliced so that both pans have the same-sized pieces? Draw on the pictures to show your work. If Nelda has served 6 pieces from one pan so far, what fraction of one pan has she served?

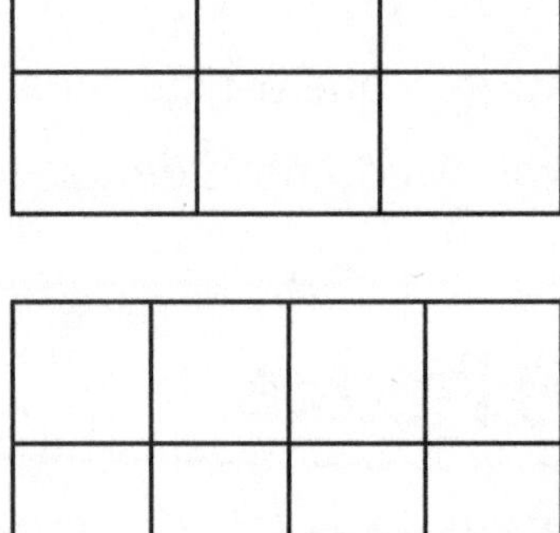

15. **Number Sense** What is the price of premium gasoline rounded to the nearest dollar? rounded to the nearest dime? rounded to the nearest penny?

DATA

Gasoline Prices

Grade	Price (per gallon)
Regular	$4.199
Premium	$4.409
Diesel	$5.019

Assessment Practice

16. Choose all the numbers that could be common denominators for $\frac{2}{3}$ and $\frac{3}{4}$.

- ☐ 8
- ☐ 12
- ☐ 16
- ☐ 36
- ☐ 48

17. Choose all the numbers that could be common denominators for $\frac{11}{12}$ and $\frac{4}{5}$.

- ☐ 12
- ☐ 17
- ☐ 30
- ☐ 60
- ☐ 125

Name ____________________

Activity

Lesson 7-3
Add Fractions with Unlike Denominators

I can ...
add fractions with unlike denominators.

Content Standards 5.NF.A.1 Also 5.NF.A.2
Mathematical Practices MP.1, MP.3, MP.4

Solve & Share

Over the weekend, Eleni ate $\frac{1}{4}$ box of cereal, and Freddie ate $\frac{3}{8}$ of the same box. What portion of the box of cereal did they eat in all? ***Solve this problem any way you choose.***

You can use fraction strips to represent adding fractions. *Show your work!*

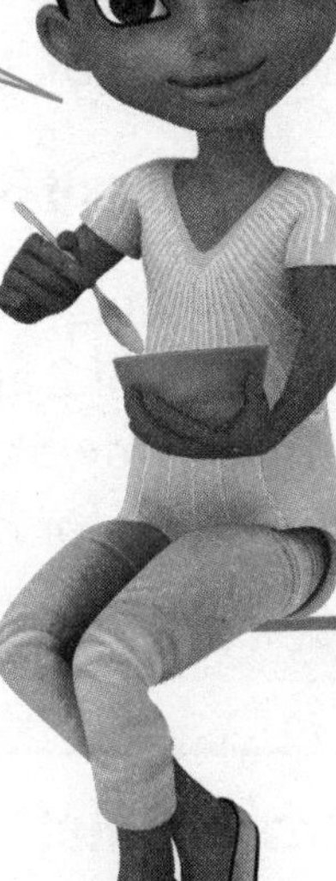

Look Back! **Make Sense and Persevere**
What steps did you take to solve this problem?

How Can You Add Fractions with Unlike Denominators?

A

Alex rode his scooter from his house to the park. Later, he rode from the park to baseball practice. How far did Alex ride?

You can add to find the total distance that Alex rode his scooter.

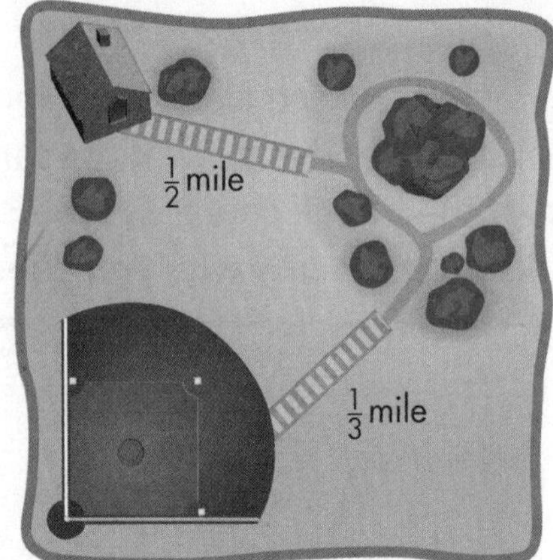

B

Step 1

Change the fractions to equivalent fractions with a common, or like, denominator.

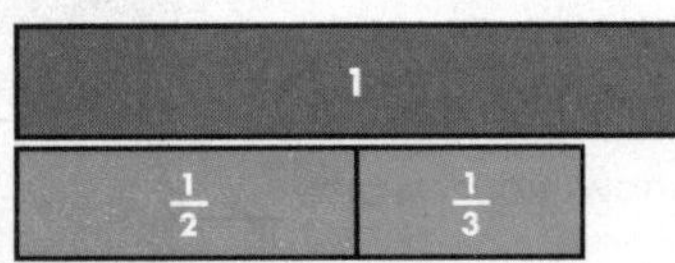

Multiples of 2: 2, 4, 6, 8, 10, 12, . . .

Multiples of 3: 3, 6, 9, 12, . . .

The number 6 is a common multiple of 2 and 3, so $\frac{1}{2}$ and $\frac{1}{3}$ can both be rewritten with a common denominator of 6.

C

Step 2

Write equivalent fractions with a common denominator.

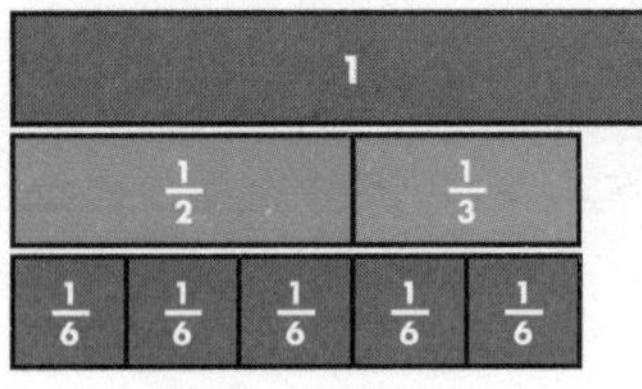

$$\frac{1}{2} \times \frac{3}{3} = \frac{3}{6}$$

$$\frac{1}{3} \times \frac{2}{2} = \frac{2}{6}$$

D

Step 3

Add the fractions to find the total number of sixths.

$$\begin{array}{r} \frac{1}{2} = \frac{3}{6} \\ + \frac{1}{3} = \frac{2}{6} \\ \hline \frac{5}{6} \end{array}$$

Alex rode his scooter $\frac{5}{6}$ mile.

Convince Me! **Construct Arguments** In the example above, would you get the same sum if you used 12 as the common denominator? Explain.

Name ____________________

Practice Tools Assessment

Another Example

Find $\frac{5}{12} + \frac{1}{4}$.

$\frac{5}{12} + \frac{1}{4} = \frac{5}{12} + \frac{3}{12}$ Write equivalent fractions with common denominators.

$= \frac{5+3}{12} = \frac{8}{12}$ or $\frac{2}{3}$ Find the total number of twelfths by adding the numerators.

Guided Practice

Do You Understand?

1. In the example at the top of page 278, if the park was $\frac{1}{8}$ mile from baseball practice instead of $\frac{1}{3}$ mile, how far would Alex ride his scooter in all?

2. **Vocabulary** Rico and Nita solved the same problem. Rico got $\frac{6}{8}$ for an answer, and Nita got $\frac{3}{4}$. Which answer is correct? Use the term *equivalent fraction* in your explanation.

Do You Know How?

Find the sum. Use fraction strips to help.

3. $\frac{1}{2} + \frac{1}{4} = \frac{\square}{\square} + \frac{\square}{\square} = \frac{\square}{\square}$

1		
$\frac{1}{2}$		$\frac{1}{4}$
$\frac{1}{4}$	$\frac{1}{4}$	$\frac{1}{4}$

Independent Practice

In **4** and **5**, find each sum. Use fraction strips to help.

Remember that you can use multiples to find a common denominator.

4. $\frac{1}{2} + \frac{2}{5} = \frac{\square}{\square} + \frac{\square}{\square} = \frac{\square}{\square}$

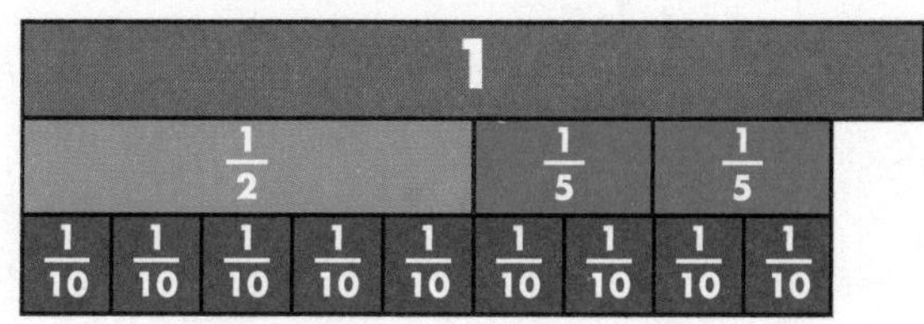

5. $\frac{1}{6} + \frac{1}{3} + \frac{1}{6} =$

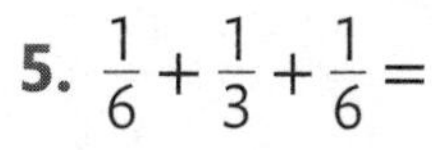

$\frac{\square}{\square} + \frac{\square}{\square} + \frac{\square}{\square} = \frac{\square}{\square} = \frac{\square}{\square}$

1			
$\frac{1}{6}$	$\frac{1}{3}$		$\frac{1}{6}$
$\frac{1}{6}$	$\frac{1}{6}$	$\frac{1}{6}$	$\frac{1}{6}$

Problem Solving

6. Explain why the denominator 6 in $\frac{3}{6}$ is not changed when adding the fractions.

$$\begin{array}{r} \frac{3}{6} = \frac{3}{6} \\ + \frac{1}{3} = \frac{2}{6} \\ \hline \frac{5}{6} \end{array}$$

7. **Model with Math** About $\frac{1}{10}$ of the bones in your body are in your skull. Your hands have about $\frac{1}{4}$ of the bones in your body. Write and solve an equation to find the fraction of the bones in your body that are in your hands or skull.

8. **enVision® STEM** Of 36 chemical elements, 2 are named for women scientists and 25 are named for places. What fraction of these 36 elements are named for women or places? Show your work.

9. **Higher Order Thinking** Roger made a table showing how he spends his time in one day. How many days will go by before Roger has slept the equivalent of one day? Explain how you found your answer.

DATA

Amount of Time Spent on Activities in One Day

Activity	Part of Day
Work	$\frac{1}{3}$ day
Sleep	$\frac{3}{8}$ day
Meals	$\frac{1}{8}$ day
Computer	$\frac{1}{6}$ day

Assessment Practice

10. Which equations are true when $\frac{1}{2}$ is placed in the box?

- ▢ $\square + \frac{5}{5} = \frac{3}{2}$
- ▢ $\frac{1}{10} + \frac{2}{5} = \square$
- ▢ $\frac{1}{2} + \square = \frac{1}{4}$
- ▢ $\frac{1}{6} + \frac{1}{3} = \square$

11. Which equations are true when $\frac{4}{7}$ is placed in the box?

- ▢ $\frac{1}{14} + \square = \frac{9}{14}$
- ▢ $\frac{2}{4} + \frac{2}{3} = \square$
- ▢ $\square + \frac{2}{7} = \frac{6}{7}$
- ▢ $\frac{1}{10} + \square = \frac{47}{70}$

Name ____________________

Activity

Lesson 7-4

Subtract Fractions with Unlike Denominators

I can ...

subtract fractions with unlike denominators.

Content Standards 5.NF.A.1 Also 5.NF.A.2
Mathematical Practices MP.3, MP.4, MP.8

Solve & Share Rose bought the length of copper pipe shown below. She used $\frac{1}{2}$ yard to repair a water line in her house. How much pipe does she have left? ***Solve this problem any way you choose.***

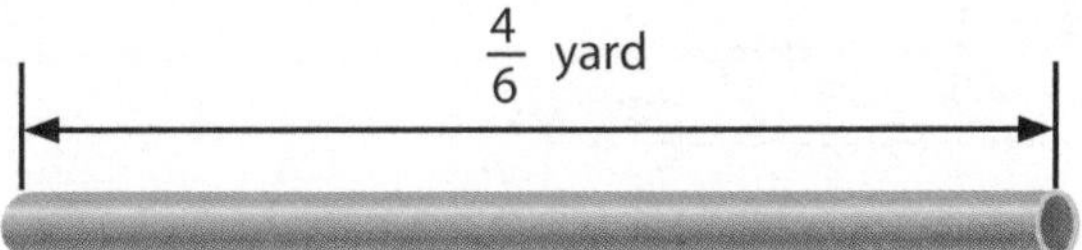

You can use mental math to find equivalent fractions so that $\frac{1}{2}$ and $\frac{4}{6}$ will have like denominators. *Show your work!*

Look Back! Generalize How is subtracting fractions with unlike denominators similar to adding fractions with unlike denominators?

 Visual Learning 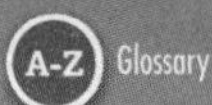 Glossary

How Can You Subtract Fractions with Unlike Denominators?

Visual Learning Bridge

A

Linda used $\frac{1}{4}$ yard of the fabric she bought for a sewing project. How much fabric did she have left?

You can use subtraction to find how much fabric was left.

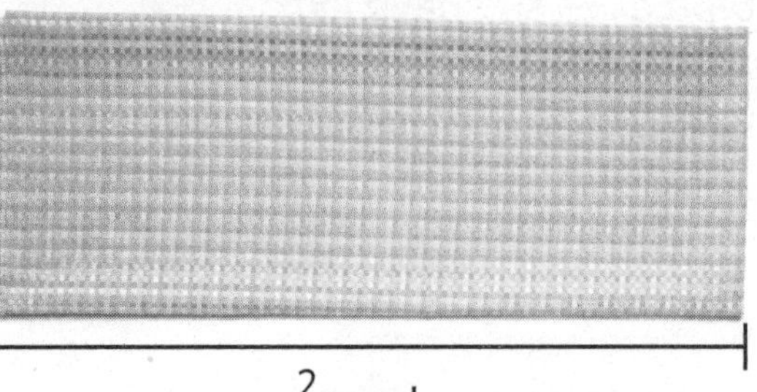

B Step 1

Find a common multiple of the denominators.

Multiples of 3: 3, 6, 9, 12, . . .

Multiples of 4: 4, 8, 12, . . .

The number 12 is a multiple of 3 and 4. Write equivalent fractions with a denominator of 12 for $\frac{2}{3}$ and $\frac{1}{4}$.

C Step 2

Use the Identity Property to rename the fractions with a common denominator.

$\frac{2}{3} \times \frac{4}{4} = \frac{8}{12}$

$\frac{2}{3} = \frac{8}{12}$

$\frac{1}{4} \times \frac{3}{3} = \frac{3}{12}$

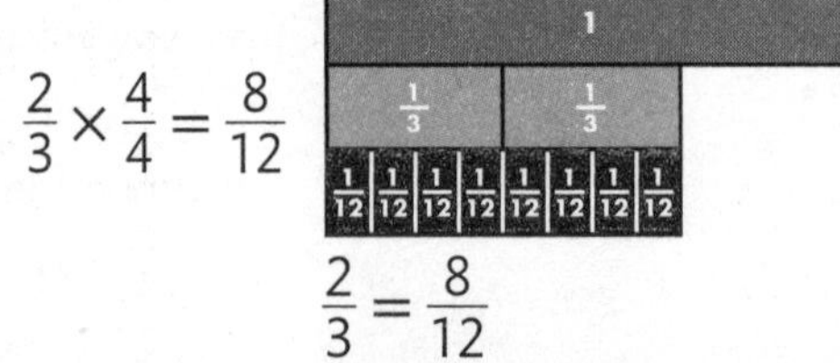

$\frac{1}{4} = \frac{3}{12}$

D Step 3

Subtract the numerators.

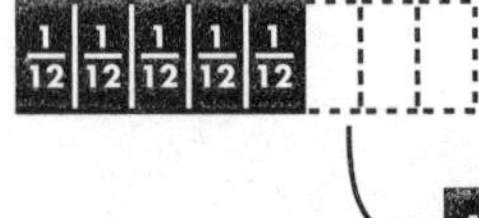

$$\begin{array}{r} \frac{2}{3} = \frac{8}{12} \\ - \frac{1}{4} = \frac{3}{12} \\ \hline \frac{5}{12} \end{array}$$

Linda has $\frac{5}{12}$ yard of fabric left.

Convince Me! **Critique Reasoning** Suppose Linda had $\frac{2}{3}$ of a yard of fabric and told Sandra that she used $\frac{3}{4}$ of a yard. Sandra says this is not possible. Do you agree? Explain your answer.

Name

Practice Tools Assessment

Guided Practice

Do You Understand?

1. In the example on page 282, is it possible to use a common denominator greater than 12 and get the correct answer? Why or why not?

2. In the example on page 282, if Linda had started with one yard of fabric and used $\frac{5}{8}$ of a yard, how much fabric would be left?

Do You Know How?

For **3-6**, find each difference.

3. $\frac{4}{7} = \frac{12}{21}$
$- \frac{1}{3} = \frac{7}{21}$

4. $\frac{5}{8}$
$- \frac{1}{4}$

5. $\frac{7}{8}$
$- \frac{1}{3}$

6. $\frac{4}{5} = \frac{24}{30}$
$- \frac{1}{6} = \frac{5}{30}$

Independent Practice

Leveled Practice In **7-16**, find each difference.

7. $\frac{1}{4} = \frac{\square}{8}$
$- \frac{1}{8} = \frac{\square}{8}$
$\frac{\square}{\square}$

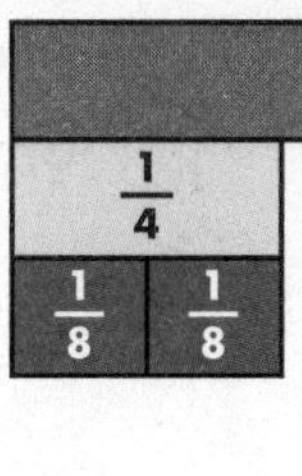

8. $\frac{2}{3} = \frac{\square}{6}$
$- \frac{1}{2} = \frac{\square}{6}$
$\frac{\square}{\square}$

9. $\frac{2}{3}$
$- \frac{5}{9}$

10. $\frac{4}{5}$
$- \frac{1}{4}$

11. $\frac{3}{2}$
$- \frac{7}{12}$

12. $\frac{6}{7}$
$- \frac{1}{2}$

13. $\frac{7}{10} - \frac{2}{5}$

14. $\frac{13}{16} - \frac{1}{4}$

15. $\frac{2}{9} - \frac{1}{6}$

16. $\frac{6}{5} - \frac{3}{8}$

Problem Solving

17. **Model with Math** Write and solve an equation to find the difference between the location of Point *A* and Point *B* on the ruler.

18. **Algebra** Write an addition and a subtraction equation for the diagram. Then, find the missing value.

x	
$\frac{1}{4}$	$\frac{3}{8}$

19. Why do fractions need to have a common denominator before you add or subtract them?

20. **Number Sense** Without using paper and pencil, how would you find the sum of 9.8 and 2.6?

21. **Higher Order Thinking** Find two fractions with a difference of $\frac{1}{5}$ but with neither denominator equal to 5.

Assessment Practice

22. Choose the correct numbers from the box below to complete the subtraction sentence that follows.

$\frac{5}{6}$	$\frac{2}{3}$	$\frac{1}{30}$	$\frac{6}{7}$	$\frac{1}{2}$

$\square - \frac{1}{3} = \square$

23. Choose the correct numbers from the box below to complete the subtraction sentence that follows.

$\frac{11}{12}$	$\frac{1}{6}$	$\frac{1}{4}$	$\frac{1}{2}$	$\frac{3}{4}$

$\square - \square = \frac{7}{12}$

Name ___

Lesson 7-5
Add and Subtract Fractions

I can ...
write equivalent fractions to add and subtract fractions with unlike denominators.

Content Standards 5.NF.A.1 Also 5.NF.A.2
Mathematical Practices MP.1, MP.2, MP.3

Solve & Share

Tyler and Dean ordered pizza. Tyler ate $\frac{1}{2}$ of the pizza and Dean ate $\frac{1}{3}$ of the pizza. How much of the pizza was eaten, and how much is left? ***Solve this problem any way you choose.***

Reasoning You can use number sense to help you solve this problem. *Show your work!*

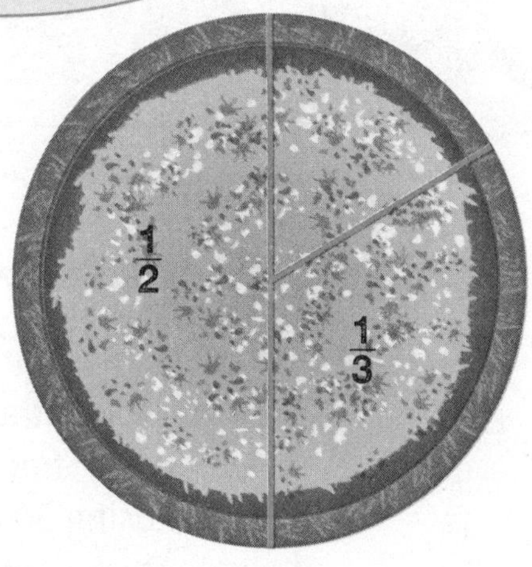

Look Back! How can you check that your answer makes sense?

How Can Adding and Subtracting Fractions Help You Solve Problems?

A

Kayla had $\frac{9}{10}$ gallon of paint. She painted the ceilings in her bedroom and bathroom. How much paint does she have left after painting the two ceilings?

You can use both addition and subtraction to find how much paint she has left.

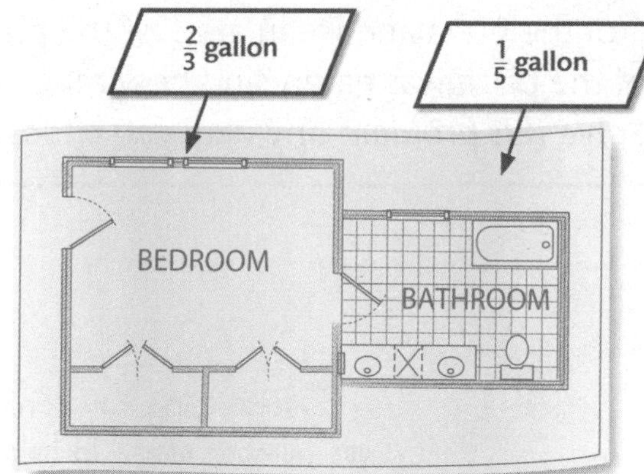

B

Step 1

Add to find out how much paint Kayla used for the two ceilings.

To add, write each fraction using 15 as the denominator.

$$\begin{array}{r} \frac{2}{3} = \frac{10}{15} \\ + \frac{1}{5} = \frac{3}{15} \\ \hline \frac{13}{15} \end{array}$$

Kayla used $\frac{13}{15}$ gallon of paint.

C

Step 2

Subtract the amount of paint Kayla used from the amount she started with.

To subtract, write each fraction using 30 as the denominator.

$$\begin{array}{r} \frac{9}{10} = \frac{27}{30} \\ - \frac{13}{15} = \frac{26}{30} \\ \hline \frac{1}{30} \end{array}$$

Kayla has $\frac{1}{30}$ gallon of paint left.

Convince Me! **Make Sense and Persevere** For the problem above, how would you use estimation to check that the answer is reasonable?

Name ____________________

Practice  Tools  Assessment

Guided Practice

Do You Understand?

1. In the example on page 286, how much more paint did Kayla use to paint the bedroom ceiling than the bathroom ceiling?

2. **Number Sense** Kevin estimated the difference of $\frac{9}{10} - \frac{4}{8}$ to be 0. Is his estimate reasonable? Explain.

Do You Know How?

For **3–6**, find the sum or difference.

3. $\frac{1}{15} + \frac{1}{6}$

4. $\frac{7}{16} - \frac{1}{4}$

5. $\frac{7}{8} - \frac{3}{6}$

6. $\frac{7}{8} + \left(\frac{4}{8} - \frac{2}{4}\right)$

Independent Practice

In **7–22**, find the sum or difference.

7. $\frac{4}{50} + \frac{3}{5}$

8. $\frac{2}{3} - \frac{7}{12}$

9. $\frac{9}{10} + \frac{2}{100}$

10. $\frac{4}{9} + \frac{1}{4}$

11. $\frac{17}{15} - \frac{1}{3}$

12. $\frac{7}{16} + \frac{3}{8}$

13. $\frac{2}{5} + \frac{1}{4}$

14. $\frac{1}{7} + \frac{1}{2}$

15. $\frac{1}{2} - \frac{3}{16}$

16. $\frac{7}{8} - \frac{2}{3}$

17. $\frac{11}{12} - \frac{4}{6}$

18. $\frac{7}{18} + \frac{5}{9}$

19. $\left(\frac{7}{8} + \frac{1}{12}\right) - \frac{1}{2}$

20. $\left(\frac{11}{18} - \frac{4}{9}\right) + \frac{1}{6}$

21. $\frac{13}{14} - \left(\frac{1}{2} + \frac{2}{7}\right)$

22. $\frac{1}{6} + \left(\frac{15}{15} - \frac{7}{10}\right)$

Problem Solving

23. The table shows the amounts of ingredients needed to make a pizza. How much more cheese do you need than pepperoni and mushrooms combined? Show how you solved the problem.

DATA

Ingredient	Amount
Cheese	$\frac{3}{4}$ c
Pepperoni	$\frac{1}{3}$ c
Mushrooms	$\frac{1}{4}$ c

24. Charlie's goal is to use less than 50 gallons of water per day. His water bill for the month showed that he used 1,524 gallons of water in 30 days. Did Charlie meet his goal this month? Explain how you decided.

25. Construct Arguments Jereen spent $\frac{1}{4}$ hour on homework before school, another $\frac{1}{2}$ hour after she got home, and a final $\frac{1}{3}$ hour after dinner. Did she spend more or less than 1 hour on homework in all? Explain.

26. Carl has three lengths of cable, $\frac{5}{6}$ yard long, $\frac{1}{4}$ yard long, and $\frac{2}{3}$ yard long. If he uses 1 yard of cable, how much cable is left? Explain your work.

1 yard		x
$\frac{1}{4}$	$\frac{5}{6}$	$\frac{2}{3}$

27. Higher Order Thinking Find two fractions with a sum of $\frac{2}{3}$ but with neither denominator equal to 3.

Assessment Practice

28. What fraction is missing from the following equation?

$$1 - \square = \frac{1}{4} + \frac{3}{8}$$

Ⓐ $\frac{4}{12}$

Ⓑ $\frac{3}{8}$

Ⓒ $\frac{5}{12}$

Ⓓ $\frac{8}{8}$

29. What is the value of the expression?

$$\frac{1}{4} + \frac{1}{4} + \frac{3}{8}$$

Ⓐ $\frac{5}{8}$

Ⓑ $\frac{7}{8}$

Ⓒ $\frac{7}{16}$

Ⓓ $\frac{7}{32}$

Name ____________________ Activity

Solve & Share

Alex has five cups of strawberries. He wants to use $1\frac{3}{4}$ cups of strawberries for a fruit salad and $3\frac{1}{2}$ cups for jam. Does Alex have enough strawberries to make both recipes? ***Solve this problem any way you choose.***

Lesson 7-6

Estimate Sums and Differences of Mixed Numbers

I can ...

estimate sums and differences of fractions and mixed numbers.

Content Standards 5.NF.A.2 Also 5.NF.A.1
Mathematical Practices MP.1, MP.3, MP.8

Generalize You can estimate because you just need to know if Alex has enough. *Show your work!*

Look Back! Does it make sense to use 1 cup and 3 cups to estimate if Alex has enough strawberries? Explain.

What Are Some Ways to Estimate?

A

Jamila's mom wants to make a size 10 dress and jacket. About how many yards of fabric does she need?

Estimate the sum $2\frac{1}{4} + 1\frac{5}{8}$ to find how many yards of fabric she needs.

DATA

Fabric Required (in yards)		
	Size 10	**Size 14**
Dress	$2\frac{1}{4}$	$2\frac{7}{8}$
Jacket	$1\frac{5}{8}$	$2\frac{1}{4}$

B

One Way

Use a number line to round fractions and mixed numbers to the nearest whole number.

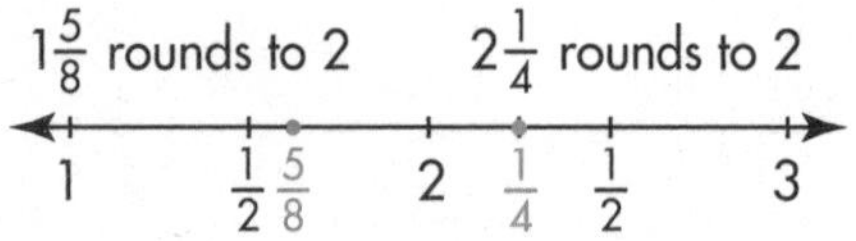

$1\frac{5}{8}$ rounds to 2 $\quad$ $2\frac{1}{4}$ rounds to 2

Number line labels: 1, $\frac{1}{2}$, $\frac{5}{8}$, 2, $\frac{1}{4}$, $\frac{1}{2}$, 3

So, $2\frac{1}{4} + 1\frac{5}{8} \approx 2 + 2$, or 4.

Jamila's mom needs about 4 yards of fabric.

C

Another Way

Use $\frac{1}{2}$ as a benchmark fraction.

Replace each fraction with the nearest $\frac{1}{2}$ unit.

$1\frac{5}{8}$ is close to $1\frac{1}{2}$.

$2\frac{1}{4}$ is halfway between 2 and $2\frac{1}{2}$.

So, $2\frac{1}{4} + 1\frac{5}{8}$ is about $2\frac{1}{2} + 1\frac{1}{2} = 4$.

Convince Me! **Critique Reasoning** In Box C above, why does it make sense to replace $2\frac{1}{4}$ with $2\frac{1}{2}$ rather than 2?

Name ____________________

Practice Tools Assessment

Guided Practice

Do You Understand?

1. To estimate with mixed numbers, when should you round to the next greater whole number?

2. When should you estimate a sum or difference?

Do You Know How?

In **3–5**, round to the nearest whole number.

3. $2\frac{3}{4}$ **4.** $1\frac{5}{7}$ **5.** $2\frac{3}{10}$

In **6** and **7**, estimate each sum or difference using benchmark fractions.

6. $2\frac{5}{9} - 1\frac{1}{3}$ **7.** $2\frac{4}{10} + 3\frac{5}{8}$

Independent Practice

Leveled Practice In **8–11**, use the number line to round the mixed numbers to the nearest whole numbers.

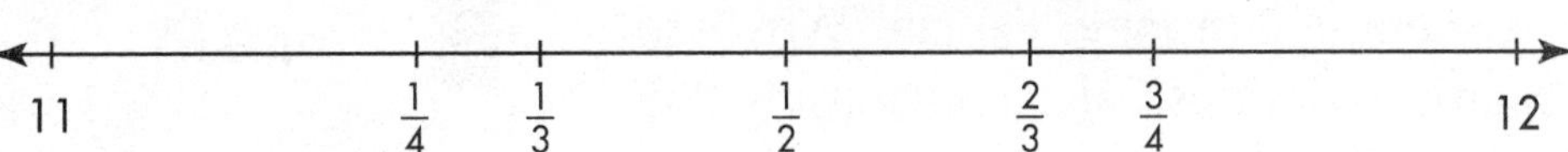

8. $11\frac{4}{6}$ **9.** $11\frac{2}{8}$ **10.** $11\frac{8}{12}$ **11.** $11\frac{4}{10}$

In **12–20**, estimate each sum or difference.

12. $2\frac{1}{8} - \frac{5}{7}$ **13.** $12\frac{1}{3} + 2\frac{1}{4}$ **14.** $2\frac{2}{3} + \frac{7}{8} + 6\frac{7}{12}$

15. $1\frac{10}{15} - \frac{8}{9}$ **16.** $10\frac{5}{6} - 2\frac{3}{8}$ **17.** $12\frac{8}{25} + 13\frac{5}{9}$

18. $48\frac{1}{10} - 2\frac{7}{9}$ **19.** $33\frac{14}{15} + 23\frac{9}{25}$ **20.** $14\frac{4}{9} + 25\frac{1}{6} + 7\frac{11}{18}$

Problem Solving

21. Use the recipes to answer the questions.

a Estimate how many cups of Fruit Trail Mix the recipe can make.

b Estimate how many cups of Traditional Trail Mix the recipe can make.

c Estimate how much trail mix you would have if you made both recipes.

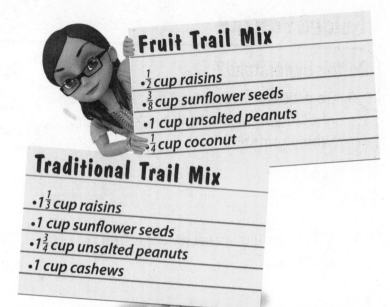

Fruit Trail Mix

- $\frac{1}{2}$ cup raisins
- $\frac{3}{8}$ cup sunflower seeds
- 1 cup unsalted peanuts
- $\frac{1}{4}$ cup coconut

Traditional Trail Mix

- $1\frac{1}{3}$ cup raisins
- 1 cup sunflower seeds
- $1\frac{3}{4}$ cup unsalted peanuts
- 1 cup cashews

22. Kim is $3\frac{5}{8}$ inches taller than Colleen. If Kim is $60\frac{3}{4}$ inches tall, what is the best estimate of Colleen's height?

23. Higher Order Thinking Last week Jason walked $3\frac{1}{4}$ miles each day for 3 days and $4\frac{5}{8}$ miles each day for 4 days. About how many miles did Jason walk last week?

24. Make Sense and Persevere Cal has $12.50 to spend. He wants to ride the roller coaster twice and the Ferris wheel once. Does Cal have enough money? Explain. What are 3 possible combinations of rides Cal can take using the money he has?

DATA

Ride Prices

Ride	Cost
Carousel	$3.75
Ferris Wheel	$4.25
Roller Coaster	$5.50

Assessment Practice

25. Liam used $2\frac{2}{9}$ cups of milk for a pancake recipe and drank another $9\frac{3}{4}$ cups of milk. About how much milk did he use in all?

Ⓐ 8 cups
Ⓑ 10 cups
Ⓒ 12 cups
Ⓓ 13 cups

26. Annie has $13\frac{1}{12}$ yards of string. She uses $1\frac{9}{10}$ yards to fix her backpack. About how much string does she have left?

Ⓐ 11 yards
Ⓑ 12 yards
Ⓒ 14 yards
Ⓓ 15 yards

Name ______________________________

Lesson 7-7
Use Models to Add Mixed Numbers

I can ...
add mixed numbers using models.

Content Standards 5.NF.A.2 Also 5.NF.A.1
Mathematical Practices MP.1, MP.3, MP.5

Solve & Share Martina is baking bread. She mixes $1\frac{3}{4}$ cups of flour with other ingredients. Then she adds $4\frac{1}{2}$ cups of flour to the mixture. How many cups of flour does she need? ***Solve this problem any way you choose.***

Use Appropriate Tools
You can use fraction strips to help add mixed numbers.
Show your work!

Look Back! Explain how you can estimate the sum above.

How Can You Model Addition of Mixed Numbers?

A

Bill has 2 boards he will use to make picture frames. What is the total length of the boards Bill has to make picture frames?

You can find a common denominator to add the fractions.

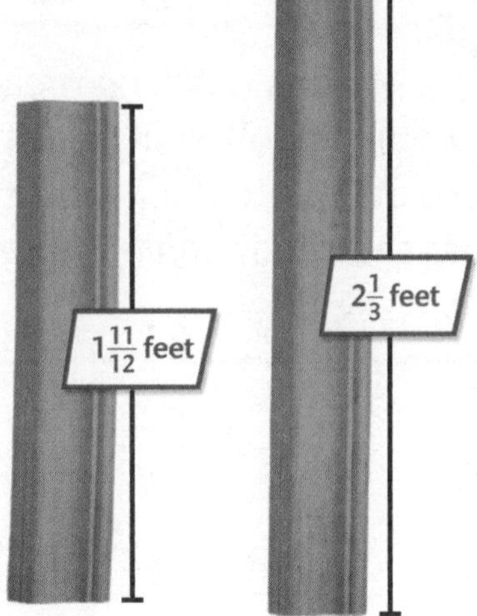

B

Step 1

Rename the fractional parts as equivalent fractions with a like denominator. Add the fractions.

$$2\frac{4}{12} + 1\frac{11}{12} = \frac{15}{12}$$

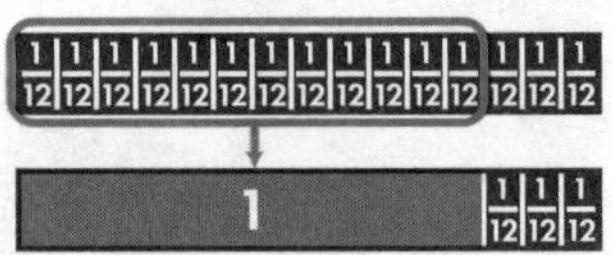

Rename $\frac{15}{12}$ as $1\frac{3}{12}$.

C

Step 2

Add the whole number parts.

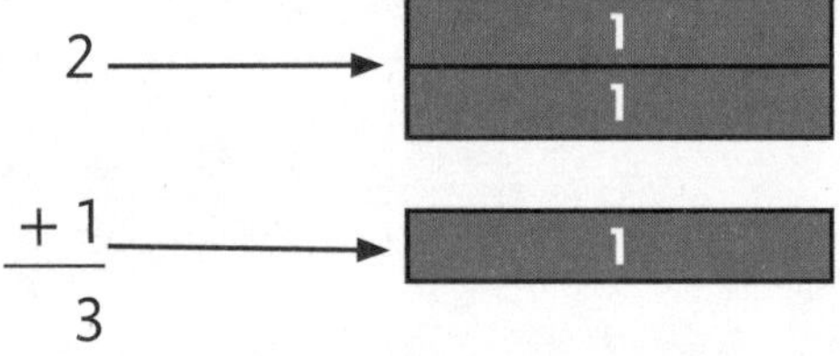

$$2 + 1 = 3$$

Then add the sum of the fractional parts.

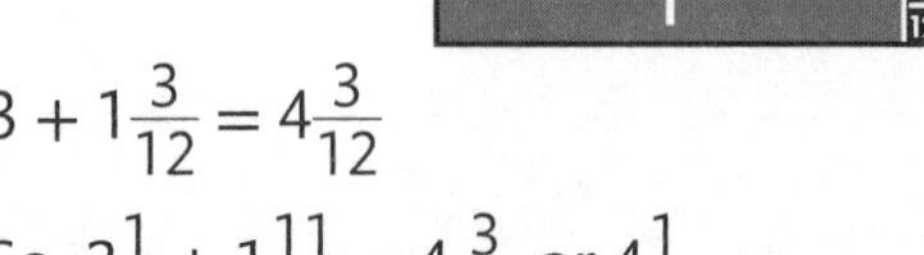

$3 + 1\frac{3}{12} = 4\frac{3}{12}$

So, $2\frac{1}{3} + 1\frac{11}{12} = 4\frac{3}{12}$ or $4\frac{1}{4}$

The total length of the boards is $4\frac{1}{4}$ feet.

Convince Me! Critique Reasoning Tom has 2 boards that are the same length as Bill's. He says that he found the total length of the boards by adding 28 twelfths and 23 twelfths. Does his method work? Explain.

Name ____________________

Practice Tools Assessment

Guided Practice

Do You Understand?

1. When adding two mixed numbers, does it ever make sense to rename the fractional sum? Explain.

Do You Know How?

In **2–5**, use fraction strips to find each sum.

2. $1\frac{1}{10} + 2\frac{4}{5}$

3. $1\frac{1}{2} + 2\frac{3}{4}$

4. $3\frac{2}{3} + 1\frac{4}{6}$

5. $3\frac{1}{6} + 2\frac{2}{3}$

Independent Practice

Leveled Practice In **6** and **7**, use each model to find the sum.

6. Charles used $1\frac{2}{3}$ cups of walnuts and $2\frac{1}{6}$ cups of cranberries to make breakfast bread. How many cups of walnuts and cranberries did he use in all?

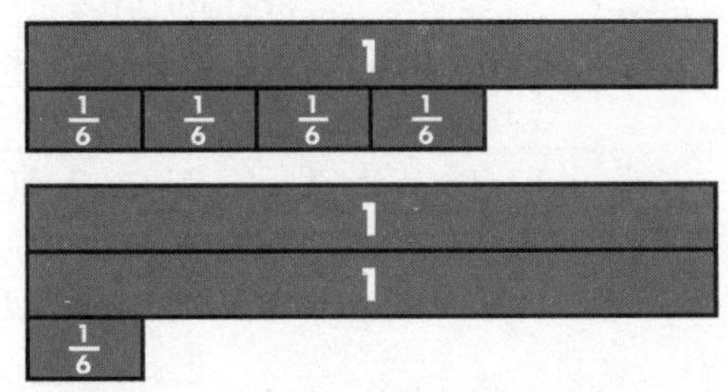

7. Mary worked $2\frac{3}{4}$ hours on Monday and $1\frac{1}{2}$ hours on Tuesday. How many hours did she work in all on Monday and Tuesday?

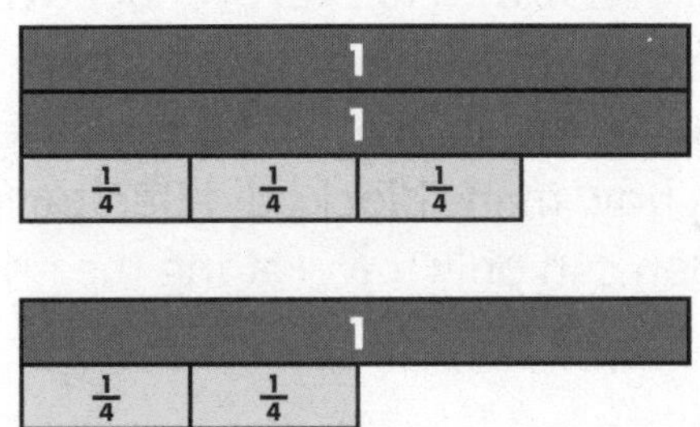

In **8–16**, use fraction strips to find each sum.

8. $2\frac{6}{10} + 1\frac{3}{5}$

9. $4\frac{5}{6} + 1\frac{7}{12}$

10. $4\frac{2}{5} + 3\frac{7}{10}$

11. $3\frac{1}{2} + 1\frac{3}{4}$

12. $1\frac{7}{8} + 5\frac{1}{4}$

13. $2\frac{6}{12} + 1\frac{1}{2}$

14. $3\frac{2}{5} + 1\frac{9}{10}$

15. $2\frac{7}{12} + 1\frac{3}{4}$

16. $2\frac{7}{8} + 5\frac{1}{2}$

Problem Solving

17. Lindsey used $1\frac{1}{4}$ gallons of tan paint for the ceiling and $4\frac{3}{8}$ gallons of green paint for the walls of her kitchen. How much paint did Lindsey use in all? Use fraction strips to help.

18. Paul said, "I walked $2\frac{1}{2}$ miles on Saturday and $2\frac{3}{4}$ miles on Sunday." How many miles is that in all?

19. Higher Order Thinking Tori is making muffins. The recipe calls for $2\frac{5}{6}$ cups of brown sugar for the muffins and $1\frac{1}{3}$ cups of brown sugar for the topping. Tori has 4 cups of brown sugar. Does she have enough brown sugar to make the muffins and the topping? Explain.

You can use fraction strips or a number line to compare amounts.

In **20** and **21**, use the map. Each unit represents one block.

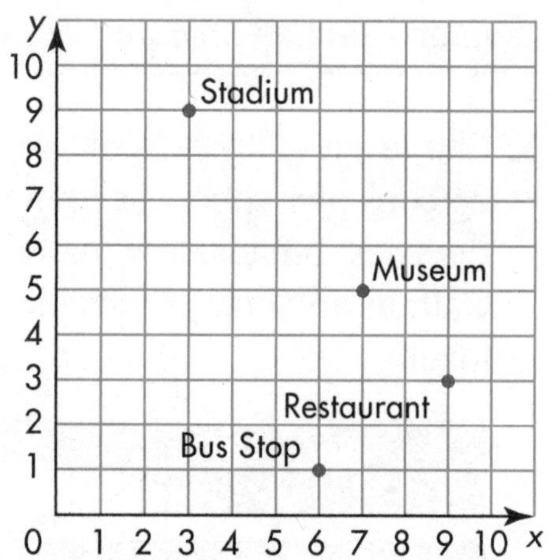

20. Ben left the museum and walked 4 blocks to his next destination. What was Ben's destination?

21. Make Sense and Persevere Ben walked from the restaurant to the bus stop. Then, he took the bus to the stadium. If he took the shortest route, how many blocks did Ben travel? Note that Ben can only travel along the grid lines.

Assessment Practice

22. Marta used $2\frac{3}{4}$ cups of milk and $1\frac{1}{2}$ cups of cheese in a recipe. How many cups of cheese and milk did Marta use?

Ⓐ 3 cups

Ⓑ $3\frac{4}{6}$ cups

Ⓒ $4\frac{1}{4}$ cups

Ⓓ $4\frac{3}{4}$ cups

23. Garrett ran $21\frac{1}{2}$ miles last week. He ran $17\frac{7}{8}$ miles this week. How many miles did he run in all?

Ⓐ 38 miles

Ⓑ $38\frac{1}{2}$ miles

Ⓒ $39\frac{3}{8}$ miles

Ⓓ $39\frac{7}{8}$ miles

Name ______________________

Activity

Lesson 7-8
Add Mixed Numbers

I can ...
add mixed numbers.

Content Standards 5.NF.A.1 Also 5.NF.A.2
Mathematical Practices MP.3, MP.7

Joaquin used two types of flour in a muffin recipe. How much flour did he use in all? ***Solve any way you choose.***

Use Structure
Use what you know about adding fractions. *Show your work!*

Basic Muffins

$\frac{1}{2}$ c milk

$\frac{1}{3}$ c melted butter

2 eggs

$1\frac{1}{2}$ c whole wheat flour

$1\frac{2}{3}$ c buckwheat flour

1 tsp baking powder

Look Back! How is adding mixed numbers with unlike denominators the same as adding fractions with unlike denominators? How is it different?

Visual Learning Bridge

Essential Question How Can You Add Mixed Numbers?

A

Rhoda mixes $1\frac{1}{2}$ cups of sand with $2\frac{2}{3}$ cups of potting mixture to prepare soil for her cactus plants. After mixing them together, how many cups of soil does Rhoda have?

You can use addition to find the total amount of soil.

B Step 1

Find $2\frac{2}{3} + 1\frac{1}{2}$.

Write equivalent fractions with a common denominator.

$$2\frac{2}{3} = 2\frac{4}{6}$$
$$+\ 1\frac{1}{2} = 1\frac{3}{6}$$

C Step 2

Add the fractions.

$$2\frac{2}{3} = 2\frac{4}{6}$$
$$+\ 1\frac{1}{2} = 1\frac{3}{6}$$
$$\frac{7}{6}$$

D Step 3

Add the whole numbers.

$$2\frac{2}{3} = 2\frac{4}{6}$$
$$+\ 1\frac{1}{2} = 1\frac{3}{6}$$
$$3\frac{7}{6}$$

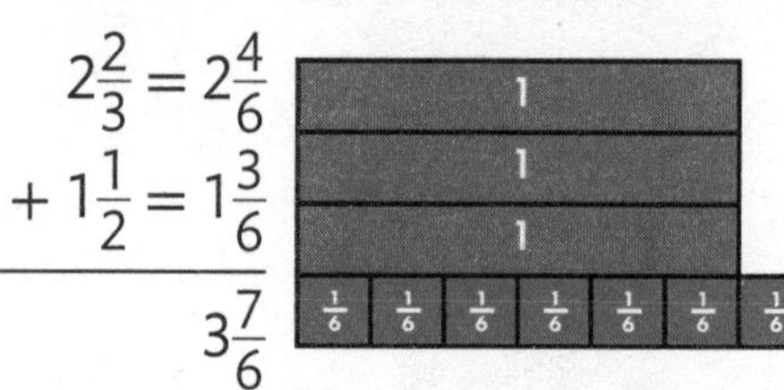

Rewrite $\frac{7}{6}$ as a mixed number.

$$3\frac{7}{6} = 3 + 1\frac{1}{6} = 4\frac{1}{6}$$

Rhoda has $4\frac{1}{6}$ cups of soil.

Convince Me! **Critique Reasoning** Kyle used 9 as an estimate for $3\frac{1}{6} + 5\frac{7}{8}$. He got $9\frac{1}{24}$ for the exact sum. Is his calculated answer reasonable? Explain.

Name ________________________________

Practice Tools Assessment

Guided Practice

Do You Understand?

1. How is adding mixed numbers like adding fractions and whole numbers?

2. Look at the example on page 298. Why is the denominator 6 used in the equivalent fractions?

Do You Know How?

In **3–6**, estimate and then find each sum.

3. $1\frac{7}{8} = 1\frac{\square}{8}$
$+\,1\frac{1}{4} = 1\frac{\square}{8}$

4. $2\frac{2}{5} = 2\frac{\square}{30}$
$+\,5\frac{5}{6} = 5\frac{\square}{30}$

5. $4\frac{1}{9} + 1\frac{1}{3}$

6. $6\frac{5}{12} + 4\frac{5}{8}$

Independent Practice

Leveled Practice In **7–18**, estimate and then find each sum.

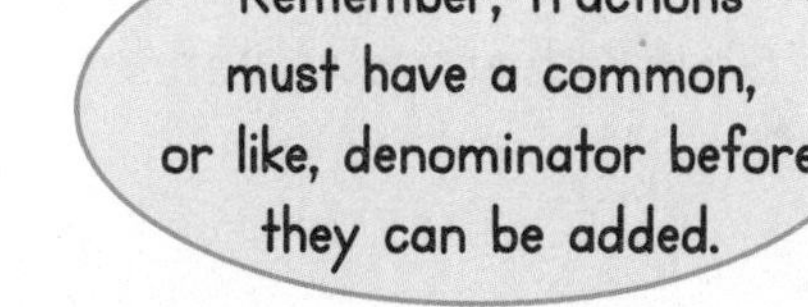

Remember, fractions must have a common, or like, denominator before they can be added.

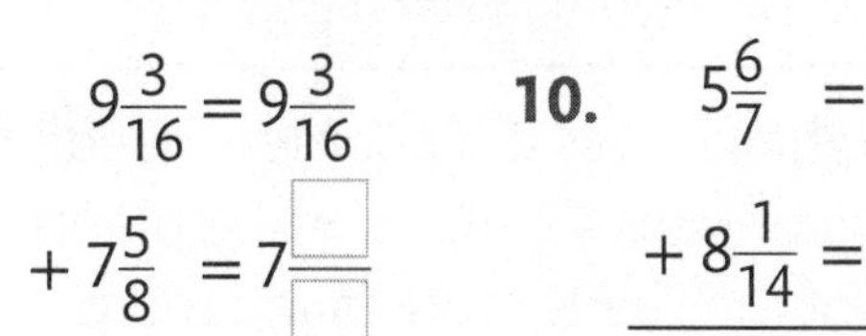

7. $3\frac{1}{6} = 3\frac{\square}{6}$
$+\,5\frac{2}{3} = 5\frac{\square}{6}$

8. $11\frac{1}{2} = 11\frac{\square}{10}$
$+\,10\frac{3}{5} = 10\frac{\square}{10}$

9. $9\frac{3}{16} = 9\frac{3}{16}$
$+\,7\frac{5}{8} = 7\frac{\square}{\square}$

10. $5\frac{6}{7} = 5\frac{\square}{\square}$
$+\,8\frac{1}{14} = 8\frac{1}{14}$

11. $4\frac{1}{10}$
$+\,6\frac{1}{2}$

12. $9\frac{7}{12}$
$+\,4\frac{3}{4}$

13. 5
$+\,3\frac{1}{8}$

14. $8\frac{3}{4}$
$+\,7\frac{3}{4}$

15. $2\frac{3}{4} + 7\frac{3}{5}$

16. $3\frac{8}{9} + 8\frac{1}{2}$

17. $1\frac{7}{12} + 2\frac{3}{8}$

18. $3\frac{11}{12} + 9\frac{1}{16}$

Problem Solving

19. Use the map to find the answer.

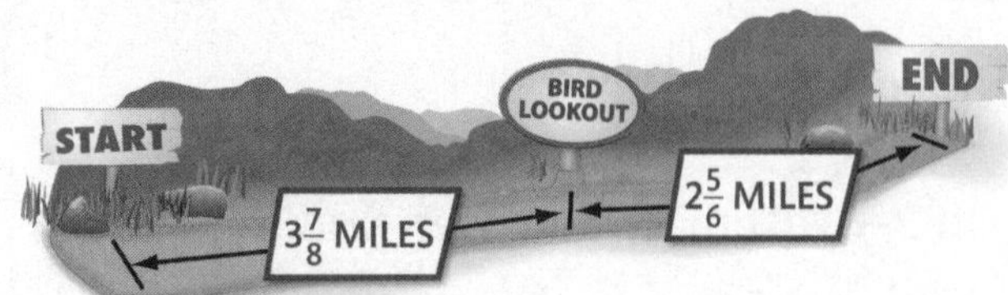

a What is the distance from the start to the end of the trail?

b Louise walked from the start of the trail to the bird lookout and back. Did she walk a longer or shorter distance than if she had walked from the start of the trail to the end? Explain.

c Another day, Louise walked from the start of the trail to the end. At the end, she realized she forgot her binoculars at the bird lookout. She walked from the end of the trail to the bird lookout and back. What is the total distance she walked?

20. Higher Order Thinking Twice a day Cameron's cat eats 4 ounces of dry cat food and 2 ounces of wet cat food. Dry food comes in 5-pound bags. Wet food comes in 6-ounce cans.

a How many cans of wet food should he buy to feed his cat for a week?

b How many ounces of wet cat food will be left over at the end of the week?

c How many days can he feed his cat from a 5-pound bag of dry food?

21. Julia bought 12 bags of cucumber seeds. Each bag contains 42 seeds. If she plants one half of the seeds, how many seeds does she have left?

22. Critique Reasoning John added $2\frac{7}{12}$ and $5\frac{2}{3}$ and got $7\frac{1}{4}$ as the sum. Is John's answer reasonable? Explain.

Assessment Practice

23. What is the missing number in the following equation?

$3\frac{1}{3} + \frac{4}{\square} = 4\frac{2}{15}$

24. Arnie skated $1\frac{3}{4}$ miles from home to the lake. He skated $1\frac{1}{3}$ miles around the lake, and then skated back home. Write an addition sentence to show how many miles Arnie skated in all.

Name ______________________________

Activity

Lesson 7-9

Use Models to Subtract Mixed Numbers

I can ...

use models to subtract mixed numbers.

Content Standards 5.NF.A.1 Also 5.NF.A.2
Mathematical Practices MP.4, MP.5, MP.8

Solve & Share

Clara and Erin volunteered at an animal shelter a total of $9\frac{5}{6}$ hours. Clara worked for $4\frac{1}{3}$ hours. How many hours did Erin work? ***You can use fraction strips to solve this problem.***

Generalize
How can you use what you know about adding mixed numbers to help you subtract mixed numbers?
Show your work!

Look Back! How can you estimate the difference for the problem above? Explain your thinking.

How Can You Model Subtraction of Mixed Numbers?

Visual Learning Bridge

A

James needs $1\frac{11}{12}$ inches of pipe to repair a small part of a bicycle frame. He has a pipe that is $2\frac{1}{2}$ inches long. Does he have enough pipe left over to fix a $\frac{3}{4}$-inch piece of frame on another bike?

Rename $2\frac{1}{2}$ as $2\frac{6}{12}$ so that the fractions have a common denominator.

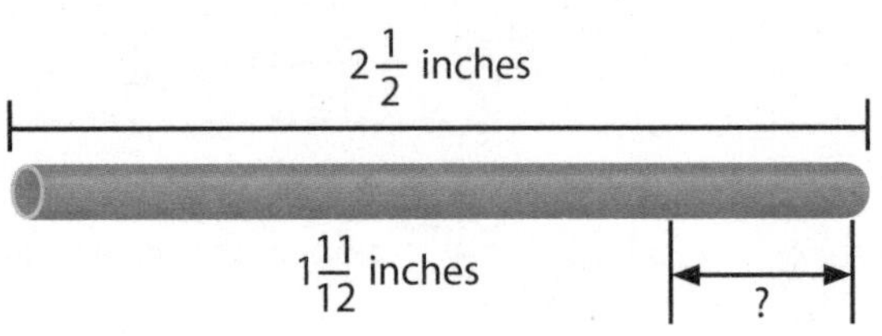

B

Step 1

Model the number you are subtracting from, $2\frac{6}{12}$.

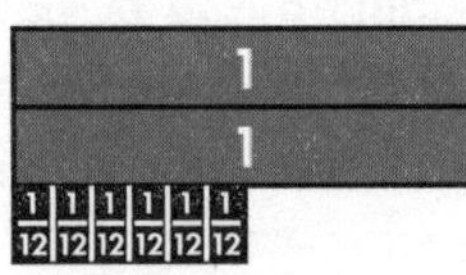

If the fraction you will be subtracting is greater than the fraction part of the number you model, rename 1 whole.

Since $\frac{11}{12} > \frac{6}{12}$, rename 1 whole as $\frac{12}{12}$.

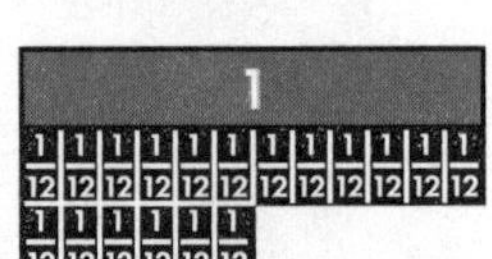

C

Step 2

Use your renamed model to cross out the number that you are subtracting, $1\frac{11}{12}$.

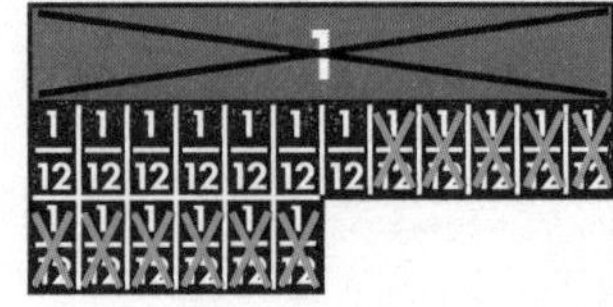

There are $\frac{7}{12}$ left.

So, $2\frac{1}{2} - 1\frac{11}{12} = \frac{7}{12}$.

James will have $\frac{7}{12}$ inch of pipe left. He does not have enough for the other bike.

Convince Me! **Use Appropriate Tools**

Use fraction strips to find $5\frac{1}{2} - 2\frac{3}{4}$.

Name ______________________________

Practice Tools Assessment

Guided Practice

Do You Understand?

1. When subtracting two mixed numbers, is it always necessary to rename one of the wholes? Explain.

Do You Know How?

In **2–5**, use fraction strips to find each difference.

2. $4\frac{5}{6} - 2\frac{1}{3}$

3. $4\frac{1}{8} - 3\frac{3}{4}$

4. $5\frac{1}{2} - 2\frac{5}{6}$

5. $5\frac{4}{10} - 3\frac{4}{5}$

Independent Practice

In **6** and **7**, use each model to find the difference.

6. Terrell lives $2\frac{5}{6}$ blocks away from his best friend. His school is $4\frac{1}{3}$ blocks away in the same direction. If he stops at his best friend's house first, how much farther do they have to walk to school?

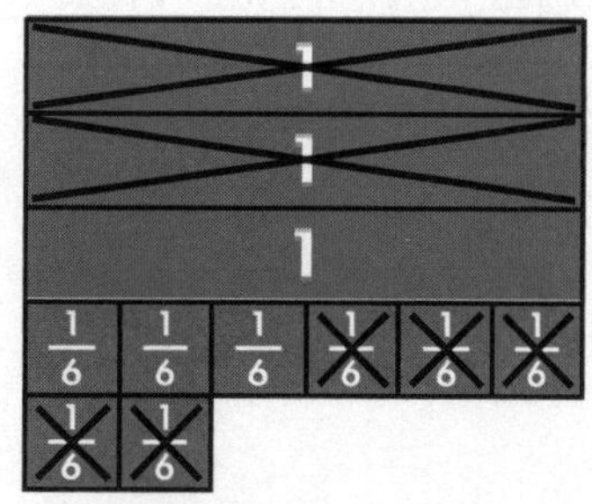

7. Tina bought $3\frac{1}{2}$ pounds of turkey and $2\frac{1}{4}$ pounds of cheese. She used $1\frac{1}{2}$ pounds of cheese to make macaroni and cheese. How much cheese does she have left?

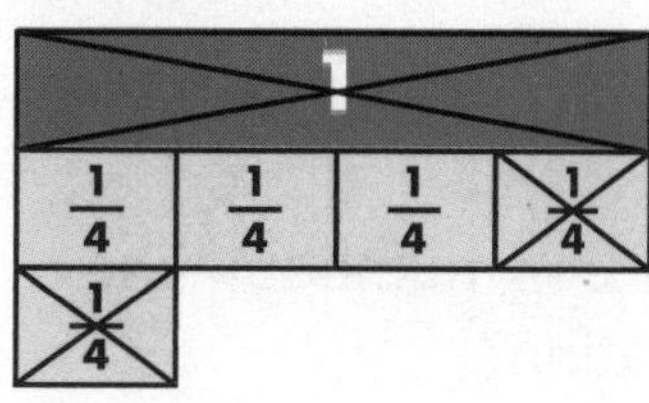

In **8–15**, use fraction strips to find each difference.

8. $12\frac{3}{4} - 9\frac{5}{8}$

9. $8\frac{1}{6} - 7\frac{2}{3}$

10. $13\frac{7}{9} - 10\frac{2}{3}$

11. $3\frac{1}{12} - 2\frac{3}{4}$

12. $6\frac{3}{4} - 3\frac{11}{12}$

13. $4\frac{3}{5} - 1\frac{1}{10}$

14. $6\frac{1}{2} - 3\frac{7}{10}$

15. $6\frac{2}{3} - 4\frac{2}{9}$

Problem Solving

For **16** and **17**, use the table at the right.

16. How much longer is a Red Oak leaf than a Sugar Maple leaf? Write an equation to model your work.

17. How much longer is a Red Oak leaf than a Paper Birch leaf? Write an equation to model your work.

Tree Leaf Lengths

Tree	Leaf Length (in.)
Sugar Maple	$6\frac{3}{4}$
Red Oak	$8\frac{1}{2}$
Paper Birch	$3\frac{5}{8}$

18. Higher Order Thinking Lemmy walked $3\frac{1}{2}$ miles on Saturday and $4\frac{3}{4}$ miles on Sunday. Ronnie walked $5\frac{3}{8}$ miles on Saturday. Who walked farther? How much farther?

19. Model with Math Jamal is buying lunch for his family. He buys 4 drinks that each cost \$1.75 and 4 sandwiches that each cost \$7.50. If the prices include tax and he also leaves a \$7 tip, how much does he spend in all? Write equations to show your work.

Assessment Practice

20. What is the missing number in the following equation?

$5\frac{2}{\square} - 1\frac{4}{9} = 4\frac{2}{9}$

21. What is the missing number in the following equation?

$12\frac{1}{2} - 10\frac{11}{12} = 1\frac{7}{\square}$

Name ____________________ Activity

Solve & Share

Evan walks $2\frac{1}{8}$ miles to his aunt's house. He has already walked $\frac{3}{4}$ mile. How much farther does he have to go? ***Solve this problem any way you choose.***

Lesson 7-10
Subtract Mixed Numbers

I can ...
subtract mixed numbers.

Content Standards 5.NF.A.1 Also 5.NF.A.2
Mathematical Practices MP.3, MP.6, MP.7

Use Structure
Use what you know about subtracting fractions. *Show your work!*

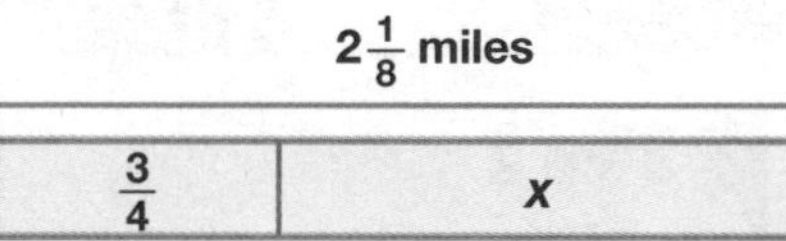

Look Back! Jon said, "Changing $\frac{3}{4}$ to $\frac{6}{8}$ makes this problem easier." What do you think Jon meant?

Essential Question

How Can You Subtract Mixed Numbers?

Visual Learning Bridge

A

A golf ball measures about $1\frac{2}{3}$ inches across the center. What is the difference between the distance across the center of the hole and the golf ball?

You can use subtraction to find the difference.

B

Step 1

Write equivalent fractions with a common denominator.

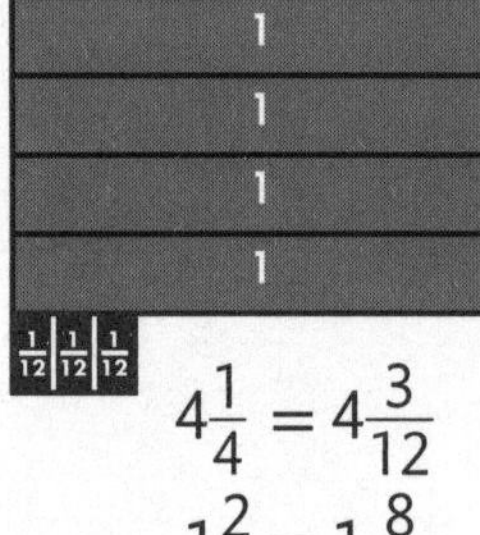

$$\begin{array}{r} 4\frac{1}{4} = 4\frac{3}{12} \\ -\ 1\frac{2}{3} = 1\frac{8}{12} \\ \hline \end{array}$$

Since $\frac{8}{12} > \frac{3}{12}$, you can rename 1 as $\frac{12}{12}$ to subtract.

C

Step 2

Rename $4\frac{3}{12}$ to show more twelfths.

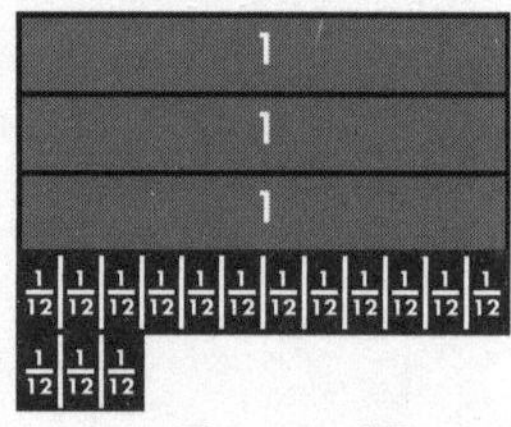

$$\begin{array}{r} 4\frac{3}{12} = 3\frac{15}{12} \\ -\ 1\frac{8}{12} = 1\frac{8}{12} \\ \hline \end{array}$$

D

Step 3

Subtract the fractions. Then subtract the whole numbers.

$$\begin{array}{r} 4\frac{1}{4} = 4\frac{3}{12} = 3\frac{15}{12} \\ -\ 1\frac{2}{3} = 1\frac{8}{12} = 1\frac{8}{12} \\ \hline 2\frac{7}{12} \end{array}$$

The hole is $2\frac{7}{12}$ inches wider.

Convince Me! **Critique Reasoning** Estimate $8\frac{1}{3} - 3\frac{3}{4}$. Tell how you got your estimate. Susi subtracted and found the actual difference to be $5\frac{7}{12}$. Is her answer reasonable? Explain.

Name ______________________________

Practice Tools Assessment

Another Example

Sometimes you may have to rename a whole number to subtract.
Find the difference of $6 - 2\frac{3}{8}$.

$$\begin{array}{r} 6 \\ -\ 2\frac{3}{8} \\ \hline \end{array} \longrightarrow \text{rename} \longrightarrow \begin{array}{r} 5\frac{8}{8} \\ -\ 2\frac{3}{8} \\ \hline 3\frac{5}{8} \end{array}$$

Guided Practice

Do You Understand?

1. In the example above, why do you need to rename the 6?

2. In the example on page 306, could two golf balls fall into the hole at the same time? Explain your reasoning.

Do You Know How?

In **3–6**, estimate and then find each difference.

3. $$\begin{array}{r} 7\frac{2}{3} = 7\frac{\square}{6} = 6\frac{\square}{6} \\ -\ 3\frac{5}{6} = 3\frac{\square}{6} = 3\frac{\square}{6} \\ \hline \end{array}$$

4. $$\begin{array}{r} 5 \ = \square\frac{\square}{4} \\ -\ 2\frac{3}{4} = 2\frac{3}{4} \\ \hline \end{array}$$

5. $6\frac{3}{10} - 1\frac{4}{5}$

6. $9\frac{1}{3} - 4\frac{3}{4}$

Independent Practice

In **7–18**, estimate and then find each difference.

Remember to check that your answer makes sense by comparing it to the estimate.

7. $$\begin{array}{r} 8\frac{1}{4} = 8\frac{\square}{8} = 7\frac{\square}{8} \\ -\ 2\frac{7}{8} = 2\frac{\square}{8} = 2\frac{\square}{8} \\ \hline \end{array}$$

8. $$\begin{array}{r} 3\frac{1}{2} = 3\frac{\square}{6} \\ -\ 1\frac{1}{3} = 1\frac{\square}{6} \\ \hline \end{array}$$

9. $$\begin{array}{r} 4\frac{1}{8} \\ -\ 1\frac{1}{2} \\ \hline \end{array}$$

10. $$\begin{array}{r} 6 \\ -\ 2\frac{4}{5} \\ \hline \end{array}$$

11. $6\frac{1}{3} - 5\frac{2}{3}$

12. $9\frac{1}{2} - 6\frac{3}{4}$

13. $8\frac{3}{16} - 3\frac{5}{8}$

14. $7\frac{1}{2} - \frac{7}{10}$

15. $15\frac{1}{6} - 4\frac{3}{8}$

16. $13\frac{1}{12} - 8\frac{1}{4}$

17. $6\frac{1}{3} - 2\frac{3}{5}$

18. $10\frac{5}{12} - 4\frac{7}{8}$

Problem Solving

19. The average weight of a basketball is $21\frac{1}{10}$ ounces. The average weight of a baseball is $5\frac{1}{4}$ ounces. How many more ounces does the basketball weigh? Write the missing numbers in the diagram.

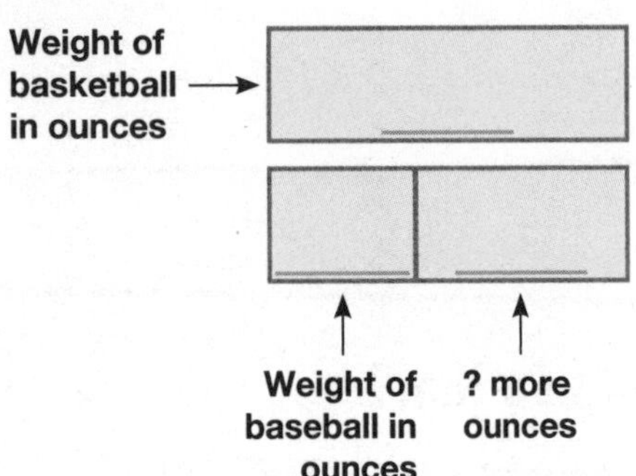

20. **enVision®** STEM The smallest mammals on Earth are the bumblebee bat and the Etruscan pygmy shrew. The length of a certain bumblebee bat is $1\frac{9}{50}$ inches. The length of a certain Etruscan pygmy shrew is $1\frac{21}{50}$ inches. How much smaller is the bat than the shrew?

21. **Be Precise** How are the purple quadrilateral and the green quadrilateral alike? How are they different?

22. **Higher Order Thinking** Sam used the model to find $2\frac{5}{12} - 1\frac{7}{12}$. Did Sam model the problem correctly? Explain. If not, show how the problem should have been modeled and find the difference.

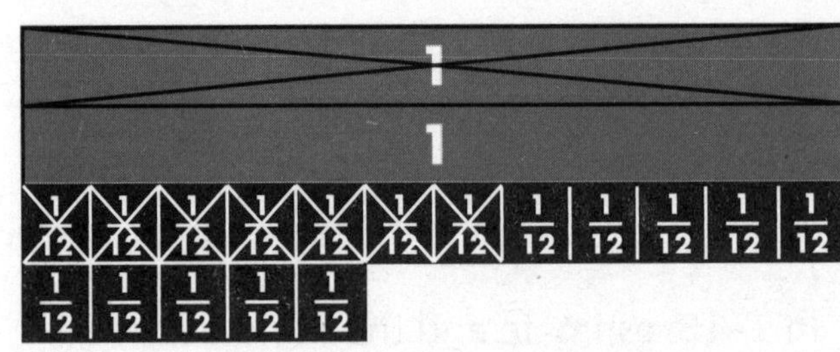

Assessment Practice

23. Choose the correct number from the box below to complete the subtraction sentence that follows.

1	2	3	4	5

$3\frac{5}{8} - 1\frac{\square}{4} = 2\frac{3}{8}$

24. Choose the correct number from the box below to complete the subtraction sentence that follows.

2	4	5	10	15

$14\frac{1}{10} - 3\frac{1}{\square} = 10\frac{3}{5}$

Name ______________________________

Lesson 7-11
Add and Subtract Mixed Numbers

I can ...
add and subtract mixed numbers.

Content Standards 5.NF.A.1 Also 5.NF.A.2
Mathematical Practices MP.1, MP.2, MP.6

Solve & Share

Tim has 15 feet of wrapping paper. He uses $4\frac{1}{3}$ feet for his daughter's present and $5\frac{3}{8}$ feet for his niece's present. How much wrapping paper does Tim have left? ***Solve this problem any way you choose.***

Look Back! In the problem above, how could you have estimated the amount of wrapping paper that is left?

How Can Adding and Subtracting Mixed Numbers Help You Solve Problems?

A

Clarisse has two lengths of fabric to make covers for a sofa and chair. The covers require $9\frac{2}{3}$ yards of fabric. How much fabric will Clarisse have left?

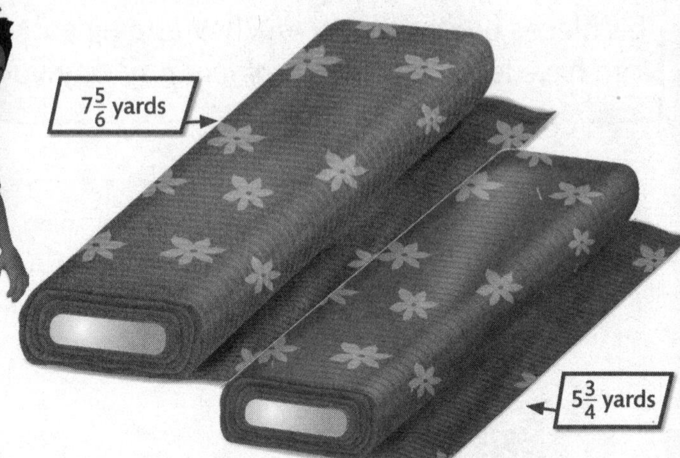

Find a common denominator when adding and subtracting fractions.
$7\frac{5}{6}$ yards
$5\frac{3}{4}$ yards

B

Step 1

Add to find out how much fabric Clarisse has in all.

$$\begin{array}{r} 5\frac{3}{4} = 5\frac{9}{12} \\ +\ 7\frac{5}{6} = 7\frac{10}{12} \\ \hline 12\frac{19}{12} = 13\frac{7}{12} \end{array}$$

Clarisse has $13\frac{7}{12}$ yards of fabric in all.

C

Step 2

Subtract the amount she will use from the total length of fabric.

$$\begin{array}{r} 13\frac{7}{12} = 12\frac{19}{12} \\ -\ 9\frac{2}{3} \ = \ 9\frac{8}{12} \\ \hline 3\frac{11}{12} \end{array}$$

Clarisse will have $3\frac{11}{12}$ yards of fabric left.

Convince Me! **Make Sense and Persevere** Clarisse has $14\frac{3}{4}$ yards of fabric to cover another sofa and chair. The new sofa needs $9\frac{1}{6}$ yards of fabric and the new chair needs $4\frac{1}{3}$ yards of fabric. Estimate to decide if Clarisse has enough fabric. If so, how much fabric will she have left?

Name ______________________________

Practice Tools Assessment

Guided Practice

Do You Understand?

1. In the example on page 310, why do you add before you subtract?

2. In the example on page 310, does Clarisse have enough fabric left over to make two cushions that each use $2\frac{1}{3}$ yards of fabric? Explain.

Do You Know How?

In **3–5**, find the sum or difference.

3. $5\frac{1}{9} - 2\frac{2}{3}$

4. $2\frac{1}{4} + 8\frac{2}{3}$

5. $6\frac{7}{25} - 3\frac{9}{50}$

In **6–9**, solve. Do the addition in the parentheses first.

6. $4\frac{3}{5} + 11\frac{2}{15}$

7. $8\frac{2}{3} - 3\frac{3}{4}$

8. $\left(7\frac{2}{3} + 3\frac{4}{5}\right) - 1\frac{4}{15}$

9. $8\frac{2}{5} - \left(3\frac{2}{3} + 2\frac{3}{5}\right)$

Independent Practice

In **10–14**, find each sum or difference.

10. $9\frac{1}{3} - 4\frac{1}{6}$

11. $12\frac{1}{4} - 9\frac{3}{5}$

12. $6\frac{3}{5} + 1\frac{3}{25}$

13. $3\frac{4}{9} + 2\frac{2}{3}$

14. $5\frac{31}{75} - 3\frac{2}{25}$

In **15–20**, solve. Do the operation in the parentheses first.

15. $\left(2\frac{5}{8} + 2\frac{1}{2}\right) - 4\frac{2}{3}$

16. $\left(5\frac{3}{4} + 1\frac{5}{6}\right) - 6\frac{7}{12}$

17. $4\frac{3}{5} + \left(8\frac{1}{5} - 7\frac{3}{10}\right)$

18. $\left(13 - 10\frac{1}{3}\right) + 2\frac{2}{3}$

19. $\left(2\frac{1}{2} + 3\frac{1}{4}\right) - 1\frac{1}{4}$

20. $2\frac{3}{14} + \left(15\frac{4}{7} - 6\frac{3}{4}\right)$

Problem Solving

In **21–23**, use the table below.

DATA

Frog Species	Body Length (cm)	Maximum Jump (cm)
Bullfrog	$20\frac{3}{10}$	$213\frac{1}{2}$
Leopard frog	$12\frac{1}{2}$	$162\frac{1}{2}$
South African sharp-nosed frog	$7\frac{3}{5}$	$334\frac{2}{5}$

21. Be Precise How much longer is the maximum jump of a South African sharp-nosed frog than the maximum jump of a leopard frog?

22. How many centimeters long is a bullfrog? Round to the nearest whole number.

23. Higher Order Thinking Which frog jumps about 10 times its body length? Explain how you found your answer.

24. A-Z **Vocabulary** Write three numbers that are **common denominators** of $\frac{7}{15}$ and $\frac{3}{5}$.

25. Marie plants 12 packages of vegetable seeds in a community garden. Each package costs $1.97 with tax. What is the total cost of the seeds?

Assessment Practice

26. Which equations are true when $5\frac{3}{8}$ is placed in the box?

- ☐ $\square - 4\frac{1}{6} = 1\frac{1}{12}$
- ☐ $10\frac{11}{12} - 5\frac{3}{8} = \square$
- ☐ $\square + 1\frac{1}{4} = 6\frac{5}{8}$
- ☐ $3\frac{1}{8} + 1\frac{3}{4} + \frac{1}{2} = \square$

27. Which equations are true when $3\frac{1}{3}$ is placed in the box?

- ☐ $3\frac{1}{3} - \square = 0$
- ☐ $2\frac{2}{5} + \square = 5\frac{3}{8}$
- ☐ $9\frac{1}{12} - 6\frac{3}{4} = \square$
- ☐ $\square - 3\frac{1}{9} = \frac{2}{9}$

Name ____________________

Activity

Problem Solving

Lesson 7-12

Model with Math

I can ...

apply the math I know to solve problems.

Mathematical Practices MP.1 Also MP.2, MP.4
Content Standard 5.NF.A.2

Solve & Share Annie found three seashells at the beach. How much shorter is the Scotch Bonnet seashell than the combined lengths of the two Alphabet Cone seashells? ***Solve this problem any way you choose. Use a diagram to help.***

Thinking Habits

Be a good thinker! These questions can help you.

- How can I use math I know to help solve this problem?
- How can I use pictures, objects, or an equation to represent the problem?
- Can I write an equation to show the problem?

Look Back! Model with Mathematics What is another way to represent this problem?

How Can You Represent a Problem with a Bar Diagram?

Visual Learning Bridge

A

The first step of a recipe is to mix the flour, white sugar, and brown sugar. Will a bowl that holds 4 cups be large enough?

Use a model to represent the problem.

Cupcakes

- $1\frac{3}{4}$ cups flour
- $\frac{1}{2}$ cup brown sugar
- $1\frac{1}{4}$ cups white sugar
- $2\frac{1}{2}$ teaspoons baking powder
- $\frac{1}{2}$ teaspoon salt
- $\frac{2}{3}$ cup butter
- 2 eggs
- 1 cup milk

What do I need to do to solve the problem?

I need to find the total amount of the first three ingredients and compare that amount to 4 cups.

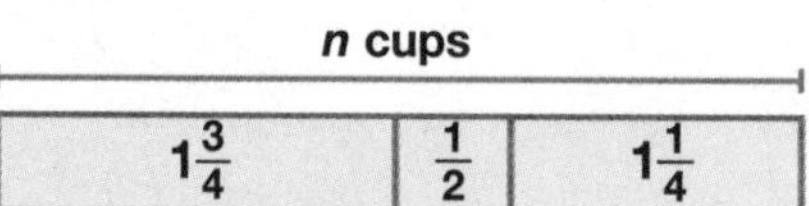

Here's my thinking...

B

How can I model with math?

I can

- use math I know to help solve this problem.
- use a diagram to represent and solve this problem.
- write an equation involving fractions or mixed numbers.
- decide if my results make sense.

C

I will use a bar diagram and an equation to represent the situation.

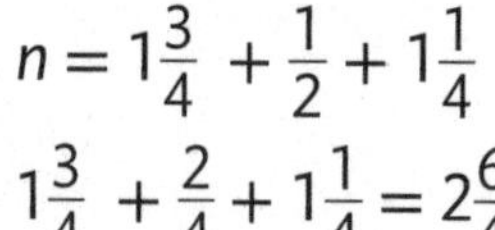

$n = 1\frac{3}{4} + \frac{1}{2} + 1\frac{1}{4}$

$1\frac{3}{4} + \frac{2}{4} + 1\frac{1}{4} = 2\frac{6}{4}$

I can write this answer as a mixed number. $2\frac{6}{4} = 3\frac{2}{4}$ or $3\frac{1}{2}$

There are $3\frac{1}{2}$ cups of ingredients, and $3\frac{1}{2}$ is less than 4. So, the 4-cup bowl is large enough.

Convince Me! **Model with Mathematics** How many more cups of ingredients could still fit in the bowl? Use a bar diagram and an equation to represent the problem.

Name ______________________________

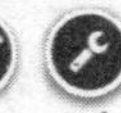

Practice Tools Assessment

Guided Practice

Phillip wants to run a total of 3 miles each day. Monday morning, he ran $1\frac{7}{8}$ miles. How many more miles does he still need to run?

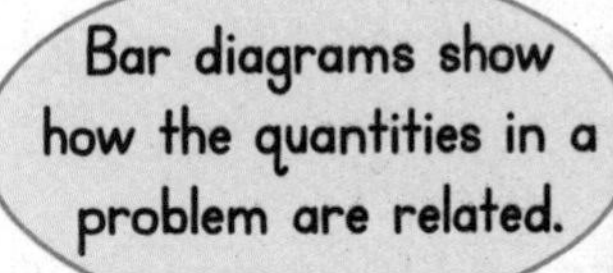

Bar diagrams show how the quantities in a problem are related.

1. Draw a diagram to represent the problem.

2. Write and solve an equation for this problem. How did you find the solution?

3. How many more miles does Phillip still need to run?

Independent Practice

Model with Math

A landscaper used $2\frac{1}{2}$ tons of sunburst pebbles, $3\frac{1}{4}$ tons of black polished pebbles, and $\frac{5}{8}$ ton of river pebbles. What was the total weight of the pebbles?

4. Draw a diagram and write an equation to represent the problem.

5. Solve the equation. What fraction computations did you do?

6. How many tons of pebbles did the landscaper use?

Problem Solving

Performance Task

Camp Activities

During the 6-hour session at day camp, Roland participated in boating, hiking, and lunch. The rest of the session was free time. How much time did Roland spend on the three activities? How much free time did he have?

DATA

Camp Activities	
Swiming	$\frac{3}{4}$ hour
Boating	$1\frac{1}{2}$ hours
Crafts	$1\frac{3}{4}$ hours
Hiking	$2\frac{1}{2}$ hours
Lunch	$1\frac{1}{4}$ hours

7. **Make Sense and Persevere** What do you know and what do you need to find?

When you model with math, you use the math you know to solve new problems.

8. **Reasoning** Describe the quantities and operations you will use to find how much time Roland spent on the planned activities. Which quantities and operations will you use to find how much free time Roland had?

9. **Model with Math** Draw a diagram and use an equation to help you find how much time Roland spent on the activities. Then, draw a diagram and use an equation to help you find how much free time Roland had.

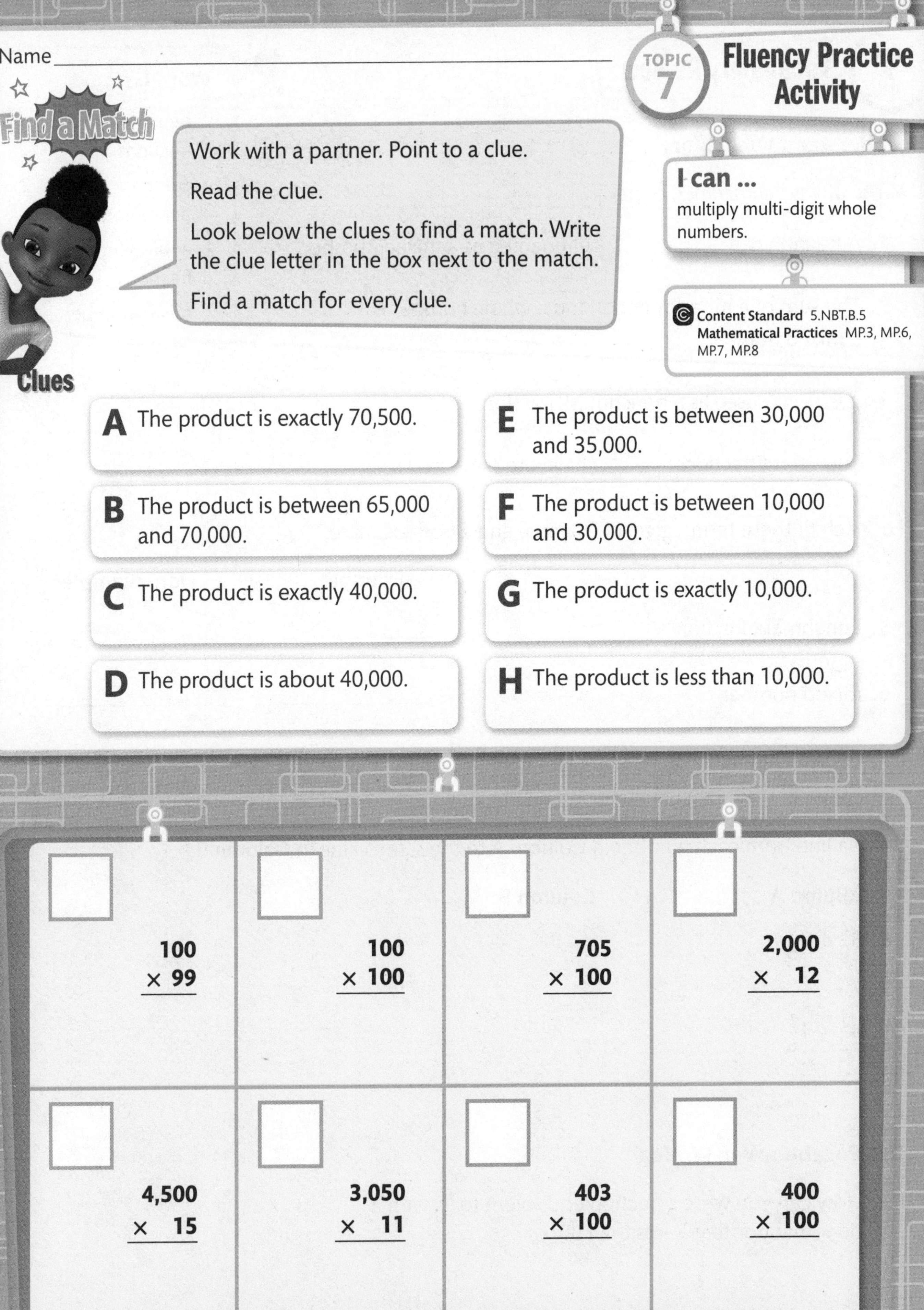

Name ____________________

Find a Match

TOPIC 7 Fluency Practice Activity

Work with a partner. Point to a clue.

Read the clue.

Look below the clues to find a match. Write the clue letter in the box next to the match.

Find a match for every clue.

I can ...
multiply multi-digit whole numbers.

Content Standard 5.NBT.B.5
Mathematical Practices MP.3, MP.6, MP.7, MP.8

Clues

A The product is exactly 70,500.

B The product is between 65,000 and 70,000.

C The product is exactly 40,000.

D The product is about 40,000.

E The product is between 30,000 and 35,000.

F The product is between 10,000 and 30,000.

G The product is exactly 10,000.

H The product is less than 10,000.

☐ 100×99	☐ 100×100	☐ 705×100	☐ $2{,}000 \times 12$
☐ $4{,}500 \times 15$	☐ $3{,}050 \times 11$	☐ 403×100	☐ 400×100

TOPIC 7

Vocabulary Review

Word List

- benchmark fractions
- common denominator
- equivalent fractions
- mixed number

Understand Vocabulary

Write *always, sometimes,* or *never.*

1. A fraction can ________ be renamed as a mixed number.
2. The sum of a mixed number and a whole number is ________ a mixed number.
3. $\frac{1}{5}$ is ________ used as a benchmark fraction.
4. Equivalent fractions ________ have the same value.

For each of these terms, give an example and a non-example.

	Example	Non-example
5. benchmark fraction	________	________
6. mixed number	________	________
7. equivalent fractions	________	________

Draw a line from each number in Column A to the same value in Column B.

Column A	Column B
8. $3\frac{4}{9} + 2\frac{5}{6}$	$5\frac{2}{3}$
9. $7 - 2\frac{2}{3}$	$\frac{3}{5}$
10. $4\frac{1}{2} + 1\frac{1}{6}$	$4\frac{1}{3}$
11. $\frac{7}{12} + \frac{5}{8}$	$\frac{29}{24}$
	$6\frac{5}{18}$

Use Vocabulary in Writing

12. How can you write a fraction equivalent to $\frac{60}{80}$ with a denominator that is less than 80?

Name ____________________

TOPIC 7

Reteaching

Set A pages 269–272

Estimate the sum or difference by replacing each fraction with 0, $\frac{1}{2}$, or 1.

Estimate $\frac{4}{5} + \frac{5}{8}$.

Step 1 $\frac{4}{5}$ is close to 1.

Step 2 $\frac{5}{8}$ is close to $\frac{4}{8}$ or $\frac{1}{2}$.

Step 3 $1 + \frac{1}{2} = 1\frac{1}{2}$

So, $\frac{4}{5} + \frac{5}{8}$ is about $1\frac{1}{2}$.

Estimate $\frac{7}{12} - \frac{1}{8}$.

Step 1 $\frac{7}{12}$ is close to $\frac{6}{12}$ or $\frac{1}{2}$.

Step 2 $\frac{1}{8}$ is close to 0.

Step 3 $\frac{1}{2} - 0 = \frac{1}{2}$

So, $\frac{7}{12} - \frac{1}{8}$ is about $\frac{1}{2}$.

Remember that you can use a number line to decide if a fraction is closest to 0, $\frac{1}{2}$, or 1.

Estimate each sum or difference.

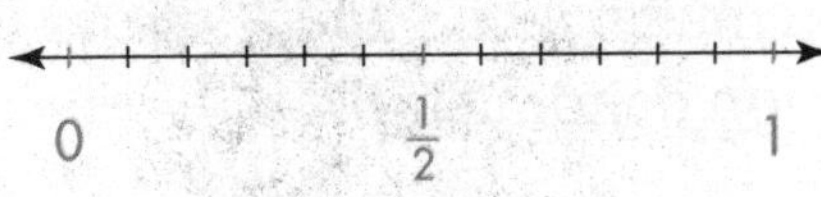

1. $\frac{2}{3} + \frac{5}{6}$
2. $\frac{7}{8} - \frac{5}{12}$
3. $\frac{1}{8} + \frac{1}{16}$
4. $\frac{5}{8} - \frac{1}{6}$
5. $\frac{1}{5} + \frac{1}{3}$
6. $\frac{11}{12} - \frac{1}{10}$
7. $\frac{9}{10} + \frac{1}{5}$
8. $\frac{3}{5} - \frac{1}{12}$

Set B pages 273–276

Find a common denominator for $\frac{4}{9}$ and $\frac{1}{3}$. Then rename each fraction as an equivalent fraction with the common denominator.

Step 1 Multiply the denominators: $9 \times 3 = 27$, so 27 is a common denominator.

Step 2 Rename the fractions:

$\frac{4}{9} = \frac{4}{9} \times \frac{3}{3} = \frac{12}{27}$

$\frac{1}{3} = \frac{1}{3} \times \frac{9}{9} = \frac{9}{27}$

So, $\frac{4}{9} = \frac{12}{27}$ and $\frac{1}{3} = \frac{9}{27}$.

Remember you can check to see if one denominator is a multiple of the other. Since 9 is a multiple of 3, another common denominator for the fractions $\frac{4}{9}$ and $\frac{1}{3}$ is 9.

Find a common denominator. Then rename each fraction as an equivalent fraction with the common denominator.

1. $\frac{3}{5}$ and $\frac{7}{10}$
2. $\frac{5}{6}$ and $\frac{7}{18}$
3. $\frac{3}{7}$ and $\frac{1}{4}$

Set C pages 277–280, 281–284, 285–288

Find $\frac{5}{6} - \frac{3}{4}$.

Step 1 Find a common denominator by listing multiples of 6 and 4.

6: 6, 12, 18, 24, 30, 36, 42
4: 4, 8, 12, 16, 20, 24, 28, 32

12 is a common multiple of 6 and 4, so use 12 as the common denominator.

Step 2 Use the Identity Property to write equivalent fractions.

$\frac{5}{6} = \frac{5 \times 2}{6 \times 2} = \frac{10}{12}$ $\frac{3}{4} = \frac{3 \times 3}{4 \times 3} = \frac{9}{12}$

Step 3 Subtract.

$\frac{10}{12} - \frac{9}{12} = \frac{1}{12}$

Remember to multiply the numerator and denominator by the same number when writing an equivalent fraction.

1. $\frac{2}{5} + \frac{3}{10}$
2. $\frac{1}{9} + \frac{5}{6}$
3. $\frac{3}{4} - \frac{5}{12}$
4. $\frac{7}{8} - \frac{2}{3}$
5. $\frac{1}{12} + \frac{3}{8}$
6. $\frac{4}{5} - \frac{2}{15}$
7. Teresa spends $\frac{1}{3}$ of her day at school. She spends $\frac{1}{12}$ of her day eating meals. What fraction of the day does Teresa spend at school or eating meals?

Set D pages 289–292

Estimate $5\frac{1}{3} + 9\frac{9}{11}$.

To round a mixed number to the nearest whole number, compare the fraction part of the mixed number to $\frac{1}{2}$.

If the fraction part is less than $\frac{1}{2}$, round to the nearest lesser whole number.

$5\frac{1}{3}$ rounds to 5.

If the fraction part is greater than or equal to $\frac{1}{2}$, round to the nearest greater whole number.

$9\frac{9}{11}$ rounds to 10.

So, $5\frac{1}{3} + 9\frac{9}{11} \approx 5 + 10 = 15$.

Remember that ≈ means "is approximately equal to."

Remember that you can also use benchmark fractions such as $\frac{1}{4}, \frac{1}{3}, \frac{1}{2}, \frac{2}{3}$, and $\frac{3}{4}$ to help you estimate.

Estimate each sum or difference.

1. $3\frac{1}{4} - 1\frac{1}{2}$
2. $5\frac{2}{9} + 4\frac{11}{13}$
3. $2\frac{3}{8} + 5\frac{3}{5}$
4. $9\frac{3}{7} - 6\frac{2}{5}$
5. $8\frac{5}{6} - 2\frac{1}{2}$
6. $7\frac{3}{4} + 5\frac{1}{8}$
7. $11\frac{5}{12} + \frac{7}{8}$
8. $13\frac{4}{5} - 8\frac{1}{6}$
9. A mark on the side of a pier shows the water is $4\frac{7}{8}$ feet deep. At high tide, the water level rises $2\frac{1}{4}$ feet. About how deep is the water at high tide?

Name ________________________________

Reteaching Continued

Set E pages 293–296

Find $1\frac{1}{4} + 1\frac{7}{8}$.

Step 1 Rename the fractions with a common denominator. Model the addends and add the fractional parts.

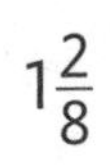

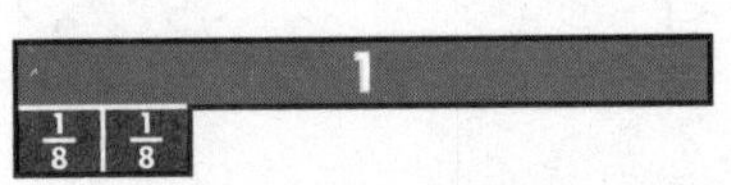

$+ 1\frac{7}{8}$

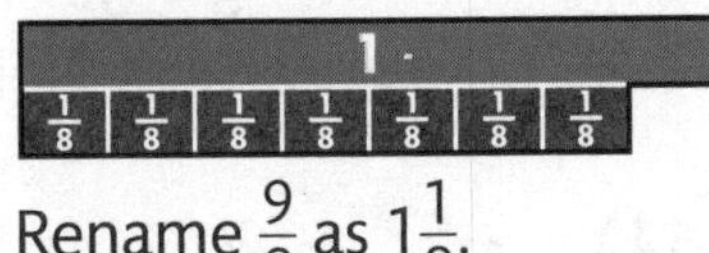

$\frac{9}{8}$ Rename $\frac{9}{8}$ as $1\frac{1}{8}$.

Step 2 Add the whole numbers to the regrouped fractions.

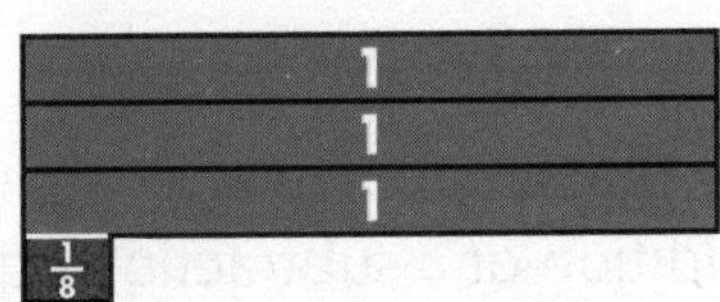

So, $1\frac{1}{4} + 1\frac{7}{8} = 3\frac{1}{8}$.

Remember that you may need to rename a fraction as a mixed number.

Use a model to find each sum.

1. $2\frac{5}{6} + 1\frac{5}{6}$
2. $1\frac{1}{2} + 3\frac{3}{4}$
3. $2\frac{3}{10} + 2\frac{4}{5}$
4. $2\frac{1}{4} + 5\frac{11}{12}$
5. $6\frac{2}{3} + 5\frac{5}{6}$
6. $7\frac{1}{3} + 8\frac{7}{9}$
7. $8\frac{4}{10} + 2\frac{3}{5}$
8. $3\frac{1}{3} + 9\frac{11}{12}$

Set F pages 301–304

Find $2\frac{1}{3} - 1\frac{5}{6}$. Rename $2\frac{1}{3}$ as $2\frac{2}{6}$.

Step 1 Model the number you are subtracting from, $2\frac{1}{3}$ or $2\frac{2}{6}$. Since $\frac{5}{6} > \frac{2}{6}$, rename 1 whole as $\frac{6}{6}$.

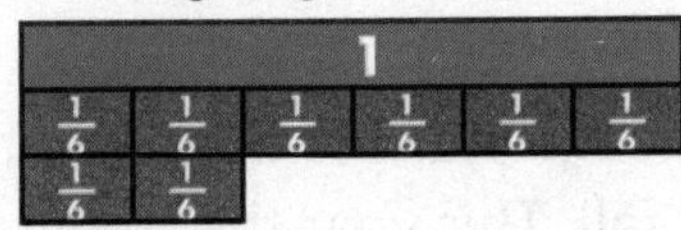

Step 2 Cross out the number you are subtracting, $1\frac{5}{6}$.

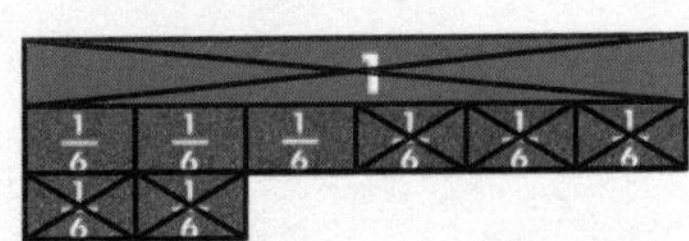

The answer is the amount that is left.

So, $2\frac{1}{3} - 1\frac{5}{6} = \frac{3}{6}$ or $\frac{1}{2}$.

Remember that the difference is the part of the model that is not crossed out.

Use a model to find each difference.

1. $15\frac{6}{10} - 3\frac{4}{5}$
2. $6\frac{3}{4} - 5\frac{1}{2}$
3. $4\frac{1}{6} - 1\frac{2}{3}$
4. $12\frac{1}{4} - 7\frac{1}{2}$
5. $9\frac{7}{10} - 3\frac{4}{5}$
6. $5\frac{5}{8} - 3\frac{1}{4}$

Set G pages 297–300, 305–308, 309–312

Gil had two lengths of wallpaper, $2\frac{3}{4}$ yards and $1\frac{7}{8}$ yards long. He used some and now has $1\frac{5}{6}$ yards left. How many yards of wallpaper did Gil use?

Step 1

Add to find the total amount of wallpaper Gil had.

$$\begin{array}{r} 2\frac{3}{4} = 2\frac{18}{24} \\ +\,1\frac{7}{8} = 1\frac{21}{24} \\ \hline 3\frac{39}{24} \end{array}$$

Step 2

Subtract to find the amount of wallpaper Gil used.

$$\begin{array}{r} 3\frac{39}{24} = 3\frac{39}{24} \\ -\,1\frac{5}{6} = 1\frac{20}{24} \\ \hline 2\frac{19}{24} \end{array}$$

Gil used $2\frac{19}{24}$ yards of wallpaper.

Remember when you add or subtract mixed numbers, rename the fractional parts to have a common denominator.

Solve. Do the operation in the parentheses first.

1. $5\frac{1}{2} + 2\frac{1}{8}$
2. $7\frac{5}{6} - 3\frac{2}{3}$
3. $3\frac{1}{4} + 1\frac{5}{6}$
4. $9 - 3\frac{3}{8}$
5. $\left(2\frac{1}{6} + 3\frac{3}{4}\right) - 1\frac{5}{12}$
6. $\left(4\frac{4}{5} + 7\frac{1}{3}\right) - 1\frac{7}{15}$

Set H pages 313–316

Think about these questions to help you **model with math**.

Thinking Habits

- How can I use math I know to help solve this problem?
- How can I use pictures, objects, or an equation to represent the problem?
- How can I use numbers, words, and symbols to solve the problem?

Remember that a bar diagram can help you write an addition or a subtraction equation.

Draw a bar diagram and write an equation to solve.

1. Justin jogs $3\frac{2}{5}$ miles every morning. He jogs $4\frac{6}{10}$ miles every evening. How many miles does he jog every day?

2. Last year Mia planted a tree that was $5\frac{11}{12}$ feet tall. This year the tree is $7\frac{2}{3}$ feet tall. How many feet did the tree grow?

Name ______________________________

TOPIC 7

Assessment Practice

1. Estimate the sum of $\frac{3}{4}$ and $\frac{1}{5}$. Write an equation.

2. Select all the expressions that are equal to $\frac{2}{3}$. Explain.

- ☐ $\frac{1}{6} + \frac{1}{2}$; I found a common denominator and then added the numerators to get $\frac{2}{3}$.
- ☐ $\frac{2}{9} + \frac{7}{18}$; I added the numerators and denominators to get $\frac{2}{3}$.
- ☐ $\frac{5}{12} + \frac{1}{4}$; I added the numerators and denominators to get $\frac{2}{3}$.
- ☐ $1\frac{1}{6} - \frac{1}{3}$; I found a common denominator and then subtracted the numerators to get $\frac{2}{3}$.
- ☐ $2 - 1\frac{1}{3}$; I found a common denominator and then subtracted the numerators to get $\frac{2}{3}$.

3. Tim has $\frac{5}{12}$ of a jar of blackberry jam and $\frac{3}{8}$ of a jar of strawberry jam. Write $\frac{5}{12}$ and $\frac{3}{8}$ using a common denominator. What fraction represents the total amount of jam Tim has?

4. Sandra drove for $\frac{1}{3}$ hour to get to the store. Then she drove $\frac{1}{5}$ hour to get to the library. What fraction of an hour did Sandra drive in all? Explain.

5. The bar diagram below shows the fractional parts of a pizza eaten by Pablo and Jamie.

? pizza eaten

$\frac{1}{3}$	$\frac{1}{4}$

A. Rename each fraction using a common denominator.

B. Use the renamed fractions to write and solve an equation to find the total amount of pizza eaten.

6. Choose the correct sum for each expression.

	$\frac{5}{12}$	$1\frac{1}{6}$	$\frac{5}{8}$	$\frac{19}{20}$
$\frac{1}{4}+\frac{3}{8}$	☐	☐	☐	☐
$\frac{1}{4}+\frac{7}{10}$	☐	☐	☐	☐
$\frac{1}{4}+\frac{11}{12}$	☐	☐	☐	☐
$\frac{1}{4}+\frac{1}{6}$	☐	☐	☐	☐

7. Benjamin and his sister shared a large sandwich. Benjamin ate $\frac{3}{5}$ of the sandwich and his sister ate $\frac{1}{7}$ of the sandwich.

A. Estimate how much more Benjamin ate than his sister. Explain how you found your estimate.

B. How much more did Benjamin eat than his sister? Find the exact amount.

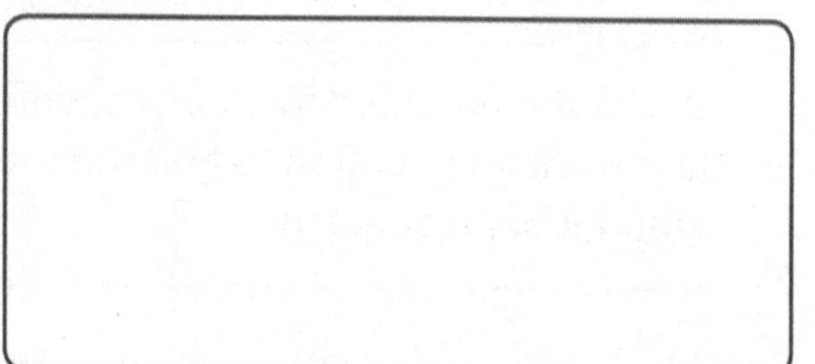

8. Alicia had $3\frac{1}{8}$ feet of wood. She used $1\frac{3}{4}$ feet of wood. Estimate the amount of wood Alicia has left.

Ⓐ 2 feet

Ⓑ 1 foot

Ⓒ 0 feet

Ⓓ 3 feet

9. Explain why you must rename $2\frac{7}{12}$ in order to find $2\frac{7}{12}-\frac{5}{6}$.

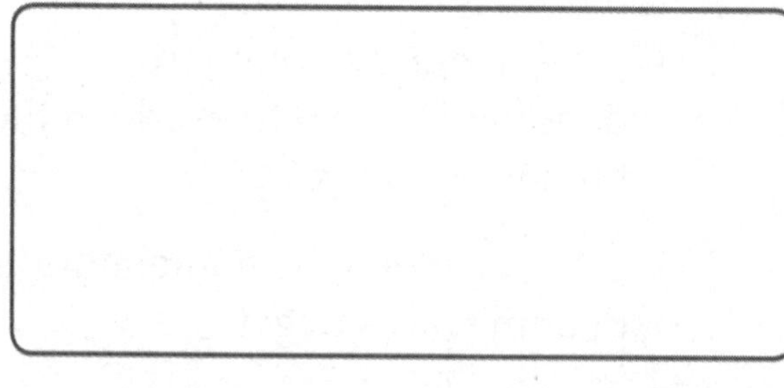

10. Mona bought $3\frac{3}{8}$ pounds of cheddar cheese. She used $2\frac{3}{4}$ pounds to make sandwiches. Write and solve an expression to find how much cheese is left.

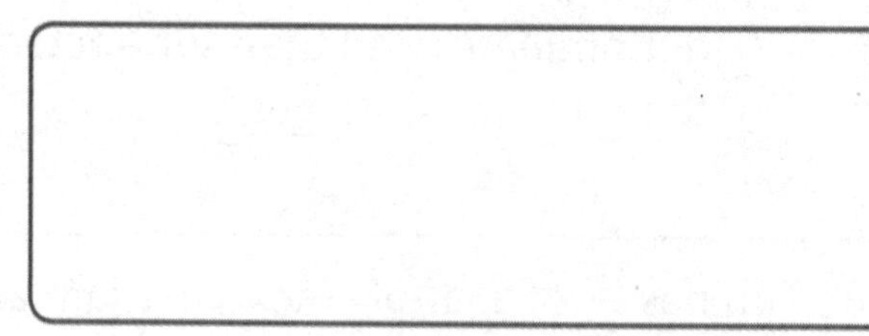

11. Marie needs $2\frac{1}{4}$ yards of fabric. She already has $1\frac{3}{8}$ yards. Which equation shows how many more yards of fabric Marie has to buy?

Ⓐ $2\frac{1}{4}+1\frac{3}{8}=1\frac{1}{8}$

Ⓑ $\frac{1}{4}+\frac{3}{8}=\frac{3}{4}$

Ⓒ $2\frac{1}{4}-1\frac{3}{8}=\frac{7}{8}$

Ⓓ $\frac{3}{8}-\frac{1}{4}=\frac{1}{8}$

Name ____________________

12. During a trip, Martha drove $\frac{1}{6}$ of the time, Chris drove $\frac{1}{4}$ of the time, and Juan drove the rest of the time. What fraction of the time did Juan drive?

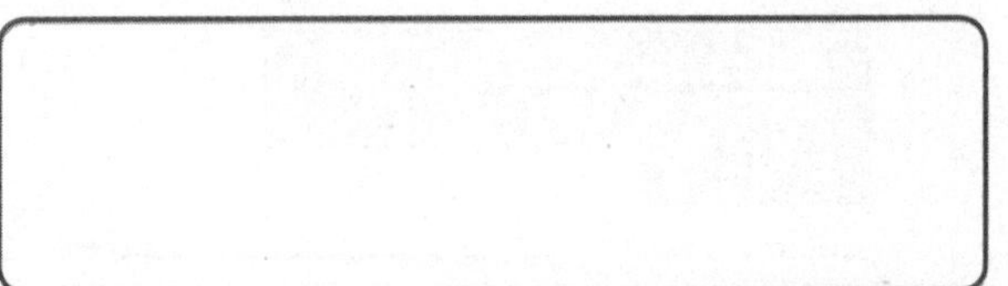

13. Gilberto worked $3\frac{1}{4}$ hours on Thursday, $4\frac{2}{5}$ hours on Friday, and $6\frac{1}{2}$ hours on Saturday. How many hours did he work in all during the three days?

Ⓐ $13\frac{1}{10}$ hours

Ⓑ $13\frac{3}{20}$ hours

Ⓒ $14\frac{1}{10}$ hours

Ⓓ $14\frac{3}{20}$ hours

14. The model below can be used to find the sum of two mixed numbers. What is the sum? What is the difference? Show your work.

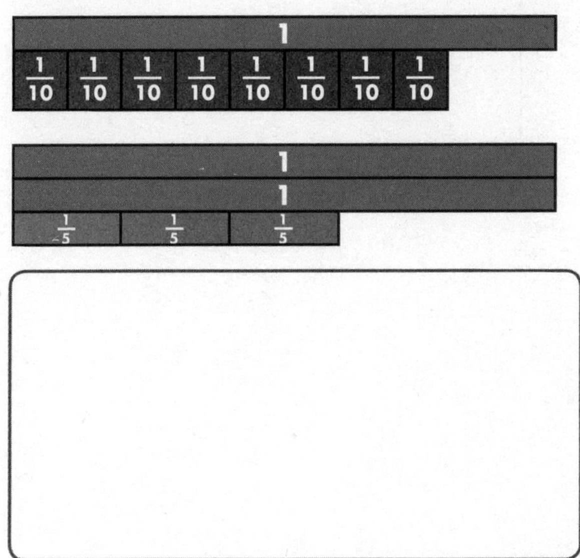

15. Estimate the sum of $1\frac{1}{3}$ and $2\frac{3}{4}$. Explain how you found your estimate.

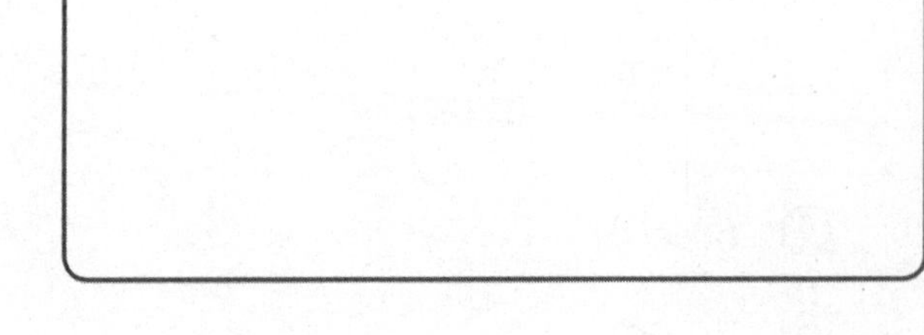

16. Find $4\frac{1}{5} - \frac{7}{10}$.

A. Explain why $4\frac{1}{5}$ must be renamed in order to do the subtraction.

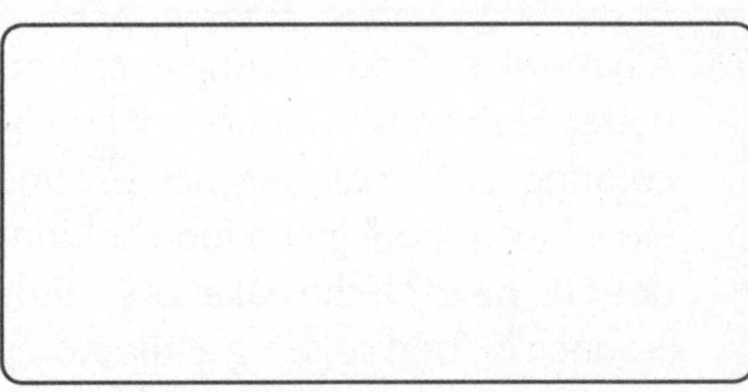

B. Explain how to rename $4\frac{1}{5}$ in order to do the subtraction.

17. Mark is making a small frame in the shape of an equilateral triangle with the dimensions shown below. What is the perimeter of the frame?

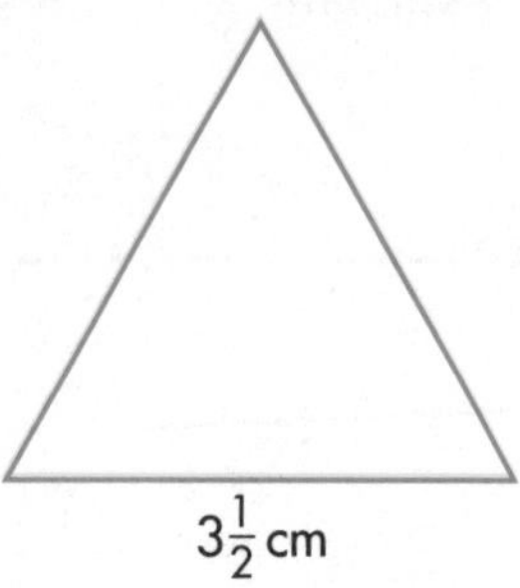

Ⓐ $6\frac{1}{2}$ cm
Ⓑ $9\frac{1}{2}$ cm
Ⓒ $9\frac{1}{6}$ cm
Ⓓ $10\frac{1}{2}$ cm

18. A baker uses food coloring to color cake batter. He needs $4\frac{1}{8}$ ounces of green food coloring. The baker only has $2\frac{1}{2}$ ounces. How much more green food coloring does he need? If the baker only finds 1 ounce of food coloring at the store, how many more ounces does the baker need?

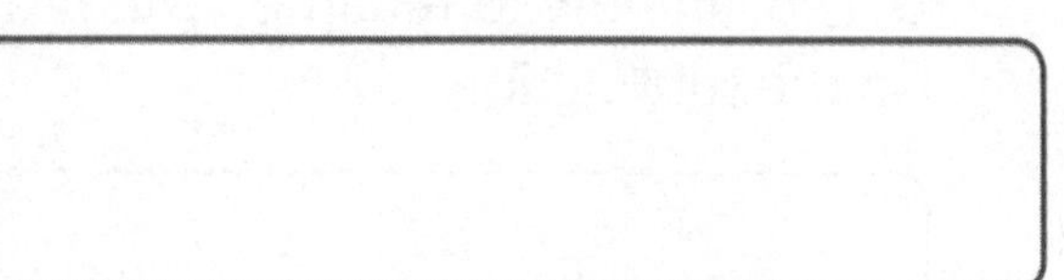

19. Models for two mixed numbers are shown below. What is the sum of the numbers? What is the difference? Show your work.

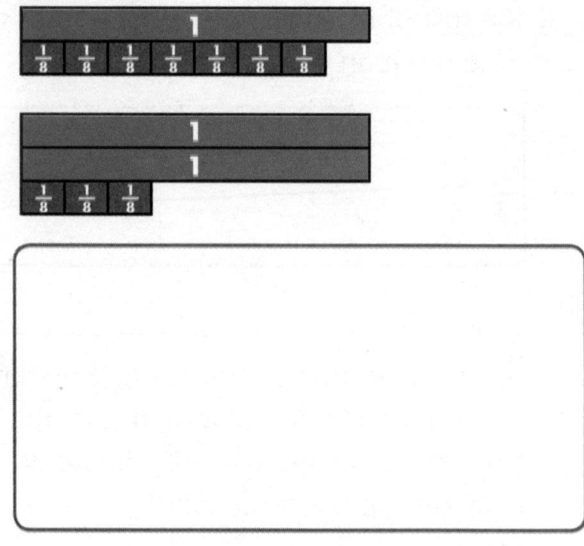

20. Dawson says that the expression $\left(2\frac{4}{10} + 8\frac{4}{5}\right) - 3\frac{1}{5}$ is equal to a whole number. Do you agree? Explain.

Name ___________

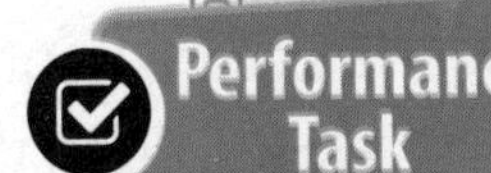

Tying Knots

Liam and Pam each have a length of thick rope. Liam has tied an overhand knot in his rope. The overhand knot is a basic knot often used as a basis for other types of knots.

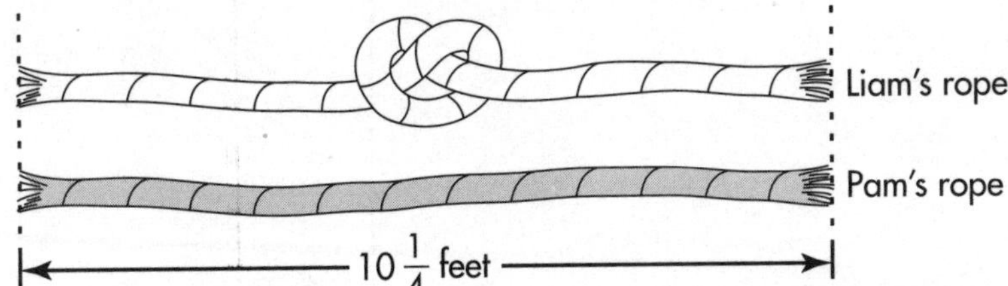

1. Liam untied the overhand knot. The full length of the rope is shown below. How much rope did the knot use?

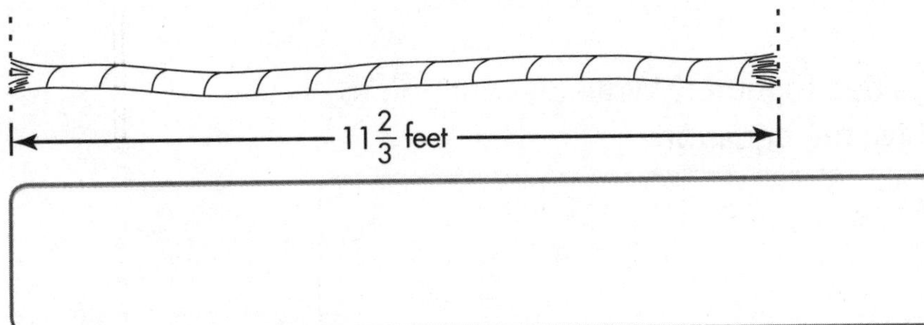

2. Liam laid his untied rope end-to-end with Pam's rope.

Part A

About how long would the two ropes be? Explain how you got your estimate.

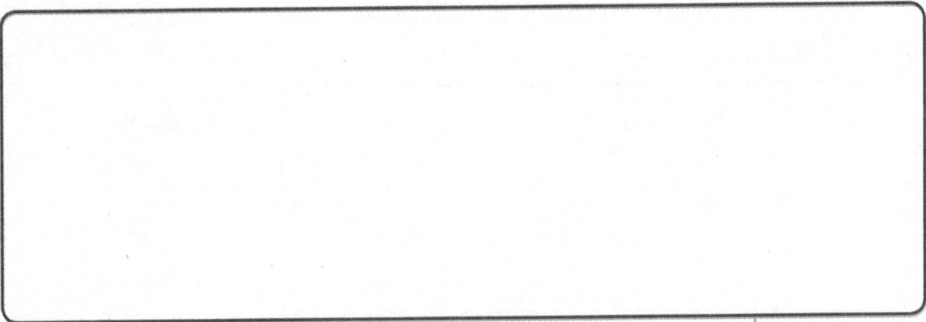

Part B

Explain whether the actual length would be greater or less than your estimate.

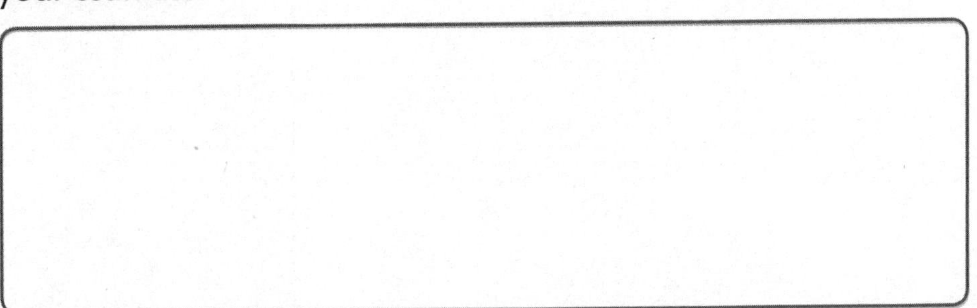

3. Liam and Pam tied their two ropes together with a square knot. The knot used $1\frac{1}{8}$ feet of rope. How long is their rope? Explain.

4. Marco has a rope that is 16 feet long. He ties his rope to Liam and Pam's rope with a square knot that uses $1\frac{1}{8}$ feet of rope.

Part A

How long are the three ropes tied together? Write an equation to model the problem. Then solve the equation.

Part B

Liam, Pam, and Marco decide to shorten the tied ropes by cutting off $\frac{2}{5}$ foot from one end and $\frac{1}{6}$ foot from the other end. About how much rope is cut off in all? Explain.

Part C

How long are the tied ropes now? Show your work.

Glossary

acute angle An angle whose measure is between 0° and 90°

acute triangle A triangle whose angles are all acute angles

Addition Property of Equality The same number can be added to both sides of an equation and the sides remain equal.

algebraic expression A mathematical phrase involving a variable or variables, numbers, and operations
Example: $x - 3$

angle A figure formed by two rays that have the same endpoint

area The number of square units needed to cover a surface or figure

array A way of displaying objects in rows and columns

Associative Property of Addition Addends can be regrouped and the sum remains the same.
Example: $1 + (3 + 5) = (1 + 3) + 5$

Associative Property of Multiplication Factors can be regrouped and the product remains the same.
Example: $2 \times (4 \times 10) = (2 \times 4) \times 10$

attribute A characteristic of a shape

axis (plural: axes) Either of two lines drawn perpendicular to each other in a graph

bar diagram A tool used to help understand and solve word problems; it is also known as a strip diagram or a tape diagram.

bar graph A display that uses bars to show and compare data

base The number that is used as a factor, when a number is written using exponents

base (of a polygon) The side of a polygon to which the height is perpendicular

base (of a solid) The face of a solid that is used to name the solid

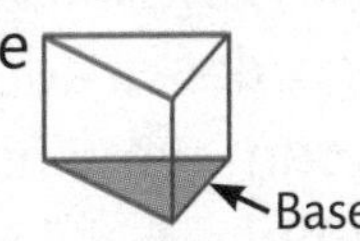

benchmark fraction Common fractions used for estimating, such as $\frac{1}{4}, \frac{1}{3}, \frac{1}{2}, \frac{2}{3}$, and $\frac{3}{4}$

braces Symbols { and } that are used with parentheses and brackets in mathematical expressions and equations to group numbers or variables together

brackets The symbols [and] that are used to group numbers or variables in mathematical expressions.

breaking apart A mental math method used to rewrite a number as the sum of numbers to form an easier problem

capacity The volume of a container measured in liquid units

Celsius A scale for measuring temperature in the metric system

centimeter (cm) A metric unit of length; 100 centimeters is equal to one meter.

circle A closed plane figure made up of all the points that are the same distance from a given point

common denominator A number that is the denominator of two or more fractions

common multiple A number that is a multiple of two or more numbers

Commutative Property of Addition The order of addends can be changed and the sum remains the same. *Example:* $3 + 7 = 7 + 3$

Commutative Property of Multiplication The order of factors can be changed and the product remains the same. *Example:* $3 \times 5 = 5 \times 3$

compatible numbers Numbers that are easy to compute with mentally

compensation Adjusting a number to make a computation easier and balancing the adjustment by changing another number

composite number A whole number greater than one with more than two factors

composite shape A figure made up of two or more shapes

coordinate grid A grid that is used to locate points in a plane using an ordered pair of numbers

coordinates The two numbers in an ordered pair

corresponding Matching terms in a pattern

corresponding terms Terms that match each other in a pair of number sequences

cube A solid figure with six identical squares as its faces

cubic unit The volume of a cube that measures 1 unit on each edge

cup (c) A customary unit of capacity; one cup is equal to eight fluid ounces.

customary units of measure Units of measure that are used in the United States

D

data Collected information

decimal A number with one or more places to the right of a decimal point

degree (°) A unit of measure for angles; also, a unit of measure for temperature

denominator The number below the fraction bar in a fraction

difference The result of subtracting one number from another

digits The symbols used to show numbers: 0, 1, 2, 3, 4, 5, 6, 7, 8, 9

Distributive Property Multiplying a sum (or difference) by a number is the same as multiplying each number in the sum (or difference) by the number and adding (or subtracting) the products.
Example: $3 \times (10 + 4) = (3 \times 10) + (3 \times 4)$

dividend The number to be divided

divisible A number is divisible by another number if there is no remainder after dividing.

Division Property of Equality Both sides of an equation can be divided by the same nonzero number and the sides remain equal.

divisor The number by which another number is divided
Example: In $32 \div 4 = 8$, 4 is the divisor.

dot plot A display of responses along a number line with dots used to indicate the number of times a response occurred
See also: line plot

E

edge A line segment where two faces meet in a solid figure

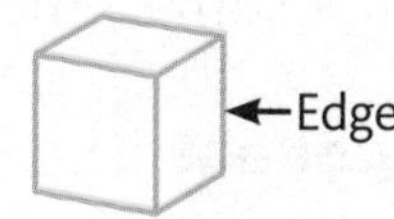

elapsed time The amount of time between the beginning of an event and the end of the event

equation A number sentence that uses an equal sign to show that two expressions have the same value
Example: $9 + 3 = 12$

equilateral triangle A triangle whose sides all have the same length

equivalent decimals Decimals that name the same amount
Example: $0.7 = 0.70$

equivalent fractions Fractions that name the same part of a whole region, length, or set

estimate To give an approximate value rather than an exact answer

evaluate Replace an expression with an equivalent value

expanded form A way to write a number that shows the place value of each digit
Example: $3 \times 1{,}000 + 5 \times 100 + 6 \times 10 + 2 \times 1$ or $3 \times 10^3 + 5 \times 10^2 + 6 \times 10^1 + 2 \times 10^0$

expanded notation A number written as the sum of the values of its digits

exponent The number that tells how many times a base number is used as a factor

face A flat surface of a solid figure

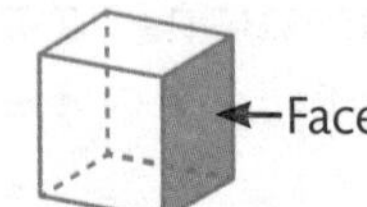

factors Numbers that are multiplied to get a product

Fahrenheit A scale for measuring temperature in the customary system

fluid ounce (fl oz) A customary unit of capacity equal to 2 tablespoons

foot (ft) A customary unit of length equal to 12 inches

formula A rule that uses symbols to relate two or more quantities

fraction A symbol, such as $\frac{2}{3}$, $\frac{5}{1}$, or $\frac{8}{5}$, used to describe one or more parts of a whole that is divided into equal parts. A fraction can name a part of a whole, a part of a set, a location on a number line, or a division of whole numbers.

frequency table A table used to show the number of times each response occurs in a set of data

gallon (gal) A unit for measuring capacity in the customary system; one gallon is equal to four quarts.

gram (g) A metric unit of mass; one gram is equal to 1,000 milligrams.

greater than symbol (>) A symbol that points away from a greater number or expression
Example: $450 > 449$

height of a polygon The length of a segment from one vertex of a polygon perpendicular to its base

height of a solid In a prism, the perpendicular distance between the top and bottom bases of the figure

hexagon A polygon with 6 sides

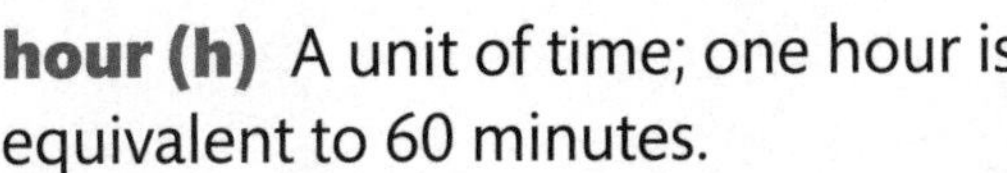

hour (h) A unit of time; one hour is equivalent to 60 minutes.

hundredth One part of 100 equal parts of a whole

Identity Property of Addition The sum of any number and zero is that number.

Identity Property of Multiplication The product of any number and one is that number.

inch (in.) A customary unit of length; 12 inches are equal to one foot.

intersecting lines Lines that pass through the same point

interval (on a graph) The difference between consecutive numbers on an axis of a graph

inverse operations Operations that undo each other
Example: Adding 6 and subtracting 6 are inverse operations.

isosceles triangle A triangle with at least two sides of the same length

kilogram (kg) A metric unit of mass; one kilogram is equal to 1,000 grams.

kilometer (km) A metric unit of length; one kilometer is equal to 1,000 meters.

less than symbol (<) A symbol that points towards a lesser number or expression
Example: $305 < 320$

line A straight path of points that goes on forever in two directions

line graph A graph that connects points to show how data change over time

line of symmetry The line on which a figure can be folded so that both halves are the same

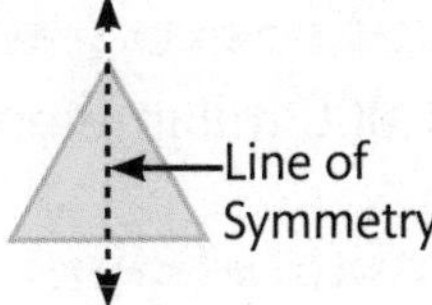

line plot A display of responses along a number line, with dots or Xs recorded above the responses to indicate the number of times a response occurred

line segment Part of a line having two endpoints

liter (L) A metric unit of capacity; one liter is equal to 1,000 milliliters

mass The measure of the quantity of matter in an object

meter (m) A metric unit of length; One meter is equal to 100 centimeters.

metric units of measure Units of measure commonly used by scientists

mile (mi) A customary unit of length equal to 5,280 feet

milligram (mg) A metric unit of mass; 1,000 milligrams is equal to one gram.

milliliter (mL) A metric unit of capacity; 1,000 milliliters is equal to one liter.

millimeter (mm) A metric unit of length; 1,000 millimeters is equal to one meter.

minute (min.) A unit of time; one minute is equivalent to 60 seconds.

mixed number A number that has a whole-number part and a fraction part

multiple The product of a given whole number and any non-zero whole number

multiple of 10 A number that has 10 as a factor

Multiplication Property of Equality Both sides of an equation can be multiplied by the same nonzero number and the sides remain equal.

multiplicative inverse (reciprocal) Two numbers whose product is one

number name A way to write a number using words

number sequence A set of numbers that follows a rule

numerator The number above the fraction bar in a fraction

numerical data Data involving numbers including measurement data

numerical expression A mathematical phrase that contains numbers and at least one operation
Example: 325 + 50

obtuse angle An angle whose measure is between 90° and 180°

135°

obtuse triangle A triangle in which one angle is an obtuse angle

octagon A polygon with 8 sides

order of operations The order in which operations are done in calculations. Work inside parentheses, brackets, and braces is done first. Next, terms with exponents are evaluated. Then, multiplication and division are done in order from left to right, and finally addition and subtraction are done in order from left to right.

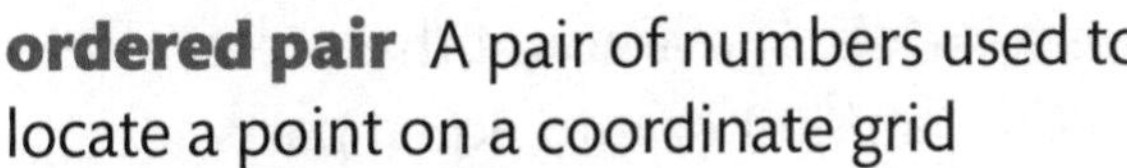

ordered pair A pair of numbers used to locate a point on a coordinate grid

origin The point where the two axes of a coordinate grid intersect; the origin is represented by the ordered pair (0, 0).

ounce (oz) A customary unit of weight; 16 ounces is equal to one pound.

overestimate An estimate that is greater than the actual answer

P

parallel lines In a plane, lines that never cross and stay the same distance apart

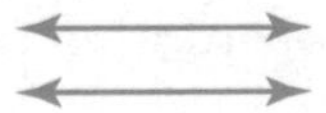

parallelogram A quadrilateral with both pairs of opposite sides parallel and equal in length

parentheses The symbols (and) used to group numbers or variables in mathematical expressions
Example: 3(15 – 7)

partial products Products found by breaking one of two factors into ones, tens, hundreds, and so on, and then multiplying each of these by the other factor

pentagon A polygon with 5 sides

perfect square A number that is the product of a counting number multiplied by itself

perimeter The distance around a figure

period In a number, a group of three digits, separated by commas, starting from the right

perpendicular lines Two lines that intersect to form square corners or right angles

pint (pt) A customary unit of capacity equal to 2 cups

place value The position of a digit in a number that is used to determine the value of the digit
Example: In 5,318, the 3 is in the hundreds place. So, the 3 has a value of 300.

plane An endless flat surface

point An exact location in space

polygon A closed plane figure made up of line segments

pound (lb) A customary unit of weight equal to 16 ounces

power The product that results from multiplying the same number over and over

prime number A whole number greater than 1 that has exactly two factors, itself and 1

prism A solid figure with two identical parallel bases and faces that are parallelograms

product The number that is the result of multiplying two or more factors

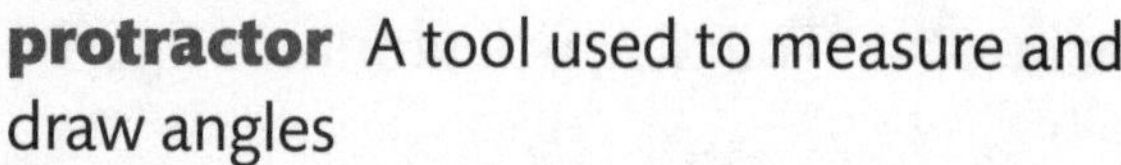

protractor A tool used to measure and draw angles

pyramid A solid figure with a base that is a polygon whose faces are triangles with a common vertex

Q

quadrilateral A polygon with 4 sides

quart (qt) A customary unit of capacity equal to 2 pints

quotient The answer to a division problem

R

ray Part of a line that has one endpoint and extends forever in one direction.

reciprocal A given number is a reciprocal of another number if the product of the numbers is one. *Example:* The numbers $\frac{1}{8}$ and $\frac{8}{1}$ are reciprocals because $\frac{1}{8} \times \frac{8}{1} = 1$.

rectangle A parallelogram with four right angles

rectangular prism A solid figure with 6 rectangular faces

regular polygon A polygon that has sides of equal length and angles of equal measure

remainder The amount that is left after dividing a number into equal parts

rhombus A parallelogram with all sides the same length

right angle An angle whose measure is 90°

right triangle A triangle in which one angle is a right angle

rounding A process that determines which multiple of 10, 100, 1,000, and so on, a number is closest to

S

sample A representative part of a larger group

scale (in a graph) A series of numbers at equal intervals along an axis on a graph

scalene triangle A triangle in which no sides have the same length

second (s) A unit of time; 60 seconds are in one minute.

sides (of an angle) The two rays that form an angle

sides of a polygon The line segments that form a polygon

solid figure (also: solid) A figure that has three dimensions (length, width, and height)

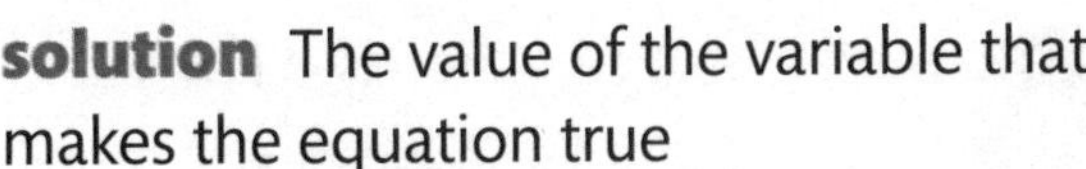

solution The value of the variable that makes the equation true

square A rectangle with all sides the same length

square unit A square with sides one unit long used to measure area

standard form A common way of writing a number with commas separating groups of three digits starting from the right
Example: 3,458,901

stem-and-leaf plot A way to organize numerical data using place value

straight angle An angle measuring 180°

Subtraction Property of Equality The same number can be subtracted from both sides of an equation and the sides remain equal.

sum The result of adding two or more addends

survey A question or questions used to gather information

symmetric A figure is symmetric if it can be folded on a line to form two halves that fit exactly on top of each other.

tablespoon (tbsp) A customary unit of capacity; two tablespoons is equal to one fluid ounce.

tenth One of ten equal parts of a whole

terms Numbers in a sequence or variables, such as *x* and *y*, in an algebraic expression

thousandth One of 1,000 equal parts of a whole

three-dimensional shape A solid with three dimensions that has volume, such as a rectangular prism

ton (T) A customary unit of weight equal to 2,000 pounds

trapezoid A quadrilateral that has exactly one pair of parallel sides

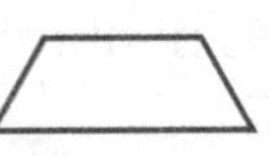

trend A relationship between two sets of data that shows up as a pattern in a graph

triangle A polygon with 3 sides

underestimate An estimate that is less than the actual answer

unknown A symbol or letter, such as *x*, that represents a number in an expression or equation

unit cube A cube that measures one unit on each side

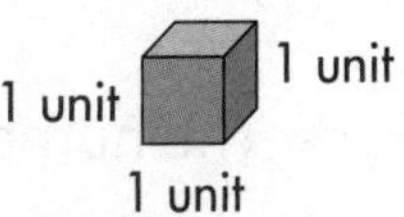

unit fraction A fraction with a numerator of 1

value (of a digit) The number a digit represents, which is determined by the position of the digit; see also *place value*

variable A letter, such as *n*, that represents a number in an expression or an equation

Venn diagram A drawing that shows how sets of numbers or objects are related

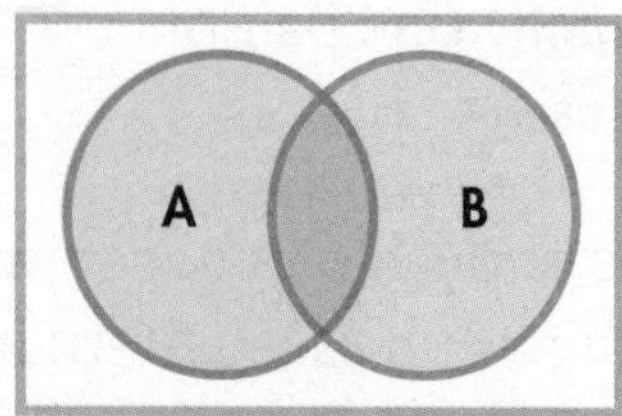

vertex (plural: vertices) **a.** The common endpoint of the two rays in an angle; **b.** A point at which two sides of a polygon meet; **c.** The point at which three or more edges meet in a solid figure

volume The number of cubic units needed to fill a solid figure

weight A measure of how light or how heavy something is

whole numbers The numbers 0, 1, 2, 3, 4, and so on

word form A way to write a number using words; see also *number name*

x-axis A horizontal number line on a coordinate grid

x-coordinate The first number in an ordered pair, which names the distance to the right or left from the origin along the *x*-axis

y-axis A vertical number line on a coordinate grid

y-coordinate The second number in an ordered pair, which names the distance up or down from the origin along the *y*-axis

yard (yd) A customary unit of length equal to 3 feet

Zero Property of Multiplication The product of any number and 0 is 0.

Photographs

Every effort has been made to secure permission and provide appropriate credit for photographic material. The publisher deeply regrets any omission and pledges to correct errors called to its attention in subsequent editions.

Unless otherwise acknowledged, all photographs are the property of Savvas Learning Company LLC.

Photo locators denoted as follows: Top (T), Center (C), Bottom (B), Left (L), Right (R), Background (Bkgd)

1 James Laurie/Shutterstock; **3** (T) Wayne Johnson/ Shutterstock, (C) Foto-bee/Alamy Stock Photo, (B) Macrovector/Shutterstock; **4** (Bkgrd) Underworld/ Shutterstock, Danny E Hooks/Shutterstock; **6** Risteski goce/Shutterstock; **12** John Foxx/Thinkstock; **18** Vladislav Gajic/Fotolia; **22** (L) James Steidl/Fotolia, (C) Hemera Technologies/Getty Images; (R) Ivelin Radkov/Fotolia; **41** Inacio pires/Shutterstock; **43** (T) Rudy Umans/Shutterstock; **43** (B) Findlay/Alamy Stock Photo; **44** (T) Elenadesign/Shutterstock; (B) Georgejmclittle/123RF; **62** (L) Tom Burlison/ Shutterstock; (R) Suphatthra olovedog/Shutterstock; **77** Samuel Liverio/Shutterstock; **79** (T) Porco_ photograph/iStock/Getty Images, (C) Iofoto/ Shutterstock, (B) M. Shcherbyna/Shutterstock; **80** (Bkgrd) China Images/Liu Xiaoyang/Alamy Stock Photo, Val lawless/Shutterstock; **92** (CL) Andreanita/Fotolia; (CR) Algre/Fotolia, (R) Eduardo Rivero/Fotolia; **96** Rikke/ Fotolia; **102** Cphoto/Fotolia; **109** Tatiana Popova/ Shutterstock; **125** Smileus/Shutterstock; **127** (T) FatCamera/E+/Getty Images, (B) Mario Houben/CSM/ REX/Shutterstock; **128** (T) AF archive/Alamy Stock Photo, (B) Kali9/E+/Getty Images; **141** Viacheslav Krylov/Fotolia; **149** Alisonhancock/Fotolia; **177** Tom Wang/Shutterstock; **179** (T) Andre Jenny/Alamy Stock Photo, (C) Chronicle/Alamy Stock Photo, (B) David Grossman/Alamy Stock Photo; **180** (Bkgrd) Kuvona/ Shutterstock, Sailou/Shutterstock; **225** Lisastrachan/ Fotolia; **227** (T) Steve Debenport/E+/Getty Images, (B) Monkey Business Images/Shutterstock; **228** (T) Accept photo/Shutterstock, (B) Ton Koene/Picture Alliance/Newscom; **265** Marcio Jose Bastos Silva/ Shutterstock; **267** (T) Arsenik/E+/Getty Images, (C) Des Westmore/Alamy Stock Photo, (B) Roman Diachkin/Shutterstock; **268** (Bkgrd) Prostock-studio/ Shutterstock, (T) Nattika/Shutterstock, (B) Boonchuay1970/Shutterstock; **298** Esanbanhao/ Fotolia; **306** Image Source/Jupiter Images; **313** (B) by-studio/Fotolia; (T) Paul Orr/Shutterstock; **329** Simone van den Berg/Fotolia; **331** (T) Philip Images/ Shutterstock, (B) Bubbers BB/Shutterstock; **332** (T) Ian Allenden/123RF, (B) ImageBROKER/REX/Shutterstock; **381** Zest_Marina/Fotolia; **383** (T) Stacey Newman/ Shutterstock, (C) Arve Bettum/Shutterstock, (B) Fluid work shop/Shutterstock; **384** (Bkgrd) Cathy Yeulet/123RF, Jarabee123/Shutterstock, **406** Bev/ Fotolia; **425** Jon Beard/Shutterstock; **427** (T) Wk1003mike /Shutterstock, (B) W. Scott McGill/Shutterstock; **428** (T) Neale Clark/Robertharding/Alamy Stock Photo, (B) Emmanuel Lattes/Alamy Stock Photo; **453** Morgan Lane Photography/Shutterstock; **455** (T) 146914/ Shutterstock, (C) Africa Studio/Shutterstock, (B) Tomasz Szymanski/Shutterstock; **456** (Bkgrd) Cathy Yeulet/123RF, Showcake/Shutterstock, (inset) Chutima Chaochaiya/Shutterstock; **485** Iktomi/Fotolia; **487** (T) Stefano Paterna/Alamy Stock Photo, (B) NASA; **488** (T) Elena Veselova/Shutterstock, (B) MaZiKab/Shutterstock; **498** Getty Images; **510** (L) Marianne de Jong/ Shutterstock; (R) Brocreative/Fotolia, **531** (T) Evgeny Karandaev/Shutterstock, (B) Volff/Fotolia; **533** Natalia Pavlova/Fotolia; **535** (T) M.R. Brennan/Shutterstock, (C) Viktoria White/Shutterstock, (B) JPL-Caltech/MSSS/ NASA; **536** (Bkgrd) LWA/Dann Tardif/Blend Images/ Alamy Stock Photo, Rawpixel.com/Shutterstock; **561** Solarseven/Shutterstock; **563** (T) Sean Pavone/ Alamy Stock Photo, (B) Kai Chiang/123RF; **564** (T) Oleksii Chumachenko/Shutterstock, (B) Alice McBroom/Pearson Education Australia Pty Ltd; **589** Pisaphotography/Shutterstock; **591** (T) Eugene Lu/Shutterstock, (C) Timothy Holle/Shutterstock, (B) Chameleons Eye/Shutterstock; **592** (Bkgrd) 123RF, Laboko/Shutterstock; **615** Leekris/Fotolia; **617** Michael J Thompson/ShutterStock; **619** (T) Pius Lee/Shutterstock, (B) Solis Images/Shutterstock; **620** (T) Rainer Lesniewski/ Alamy Stock Photo, (B) Railway fx/Shutterstock; **624** 2010/Photos to Go/Photolibrary